TOO SOON
TOO LATE

TOO SOON TOO LATE: HISTORY IN POPULAR CULTURE
IS VOLUME 22 IN THE SERIES

THEORIES OF CONTEMPORARY CULTURE
CENTER FOR TWENTIETH CENTURY STUDIES
UNIVERSITY OF WISCONSIN—MILWAUKEE
GENERAL EDITOR, Kathleen Woodward

TOO SOON

......

TOO LATE

HISTORY
IN
POPULAR
CULTURE

MEAGHAN MORRIS

Indiana University Press
Bloomington and Indianapolis

This book is a publication of
Indiana University Press
601 North Morton Street
Bloomington, Indiana 47404-3797 USA

http: //www.indiana.edu/~iupress

Telephone orders   800-842-6796
Fax orders   812-855-7931
Orders by e-mail   iuporder@indiana.edu

© 1998 by Meaghan Morris

Library of Congress Cataloging-in-Publication Data

Morris, Meaghan.
      Too soon too late : history in popular culture / Meaghan Morris.
            p.   cm. — (Theories of contemporary culture : v. 22)
      Includes bibliographical references (p.   ) and index.
      ISBN 0-253-33395-4 (alk. paper). — ISBN 0-253-21188-3 (pbk. :
alk. paper)
         1. Popular culture—Australia—History—20th century.
      2. Political culture—Australia—History—20th century.
      3. Australia—Civilization—20th century.   I. Title.   II. Series.
      DU117.14.M68   1998
      306'.0994—dc21   97-47773

         1   2   3   4   5   03   02   01   00   99   98

For
André Frankovits

CONTENTS

Part Two: Media Time

ILLUSTRATIONS

ACKNOWLEDGMENTS

Any book written over ten years incurs many debts. My first thanks must go to Kathleen Woodward, both for her kindness as a patient series editor, and for the stimulus her work on the emotions gave to a dedicated skeptic; and to André Frankovits, John Frow, Lawrence Grossberg, Patricia Mellencamp, and Paul Willemen, all of whom shaped this book directly, and persuaded me to finish it. My thanks, too, to Joan Catapano of Indiana University Press for her steadfast encouragement, Michael Baker for his sympathetic editing, and Glen Powell for giving this book an Index.

Many friends have read chapters or talked problems through with me. I have had the benefit of comment and criticism from David Bennett, Dipesh Chakrabarty, Ross Chambers, Kuan-Hsing Chen, Paul Foss, Anne Freadman, Ross Gibson, Helen Grace, Elizabeth Grosz, Ghassan Hage, Donald Horne, Ian Hunter, Laleen Jayamanne, Noel King, Adrian Martin, Brian Massumi, and Stephen Muecke. Others helped me directly with research materials and advice: thanks to Rolando Caputo, Virginia Coventry, Ann Curthoys, Michael Dean, John Docker, John Forbes, the staff of Gleebooks, Louise Johnson, James Hay, Chris Hilton, Colin Hood, Mark Jackson, Gary Jones of Bundeena Video, Pat Laughren, Jenny Lee, David Marcus, Rachel Moore, Joyce Morris, Andrew Naylor, Gil Rodman, Elvira Sprogis, Michael Taussig, Hilary Yerbury, and Anne Zahalka. Rereading ancient notes, I find that Paul Patton wrote me a letter about Sydney Tower in 1982 that I seem to have borrowed wholesale.

Conferences and seminars obliged me to socialize my ideas and gave shape to most chapters: I am grateful to Linda Baughman, Jon Bird, Edward Bruner, Sandra Buckley, Beatriz Colomina, Sally Couacaud, Peter Garrett, Stuart Koop, May Lam, Susan Magarey, Julie Marcus, Ken Ruthven, and Susan Sheridan. I had a wonderful time discussing an imaginary book with students and colleagues at the Center for Twentieth Century Studies, University of Wisconsin–Milwaukee, in 1987, and at the Unit for Criticism and Interpretive Theory, University of Illinois at Champaign-Urbana, in 1990. My bibliography does not reflect how much I have learned from sometimes baffling, but always rewarding, adventures in the United States.

Paul Willemen invited me to give the Claire Johnston Memorial Lecture at the 42nd Edinburgh International Film Festival, August 1988. Chapter 5, "Ecstasy and Economics," is based on that lecture.

Without public support for criticism and research in Australia, this book could not have been written. From 1991 to 1993, a Senior Fellowship from the Literature Board of the Australia Council gave me unbroken time to work on this book, and I have completed it as a recipient of a Senior Fellowship from the Australian Research Council.

Early versions of the following chapters appear as "At Henry Parkes Motel," *Cultural Studies* 2/1 (1988); "Things to Do with Shopping Centres," *Grafts: Feminist Cultural Criticism*, ed. Susan Sheridan (London: Verso, 1988); "'On the Beach,'" *Cultural Studies*, ed. Lawrence Grossberg, Cary Nelson, and Paula Treichler (New York: Routledge, 1992); "Great Moments in Social Climbing: King Kong and the Human Fly," *Sexuality and Space*, ed. Beatriz Colomina (Princeton: Princeton University School of Architecture, 1992); and "Ecstasy and Economics: A Portrait of Paul Keating," *Discourse* 14/3 (1992). "Lunching for the Republic" was commissioned in an earlier version for *Multicultural States: Identity and Difference*, ed. David Bennett (London: Routledge, forthcoming). The Preface began as "'Too Soon, Too Late': Reading Claire Johnston, 1970–81" in *Dissonance: Feminism and the Arts 1970–90*, ed. Catriona Moore (Sydney: Allen & Unwin, 1994). Parts of my Introduction draw on "Metamorphoses at Sydney Tower," *New Formations* 11 (1990), and "Life as a Tourist Object in Australia," *International Tourism: Identity and Change*, ed. Marie-Françoise Lanfant, John B. Allcock, and Edward M. Bruner (London: Sage, 1995). A portion of "Epilogue: Future Fear" appears as "Future Fear," *Mapping the Futures: Local Cultures, Global Change*, ed. J. Bird, B. Curtis, T. Putnam, G. Robertson, and L. Tickner (London: Routledge, 1993).

In chapter 1, the extract from *Motel Chronicles*, copyright © 1982 by Sam Shepard, is reprinted by permission of City Lights Books. In chapter 2, the image of mother and child shopping at Blacktown Westpoint is from *The Shopping Centre as a Community Leisure Resource*, Department of Environment, Housing and Community Development (Canberra: Australian Government Publishing Service, 1978); Commonwealth of Australia copyright reproduced by permission. Also in chapter 2, "Greetings from Indooroopilly Shoppingtown" is reproduced by permission of David Lee, International Colour Productions, Pty Ltd. In chapter 4, the still from *A Spire* is reproduced by permission of Chris Hilton, Aspire Films.

PREFACE: "TOO SOON TOO LATE"
In Memory of Claire Johnston, 1940–87

> . . . we see women's liberation as working for revolution,
> but not the sort of revolution which is an event that
> takes two or three days, in which there is shooting and
> hanging.
>
> —ANN CURTHOYS AND LYNDALL RYAN (1971)[1]
>
> History will never be rid of dates.
>
> —GILLES DELEUZE AND FÉLIX GUATTARI (1980)[2]

In 1991, Artspace in Sydney organized an exhibition and a national series of art projects to commemorate twenty years of feminism. The idea was to frame contemporary work with a new collective history of "Feminism and the Arts 1970–90."[3] Invited to write for an anthology that would include a (for me unreadable) manifesto by my younger self, I had great difficulty thinking of feminism as anything like an unbroken story. Feminism for me has been as much about sporadic bursts of energy, interrupted projects, blocked paths, stretches of lassitude, and invaluably prolonged digressions as it has been about a long, cumulative labor of transformation. I could think about "history" only by working through some fictions of historical *time* that have mattered to feminist critics considering what "action" might mean for feminist work in culture.

This led me to think about activism and professionalism, utopia and pragmatism, commitment and career paths, the shifts and the tensions between them all as values for middle-class feminism. But those are very large terms, and I found myself returning to the concepts of history and activism explored in a few texts by Claire Johnston, one of the first and most visionary of British feminist theorists working with film in the 1970s. I did this partly to understand why I found it hard then to read Johnston's essays (along with most other early "second wave" feminist texts), but mainly because her work—in its very difficulty for me in, as she might have said, "this specific conjuncture"—illuminated my present as a feminist critic.

It still does today. This means that I no longer have a *retrospective* relationship to Claire Johnston's work. I think I did when she died. By 1987, a sense of sharp distinction between "the seventies" and "the eighties" had been widely expressed for years in many areas of Australian cultural and political life. In the media, momentous debates about the future of the nation were packaged, using charismatic Prime Ministerial names, as "Hawke" (1980s) versus "Whitlam" (1970s).[4] In the artworld, this often took the form of an opposition of *styles*: it was not uncommon in those years for speakers at public forums to introduce themselves polemically as "an eighties person," as though whole paradigms would neatly follow suit like credit cards tumbling from a wallet. But beyond these testimonials to the enduring power of vanguardist narrative, an experience of what Laura Mulvey, in her wonderful essay on closure and the 1980s, calls "Changes," was also real, intense, and necessary then for feminism as a movement.[5]

Claire Johnston committed suicide. (She was not "an eighties person.") So in 1987, it was hard not to question her texts as though to find out what had "gone wrong." Such reading told me nothing: it was too soon for other questions, too late for an answer to matter. I was not really interested in reviewing early feminism (too late for reminiscences, too soon for sober history)[6] and, impatient to get on with other things, I meant quietly to ignore the "1970–1990" part of the *Dissonance* proposition. However, I kept on reading. Language does have its imperatives: it is amazing, as Deleuze and Guattari say, "how thoroughly politics works language from within" (83); fleeing those dates, I found myself able *because of them* to read Johnston's work, at last, in 1991.

For as time passed, a more complex, less mythical sense of how texts work in history, over time—*her* critical sense, in fact—began to assert itself. Johnston's writing, always historical, nervous of myth, became more a part of my present than it ever had been of my past. It began to be important, not something to disavow, that I was actually reading many of her texts for the first time in my life. For I came "late" to Claire Johnston's work. In the 1970s, I learned very little from British feminist film theory; I was not interested in psychoanalysis, and my own work looked instead to Gilles Deleuze and Michel Foucault.[7]

These are very personal remarks, but they help me to clarify an issue about feminism and historical time that I want to explore. Whatever their differences, most feminisms have been marked, at least in their creative political phase, by an experimental approach to the present, a desire to shape the future, and an enterprising attitude to representing the past. In other words, feminism is skeptical but *constructive*. If this made feminism untimely for history-is-dead and Shakespeare-said-it versions of art postmodernism, it still sounds safe enough as a practical orientation. However, feminism is not easily adapted to heroic *progress* narratives. If most of the dreams of historicism, from bloody revolution to the millenarian community, have been taken up, at one time or another, by some form of feminism, that basic skepticism about History has also made feminism at once resilient in surviving its failed experiments and resistant to modes of argument that base their claims on necessity.

This connection between a constructive social philosophy and a skeptical theory of history is ungrammatical not only for melancholic aesthetics, but for many of the left-wing political traditions with which feminism has been associated. It also makes feminism difficult to situate for most contemporary polemics about modernity, postmodernism, and "standards" in cultural life. Feminist discourse often stammers when it comes to validating action with a logic of events; it is not that logic is renounced, or history deemed chaotic, but that there is a struggle to name a different temporality ("*not* the sort of revolution which is an event that takes two or three days" . . .) that might make a *feminist* concept of eventfulness historically intelligible. More exactly, feminism makes political discourse "stammer."[8] To act, as I believe feminism does, to bring about concrete social changes while *at the same time* contesting the very bases of modern thinking about what constitutes "change" is to induce intense strain, almost a kind of overload, in historical articulation—and sometimes, in feminists' lives.

For there really is no easy split between a practical, everyday feminism, and the relentless but specialized struggles of feminist theory. They can and often must be distinguished, of course, but I doubt that the useful distinction now is between activists on the one hand and academics on the other, or even between the "political" and the "cultural." Professionalism, for example, has come to bear quite as intensely on community and campaign groups as on the artists who sometimes work with them. Nor does professionalism map neatly on to matters of class and race; it is not in itself a "white middle-class feminist" problem, although ease of access to it may be a white middle-class privilege. Under professionalism, something like a *general* specialization of activities takes place: it is no longer obvious that the difference between a "politics" and a "job" is one of scale, or quality of commitment, or even relevance to a community.

Claire Johnston was a cultural activist in the 1970s sense. She worked collectively in the London Women's Film Group and on the editorial board of *Screen*. She organized, with Lynda Miles, the first Women's Film Festival at Edinburgh in 1972; several Special Events at the Edinburgh Film Festival during the 1970s; and a Feminist Film Festival in 1980. She wrote some twenty essays, several of them foundational for feminist work in cinema and not one of them produced with a curriculum vitae in mind. Her last published essay, "Maeve," came out in 1981. She fought with "the phantoms of psychosis, Thatcherism and solitude,"[9] and so with money and housing nightmares. She wrote manuscripts, and destroyed them. She taught for ten years without tenure, and never published a book of her own.[10]

To read Johnston now is to confront an aspect of feminist history (and activist time) that Lesley Stern, in a beautiful tribute to Johnston, calls simply, *survival*.[11] Johnston often defined her work in intensely localized terms, as though she wanted to restrict its life: she was "intervening" at "a particular historical moment" to have "effects" in "specific situations," not creating a body of knowledge to endure as Feminist Theory. There are problems and paradoxes in this fiction, but in its hyperpolitical restlessness her thought was profoundly undogmatic. It has a cantankerous energy; it survives. She did not always sound undogmatic: there is *so much Latin* in that British Film Theory prose, a mythic Latin saying "I am an instance of rigorous scientificity"; as Stern says, the effect can be "sombre, not to say tyrannical." But there is a fink streak in Johnston; she has a way of using that Latin to make it sound like a fart in church.

Dogma in cultural criticism today is rarely somber in presentation: rabid, yes (in the mainstream media), or cool, chic, smarmy (in Stern's terms, "hebephrenic"[12]). The dominant constraint on feminism now is not the sound of scientificity, but what a U.S. literary critic calls "the look of corporate populism."[13] In this context my problem is no longer, or not only, why Johnston's activism could not endure the 1980s, what "went wrong." Now I also wonder how it survived the 1970s—in other words, what went *right*. This means reading Johnston backward in chronological terms: instead of searching her early work for tragic premonitions, I have at last learned, from her skeptical history, to begin at the beginning.

LIFE, ART, LABOR

> One is one's labour power and the drives which situate that labour power have to increasingly (in Thatcherism) engage and re-engage with the realities of one's own death, whatever one's beliefs, political affiliations or anything else.
>
> CLAIRE JOHNSTON (1987)

Let me read this remark of Johnston's by working through, digressively, a simple proposition: Deleuze and Guattari's claim in *Kafka: Toward a Minor Literature* that "living and writing, art and life, are opposed only from the point of view of a major literature."[14] This claim helps me to understand some aspects of Claire Johnston's life as a feminist critic, while Johnston's writing gives me "a point of view" on some aspects of the concept of the minor. In between, I can clarify the problems I have with both.

Most literary debates about Authorship have assumed the feasibility of a life/art opposition (author/signature, biography/text, history/form), whether by affirming it, refuting it, or refining it. Even the poststructuralist critique of Authorship was read against the grain, in literary criticism, as a pretext for opposing art and life; in the crudest form of this reading, if the "real author" didn't matter then biography and politics would be excluded from literary study. In cinema studies, Foucault's "What *is* an Author?" clearly asking *how*, not whether, authors matter, was read a little more carefully; "the advent of post-structuralism had," Patrice Petro points out, "the opposite effect on feminist criticism."[15] It enabled feminists like Johnston to revise the auteur theory influential in the 1960s, to begin discussing the place of *women* directors in the Hollywood studio system, and to create that enormous field of research now called "the female spectator."[16] However, as Petro says, Johnston was unusual in insisting that "history, biography *and* textuality" must always combine in such research.

Now, in *Kafka* (1975) Deleuze and Guattari were still attacking the psychological criticism that had infuriated Roland Barthes in "The Death of the Author," a tradition that saw "art" as a substitute for "life," and then analyzed the author through the text.[17] But their emphases differed from his. Where Barthes went on to theorize the work of the reader, Deleuze and Guattari studied the "life" of Kafka's *writing*: *Kafka* is a biography of a particular mode of creation. It is also a "manifesto for a literary/political avant-garde."[18] Famously based on an idea taken from Kafka's notes on Yiddish literature in Warsaw and Prague Jewish writing in German, the minor is a constructive concept; the book's project is "*toward* a minor literature." What is unusual about *Kafka* is that in place of an avant-garde negation of art's status in bourgeois society,[19] Deleuze and Guattari offer an *affirmative* project based on a mass historical experience: "How many people today live in a language that is not their own? Or no longer, or not yet, even know their own and know poorly the major language that they are forced to use?" (19).

While it refers directly to the experience of immigrants and colonized people, this question is echoed obliquely in the concerns of early feminist criticism and Johnston's work on "women's films made *within the system*" of Hollywood's social and cinematic codes.[20] A minor literature is not "marginal": it is what a minority constructs *in a major language,* and so it is a model of action from a colonized, suppressed, or displaced position *within* a given society. In this it differs from theories that propose, like Laura Mulvey's early work in film, to found an alternative system. "Minor" has the force of an adjective, not a noun, for Deleuze and Guattari; they do not oppose a notion of social or ethnic *minority* to that of an abstract *majority.* "Minor" and "major" are used in a musical sense: they refer not to essences or states but to different ways of doing something, "two different treatments of language, one of which consists in extracting constants from it, the other in placing it in continuous variation."[21] Like Godard, whom Deleuze and Guattari also consider "minor," Kafka is a canonical author, not an obscure or neglected writer, and so *Kafka* is itself a "minor" reading of a major literary figure. But the vast histories of oppression often masked by the term "minority" (and comically revealed by a careless phrase like "women and other minorities") are *involved* in the concept of the minor; *Kafka* is a reading of an author's work in terms of his ethnicity.

For to say that art and life are opposed only from the point of view of a major literature is not to say that this is *wrong*, and that art and life should be reintegrated (according to Peter Burger, the project of the avant-garde).[22] It is to say that, from another point of view, the problem is simply not relevant. Some of the main features of the concept of the minor explain why this should be so. Minor literature is highly deterritorialized; to make minor use of a major language is to articulate living displacement. Everything in minor literature is political: the poverty of resources in the "cramped space" of the minor means that each individual intrigue connects immediately to politics, and that the individual matters intensely—"a whole other story is vibrating within it."[23] So everything has collective value; there is no room for a "master" enunciation to develop that is *separate* from the collective. This "scarcity of talent" actually forces minor literature into great creativity; and so the minor defines "the revolutionary conditions" for *all* literature.[24]

The notion of "cramped space" may be more useful for thinking about early feminist practice than "minor," entangled as that term is in shaky analogies and by a history of its romantic use to celebrate marginality. *Kafka* has great immediacy as a description of how creative movements work. Cramped spaces can be formed by petty milieux as well as for fragile communities: in my own experience, a political movement like Women's Liberation, a peripheral feminist or national cinema, and a small journal subculture, can at least have in common an insistence that every gesture *matters.*

In milieux, history is happening in a totally intense present: there is no "spare time," no tolerance for waste; mistakes are tragically construed as disasters for the future, then stoically salvaged as "the lessons of the past"; criticism is a volatile act fraught with perils and acute emotional risks, having consequences, not "validity." This is the temporality of the project, not the profession, and Johnston's essays bear its marks: massive interpretation of what may seem, to outsiders, slight events ("Brecht in Britain: on *The Nightcleaners*"), fear of "dangers" attending bad moves or wasted lessons of history ("The Subject of Feminist Film Theory/Practice"), a passionate care for the labor it takes to try to make a difference ("Maeve").

In any cramped space, there is no material basis for opposing art and life. But in a political project, activism can make a virtue of necessity by demanding a *consistency* between living and writing, acting and thinking, life, art, and labor. There is no such ethic in *Kafka*; the artist does what he does without militancy, or injunctions to stay intense. Greatly complicated by Deleuze and Guattari's later work,[25] the minor in *Kafka* remains a cheerful and benignly elitist concept. Exactly utopian, "minor" names a process by which the solitary individual may face "diabolical powers of the future" (fascism, communism, Fordism are "knocking on the door" for Kafka), express for the collective a "possible community", and confront the diabolical with "a revolutionary machine-to-come."[26] The minor is *prophetic*. It does not name the historical process in which (as for feminism) prophecy motivates social action and is tested by social change. *Kafka* deals with bureaucracy, with terrors in daily life, with defeat and with the loss of creativity, but it is not about the everyday grind of any mundane social struggle, not about the shunting between minor and major practices that regulates experience in modern urban life—and not about the problems of sustaining an activist ethic.

In an unpublished text written in 1987, Johnston explained why she found it impossible to go on living and writing. She confronted a social order—her own "diabolical powers"—placing increasing pressure on that solitary individual, the middle-aged single woman. As a feminist intellectual, she lived for writing and teaching. As a professional feminist, she also taught and wrote for a living. Under Thatcherism, the gap between *not* writing and *not* living was becoming, for Johnston, frighteningly narrow. "Breakdown" in capitalist society means the time that you have to stop work. When this happened to Johnston, teaching was a test of the survival of the fittest, housing costs were spiraling, clinics were closing down in the name of "freedom to live in the community," while "free" community, for the jobless and the ill, might mean the street. This was "cramped space" of a deadly kind: the resources needed for personal recovery were those being most depleted by everyday working life. So Johnston saw her death as a logical outcome in "a history which is mine and a history of the 1980s and the massive changes that have taken place which ultimately bring their weight to bear on the body, and psychic life in general."

Today, much has been written about those massive changes and their weight on bodies and souls. Some of it, sincerely regretting the poverty and hyperexploitation bearing down most heavily now on women and men of color, celebrates new chances, new career paths, for ameliorist professionals such as feminists in the arts.[27] But unlike proponents of "new times" or the look of corporate populism, Johnston was not optimistic. In Thatcherism she saw a regime of total realism (no dreams of immortality) and thus of deathly prohibition—no imagining another life, no inventing different worlds, no revolutionary machines-to-come. She may have seen her future as an eternity of what Deleuze and Guattari, citing Elias Canetti, call "enantiomorphosis," the negation of becoming: "There are dead spaces just as there are dead times. 'If [enantiomorphosis is] practised often the whole world shrivels. . . . Social prohibitions against metamorphosis are perhaps the most important of all. . . . Death itself, the strictest of all boundaries, is what is interposed between classes.'"[28]

Such death is exactly what Thatcher's famous TINA slogan, "There Is No Alternative," announced. Proclaimed by the leader of a nation, this slogan (a performative, an act accomplished in the statement) is what Deleuze and Guattari call a *mot d'ordre*, an "order-word"; it is "a little death sentence, a Judgment, as Kafka put it."[29] Perhaps this is what Johnston meant by having to "engage and re-engage with the realities of one's own death" under Thatcherism: to survive was to accept *on a daily basis* this denial of possibility, this prohibition on creative power, this flat negation of life. For a feminist intellectual, engaging with one's *own* death could be as simple as knowing one's social place, learning to live with its limitations and accept or ignore its privileges, saying one thing, doing another—inscribing and reinscribing that boundary between living and writing, art and life.

And yet—in rejecting this, Johnston was also questioning the legacy of the feminism informing her own realism, her own sense of "no alternative." Among the pressures she faced, it was, she said, "*this image of feminist activity*" carrying over from the past that for her had proved "the most deadly." An activist imaginary denying the force of those "massive changes" and so unable to bear them preserves, in its own negation of becoming, a "dated" imperative lethal now to its socially paralyzed subject; any self chronically dependent for its identity on "seeing the world in a certain way" could find itself subject to an injunction, no longer to *change* that world, but simply to drop out of history.

For there is something very important to remember about the way Claire Johnston had worked. From "Women's Cinema as Counter-Cinema" (1972) to "Maeve" (1981), she successively generated new spaces of analysis in which she could say what needed to be done in the *next* new space—and then, she could formulate a strategy for doing it. She detested any myth-making, feminist, nationalist, or even just cinephilic, that saw the past as a Golden Age and the present as a state of decline. When Johnston wrote of memory, she wrote of it as a practice, not an inheritance, as a way of acting relative to place as well as time—in fact, as a mode of becoming. She saw the past as a "dynamic" vital to any struggle, but she also assumed that this dynamic must have nothing to do with lost heritage, and everything to do with creating effective ways of action in the present. Claire Johnston's thought was eventful: what she called "theory/practice" was a temporal art with social implications. She was an activist, in the sense that she made things *happen*.

When in 1972 she sketched what were to become her historic analyses of Dorothy Arzner and Ida Lupino, she did not make the case for "history" that a retrospective construction *now* of feminism *then* might lead us to expect. She did not argue for rediscovering the "lost" work of women directors, but that studying Arzner and Lupino would be a way to undermine the "monolithic view of the media as repressive" then popular with activists, and to "restore the interest of Hollywood" in the face of "puritanical" attacks from the Left. She said that a politics of entertainment and desire would be vital to women's cinema, and so it was the *future* that for her defined "the interest of women's films made within the system" in the past.[30] To read "Women's Cinema as Counter-Cinema" now is to gain a useful perspective on the self-promoting fairy tales of cultural studies today (once upon a time in the seventies, the story goes, feminists had a monolithic view of the media as repressive . . .). More importantly, it is to be asked to consider very carefully, by Johnston herself, what the point of reading her today might be.

In her essay on Pat Murphy's *Maeve*, she discussed "nostalgia" in the strict sense of longing for "home." Her reading of feminism and republicanism in Northern Ireland stresses the difference made by the film between a nostalgic memorializing, that binds Maeve's republican father to his past, preventing him from acting, and Maeve's "reactivation" of her past—her labor to tell a history of her life that makes it possible to act in future. The image that for Johnston represented this difference-made was an image of the Giant's Causeway in the closing scene of the film; three women drinking together under the rocks, while a male voice-off rants and drones in a "mad pastiche of Irish patriarchal discourse." This scene suggested to her the possibility not only of displacing a patriarchal mythology of homeland, but also of creating, for women and in cinema, "an other imaginary"—enabling another history, a different temporality.

Reflecting on survival, Laleen Jayamanne writes that the "wily ability to negotiate the intellectual domain without sacrificing the body is a skill we have barely begun to learn."[31] Johnston always saw survival as an issue vital to women: already in 1975, in an essay on *Anne of the Indies*, she saw the implications of the models of femininity as masquerade and hysteria then gaining influence in theory when she said of Tourneur's heroine, "the radical heterogeneity which her masquerade dramatised has finally been played out and frozen in the ultimate place of radical absence—death itself."[32] Her own texts were always delicate lessons in the fine art of negotiation, staying alive, lessons that she drew from the practices of other women working in cinema, and performed in her mode of writing.

Feminist "art" is not in much danger of forgetting the experimental practice of history that I have just described as "the way Claire Johnston worked." It is basic, though not exclusive, to most feminist activity, and the films that have most pervasively affected my own thinking about Australian cultural history over the two decades—Helen Grace's *Serious Undertakings*, Laleen Jayamanne's *A Song of Ceylon*, Tracey Moffatt's *Nice Coloured Girls* and *Night Cries*—have all had this practice in common. My concern in "remembering" this aspect of Johnston's work is not to recall feminism to what it has always done, but to engage with some recent theses on ethics, truth, and (an often unstated) professionalism that make feminist arts and histories an object of tacit criticism, or even direct attack.

Unlike much art criticism today, these are not products of neoconservatism, although they have a reactive edge. They belong to Marxist and liberal critical traditions nominally in sympathy with feminism: they, too, review twenty years of cultural politics, and they do so with an eye to the global tensions that have shaped the 1990s. Serious, challenging, urbanely academic, these are theories happily espousing a constructive social philosophy, but not, in practice, very comfortable with a skeptical approach to history. Some, like David Harvey's influential book *The Condition of Postmodernity*, associate feminist aesthetics with "nostalgic" ethnic nationalism and religious fundamentalism; in this view, which cannot accommodate "Maeve"'s politics of differentiation in memory, feminism can be potentially fascist.[33] Others, like Christopher Norris's *Spinoza & the Origins of Modern Critical Theory*, passionately defend the possibility of truth and Reason against a "postmodern" *pragmatist* history; for this view, which cannot grasp the activist modalities of Claire Johnston's critical reasoning, feminism has not yet happened.

Many women have noted the glossing over of feminist contributions to cultural debate in recent years (as well as the conflicting modes of recognition that constitute feminism itself) and have speculated on its causes.[34] Looking at these instances in politically engaged, energetic works of theory, I am convinced that something to do with the troubled feminist category of "experience" is involved in this corporate *unease* about the status of feminist intellectual work. The category of experience has always assumed the irrelevance of opposing living and writing, art and life.[35] When it is used as a way of posing skeptical questions of history, rather than as a way of imposing a claim to personal authority, "experience" has also been part of the struggle to name a different temporality ("*not* the sort of revolution which is an event that takes two or three days . . . ") that makes a feminist ethics of history theoretically intelligible.

This is a struggle, I suspect, that "major" cultural critics like Harvey and Norris cannot read from their experience of life and labor in an academic profession. However, I have no wish to attack their (historical) position, denounce the limitations of knowledge produced by "white middle-class males," or renounce the institutions and professions in which feminists now may work. On the contrary, it seems much more useful to ask how professional feminists may now negotiate the limitations of *our* positions. Sooner or later this will require, it seems to me, something like an experimental practice of *feminism's* history.

In the twenty-five years since Ann Curthoys and Lyndall Ryan foresaw a revolution that was "not . . . an event that takes two or three days, in which there is shooting and hanging," feminism has had its share of violent death. In 1988, Ann Curthoys provoked a series of new efforts at naming a different temporality by suggesting that, for white middle-class Australian women, a feminist eventfulness, even violent, is in no way *revolutionary*: "It's a relief . . . that we no longer live in the world of revolutionary slogans that were so common in the late 1960s and early 1970s, the blithe talk of revolution by a sector of society which knew it would never really be part of such an upheaval and would have been profoundly scared at the prospect."[36] Yet in the late 1990s the prospect of upheaval is closer, once again; how that small sector of society involved with feminist criticism will deal with more "massive changes" in future is not really an untimely question.

Sometime in the 1980s, I saw a film about untimeliness by Jean-Marie Straub and Danielle Huillet called *Trop Tôt Trop Tard* (*Too Soon Too Late*). One scene is vivid in my memory. The camera is fixed in front of a factory. It stays fixed for what soon becomes an unendurable length of time: *almost* unendurable; with foreboding, I realize that this is going to continue and that I am going to stay. This is "real time": people come and go at the gates, drifting in, pouring out, dwindling away again; a voice goes on about the history of modern Egypt and something to do with Engels. The "fiction" becomes the everyday simply happening in front of one's eyes. Slowly drawn in to this fiction, I am absorbed in time passing so slowly that it vanishes into that timeless speed called "passing in no time at all." The scene refers to a Lumière film about *La sortie des usines*. But my body is intensely in the cinema, present tense: my eyes hurt, as figures blur into flowing lines and random pulses of movement, filling and emptying the frame. I am mesmerized by this image, and yet, I endlessly look at my watch.

Working with temporality is classic practice in modern art. Real time can mythically signify "Experimentality" in cinema. What was memorable about this scene was its skeptical function in a film about colonialism, industrialism, and cinema, untimely political experiments and interminable revolutions. The increasing abstraction of its image of "the workers" did not drain the scene of history, as myth is supposed to do, but filled the screen and the cinema with a critically dense experience (in the feminist sense) of the power of representation in the history of colonized bodies. The model of eventfulness it offered viewers was neither an activist identification with the image, nor a critical distance from it, but the more difficult experience—enduring, erratic—of *involvement*.

Writing about *Too Soon Too Late*, Paul Willemen points out that Straub and Huillet's film "doesn't accept the 'too soon' or the 'too late' of political events and movements as a tragic fate legitimating . . . immobility and cynicism"; perhaps, he says, there is a need "for things being *both* too soon and too late" if "even a moment" of eventfulness is to be possible.[37] I think that this, more than anything to do with a "postmodern" pragmatism, describes the activating principle of Claire Johnston's feminist film history, and provides me with a starting point today.

TOO SOON
....
TOO LATE

INTRODUCTION: HISTORY IN CULTURAL STUDIES

> *Why does cultural studies* want *history? What does wanting it mean? What new acts of transference will items from the past help cultural studies—or make it—perform? How will it be done? How taught? Will there be any room for detailed historical work; or are students of cultural studies bound to rely on great schematic and secondary sweeps through time? Will there be any room for the historical case-study in its pedagogy? What good is it all to you anyway?*
>
> —CAROLYN STEEDMAN[1]

HISTORY, "THEORY," AND CULTURAL STUDIES

There is a methodological problem often encountered by people working in cultural studies on the very recent history of the present. Writing about the difficulties of theorizing popular culture in the United States today, Lawrence Grossberg puts it this way:

> What do you do when every event is potentially evidence, potentially determining, and at the same time, changing too quickly to allow the comfortable leisure of academic criticism?[2]

For my purposes, the problem of stabilizing an object of analysis in cultural studies needs to be posed in a slightly different way. In the phrase "comfortable leisure," there is a gesture of disengagement from a traditional literary practice that seems unnecessary in Australia, where academic critics presume neither comfort nor leisure as a condition of their work. Nevertheless, Grossberg's question defines a clearly recognizable dilemma, and one that is by no means new nor restricted to a textual criticism grappling with information flows, high-speed temporal forms, and industrial demands for career fast-tracking. It is worth remembering that already in the 1960s, Henri Lefebvre formulated the problem of *Everyday Life in the Modern World* by analyzing his own abandonment of the original project of the three-volume *Critique of Everyday Life*, the first volume of which had appeared in 1947.[3] Lefebvre said of that volume's "remainder" that:

> . . . this work was never completed or published because the author soon realized that the momentous changes taking place in society at the time had transformed his "subject" to the point of making it unrecognizable or virtually non-existent.[4]

Observing this encounter with disappearing objects in an inaugural text of the study of everyday life, one response would be to resort to one of those "great schematic and secondary sweeps through time" that allow us to recast our methodological problems in more manageable form as *symptoms* of a broader cultural "logic,"[5] social "condition,"[6] or epochal "moment"— postmodern, postcolonial, postindustrial, perhaps even posthistorical.[7] Thus accounted for, rather than solved, problems of method become occasions for rehearsing blockbuster theories of History. When thunderously huge, monolithic Subjects—the West, Modernity, Fordism—begin to stride and then to topple, in our texts, across vast stretches of world and time ("ever since the Enlightenment, . . . "), "notions of historic change take mythical, apocalyptic, or theoretical forms";[8] there is little room left for historical practice—or unsettling empirical surprises—of any kind.

Such sweeps are troubling to many historians, because they threaten to exclude historical *work* from the field of cultural studies, and to dispense with historical rules of evidence for making historical claims. But this is not only a problem for historians. When cultural critics agree to debate a (largely bibliographic) frame of reference in lieu of an object of study, we in effect use a generic brand of "theory" to avoid asking questions about the status of objects, and differing concepts of evidence and determination, in a *multidisciplinary* project. The narrative form in which we perform this avoidance is neither new nor specific to cultural studies. However well it may serve to tell a story of hyper-eventfulness and accelerating change, the form is derived—with the stylistic mediation of widely imitated philosophers such as Foucault, Lyotard, and Derrida—from the scholarly tradition of a "History of Philosophy" in which a very few big events take place (it goes without saying, in Europe) over very long periods of time: "ever since Plato, . . . "; "since Descartes, . . . "; "since Kant. . . . "

Epic rehearsal of great moments in Theory is not the only resort available to the critic caught analyzing an object that has ceased to exist or that everyone else has forgotten. My preference is to turn to history for a context prolonging the life of the ephemeral item or "case": saturating with detail an articulated place and point in time, a critical reading can extract from its objects a parable of practice that converts them into *models* with a past and a potential for reuse, thus aspiring to invest them with a future. This is a literary solution and it favors, however domestic the setting, a picaresque form of narrative: in an endless series of minuscule events, popular heroes act out theoretical logics of formidable complexity against a more or less well-defined social background.

With its own investment in the significance of documents, cases, and exceptions, any "text-based" cultural studies is prone to defer to history as a way of framing its discourse on any sort of change. Historically, this is understandable. The very formality of this deference, however, provokes Carolyn Steedman to ask exactly what our appeals to history mean *now*, and what we want them to achieve. Her point, I take it, is not to find cultural studies wanting "as" or "in" history, but to render explicit, in cross-disciplinary discussions of method, a question of desire. Why do we who want history, want *history*—for Steedman, "the most unstable" and "the most impermanent of written forms"—if not just to use a piece of it "as a building block for a different structure of explanation" (614)?

After all, history dates. "There is nothing deader and colder than old history"; written history "is not just *about* time, doesn't just *describe* time, or take *time as its setting*; rather it embeds time in its narrative structure" (614). This is partly why Deleuze and Guattari say that "history will never be rid of dates"; while history recounts "the actions and passions of the bodies that develop in a social field," it also transmits "pure acts intercalated into that development."[9] Steedman, however, asks us to consider that the historical *enterprise* may be dated. Constraints of time and money are eroding the slow, costly practice of archival research on which the modern discipline is founded; "a very odd account" of the past is being shaped by the pedagogical need to base history, cheaply and democratically, on a reading of mass-produced texts (government reports, prose fictions); the paradigm shift whereby one discipline after another "(has) cut its ties to history, strengthened its autonomy with theory"[10] continues apace across all academic culture and "the commonplace and secular world of which the academy is a part"; while historians, too, take part in "the abandonment of time in favor of 'the culture concept'" (620).

Given Steedman's own sobering response to the question of the "good" that history can be—"perhaps no good at all" (621)—it would seem unwise for a cultural studies engaged with that commonplace and secular world to turn to history for help. Whether we like it or not, cultural studies is enabled by the culture concept; it is a *product* of "the general flight from the historical," and the institutional pressures, that Steedman describes; as a pedagogy, it affirms (with Steedman) the value as well as the necessity of cheap, democratic practices. So "wanting history" might be a sort of corporate nostalgia, expressed as what she calls the "politeness" of an academy liberated from the once pervasive dominance of historical understanding, but happy to agree, for old time's sake, that "any rigorous theoretical form or mode of inquiry needs a historical perspective, a proper historicity" (620).

Yet there is, as she says herself, no real choice but to *have* history. In a host of "studies" courses, history is taught not only from reports and prose fictions but (with no regard for "the 50-year rule"[11]) from films and hastily taped TV shows; documented video editions of films and TV shows; photocopies of any sort of text that can be copied; recorded or live testimonials; "critique" expeditions to museums, galleries, tourist sites, and monumental public spaces; great wads of xeroxed theory; from magazines and the morning's newspaper. Taught this way, inflected by the concerns of Aboriginal, feminist, multicultural, and (more rarely, still) gay and lesbian scholarship, history is a set of public debates, and it is monitored, as such, in the media.[12] Whatever the balance in institutions between the new, "odd" versions of history and the traditional discipline (with which, for the moment, academic power and prestige remains), I am certain that a cultural studies that gamely declared itself post-historical—or probed too seriously its divergences from what historians of good will can cheerfully recognize as history—would be consigned in Australia to the spotlit obscurity of the art world, or the shade of the philosophy seminar.

Does this expansion of the practical activities that can be given history's name help us to deal more confidently with questions of cultural change, or does it make our concepts of culture and change more vague? In the pedagogies I am describing, "wanting history" and wanting to "change the culture" by gaining some purchase on public debate, some influence over what can count in future as a useable past, are desires not easily disentangled. "New" history is a product of mixed motives, and what is interesting about this situation is its utter lack of novelty. If a history "option" is a site of acute awareness that it is now "very difficult to make time into a principle of intelligibility, let alone a principle of identity"[13] (as Marc Augé, an anthropologist, puts it), the intelligibility and identity of history as a discipline of *statecraft* are not necessarily threatened by this: not in immigrant-based societies and settler states, where the study of culture as disjunctive and contested, and a rendering historic of time itself as a European mode of understanding,[14] may more effectively serve the purposes of nation-building than any discourse on a common past, or a connected and coherent culture.[15]

From this perspective, the impermanence of historians' discourse and disciplinary practices may be less significant than the enduring power of History as the name *of* a cultural discipline. As Dipesh Chakrabarty eloquently explains, it matters that wanting history is not a primal human desire.[16] We have to be taught to want it, to learn that history is the name of something we lack, and this particular pedagogy of desire and lack has been intimately bound up with nationalism as a project aspiring to govern change. On the other hand, given this history, a longing *for* history need not be nationalist in impulse or citizenly in force. In cultural studies, it is more likely to be organized by transnational constituents of subjectivity and experience, and by mobile figures of resistance or excess. It follows that "making history" gains lucidity and power as an *institutional* project from the very impermanence of historical discourse, and the malleability of historical practices, that Steedman describes.

Nor does "wanting history" have to depend on a sense of *lacking* history, or even on having a sense of history for which "lack" is a relevant category. Desire for history may be created and distributed pragmatically, like the "new domain of positivity" that Stephen Muecke sees "forged under the slogan 'Australia has an Aboriginal Past.'"[17] Across a continent, in a short space of time, this slogan has circulated a *demand*, as well as a desire, from the Black Australian spaces it helps to organize to the White Australian spaces it most directly, but not exclusively, addresses. Cited and amplified by many different bodies, relayed between the T-shirt shop and the archive, the media and the museum, the slogan gathers force as a demand for historical recognition, historical work, but also as a demand *for desire*; it demands that non-Aboriginal Australians learn *to want to learn* about this past, and to want this past as history.

So any simple reiteration of history's history as the *citizenly* discipline obscures complicated issues about the placing and address of differing desires for history in different public spaces. Wanting history, non-historians do not usually want just anybody's history, or even simply to be touched by the dignity and authority that historicity still endows. We may want "our own" histories, the more strongly if we do feel denied history, or subjected *to* history, in the past; or, histories that potentially may have something to do with us—histories that pressure us, solicit, engage, or confront us, histories unsettling the frameworks in which we desire and evaluate "change." In these fluid conditions, written history as the product of the exacting, vanishing labor that Steedman values as history—"the uncovering of new facts, the endless reordering of the immense detail that makes the historian's map of the past" (614)—may not be quite what we want, or all that we might be wanting. Methodological desire alone is rarely strong enough to carry amateurs through thick textual slabs of detail about people, places, and times with which we have no lived or imaginable connection. Wanting history, I read for the theory and skip the facts.

The empirically minded historian does have a problem with desire in the international as well as interdisciplinary geography of cultural studies. It surfaces near the end of Steedman's essay when she calls her account of a British situation "parochial" in its setting, a U.S. cultural studies conference. In an academic context, to be parochial (as the *Macquarie Dictionary* has it, "confined to or interested only in one's own parish, or some particular narrow district or field") is unengaging, a failure of *spatial* tact: we fail to touch or be touched by others in a discourse "large" enough to appeal to more than one parochialism. Of course, such failure never threatens all parochialisms equally. Chakrabarty reminds us that *because* of history, only the history of those "already at the centre of things" is "inherently interesting to others" (103). However, the historian risks parochialism by the very nature of her practice: new facts, an endless reordering of detail, a fine attention to particulars, have no value without a shared frame of reference to make them meaningful to others, and a way of translating what *counts* as significant change.

But this is not a problem only for British historians. In the transnational economy of cultural studies—centered in the United States with its conference and publishing circuits, managed through the functionally grand narratives of U.S. feminism, multiculturalism, postcolonialism, diaspora, postmodernism—any analysis of overly specific materials differing too much from U.S. norms runs the risk of a failure to address: the parochial becomes the *pointless*. Like speaking as an outsider ("the historian"), calling oneself parochial is a cosmopolitan solution to this; Steedman's self-description is tactful, enabling her to launch her questions pointedly at anyone who cares to respond. More usually, what we call "theory" does the work of fabricating an address to the topics deemed inherently interesting in a given transnational space.[18] Within such space, theory *is* the work of extracting a cosmopolitan point from the most parochially constructed or ephemeral "events" in Grossberg's sense—even when that point is to criticize theory's cosmopolitanism.

Hence the odd, awkward status of *theory* (rather than history) in cultural studies, where "theory" has in practice had little to do with strengthening the autonomy of the field,[19] even less to do with dissolving the autonomy of other disciplines, but a great deal to do with cross-cultural and interdisciplinary translation, negotiation, and power play. Cultural theory is a medium of diplomacy. This is why the term simultaneously refers, in media as well as academic usage, to a small but internationally recognized canon of names; to a subphilosophical jargon; and to a populist performance mode that aesthetically signposts its mixing of expository and narrative (or "academic" and "personal") rhetorics. All three practices are ways of creating a partial and often temporary commonality between people with little in common.

This is why theory can be described, on the one hand, as an "object of exchange"[20] to be criticized for its First World presumptions and its homogenizing powers, even as it is practiced, on the other hand, as a utopian work of reflection on the conditions in which translation between heterogeneous, politically unequal, and conflicting knowledges (with, perhaps, unevenly shared histories of contact) may occur. Criticizing the "currency" of theory is part of this process. So is its tactful use to relieve contextually more powerful others of the burden of their failure to desire the "facts" of our history.

Here, Steedman's questioning admits its most challenging inflection: is cultural studies, then, effectively *bound* to schematic and secondary ways of dealing with the past? In this book, my answer is "no": cultural studies entails a flexible relation both to history *and* to the sweeping claims, spatial as well as temporal, circulating as theory. However useful her challenge, Steedman's all-embracing opposition between history and theory (of which "the culture concept" works as a metonym in her text) makes it hard to think in practical ways about the third term, "cultural studies." The pressing question for practitioners is not whether cultural studies can make "room" for historical case studies. Of course it can. The question is rather what a "case study" might mean, and what it can *do*, in cultural studies.

I share Grossberg's preference for the term "context," rather than "case study," to describe a method as well as an object of cultural studies research. Grossberg defines a context as a "specific bit of everyday life" positioned *between* culture, understood as "a specific body of practices," and particular social forces, institutions, and relations of power.[21] Cultural studies works to understand how contexts are made, unmade, and remade, and how they change the meaning and value of cultural practices. A "case study" then minimally involves an act of delimiting a context. It follows that it really is impossible to generalize about the role of "time" and history in cultural (case) studies. For one of the few assumptions that unites the field is that contexts, including contexts of research, are always dynamic, and open to change.

This is why I do not set out in this book to review the vast theoretical literature now produced in many disciplines on the relations between "history" and "culture" (not to mention "time" and "space"). My focus is on a tiny sample of popular cultural constructions of "history" in the double-edged, colloquial sense of "significant past and present events" and "discourse on the past." When I do discuss theories bearing on the role played by histories in popular culture, I restrict my scope to a few texts I find useful in context; this is not a book about the philosophy of history,[22] and I write elsewhere about historicism in theories of popular culture.[23]

This book took shape very slowly as an essay in cultural studies, not cultural theory. In my understanding of this distinction, it follows that I can't adequately respond to Steedman's question of desire or Grossberg's questions of method solely in argumentative terms. I need to define a context that makes these questions matter.

PERIOD OF STUDY: 1972–1995

When I first began this project in the mid-1980s, I wanted to study the cultural politics of Development—with the capital D that hallows the word in the usage of the real-estate/tourism/leisure-industrial complex better known as the "hospitality sector"—in Australia between 1972 and 1988. These dates were chosen as a rough guide to a periodization made necessary, I thought, by tourism's growing importance to the Australian economy, its effects in the social landscape, and the resonance of both in the new *national* image-space created by regulatory changes and domestic satellite technology in 1986;[24] without historical boundaries, such a project does risk descriptive chronicling of apparently endless change. Periodization does not signify "history" in a disciplinary sense. I simply meant to limit my research.

Nineteen seventy-two is a symbolic threshold year in modern Australian history. The first Labor government[25] since 1949 was elected in a climate of euphoric political radicalism and desire for social change, but also in the last year when it was easy to assume that economic prosperity was "natural" to Australia; with the mad boom of 1973 came increasingly open talk about "postwar" prosperity as a historical "phase" that could actually be said to be over. Sixteen years later, in 1988, another Labor government (first elected in 1983 on a platform of pragmatism and a promise of social consensus) supervised the Australian Bicentenary as a huge, tourist-oriented, media spectacle—a "historical special" that lasted all year and had a strong social impact on major cities, especially Sydney.

During those sixteen years, it became a media commonplace that Australia is not a securely affluent "European" society on the edge of "Asia," but an odd, vulnerable hybrid, a "poor little rich country" (as the most dismal of economic pundits, Maximilian Walsh, entitled his 1979 book on "the shock of the seventies"); *something like* a "Third World economy" dependent on natural resources and tourism, deeply indebted and with a structurally underdeveloped manufacturing sector, yet sustaining a spendthrift society with First World expectations of living standards and an entrenched First World *self-image*.[26] No longer an outpost of Europe, Australia was now a peripheral country of the Pacific Rim, economically dominated by Japan. In the 1980s, then, government added a diffuse cultural pedagogy to its program of economic internationalization. Promoting tourism would be part of a wider process of "reconstructing Australia" in which white Australians would learn to adjust our expectations—and begin to rethink that self-image.[27]

Within this historical framework of intensely conflictual change, I chose tourism as a focus for studying, in very small "contexts," how changes were worked through, on the one hand, in the everyday living of particular communities, and, on the other, in what Donald Horne calls "*the public culture*": the mixture of rituals, beliefs, customs, practices, and images of policy and pleasure created by all those institutions, great and small, state and private, sacred and secular, that sustain a "mirage that can float over a society, purporting to be its national life, serving some interests and suppressing the very existence of others."[28] For Horne, a *public* culture is not always the same as "hegemony" understood as a negotiated common sense, and it is certainly not always *popular* culture in the sense of being widely practiced, enjoyed, and shared: "a majority of the people in a society may not appear in a public culture at all, or may be presented in some way in which they don't recognise themselves" (vii).

I was interested in the reworking of public culture in Australia during this period, including many of those beliefs in whiteness, Britishness, homosociality, ordinariness, and egalitarianism that for over a century had sustained the *feeling* of being "major" for Anglo-Celtic[29] working-class people. The federal government agenda for this reworking included a media-promoted shift in national mythology from protectionist "working man's paradise" to free trade tourist heaven. However, the *imagery* of such a shift could not be "popularized" to the same degree or in the same way as that of the no-less-engineered policy shifts, in this period, from White to Multicultural Australia, and from Classless to Cosmopolitan society[30]—not least because so many migrants imported as industrial labor after the Second World War found their cosmopolitanism useless to the tourist economy. A majority of Australians simply could not appear in a Pacific Rim tourist picture; or, to put the problem in a less unnegotiable way, the roles accorded most Australians could not be recognized as "major."[31]

At the level of *popular* mythology, then, "the improbable enclosure of tourism within an apparently nationalist commercial project"[32] always had a potential to interfere with the ideological work of multiculturalism and cosmopolitanism. Tourism is just too blatantly sectoral in its economic appeal to assuage majority fears. As Jennifer Craik succinctly puts it, the industry favors "low skilled, part-time, casualised and underpaid ('feminised') employment," and selected coastal or desert locations.[33] Packaging tourism as nationally redemptive can create new needs for old social scapegoats: migrants taking the good jobs; women, taking bad jobs and undermining unionism; Aborigines taking land, taxpayers' money, and tourists away from the cities; Asians "taking over the country" as tourists and developers. Sensible cultural studies lessons on the virtues of well-managed tourism in, say, Bali,[34] do not really address such fears, which are powerful intimations that the "majority" mirage is fading.

Nevertheless, "touristification" proceeds, in slow time, as a cultural and economic process among others. In my own fairly populous state of New South Wales, where battles over wilderness are relatively rare and the housing supply for citizens is a major environmental problem, tourism is usually experienced less directly as a threat or a panacea than as a mundane reality negotiated daily in people's lives. So I set out to study representations of space, time, and movement *at work* in and around family tourist practices (shopping and driving as well as sight-seeing) as they were carried out by residents as well as visitors in particular places.

I examined discourses involved in the production of tourist places—government reports, media stories, planning debates, promotional literature—and circulating as gossip, myth, and opinion between the users of a place. Since I think of "particularity" as a set of relations rather than an essence, I also wanted to analyze *different* tourist places on Australia's middle East Coast: a family motel in the small bush town of Tenterfield ("At Henry Parkes Motel"); three suburban shopping malls, two in Brisbane, one in the rural-industrial town of Maitland ("Things to Do with Shopping Centers"); an urban tourist tower ("Great Moments in Social Climbing"). All these sites of analysis were spaces of women's work; all were inhabited or invested in some way by working and lower-middle-class communities; and most were involved in the process of remaking socio-economically ravaged regions as "tourist landscapes."

An early outcome of my preliminary work was an interest in the persistence of ideologies (narratives and rhetorics) of Progress and Development: how and where "progress" and "development" were mobilized and disputed as values, by whom, what tasks they performed, what actions they enabled, and, since the two terms are distinct but able to act as synonyms, how they shift in relation to each other, overlapping on some occasions, conflicting on others. Progress and Development are grand narratives both, implicated as they are in modern histories, theories of history, and theories of theories of history that are hardly unique to Australia.[35] However, despite the incredulity that is now, according to Lyotard, the condition of any grand narrative's circulation,[36] they have had and still have an intensely practical resonance for local politics as well as national historiography. If Adorno is right to claim that "more than other concepts, progress vanishes upon specification of what is really meant by it, that is, what progresses and what does not,"[37] then it is vital to ask *how* progress is "specified" and, perhaps, vaporized in social conflicts over its value.

The pursuit of competing versions of Progress, with Development as an instrument or opponent, has long been considered, by widely diverging interests, the driving force of European settlement in Australia; by the early twentieth century, "the law of progress and the survival of the fittest"[38] was a core justification for the White Australia Policy and for Aboriginal dispossession. In 1977, Bob Connell bluntly put it this way:

Modern conservatism is different in a number of ways from the aristo-cratic and religious European conservatism of the nineteenth century. It is secular, optimistic, and ties its defence of private property to a doctrine of prosperity and progress. This is nowhere more clear than in those coun-tries, like Australia, which were colonies of settlement in the nineteenth century. 'Progress' was almost the condition of their existence: killing off the blacks and filling up the country with whites and their buildings was the process with which local politics began.[39]

Written in 1977, Connell's account of conservatism needs refinement to-day. In "Ecstasy and Economics," I argue that neoliberal economics, politi-cally projected as neo-conservatism, has largely displaced that secular, opti-mistic doctrine of prosperity and progress with a mystical pessimism emphasizing *survival* and *management*. However, Connell's stress on the shaping importance of Progress retains its analytical force. Today, when ap-peals to "progress" are as likely to arouse groans as applause in public de-bates about the purpose of a development, Progress is still invoked as a *foun-dational* value, whether coded as a spirit to be recaptured or as a loss to lament but accept—that is, as a myth of origins, if no longer of destiny.

Histories of race and racism, nation-building and nationalism, class con-flict and labor relations, immigration, and the struggles for population con-trol waged over and through women's bodies and sexualities, cannot easily be written here without reference to what Paul Gilroy calls, somewhat dis-missively, "the mesmeric idea of history *as* progress."[40] In "Things to Do with Shopping Centers," I suggest that even a cursory study reveals the te-nacity of the idea's mesmerizing power in social contexts where "History" in the disciplinary sense is not overtly at issue—for example, debates about housing, health, community services, leisure facilities, the environment, new technology. At the same time, rhetorics of evolution, elevation, ad-vancement, "upward mobility," and cohesively linear time have served with as much tenacity to articulate the aspirations of radicals, reformers, and dissenters as they have to validate and channel colonial power: as Donald Denoon reminds us, "settler historiography was not only Eurocentric but forward-looking. A golden age lay not in the past but in the near future."[41]

So the voiding of Progress, in the 1980s, from neo-liberal narratives of Australia's *future* ("poor little rich country") was in itself a historic shift that brought no joy to progressive critics of "history as progress." It was one of the ways in which economic models of development were being sundered, at this time, from other, untimely elements of the concept's complex nine-teenth-century content—social reform, human betterment, the struggle for justice, dreams of a more equitable distribution of property, income, and resources. Indeed, despite its title Max Walsh's *Poor Little Rich Country* in 1979 was only partly a self-pitying fable of white decline. More forcefully, it was an early move to popularize the rejection of ideas of *social* progress as too "costly" that would permeate the public culture of the 1980s.

The socially traumatic, contested, and still unfinished reworking of relations between the old "public" (social) and the new "privatized" (corporate) models of progress is an organizing theme of this book. While I do not try to survey currently "active" theories of progress (a forbidding task, even for the period I discuss), I do examine six *contexts* in which the circulation of a story or a figure of progress—whether an emblematically singular character (a late-nineteenth-century self-made man in "At Henry Parkes Motel," King Kong and the Human Fly in "Great Moments in Social Climbing," a late-twentieth-century "upwardly mobile" man in "Ecstasy and Economics") or an overtly corporate parable of a collective aspiration (small town revival in "Things to Do with Shopping Centers," national renewal in "On the Beach" and "Lunching for the Republic")—defines a *revisionary* space in which a local boundary between public and corporate is redrawn or disputed, and a struggle over "history" conducted.

As it turned out, my interest in these issues made it impossible to end my study of "tourist places" with the Bicentenary or to focus only on cultural responses to tourism. The touristic, ahistorical form of the mass media Bicentenary (the version most Australians had in common) paradoxically fostered a wide interest in "history" in every sense of that term.[42] For all the homogenizing activities aimed at an international tourist market, the Bicentenary celebrations pluralized, or rather *multiplied*, historical consciousness in Australian cultural life. It gave a new legitimacy to critical accounts of the colonial past—distributed by museums, TV shows, radio, films, pop songs, festivals, personal memoirs, and magazine stories as well as academic books—and to sophisticated public attacks (most obviously, by Aborigines) on the idea of history as progress.

More social activists in this period began to think of the media as offering *time*, as well as "space," for action and argument. Dedicated to the power of positive thinking and conflict resolution, as any state-sponsored enterprise on such a scale must be, the Bicentenary welcomed constructive feminist, migrant, working-class, local, family, and, above all, Aboriginal historical experiments with financially open arms, and endowed them, for a time, with a respectability that flowed on to other kinds of news and entertainment. As a result of both these developments, it shaped a lively space of public debate about the meaning of a *national* history.[43]

However, the visible fluency in this debate of "special interest groups," including feminists, also began to foster resentment among rural and white working-class people who felt excluded or attacked by the revisionary mood of all this talk about the past, while coping with economic reforms that seemed most obviously to benefit big business, on the one hand, and tertiary-educated, media-smart, middle-class lobbyists for "minority" interests on the other.[44] While I thought that the Bicentenary inflected rather than initiated conflicts about the politics of development, the time-released complexity of its impact led me to consider more closely how those conflicts in turn were being shaped by media images *of* economic policy and social activism.

I came to see the unity of my own project as deriving from the tension between the social *values* commemorated and "built in" to the working-class landscapes I knew,[45] the neo-liberal economic *beliefs* of the Labor regime (shaped by the political losses of the 1970s, foregrounded in the boom years of the 1980s then shrouded with something like shame in the recession that followed) and the historic *myths* of Labor as the party of social progress, creative nationalism, and historical consciousness. Dusted down for the Bicentenary, these myths were powerfully renewed for the new, socially progressive, cultural elites (in ways that I discuss in "Lunching for the Republic") in the early 1990s.

The media figure of Paul Keating, Treasurer in the Hawke Labor government of 1983–91, and Australian Prime Minister 1991–95, became central to my effort to understand popular debate about history. Widely represented as embodying economic rationalism and globalization during the 1980s, Keating "morphed" in 1990 into a bearer of history and nationalism. The critical, revisionary accounts of colonial history admitted to the mainstream during the Bicentenary became, for four brief but heady years, institutionally dominant accounts. They even crept into the tourist industry: most obviously through museums, and the promotion of Aboriginal culture, but also through state support for an export image of Australia as an urbane, socially liberal,[46] *multiculturalist* heaven.

Given that the contradictions between this culturalist program and the economic realities of life for most rural and working-class people had been obvious for a decade before the "Keating era" began, it is not surprising that the era ended with a devastating defeat for Labor at the federal election of March 1996.[47] For historians, it will be a long time before this period can seriously be evaluated. As a cultural critic, however, I am concerned with the role played by images and stories of the past in the conflicts of the present. For me, the value of analyzing both phases of the Keating *mythos*, "economics" (the 1980s) and "history" (the 1990s), is that it shows how profoundly so-called "local" and "everyday" issues of identity, community, and cultural power—so acutely raised by the *social* pressures of a tourist economy—are shaped by and responsive to the "global" struggle over the future of the nation-state. This is the concern of the first four chapters of the book.

The last two chapters examine from a feminist perspective the national *political* terrain of this struggle. Like many an experiment in "sensitive" and "sustainable" tourism, the Keating government attempted to fuse a cultural politics of national identity–promotion with an economic policy of internationalism. I do not presume to say whether this formula ("and . . . and") succeeded or failed at its social balancing act; even for a cultural critic it is too soon to tell, and the story of the nation-state form is far from over. I do say, however, what kinds of problems and opportunities can arise for feminist intellectuals on a political terrain so defined, and what kinds of "cultural politics" such a balancing act makes possible. That is the concern of my final chapter.

Alas, the methodological dilemmas of criticism cannot neatly be contained by an act of periodization. During the years I spent puzzling over issues of economy and culture, every place I was studying *changed*. All of them renovated their identities at least once. Some won, for a while, and others lost in the "regional wars for jobs and dollars"[48] that forced so many towns to compete, often against the odds, to become what David Harvey calls "centres of consumption."[49] Even the place or the object which first aroused my interest in these issues mutated—and it had seemed to be, on the surface of things, a massive overstatement of immutability.

METAMORPHOSES AT SYDNEY TOWER

Sydney Tower is a tourist-telecommunications monument in the center of Sydney's Central Business District (CBD), and it rises out of a historic shopping center called "Centrepoint." When it first opened in 1981, Sydney Tower was heralded as inaugurating a CBD ("downtown") revival,[50] and it was a focus of heated argument about its aesthetics and furious gossip about its function. In what turned out to be an inaugural gesture for my own research, I wrote an essay about it.[51] While it may seem self-indulgent to discuss the problems with that essay (given the parallel I've just created between "my" criticism and Sydney Tower's history), it is a way of summarizing the problems this history poses for a certain kind of cultural criticism (including the problem of parallelism).

In 1981, I was struggling to disengage from the French semiotic tradition in which I had been schooled, and so I did the obvious. I structured my reading of Sydney Tower around a point-by-point demonstration that it was *not* like the object of Roland Barthes's essay, "The Eiffel Tower."[52] This contrast was not quite as arbitrary as it looks, given the flagrant dissimilarities between the two structures. Long before Sydney Tower was built, it was promoted as "The Eiffel Tower of the Southern Hemisphere" ("only higher").

For a long time the Eiffel Tower has been the model of models of "modernity" as an engineering feat. Reference to it marks the history of the American skyscraper, "beating" the Eiffel Tower being the mission of the Chrysler Building, and thus of the cloning of *American* skylines around the world.[53] I wanted to know *how* this metacliché was used in Sydney in the 1970s. Differentiating the Parisian and Sydney towers by way of a critique of an essay by Barthes, my own model of models at that time, seemed a logical way of learning to think from Sydney in 1981 rather than Paris in the 1950s. It also attended faithfully to Barthes's own critique of *Mythologies* in "Change the

Object Itself."[54] I thought that if I showed how my Sydney Tower differed from Barthes's Eiffel Tower, I might change the object (in his terms) as it presents itself to speech—helping to transform the developers' serial object, "Eiffel-Sydney Tower," into a locally articulated *event.*

Looking back, this idea seems to me not only formalist but insanely devious. It was also unsuccessful. I merely supplemented Barthes as my model of models with a mix of Foucault on surveillance, Baudrillard on implosion, and feminist film theory on voyeurism. Certainly, I was picking up on a real convergence between local intellectual passions and the spatial stories circulating about the Tower. Sydney Tower was an urban talking-point for years, an inexhaustible source of rumor and anecdote. Looking at the opaque stem holding up the turret, many people believed, and a colleague of mine (it was rumored) taught as fact, that "THEY"—the police, the CIA—had their offices in there, all the way up to the top, so they could watch everything we were doing (surveillance). As for implosion, the media frenziedly described Sydney Tower as attracting bodies and money to the city center from outer suburbia and "all over the world," then fretted about urban parking and circulation systems collapsing under pressure.[55] Voyeurism was popular in a ribald rather than a critical-paranoid mode. The great width of the bottom of the turret on top of the phallic spire made it look like a dress, provoking talk about the ambiguity of the Tower's sex and the excitement (which is real enough) of looking up at it from below.

In producing a mirror exchange between theory and gossip, people "working on the Tower" had an intense if fuzzy experience of pertinence in that work. It was one of those times when there is coincidence or a *buzz* between theoretical terms and those more widely circulating in the public culture, in an effect that we readily call "relevance." At other times, when there is no such co-incidence, we may too easily assume that the relationship between theory and public culture is therefore one of irrelevance. So I want to contextualize that long-gone buzz about Sydney Tower by looking in more detail at the representation of history to be found *inside* it in 1981.

The turret interior was elaborately and self-reflexively decorated. Each of the two observation decks had a gallery of photographs running round above the rim of the "view," and each level had its own theme. The lower deck commemorated the development of Sydney as a locale: old photographs of pioneer cottages and rough roads contrasted with the sublimity and modernity of the urban Panorama outside. The upper deck gave a formalist history of "the tower," and of tourist activities. Linking both levels was the theme of the end of the "tyranny of distance" (one of the great popular clichés of Australian postwar historiography),[56] thanks to telecommunications. From informational displays to toys, new technology was everywhere invoked as enabling Australia's integration into the age of global simultaneity: no more time lag, no more isolation by vast space from the rest of the world and from each other.

This imagery proclaimed the fulfillment of a mission that the developers had set themselves in the rhetoric used for over twenty years to "get the Tower off the ground." As a "talking" or telecommunications tower, Sydney Tower was to *be* an annunciation of modernity. It would enable Sydney to "grow up," as journalists and architects put it at the time, and to become a "world city"; Sydney would be integrated *at last!* (if a little late) into the modern age inaugurated long ago by the model of modern models, the Eiffel Tower.

As with all such annunciations and the linear temporality they entail, there could be nothing new about this. In fact, there seemed to be nothing new about Sydney Tower. It imitated a number of tourist-telecommunications towers worldwide (the London Post Office tower, Toronto's CN tower),[57] and no sooner was it finished than critics were complaining that it was an old-fashioned building. However, in a history of Australian modernity, this archaism constitutes its instant classicism. As David Bromfield has shown of Perth in the interwar period, "the modern" was only marginally understood by Australians as implying the future, youth, originality, innovation, rupture, the unknown, and so forth.[58] The modern is much more commonly a known history, something that has *already happened elsewhere* and needs to be reproduced with a local content. Along with its dated thrust ethos and failed funk aesthetic, Sydney Tower's Eiffelesque aspirations placed it squarely in the great tradition of Australian "positive unoriginality."[59]

At least, that is how things look if you frame the problem of the modern in terms derived from aesthetic debate. I think there was something "new" or symbolically inaugural about Sydney Tower: with its self-reflexive celebration of tourism as a *means* of becoming-modern, it was the first, big architectural announcement of Sydney's emerging "vocation" for tourism,[60] and the first big monument to doubly hail Sydney residents as "citizen-tourists" (in Robert Somol's phrase)[61]—citizens at one with foreign tourists in our admiring gaze at our city, yet also the living *objects* of that self-same tourist gaze. The talking turret supplied photos of Sydney people, perhaps some of us visiting the Tower, waving at the camera from their/our nicely restored wrought-iron balconies, wandering around their/our freshly repainted Chinatown, strolling their/our exotic zoos and museums. Here began what has long since become an explicit, sometimes state-funded discourse on the need to remodel local culture for the needs of a tourist economy: to improve our manners (learning strange phrases such as "have a nice day"); to change our attitudes to labor (learning that service is a virtue, not a chore); to mask the prejudices running through the old majority culture (learning that racist and sexist talk is bad for business).[62]

However, the most striking component of Sydney Tower's self-production involved an *un*masked history of "race" in the audiovisual theatrettes on both levels of the turret. In harmony with the photographs, the lower theatrette defined Sydney as a tourist locale with pictures of people waving from boats, streets, and houses at objects not represented. All these images of *pointing* ("you are here") were in snapshot style, except one. The last was a simulated "naive" painting of the foundation of the city: natives on the foreshore pointed at a sailing ship in the Harbour, the Europeans on board pointed back, and the soundtrack intoned these words: "*You* can imagine *their* surprise when the first settlers sailed in to this magnificent Harbour." This was genesis: the first white gaze at Aborigines, first objects of tourism in a brave new land; "we" Europeans (for this display did not address Koori tourists) imagine "their" surprise at the wonder of "us," while we gaze at "this" (not their) magnificent harbor. Then on the upper level came a sequel, "Evolution of the Tower: From Tree House to Sydney Tower." The higher display *began* with a simulated naive painting of a creation story: caveman, attacked by animals, invents the treehouse; elevated, cavewoman sees a volcano erupting in the distance; she *points*, and the universal language of tourism is born. Naive images gave way to a postcard mode, and a series of model towers (London, Pisa, Eiffel) "ascended" from the ancestral tree house until, in climactic bursts of repetition of a single identical image, the pure, final form of Sydney Tower was attained.

Walking in the sky in 1981, the impact of this narrative of Progress was strong. Prissy as it may sound, I was deeply shocked by these displays—a rare experience, for me, in Australian family entertainment space. (In contrast, I am shocked by G-rated culture in the United States all the time; but I am not majoritarian there to anything like the same degree.) I *knew* that story. As a child in the 1950s, I learned it from newsreels at the cinema and from drawings and history lessons in the state-supplied school magazines that taught me my social Darwinism, the story that for so long gave White Australia a way of fixing boundaries of community and securing national identity. The displacement of this story by multiculturalism was recent enough in 1981 for "Evolution of the Tower" to be appalling in its bald reaffirmation of a brutal truth about the principles of "Australian History." Over the next few years, its impact was intensified for me by the opening of a more public discussion by Aboriginal people of their own negotiations of an ever-increasing tourist and art-market interest in their cultures and histories.[63] For this reason, Sydney Tower's autobiography seemed an ideal place to begin a study of the narratives and rhetorics of Progress in contemporary Australia.

So you can imagine *my* surprise when I went back to the Tower one day in 1989, with the reordering of detail in mind, and it was almost all gone. Worse, it was as though none of the representations I was laboring over had ever been there. I pestered every employee I could find with questions about the renovations, but none of the part-time, casualized, and underpaid staff had been around long enough to remember the decor of the Tower having ever been any different from the way it was on that day. So the episode ended with a crazed cultural critic staggering around the turret, crying, "What have you done with the evidence?"

The lower deck had become a cafeteria, and its theatrette had vanished. Sepia photographs had been replaced by plastic bas-reliefs with a wildflower motif, in a rectangular design alluding not to wildflowers but to cafeteria trays. The "Evolution of the Tower" survived on the upper level, but as a self-contained story with no anaphoric reference linking its "primitive" figures to Aboriginal people, whose existence was now admitted only by the toy boomerangs in the souvenir shop. All the other images linking the Tower to Sydney's history had also disappeared. Instead of narrating the founding of place, the gallery celebrated international tourist *time*: ads for duty-free fur and opal shops, portraits of transport systems (trains, boats, hydrofoils, even a charter bus drawn up near a Qantas jet), and snapshots of other destinations—anonymous motel pools, distant tropical and rural resorts.

These images promoted only the possibility of going somewhere else. No longer a centralizing metonym of the City, Sydney Tower had become a prelude offering an "overview," not of space to be consumed but of an itinerary of movements to be performed. Sydney residents were simply ignored—unless we, too, were going elsewhere and could qualify for duty-free shopping. Otherwise, looking out at our city, we could at best overlook the programs of other people's pleasures and gain a vague pride of place therefrom.

Foolishly, I had failed to expect such a drastic change. Of course, I had expected to revise my frames of reference and reformulate problems accordingly. In the years since my first visit to the Tower, new accounts of Australian colonialism had appeared, rapidly entering the public culture and shattering the complacency with which I, like many other white feminists, had thought about history, place, and "home."[64] In 1989, I also knew that I was gazing at a socio-economic "panorama" vastly different from 1981, when the city was still sluggish from the great property market crashes of the mid-1970s. Now, the view was of a frenzy of construction interfering with the tourist dream it aspired to accommodate.[65] From the turret, cranes vied with skyscrapers for visual attention. On the ground, the roar of jackhammers pulverizing your ears, walking in the city was a nightmare; whole guide books became dated overnight as buildings disappeared and city blocks mutated. I knew, too, that if the Sydney skyline is always a projection of class societies elsewhere,[66] the 1989 skyline was being created by the emergent class systems of the Pacific Rim, not those of the age of the Eiffel Tower.

All this knowledge, however, was of little practical assistance in deciding what to *do* with the discovery that my "founding" site had changed in almost embarrassing congruence with the socio-economic landscape. Here, Grossberg's question returns: "what do you do when every event is . . . changing too fast to allow the comfortable leisure of academic criticism?" Well, you can ask, first of all, *why* this kind of change is a problem. After all, you can argue that change itself should be the object of study, rather than an "event" construed as a "text" read as a symptom of a "condition" to be diagnosed by cultural critics. Studying change rather than texts, objects, or even practices in popular culture is in part what Grossberg suggests we might do, and I would agree with his shift of emphasis.[67]

However, studying change creates a problem for analyzing "places," which tend to change at a rate that may be called geological in comparison with TV, music, or fashion but that is drastic when it happens. This is the problem of *description* in the writing of a cultural study. Cognate in some ways with the plot summary in film criticism, description also involves problems of exchange between local as well as national cultures in a not quite postimperial world. Barthes, for example, could call the Eiffel Tower "present to the entire world"—a reasonable proposition, especially if one adds the restriction, "of likely readers of this book"—and this fiction of presence and stability over time meant that he didn't have to *describe* it.

Writing of turret interiors in Sydney, or, even more acutely, of motels and shopping centers in towns that many Australians have never heard of, I cannot take presence or durability for granted in quite the same way, any more than critics of U.S. cable TV can assume familiarity, even from other critics, with any but already canonical shows. In this sense, obscurity and proliferation create comparable problems. Faced with this need to describe, to create a referent, the most resolutely "textual" of cultural studies can drift, just like the "consumer activity" research so often taken to be its opposite, into practicing a version of the *ethnographic present*—that disciplined failure of reflexivity that can, as Eric Michaels notes, "be obscured but not changed by writing about it."[68] Describing them, we monumentalize and often also render *timeless* the "places" we discuss. Then when they change, as they almost always do, an apocalyptic erasure of a world appears to have occurred.

What interests me most about description is not the epistemological or metaphysical issues it can be made to raise, but the technical, rhetorical issue of the strategies of reference involved in producing particular descriptions—and the disciplinary problems these strategies can create. If I am honest about it, what annoyed me most about the inner transformation of Sydney Tower was the *tense* change it imposed on my account. Taking away the security of my "mythographic" present, it forced me to shift register from "discourse" to "history" (in Benveniste's rather than Steedman's sense of those terms),[69] and thus to enter a different relationship to my material. I found myself writing a fuzzy sort of historical narrative, and this threatened the legitimacy of my research. Despite encroachments from Economics, History is still the most privileged discourse of liberal intellectual authority in Australia, and I am not a historian. Moreover, the "past" of Sydney Tower is not easily passed off as a hitherto suppressed dimension of national experience important enough to justify resorting to personal narrative. Why should the past of Sydney Tower matter at all, except as an "investment" of a researcher's time and energy?[70]

"THEORY" AS PROGRESS

Cultural studies traditionally offers a number of ways of circumventing a close encounter with this problem.

I could paraphrase various certified general accounts of the culture of late capitalism—such as Baudrillard's theory of "hyperreality" or Jameson's story of postmodernism as a death of "real" history—and then read the renovation of Sydney Tower allegorically as a local variation on these.[71] This would be an Australian "modernist" solution. It would also take me away from cultural studies (analysis of contexts) and back to theory (those "great schematic and secondary sweeps through time").

I could find something empowering in the developments I have described.[72] This has been done with Darling Harbour, a newer citizen-tourist development, and a related monorail that runs through the Sydney CBD. In the controversy over the monorail, some cultural critics argued that its opponents had a morbid Frankfurt School hostility to the popular, and that the monorail experience should be separated from the question of why the Labor government that funded it under pressure from Transfield-Kumagai, the Darling Harbour developer, was also responsible for hospitals in working-class suburbs with walls patched together with chicken wire.[73] This solution achieves equanimity about materially changing objects by fundamentally ignoring difference and eventfulness; the ethnographic present is used to extract the same moral ("life is complex and some good comes of everything") from endlessly diverse situations. Since this moral is independent of its vehicles, it precedes, survives, and can, if necessary, redeem any actual event.

Or, I could reiterate from my old analysis the notion of *implosion*, taking the now disinvested Tower as an emblem of the postpanoptic collapse of meaning and distinction into the "dead center" of the urban core that Robert Somol described in his classic analysis of Chicago's State of Illinois Center—an "urban ruin" that would be, for any story of the Progress of simulation, much more *advanced* than the jaunty verticality of Sydney Tower.[74] This solution returns to aesthetics by declaring the end of social progress and the birth of a dystopian age of "style," confirming both the futility of activism and the death of the critical spirit.

I think that all these possibilities, whatever their separate attractions and disadvantages, share a common flaw. Each is a way of reading a singular site as if *it were* an allegorical exposition of theoretical problems taken as given, and thus an illustration of general forces already known to be at work in the world. My problem is not with "general forces" (talking about tourism that would be absurd) but illustration. Often doing duty as description, this sort of exposition creates a complicity between the aesthetic problematic of the exemplary object, the singular site, "the" text, and what remains, despite rhetorical disavowal, a linear model of historical time in which the inevitable—whether it be the spatial fix of late capitalism, the moral imperative to find empowerment, or the apotheosis of simulation—is realized in *a* time which is not that of urban development, the popular, or "late" capitalism, but that of the enunciating subject of the discourse in which this complicity is produced. In other words: the grand narrative of history as progress is restored and miniaturized, in these accounts, by little parables of "theory as progress."[75]

For example, Somol's witty (and now, "pomo period") conclusion that we must "abandon the language of struggle," because "in quicksand, movement only tends to swallow one faster," depends for its effect on a prior claim that the "world" has largely "moved beyond" the techniques of power that once made activism effective:

> Foucault's project may well have made sense . . . a generation ago, but we are on the side of urban fall-in. Similarly, from our reversed perspective, the currently "progressive" architects and planners who continue to move away from forty-five are unintelligible to those of us on the down side of sixty-eight. Their nova is our black hole. We remember things in their future, although to them we have yet to be born. (115)

In "generational" formulations of this kind (which recur unvaryingly, at the level of form, decade after decade in critical debate), it is in the present tense of the rhetorical "we" that a progressive subject of linear, albeit dystopian, Development is reconstituted, along with a vanguardist, albeit cynical, model of intellectual practice. This "time" belongs to the mundane temporality of a *market* in cultural attitudes and ideas, and its relevance (which is perfectly real) is not to the past or future of urban struggles but to the jostling for position and credibility that is business as usual for that market.

However, it is no use to assert this if one does so moralistically to reiterate as doctrine (from an imaginary position transcending the "market") the notions of unequal development and differential temporality.[76] For practical purposes it is important to ask anew, for each case study or context, *why* a model of temporality evenly unfolding might be a problem. My problem, this time, is that I began by asking questions about the social and cultural uses of contemporary stories of history as Progress, only to find myself retrieving the "theory" I had before the questions.

So one thing I can do in response to changing objects is refuse to be "sucked in" (in Somol's phrase) by the self-promotional rhetoric of particular events or sites. This is one reason for studying several places in a tourist economy, defining a context of relationships, differences, and relative rates of change. If Sydney Tower no longer addresses city residents, other developments do. To ignore this by narrating the Tower's changes in apocalyptic form concedes too much to property developers' proclivity for declaring each monument to capital an "epochal" statement. It follows that an analysis of Sydney Tower's changes would not necessarily be an adequate prelude to going further afield, as an ethnographer or sociologist usefully might, in order to ask why "Green Hills" shopping mall in East Maitland mutated, around the same time, from an outdoor village square to a history-effect enclosure called "The Hunter"; or why, 500 miles north, the gracious history-effect enclosure of Henry Parkes Motel vanished in an explosion of lurid hot pink paint.

HISTORY, "TIMING," AND THE POPULAR

Voluminously analyzed by social theorists and geographers in recent years, global economic, political, and technological shifts have enabled the changes I discuss in this book. Those shifts are not my subject here, although their pressure shapes the substance of every chapter: from the remodeling of a failing country town as a national historic site in "At Henry Parkes Motel" to the recasting of a nation as an open international marketplace in "Lunching for the Republic," each context I discuss is one in which people confront the collapsing of old economies of "work" and "home"; the fraying of social bonds and political alliances that once secured, for some, a progressive sense of history; and an abrading of familiar boundaries of "culture." Within these contexts, I examine the ways in which mass-mediated but niche-marketed (rhetorically directed, socially pitched) images and stories about "great changes" can, in definite circumstances, help to bring changes about.

As my emphasis on aesthetic change will suggest, my questions and research methods derive from the disciplines of so-called textual criticism[77] rather than social science, and from rhetoric rather than philosophy. I do borrow, gratefully, from other disciplines. However, when I offer a historical account of the production of an object or touch on questions of social usage, I do so for purposes defined by my critical project. Such borrowings help me to question aesthetic propositions *about* the historical and social effects of cultural practices. The "aesthetic" in my sense includes institutional ways of using images and stories to legitimize powers and policies as well as to produce cultural values, historical memories, desires, and ethical ideals.

In the process, I deal with two immensely polysemic terms, "history" and "popular culture," so I must mark the limits of my pretension to address the issues that they raise. I use these terms in several senses and do not stop to define my usage every time: I never ask "what is history?" or "what is popular culture?" (questions of cultural theory), attempt a history of the concept of culture, or engage with work in cultural theory on the philosophy of history (which theory-shorthand often conflates with "history");[78] more painfully, I also forgo discussing the now vast feminist literature on the relations between history and culture. I simply ask what is *meant* in particular empirical contexts by history, the popular, and culture. "Meaning," I take as a matter of social negotiation, not semantic definition;[79] when I analyze meaning, I do so in terms of the force and form of *mixed* practices (in Deleuze and Guattari's terms, "regimes of signs")[80] that I assume to be collective ("general") and situated ("particular") in ways that it is my task as a critic to specify.

Although I do not presume to offer here a history *of* the present, my concern is with struggles over the meaning and value of history *in* the present, where "the present" is assumed to have temporal depth—not least, because of the work of memory. I reject the amnesiac model of postmodern consciousness espoused by some theorists of popular culture (and built in to Sydney Tower's administration), a model for which "now" is, in William Gibson's words, "a narrow and literal thing, News-governed . . . Cable-fed. A present honed to whatever very instant of a helicopter traffic report."[81] For me, the present includes amnesiac moments, impulses, and forces. However, just as Sydney Tower is merely one place in a complex tourist economy, not a metonym of a universal spatial form ("*the* tower") or historical phase ("postmodernity"), so the traffic-report "now" is only a fraction of the present, not its essence. I see no point in criticism that reproduces and renders absolute the effects of precarious employment; from the fact that "feminized" workers at a tourist site know nothing of its past (or remember what a cultural critic wants them to remember), it does not follow that they have no memories and no sense of a past.

It *may* follow that criticism needs to rethink what history means when its "sense" is no longer shaped (there, at least, where once it was) by enduring and stable relationships to place projected as "work," "home," "nation." Here, I examine what people say and do in the *name* of history in a very small set of sites. This saying and doing includes telling stories and circulating images of the past, but also developing promotional strategies for commercial as well as community-building purposes; it involves romantic or nostalgic quests for personal and social identity as well as the rigorous search for truth;[82] it entails what Noel Pearson calls "creation, maintenance and deconstruction of popular belief."[83] However, the sense of history that I as a cultural critic most frequently bring to bear on these materials is one specific to the study of *forms* of practice; I emphasize the historicity of genres, narratives, clichés, vernacular turns of phrase and, in chapters 3 and 4, I defend the material distinctness of this level of analysis.[84]

I approach popularity in a similar way. While I never equate the popular with folklore, with mass culture, with the media, with "the majority," with vast numbers of consumers, with the *demos* or with the opposite of "art," all these uses of the term are retraced and reworked in mine; my discourse, too, is enabled by a history of scholarship and debate. While the popular can also be described as an empty category, and one useful way of doing cultural studies is to examine how it works for particular practices of "distinction" (in Bourdieu's phrase), that is not my purpose here.[85] What I do consistently examine is the dynamic, uneasy relationship between *public* culture in Donald Horne's sense—including media, governmental, and corporate images of policy—and the *popular* in Michel de Certeau's sense of an "art of timing," a way of doing things, rather than a space or zone of culture.[86]

This model of the popular has its drawbacks, and I discuss some of these in "Great Moments in Social Climbing." However, it does allow me to distinguish the media-saturated, institutionally sustained and, in de Certeau's terms, *strategic* production of "public" discourse on Australian culture and history from the actual practices, whether everyday (shopping at Green Hills) or extraordinary (climbing Sydney Tower), that serve as materials for that public elaboration of a national life. These practices, the "tactical" things people do, may in turn serve as ways of responding to, contesting or appropriating the "public image" created about them and for them by institutions.

For de Certeau, tactics is an art of taking *time* away from strategic institutions and "places." However, the public/popular distinction for me does not entail an opposition between the official and the vernacular, or the academy and the street; public (institutional/strategic) and popular (practical/tactical) are asymmetrical categories. I am interested in the varying forms and degrees of *involvement* between public culture and popular practices in my period of study, and I take genres, narratives, and rhetorical traditions to be material and historically persistent, as well as productive, modes of such involvement.

Let me be clear, however. The popular practices I discuss are not always socially progressive or heroically subversive. I don't identify with all of them, and I try not to exaggerate the import of any of them. In fact, a case could be made that Australian *public* culture over the past twenty-five years has produced a "mirage" of liberal social experiment (with which I do identify), that has been contested, resisted, and evaded by a "popular" conservatism. While this would be an abusive simplification, the context in which it arises as a possible interpretation of public/popular relations is one in which I want to insist, again, on recognizing different temporalities.

Like the political debates between competing interest groups on television examined in "Media Time," theoretical debates in cultural studies have their own speeds and rates of change. Sometimes they move very fast, much faster than other lines of thinking in a society. Keeping up with the rate of change in our discipline can lead us to ignore the way that a rhetoric or a problematic deemed "dead" or "dated" in one context can be alive and kicking in another. Always occurring too soon, too late, "progress" is an obvious case. My view of my social place as an intellectual is that I need to think not only from a time (which I do inhabit) "late" in the day after centuries of argument about theories of theories of history, but also from those moments of popular timing in which people living in the path of tourist developments too soon say: "it's sad, but you can't stop progress."

INVOLVEMENT: DESIRE AND HISTORY

This raises the question of my own involvement in this study. Following an old, much disputed feminist principle, I mostly confine myself here to tourist landscapes, local histories, and cultural traditions of which I have extensive personal experience. This means that the popular culture I discuss is primarily white, Anglo-Celtic, heterosexually centered, and working-class or petit-bourgeois Australian. However, I do this in a spirit of recognizing and articulating in a critical practice the *otherness* in this culture.

My commitment to doing this is to some degree political. Slavoj Žižek has argued that the "blind spot" of white liberal intellectuals in the West is to recoil from the "red-neck horror" or "populist proto-fascism" of their own traditional cultures while saluting the "autochthonous ethnical communities *of the other*."[87] The history of white feminism's trouble in seeing how racism and colonialism "matter" suggests that Žižek is looking at the wrong blind spot.[88] However, he may be right to say that such recoil, when it occurs, involves a hatred of "one's own" enjoyment that conceals a persecutory ambivalence toward the other's fantasmatic enjoyment. I am certain that it is crucial to take seriously the anxieties and fears pervading self-identified majority cultures profoundly threatened by social and economic change.

By doing so, those of us who grew up in such cultures can perhaps restore some intellectual and political force to the insistence that the popular is complex and contradictory. Take tourism, for example. My short history of Sydney Tower might be taken to confirm many people's fears of what global tourism can mean, with its abrupt abolition of mediating signs of locality and history. Yet it also suggests the ambiguity of a moment in which a society that has produced its own identity historically by dispossessing others now finds itself subject to fears, and sometimes enjoyable fantasies, of displacement. Economically motivated cultural restructuring involves not only a process of revising and contesting inherited accounts of the past, but also the production and circulation of new polemical images of what a desirable *future* might be for a society being "touristified."

In such a context there can be no simple answer to Carolyn Steedman's question, "why does cultural studies want history?" Wanting history can mean many things, some of them defensive. We may want "history" as a form of reassurance that things will turn out as badly as we fear they might (and in "Lunching for the Republic" I discuss a feminist argument that takes this form). My impulse is rather the opposite: I tend to want history as a source of a liberating certainty that anything could happen. The image of the Qantas jet in Sydney Tower's gallery, for example, has quite a different value if we use it to frame another story of history and international tourism—one not so easily understood through "mythical, apocalyptic or theoretical" notions of historic change.

Ngukurr: Weya Wi Na ("Ngukurr: Where Are We Now") is a videotape produced in 1988 as a program for broadcast on Aboriginal television in Central Australia.[89] Made by members of the multilingual Ngukurr community in the Northern Territory, the tape constructs a history of that community as it developed after white settlers, missionaries, and teachers arrived in the North. This history is narrated both as a story and an argument for a syncretic cultural politics to sustain the community's autonomy in the present and the future.

The theme of cultural syncretism is established at the beginning when an old man scolds young people for playing "too much rap, disco. Rap—that's whitefella music."[90] Without undermining his insistence that the young people should learn their own dances, the film suggests that no cultural form is intrinsically "whitefella" property; aesthetically eclectic, it mixes several genres and internationally familiar visual and musical styles with Aboriginal traditional elements. In this way, it performs a complex, visually beautiful argument in favor of a practice of self-determination to enable Aborigines to appropriate on their own terms technical knowledges and cultural goods from other societies, thus further securing their independence from both welfare bureaucracy and assimilationist cultural and political pressures.

As part of a history of collective achievement, the film includes community discussions about a language policy for the school. The adults want the children to learn English as well as their own languages and culture, and they plan a field trip to research potential models. They choose Singapore as a multilingual society where English is used in schools while other languages are spoken at home and in social life. The next sequence documents a tourist expedition in which there is more mutuality to cultural exchange than most tours require or even permit. At a Chinese school, the children sing in English for their visitors; in return, the tourists perform Aboriginal music and teach children how to dance. In casual scenes at the airport, the zoo, the streets, and the markets, the discovery that black Australians exist is represented as educational for Singaporeans of many races; on a trip to Malacca, Aboriginal and Portuguese-Malaysian women exchange experiences. The whole journey, an adventure in "cultural tourism" undertaken with precise, pragmatic aims, is considered a success and its story is incorporated into a lesson at school back home at Ngukurr.

As a white urban viewer watching this tape (and as one for whom the white as well as the black communities of the Northern Territory inhabit a remote space that I have only ever imagined visiting precisely as a tourist),[91] *Ngukurr: Weya Wi Na* challenged my thinking about tourism and history in three fundamental ways.

Most disconcerting to me was the irrelevance of my own concept of "Australia" to the cultural and historical map constructed by the film. Not only is tourism represented as an encounter between Aboriginal and Asian societies unmediated by significant European agents, but White Australia figures in the film *only* as "history," a sign of the past (for example, archival footage of the missionary school that preceded the community school of today), and as a technological membrane,[92] represented by a Qantas jet, through which Aboriginal people can pass to an elsewhere in the present. An explicit link between the archival footage and the jet is provided by the older man's comment, heard in voice-over as the group boards the plane to Singapore, that he had always wanted to travel overseas but was refused a passport in 1966.[93]

In short, both the international tourist industry and the Australian nation-state function as enabling mechanisms for a social practice carried out without reference to the othering force of contemporary white Australia. What emerges is an "and . . . and," not an "either . . . or," way of operating. Singapore and Malacca certainly figure in the film as *different* from Ngukurr (though not especially different from each other). However, this difference is conceptualized as a basis for constructing *limited* and thus non-specular similarities, such as multilingualism, through a cross-border exchange from which the Ngukurr people derive their own use value.

The second challenge follows from this. For years, Aboriginal culture has been debated as an *object* of tourism. Aboriginal intellectuals, bureaucrats, and community leaders have participated in this debate, and it has long included arguments that developing new "traditions for tourism"[94] can be a useful activity, increasing Aboriginal culture's prestige in the wider Australian society and generating income to secure economic independence from the state. "Traditional" culture, it is often said, is not a remainder of a pristine cultural source, but an already hybridized historical product, and its maintenance can be assisted by appropriating and transforming things from other societies.

As I have suggested, *Ngukurr: Weya Wi Na*, as I see it, explores this sort of strategy. However, it is not about Aboriginal culture as a tourist object. It positions people as *subjects* of a tourist practice, as well as of a history, a pedagogy, and an economy. So it goes well beyond asking how new traditions maintain the old; change is not only a part but a precondition of Ngukurr's history. Rather, the tape asks how the processes of change can be *planned and managed in future* by the people who will be affected, and the making of the tape is just one of a number of practical projects to make this possible. In this way, *Ngukurr: Weya Wi Na* ignores the critique of white Australian historiography in order to tell a different story—one in which a tourist narrative is incorporated into an ongoing Aboriginal history of survival, struggle, and self-determination.

The third challenge which I see in *Ngukurr: Weya Wi Na* concerns the doubts I have about my formulation of the first two. It is easy to declare, in an orthodox cultural studies move, that this tape offers an exemplary instance of how new possibilities open up for an oppressed and marginalized group of people under the "complex and contradictory" conditions provided by tourism. I think such a reading of *Ngukurr: Weya Wi Na* would represent an impacted version of my own "desire for history," projecting on to Aborigines my own anxieties about Australia's past and future and displacing these with a story about one of their stories. If it is often tempting for some (by no means all) white Australians now to idealize Aboriginal ways of life at a safe distance from their struggles, it is always too easy to draw from selected success stories a promise of reassuringly generalized "survival" in a global tourist economy. Steedman might well call this use of history an "act of transference," although it isn't a new one. Aboriginal culture has long been invested by white Australians (among others) with a superior wisdom that could help the rest of us solve our problems.

There is nothing intrinsically wrong with transference. In academic work, it is unavoidable. Steedman's point is that we need to think about *what* we are doing, when we do it, and why. So my way of responding to her question, "why does cultural studies want history. . . . what good is it all to you anyway?" is to remember that the stories of Sydney Tower and Ngukurr, and the historiographies of "Evolution of the Tower" and *Ngukurr: Weya Wi Na*, are not disconnected from each other: like the image of the Qantas jet, a history of tourist place-making and media time links them in more ways than one. There is a level at which it *matters* that the designers of Sydney Tower's audiovisuals and the film-makers from Ngukurr inhabit the same continent, may encounter some of the same political systems and institutions, and share the same time[95]—however divergent their interests, however disjunct their experiences of temporality and history, however incommensurable their ways of living, however great the inequality of the value accorded those ways by the power arrangements of my society.

Cultural studies is a practice that encourages us to try to understand critically the present context of their co-existence, as well as the specificity of each, and to work to create future contexts in which the terms of their co-existence might be different. History, I think, is good for doing that work, not least because history is the name that Australian public and, sometimes, popular culture gives this process of creation at present.

PART ONE

· · · · · · · · · · · ·

TOURIST PLACES

AT HENRY PARKES MOTEL

A motel is a motel anywhere. . . .

—Robert Venturi

I. BRICK WALL

On the 24th October 1889 Sir Henry Parkes Colonial Secretary and Past member for Tenterfield made his Historic Federation Speech. As a result of this Speech the Commonwealth of Australia was formed.

The Sydney Mail *referred to Sir Henry Parkes as Australia's Most Farsighted Statesman. This Motor Inn is located 180 metres from the Place where that Famous Speech was delivered. It is called "The Henry Parkes" in Honour of this Great Statesman.*

There is a legend inscribed on the street-front wall of the Henry Parkes Motor Inn, Tenterfield.

It tells a story about one of the representative Great Men of colonial New South Wales—an immigrant, self-made man, traveler, poet, journalist, and an indefatigable patriarch in his family and political life—founding the modern nation with a speech-act.[1]

It is also the story of a journey famous only for being interrupted in a small rural town. Parkes was returning to Sydney by train from Brisbane after talks with Queensland leaders, and stopped in Tenterfield to issue the equivalent of a press release—an after-dinner Oration. The story of his speech is repeated now to attract the attention of travelers passing through that town today.

I would like to be able to say that a reading of this Legend *in situ* provides a useful starting point for a feminist essay on history in popular culture. It raises familiar questions about the past represented in the present (myths of nationality, origin, engendering). It does so in a context formed by everyday cultural activities—driving, stopping at a motel, tourism, small town life—in which the Legend is used to engender effects of *place*. It attempts to persuade passing tourists to stop, and to define the town to its residents. To thematize relations between past and present, mobility and placement, is the minimal semiotic (promotional) program of any memorial-motel. The *Henry Parkes* in this respect is usefully self-reflexive.

A feminist reading could also ask whether the myths of national and local history produced in the practices of tourism may also imply, and intersect with, a gendering of the spatio-temporal operations (movement/placement) on which those practices depend. This is a question about representation: figures (moving) in a landscape. But a feminist reading would also want to invest any motel context with effective social significance. Motels are often used today as sites of a road-runner angst (the *Paris, Texas* model). In that guise, they usually signify a transcendental homelessness. But with its peculiar function as a place of escape yet a home-away-from-home, the motel can be rewritten as a transit-place for women able to use it. On the one hand, motels have had liberating effects in the history of women's mobility. They can offer increased safety to that figure whom Trollope once described as the Unprotected Female Tourist, and promise decreased bother to women on "holiday" with their families.[2] On the other hand, they fix new sites of placement for domestic, affective and sexual labor, paid as well as unpaid.[3]

So the motel can be used to frame and displace, without effacing, the association of men with travel and women with home that organizes so many historic Australian "legends," in academic as well as popular and recycled touristic forms.[4] A memorial-motel is a complex site of production, and one in which conflictual social relations cannot sensibly be ignored.

But if the text of a motel Legend seems to represent a likely point of departure, a tour of recent cultural studies can make it surprisingly hard to get there. For each direction of research I've mentioned, there is a different kind of objection.

Firstly, there's a problem about what counts as the proper use of *time* in analysis of popular culture. Iain Chambers, for example, declares in *Popular Culture* that since "in the end, it is not individual signs, demanding isolated attention, but the resulting connections or 'bricolage'—the style, the fashion, the image—that count," we should, in response to popular culture, refrain from resubjecting it to "the contemplative stare" of "official culture."[5] To linger too long at a motel wall, or to "read" its inscription too closely, requires a tempo inappropriate to my object: such reading "demands moments of attention that are separated from the run of daily life." The past-in-the-present is now a look, not a text.

Then there is a problem about *placement.* For Georges van den Abbeele in "Sightseers: The Tourist as Theorist," studious reading does not contradict the daily pursuits of tourism. He sees them as fellow travelers: tourism is already a mode of cultural studies, and a contemplative mode at that.[6] It can involve research, interpretation, and prolonged moments of intense attention. Yet for him too, there is a trap involved in lingering at an inscription. The Legend of Henry Parkes is what he calls, following Dean MacCannell, a *marker*—a sign constructing a "sight."[7] In studying it, both tourist and theorist can be caught up in a metaphysical quest. Each is motivated by desire "to make present to himself a conceptual schema which would give him immediate access to a certain authenticity (the 'real nature' of his object of study)."

So if I insist to the first objection that the Legend of Parkes is a tourist tale of politics made on the run, and to the second that it marks for critical inspection a (phallo)logocentric myth, from either side this motel wall represents, as an object of reading, a desire to limit movement by constructing a singular place. Here comes a third kind of difficulty. For numerous theorists of travel (Fussell, Baudrillard, and Virilio, for example) there is no such "place" to start with. The trouble with a *motel* as a site of analysis is not the familiar gap between a text (a particular motel-in-place) and reading practices (the multiplicity of its uses). Nor is it the pertinence of talking in this way about a bit of the built environment, or a segment of everyday life. The trouble is that, whatever they may say, motels in fact *demolish* sense-regimes of place, locale, and "history." For these theorists, motels memorialize only movement, speed, and perpetual circulation.

So the project of reading should retreat, perhaps, and recommence, with a view on the run from the road. This is to follow the line of least resistance, a "populist" approach—though to depart, in order to arrive, is a time-consuming, place-fixating activity. One reason for pursuing it, though, is that it's the kind of popular practice that motels work to foster. Another is that it lets me discard, en route, some encumbrances.

The Glimpse

You can see from the highway it's a tempting motel, an obvious place to stop. If you come in to town from the South, one surge brings you over the mountain and down a slope to the Motor Inn at the bottom. A radiant promise of SPA POOL SAUNA GYM (and in these cold climes, CENTRAL

HEATING) flares out, day and night, at the delicate moment dividing a long, hard haul from Sydney from an easy cruise into Brisbane. This is the last town before the Queensland border. As a scenic view on the north-bound road, the *Henry Parkes* is perfectly timed.

From the North, the approach is less dramatic. Tenterfield is only the first real town in New South Wales, and you would already have driven through most of it. It's pretty, with willows and old stone buildings, but after some three blocks of deserted main street there's not a great deal to stop for. But there's a long, level view of the *Henry Parkes* on the other side of the high-way. Its design is imposing enough to beg serious attention: verandahs curving grandly around a garden courtyard, white-sashed Georgian windows, and on the front wall of the nearest wing, a large commemorative scroll. Clearly a motel, it might also be a gracious residence; a country resort; a health center; a historic public building. From this direction, the *Henry Parkes* suggests serious leisure instead of a night's salvation.

Scan

Personified models of action (the weary itinerant coming to rest, the re-flective tourist sampling the country . . .) are commonly produced by travel narratives set in and around motels. Any well-designed motel can cite and mobilize a number of these without imposing any one too explicitly. Indeed, the motel form (or chronotope, in Bakhtin's terms) has become so richly mythic in our culture that any one motel anywhere must constrain the pos-sibilities.[8] An amorphous, general motelness can be commercially uncon-vincing at any price except to connoisseurs of the basic.

It isn't simply a matter of suggesting, for "high speed comprehension" across vast space,[9] a competitive definition of style (cost, ambience, clien-tele). Motels are transit spaces, charged with narrative potential. A motel should promise a scenario, and exactly the one you want: a hiding place, a good night's sleep, a stint of poignant alienation, a clandestine adventure, time off housework, a monastic retreat . . . promises that need have nothing to do with what anyone subsequently does. Veering off the road and into the drive of any motel setting, we seek shelter, rest, and safety, but we also assess a script (even, or even especially, at the lone motel, in the middle of nowhere, no commercial rivals for miles).

The *Henry Parkes* is distinguished from its close competition by the sense of a "complex" it generates. The major rival is straight across the road—the Jumbuck, a Homestead Inn. The familiar "H" sign for the chain aficionado is in thick nailed board, and its woodiness is the single concession, apart from the motel's name,[10] to a code of bush nostalgia. The Jumbuck is ag-gressively *serial* in theme ("You're Home," wherever you are): the asphalt yard is for parking, no nonsense with stately courtyards; a few routine flow-ers, no pretentiously landscaped shrubs; and, unusually for a New England motel, no effort at Georgian sashing. The sliding windows are uncompro-

misingly functional, with mean proportions outlined by the plain alu-
minium of a hardline, no-frills modernism. The Jumbuck makes minimal
use of allusiveness to other building forms. It could be, at best, a raw new
home in a brand-name housing settlement. Anywhere else, the same design
might merely be motel-basic. But opposite the florid expanse of the *Henry
Parkes* it claims austerity and rigor. The Jumbuck is a real motel, for travelers
on serious business.

So the reflective tourist arrives at a scholastic dilemma where Miles St.
meets Rouse St., Tenterfield. On one side of the road, a myth of the Modern
Universal: seriality, chain self-reference, territorialization by repetition-and-
difference; "*a Homestead is a Homestead everywhere.*" On the other, Postmodern Particularity: bricolage individuality-effect, pluralist pastiche coding,
localization by simulated aura: "*this motel is The Motel in Tenterfield.*"

In each case, the major signifiers of these myths are equally myths of
Australianness (the motel signs: Jumbuck, Henry Parkes) and of Home (the
suburban referent of their design). But these function quite differently on
either side of the road. The Jumbuck is a national-*identity* synecdoche, as
internationalizing in form as a Tudor Inn or a Ten Gallon Hat; its model of
"home" is a standardized housing. The *Henry Parkes*, in contrast, advertises
personality: a locale appropriates a "historic" name, to claim special regional
significance; and the "home" it offers is a middle-class splendor, customized
to connote "uniqueness." The Jumbuck is a motel to use, the *Henry Parkes* a
place to visit.

Quandary

On the road, the choice can be quickly reduced to price, availability,
mood. So for some reflective tourists, there could be no choice involved.
A motel, by definition, can never be a true *place*: the locality-effect of the
Henry Parkes is an optical illusion.

Following an influential distinction derived from Daniel Boorstin, for
example, any motel is necessarily one of the "pseudo-places" defining the
tourist world.[11] For Paul Fussell, the characteristic sign of the pseudo-place
is, from Disneyland to the airport, Switzerland to the shopping center, a
calculated readability.[12] True places are opaque to the passing observer, and
"require" active response—ideally, the rich interpretation that was "literature" in the lost era of "travel." Pseudo-places achieve an artificial transparency, inducing the passivity typical of "tourism." It follows that motels jux-
taposed in space can only be rival pseudo-places. In Tenterfield, itself part
place, part pseudo-place, the most that could be said in these terms is that
while The Jumbuck celebrates its pseudo-status, the *Henry Parkes* tries to
hide it. The difference is mere variation apprehended in a high-speed, empiricist *flash*. Indeed, the rapidity with which I can "recognize" the difference would be a sign of its pseudo-status.

Given its dependence on cultural elitism and on a realist epistemology, the idea of the "pseudo" has shown a surprising tenacity in cultural studies. Jean Baudrillard's concept of hyperreality owes a good deal to Boorstin's work, and can be written back into its terms.[13] In Baudrillard's world of third-order simulacra, the encroaching pseudo-places finally merge to eliminate places entirely. This merger is a founding event: once it has taken place, the true, like the real, begins to be reproduced in the image of the pseudo, which begins to become the true. This event is also foundational for Baudrillard's theory, since it is only after such a "merger" that the concept of the pseudo (which Baudrillard often calls the Imaginary) can at last be abandoned by theory. When there is no more difference between place and pseudo-place, new terms must be announced to match the spaces of our experience (simulation, seduction, ob-scenity). The "pseudo" lingers, however, like a ghost of the annunciation: without some sign of a once-present difference that has now disappeared, the new order could not be proclaimed.

In this optic, my two motels can only be "recognized" as generators of a hyperreal country-town. Adjacent features—old houses, paddocks, sheep—become, like "rural" faces in the street, indifferently either vestiges of the old order of the Real, or simulacra of the old (more true than the true, more rural than the rural) for the new order of hyperreality.

For both Fussell and Baudrillard, the irreality of motels is of an objective order. Both write allegories of subjects in movement halting here and there in an obdurately recognizable landscape: where Fussell's tourist requires the known, Baudrillard's theorist always finds it.

Acceleration

A different rejection of the *Henry Parkes* can be produced by simply not stopping—writing the subject as a zooming observer, and tourism as a history of *speed.* For Paolo Prato and Gianluca Trivero, scanning Fussell's use of Boorstin *via* the work of Paul Virilio:

> Speed undoes places (events [*faits*] become non-events [*défaits*], Paul Virilio) and a succession of pseudo-places reduces the complexity of the environment to hotel chains, motorway restaurants, service stations, airports, shopping centres, underpasses, etc.[14]

And indeed, for Virilio speed consumes time, narrative, and subjectivity as well as space: speed is itself a "non-place," and the users of transit spaces, transit-towns (like airports) are spectral: "tenants . . . for a few hours instead of years, their fleeting presence is in proportion to their unreality and to that of the speed of their voyage."[15]

In the "accelerated impressionism"[16] of an aesthetics of disappearance, "the" landscape becomes a blur, a streak, and no sense of place can survive.

However, if there is a specter haunting transit-space in these racy formulations it is the figure of the *peasant* rather than the short-term tenant. Duration, stability, accumulated experience, reality itself are assumed, in this discourse, to be products of relative immobility in a permanent and singular place: which is to say, they are rhetorically immobilized *categories*. They don't really move in history, or transform in response to transition. The founding myth for these writers is not geographic (a progressive encroachment of the pseudo-sphere) but historical: the trauma of "humanity's" first train ride, the thrill of first contact with cinema.[17] Unlike Baudrillard's hyperrealist, however, the subject of Virilian zoom analysis is eternally fixed in his originary traumatic moment. Hurtling on in the accelerating placelessness of speed, he is a figure in chronic stasis.

U-Turn

However, Virilio's notion of the "lodgement" as a "*strategic installation*" (establishing "fixed address" as a monetary and social value in the history of mobilization) allows for slowing the pace.[18] A motel is a type of installation that mediates, in spatial, social, and monetary terms, between a fixed address, or domicile, and, in the legal sense, "vagrancy." It performs this function precisely as a transit place, a fixed address for temporary lodgment.

Furthermore, the installation of any one motel can easily be seen as strategic. There is not only rhetorical competition with neighbors ("address" projected in space), but a conative effort at stopping the traffic over days as well as moments, to slow transients into tourists and divert energy to places (the motel and its vicinity). The aim of a specialist motel like the *Henry Parkes* is an elaboration on this—an attempt from a small-town highway spot to alter urban maps of significance. The ploy assumes the transience and plasticity, not the fixity, of meanings constructed in space. So to stop to examine such an effort is also to construct a strategic installation: rather than halting for confirmation (collecting theoretical brochures) at exemplary places or performing their disappearance (hypostasizing motion), it places reading transitionally *at* a site, in a process of place-invention.

Tour

Highway clichés aside, the *Henry Parkes* foyer is in fact a place where the "fixed" and the "mobile" meet. Adorned with all the conventional signs of tourism and moteldom, it is both a front office to one wing of the motel, and a work-space extension to the family home a few steps away on the left—with activity spilling between them.

To a new arrival looking around, the relationships between parts of the complex are hard to stabilize. Behind the family home, designed to blend with the motel, is a public sports center with a large, well-equipped gym; and the passage to it from the motel negotiates a garden-with-pool landscaped in suburban "backyard" styling. Like many motels with a sporting motif, the *Henry Parkes* can double as an informal community center; the therapeutic motel-function extends into the local leisure economy. So at any moment, and in most of the spaces defining the complex, there is constant intermingling of the "host" family's domestic life, the social activities of town residents, and the passing diversions of tourists. The motel's solidity as *place* is founded by its flexibility as *frame* for varying practices of space, time, and speed.

This art of motel extension projects rhetorical identity in space in a manner quite different from that analyzed by Venturi, Scott Brown, and Izenour for facades on the Las Vegas strip. In those highway-inflected structures, they see a functional distinction between front and back reflected in formal design: "Regardless of the front, the back of the building is styleless, because the whole is turned towards the front and no one sees the back."[19] A front/back regionalization model[20] is thus rewritten as a distinction between a surface (persuasive) rhetoric, that varies, and a deep (enabling) grammar, that does not—"the neutral, systems-motel structures behind . . . survive a succession of facelifts and a series of themes up front."

The *Henry Parkes* abandons these distinctions. The facade theme is developed, not restricted or deflated, by the intricate regions behind. The country-resort experience begins on the street and runs all the way back to the fence. As a strategic installation this motel works *against* the codes of highway-inflection—and in fact, against the pull of the highway. It intrudes into the traffic flow to inflect it toward the town.

It is as a small-business "front," then, that the *Henry Parkes* effects a rural solution to the problem defined by Venturi. Its production of itself as a "place," and of Tenterfield as a tourist setting, isn't simply a logical progression from the dynamics of highway competition but an effort to reverse and exploit the highway's effect on small towns. It is a common device used by theme-motels in locations of fragile importance, and one that still allows for variation along the lines described by Venturi. Other sports-theme motels, for example, may function primarily as body-working centers or health-and-beauty farms. In this case, place is produced in Tenterfield as a strongly built form of *residency*.

Inside the complex, the resident family, visiting locals, and motel guests all share in a pervasive production of "home." The *Henry Parkes* offers locals not only a little work and an inspiring architectural model of the "beautiful residence," but the raw material ("strangers") for further home-town promotion. The coherence of the *Henry Parkes* complex is an embracing and durable familialism. Here, the touristic, the neighborly and the proprietorial are related not by opposition (mobile vs. fixed, touristic vs. everyday, itinerant vs. domestic) but along a spectrum divided by degrees of duration, *intensities* of "staying"—temporary, intermittent, permanent.

Being There

Bannered across a brick wall, curved elegantly around a plaque and bust, is a legend of a famous Visitor. This is the motel's foundation-stone, its anchorage in History—national (the Federation of Australia), regional (the Tenterfield Oration), and personal (the motel's naming).

For a cursory glance, the ornate script of the Legend and the bronze-effect of the bust need do little more than signify period-nostalgia. For most tourists, no doubt, there it stops. Another kind of cursory glance could read, yet again, the disappearance of history in myth. On this wall, the bitter class struggles of the late nineteenth century, the machinations of a fading patriarch still grasping at political influence, the displacement of the Aboriginal people[21] and so the very history of this town, this *site*, in battles for land, wealth, power, and the right to determine "Progress"[22]—all, indifferently, are obliterated by a cloying and sentimentalized sign of the past as timeless colonial *style*.

An experienced history-tourist could even defy the anecdotal status of the Legend, and make it an accessory to the motel's familial myth. It was Parkes, after all (reformer and titular founder of housing, health, prison, transport, communications, and education programs) who married, in 1890, the dream of a white Australia to a nostalgia for Britain as "home"—casting, in a memorable and much-commemorated form, the Imperial Family legend: "The crimson thread of kinship," his descendants would repeat, "runs through us all."[23]

Yet there is an imbalance between this all-embracing interpretation of the motel-myth and the scroll's quite casual position. On the one hand, the Legend ascribes great powers to the Word (Parkes spoke, and as a result, Australia federated) and to the authority of media citation (The *Sydney Mail* creates Parkes's status). On the other hand—who reads it? what powers does a scroll exercise? the cypress pines in front of it grow taller . . . the locals can ignore it, most tourists may not see it, and who has heard now, anyway, of Henry Parkes? It has the power, at best, to send some trade down the road to see the Place of the Oration. Few travelers, one must imagine, can be expected to take their pleasure in knowingly sleeping and eating 180 meters away from a site of enunciation.

Who can say? Who knows about "the others"? This is one problem that the scroll can raise, with its story about an exemplary figure's *fiat*. What other actions are performed when we posit ideal models of a theoretical practice and a speaking position "appropriate" to popular culture? The motel gives pause to think about the question. To give *pause* is the primary function of the motel as motel anywhere.[24] Back in the rooms of this one there is, in the midst of a comfortable mix of mod-cons and period-effects, strategically installed, under a window beside the TV, that contemplative place—a desk.

II. DOMESTIC PURSUITS

Political Philosophy.

Under which thimble—quick! if you please—
Under which thimble now are the peas?
Juggle on juggle, all the day long,—
Sir, you are right!—ah no!—you are wrong!

Then it was R, and now it is C,[25]—
None of your eyes could follow the pea;
How it was smuggled nobody shows,
How it was juggled nobody knows.

Juggle on juggle, day after day,
Life is a struggle, do what we may;
Wait for our next, and then you shall see
Which is the thimble holding the pea.

Juggle on juggle all the day long,
None are quite right, and none are all wrong;
Life is a struggle ever up hill,
Life is a juggle, say what you will!

—HENRY PARKES[26]

(Of all Parkes's features as a self-made man, few caused more hilarity to critics during and after his lifetime than his untutored efforts at Poetry—except perhaps the "wandering aspirates" that gave his class origins away. He published five volumes of verse, including many poems about the joys of travel, and others about domestic bliss enjoyed at home with his wife.)

In "Sightseers: The Tourist as Theorist," Georges van den Abbeele makes this comment on the kind of itinerary I've just produced:

The ritualizing and/or institutionalizing of the voyage can also be an attempt to achieve a certain immediacy (of knowledge, of presence) through the realization of a priorly conceived project. One attempts to circumvent the delay in cognition by being there so to speak before one has begun, by preparing an "ambush" so that when the experience takes place it can be grasped as fully present. (9)

His article is an intricate commentary on Dean MacCannell's book, *The Tourist: A New Theory of the Leisure Class*. MacCannell argues that tourism emerges in a society no longer dependent on alienated labor but on "alienated leisure," in which "reality and authenticity are thought to be elsewhere" (3).[27] Tourism is a quest to find them. But this quest is made impossible by the very structure of modern tourism. It is defined by a "semiotics of attraction," in which something (the marker) represents a "sight" to someone (the tourist). Claiming to indicate the sight, the markers delimit and produce it; without the proliferation of information and itineraries, the tourist would not be able to distinguish the "sight" from its "surroundings." Thinking that he is grasping the reality of a different world, the tourist is in fact always reading the signs of tourism—that is, signs of difference.

In van den Abbeele's gloss on this argument, a tourist does research for his trip not merely to avoid discomfort in strange places, but to prepare himself, like an assiduous art student (or a pursuant of the pea of truth in politics), for *grasping* the eventual authentic "sight." So the tourist as autodidact is perpetually involved in producing and reproducing a metaphysics of presence. He hopes to "ambush" the sight, but he is always already ambushed by the marker-sight relation.

The trap laid here is unavoidable; and, in one sense, it is in fact the inevitability of "ambush" that is, like the pious moral of Parkes's Cynical philosophy, the "desk" in my writing on the wall, always already present to van den Abbeele's argument.

Rather than retrace the path toward it, I want to sidestep to consider the moves by which Tourism and Theory are read, in this argument, as exemplary, parallel instances of a teleological *drive*.[28] It is difficult to do justice in summary to van den Abbeele's text, not only because of its complexity but because of its shifting relations to the text of *The Tourist*. To simplify, I shall disarm my own ambush by exposing it at the beginning. Van den Abbeele will argue that the totalizing projects of both Tourism and Theory could be displaced by a theoretico-practical Nomadism. I will read his argument as developing from three major oppositions that he works to deconstruct—*voyage/home, Man/difference, theory/tourism*. They do not function as equivalents of each other, but I shall read each of them as marked by an implicit valorization of the first term as "masculine," that is, unmarked-human: a valorization that survives the deconstructive move and in doing so enables an elimination of politics (for example, an activism of the "toured") from van den Abbeele's trajectory.

Voyage/Home

In his reading of MacCannell, van den Abbeele accepts that a search for "destination" is endemic to tourism. Doing so allows him to develop a strong analogy between "tourism" and "theory" using the classic epistemological metaphor of the voyage. He also limits that metaphor's deployment by reading it as a model of narrative structure. The key figures connecting these operations are "*home*," or the "*domus*," and "*domestication*":

> The tourist theorizes because he is already en route and caught up in a chaotic, fragmented universe that needs to be domesticated. The very concept of "the voyage" is this domestication in that it demarcates one's traveling like the Aristotelian plot into a beginning, a middle and an end. In the case of the tourist, the beginning and the end are the same place, "home." It is in relation to this home or domus then that everything which falls into the middle can be "domesticated." (9)

In this account, the project of domestication fails not only because of the gap between marker and sight but because the tourist's interpretation always temporally "lags" behind the activity of voyaging. Domestication is an effort to catch up cognitively with the ever-fleeing experience, or the "motion," of being *en route*. It is thus an attempt to contain and deny the precedence, as well as the excess, of process over structure. The tourist's problem with "lag" here becomes, I think, a model of a more fundamental dilemma said to define the speaking-being.

Van den Abbeele's is an account of the "circular structure of referentiality," in which the *domus* really functions as the ultimate ambush awaiting the tourist. As the fixed point to which the tourist's theorizing attempts to refer, the *domus* is not only always already receding as the voyage begins (the designation "home" is an "eminently retrospective gesture") but will never be the same when the tourist attempts to "return." Home has moved on while the tourist moved away, and the tourist returns transformed by the process of "domesticating" experience elsewhere. Van den Abbeele's tourist is trapped, of course, not only by his own myth of Presence, and by the aporia of his empiricism, but by a literary variant of both—Tristram Shandy's dilemma. His Tourist, chasing "himself" in time, is a doomed but indomitable realist, forever pursuing a pea.

One problem with this account is the place it accords to "activity," "effort," and "labor." These terms are made operative only for the voyage, not "home" (the elusive ideal that motivates the journey). The *domus* is not reciprocally constructed as a site of work, theoretical or otherwise. Van den Abbeele is attentive to practical activities in tourism (boarding planes, checking in baggage, taking taxis, getting out of bed . . .), but, as the ordering of this list suggests, only in relation to the rituals of arrival and departure that extend the "voyage" into the domestic space, and make its beginning impossible to fix. That is to say, "home" is a space that is *blank* (so, impossible), and a site of recessiveness: the voyage intrudes into the home, not vice versa (except as a dream of nostalgia). The *domus*, therefore, is figuratively constructed not only as a womb, but as unproductive—a womb prior to labor.

Furthermore, if the work of tourism (research, reading the markers, theorizing the voyage) is a "domestication," it is because the domestic is understood in the romantic sense of a "taming" and a "naturalization." There is no necessary logical connection between the concepts of coherence and unity (which the tourist tries to impose on a "chaotic and fragmented universe") and those of home and womb (between which, again, there is no necessary connection). But of course, there is a powerful cultural link, one dear to a masculinist tradition inscribing "home" as the site both of frustrating containment (home as dull) and of truth to be rediscovered (home as real). The stifling home is the place from which the voyage begins, and to which, in the end, it returns.

An extreme version may be read in Sam Shepard's *Motel Chronicles*. On the left-hand page, a poem: the world-weary drifter declares, in a moment of "domesticating" his experiences while not-at-home, "I've about seen / all the nose jobs capped teeth and silly-cone tits I can handle / I'm heading back to my natural woman."[29] On the right a photograph of a woman in a house or motel laundry—her body balanced beautifully between the ironing board and the washing machine. Shepard, in this instance, is the more rigorous theorist of the *domus*. Labor is inscribed on both sides: Man on voyage (writing poem) positions Woman in *domus* (with washing).

In van den Abbeele's text, the restriction of work to the voyage prevents this sort of crudity from emerging in his schema. It also blocks reflection on the schema's cultural history; it defines, for him, a purely epistemological problem ("the metaphorics of the voyage"). A feminist reading can ask, therefore, what happens to that problem, and the voyage/*domus* opposition, if "home," rather than the voyage, is rewritten as chaos and fragmentation, labor, transience, "lag"—or in quite different terms, since these remain parasitic on the voyage.[30] For van den Abbeele, however, the possibility of rewriting "home" cannot emerge any more than a feminist desire to do so does. The tourist leaving and returning to the blank space of the *domus* is, and will remain, an indifferent "him."

Man/Difference

One reason for this blankness is that van den Abbeele follows Dean MacCannell at least some way toward displacing the "working class" with the "new leisure class" (of tourists) as a privileged site for analyzing modernity. MacCannell considers work used as a tourist-spectacle—work displays—to be the very definition of "alienated leisure"; we now work to tour other people working. In van den Abbeele's text, non-theoretical "work" drops from sight: the elision of work from the *domus* simply follows from accepting that the tourist's social "home" is a society of alienated leisure.[31]

Another reason is that van den Abbeele goes further than MacCannell in theorizing tourism, and thus "modernity," as a production of differences, and spectacles of difference. This requires a digression to look at *The Tourist* in more detail.

MacCannell argued that rather than being organized by simple dualities (capital/labor, men/women . . .), modernization is an institutionalized process of "social structural differentiation." This means "the totality of differences between social classes, life-styles, racial and ethnic groups, age grades . . . political and professional groups and the mythic representation of the past to the present" (11). In his version of this classic diagnosis of the modern condition, MacCannell sees differentiation as the "primary ground" of the feeling of freedom, and also of contradiction, conflict, and alienation, in modern society. Tourism rests on this ground, as a "collective striving" to transcend differentiation and discontinuous experience by grasping the Big Picture. The tourist as alienated but active cultural "producer" is thus, for MacCannell, a model of *modern*-man-in-general (10).

This is also why the tourist, for MacCannell, always remains an ambivalent figure. On the one hand, *"sightseeing is a ritual performed to the differentiations of society"* (13). Seeking signs of authentic difference elsewhere, the tourist carries modernization further afield (imperialism). His quest is foiled not only because tourist attractions have the same structure as the differentiations of modern society, but by the effects of his own action in spreading the "totalizing idea" of modernity. Tourism correspondingly helps to secure a "strong society" at home: therefore, it may be fundamentally conservative, as well as destructive in the field of modernity's Others.

On the other hand, the quest at least implies a discontent with "home" (modernity). The issue is complicated by the fact that, while defining the quest as "doomed," MacCannell also wants to reject denigration of tourist activity as *in*authentic. It's not just a matter of sympathy for popular culture but also of arguing that the "rhetoric of moral superiority" to tourism is, especially in the form of touristic anti-tourism, in perfect conformity with the logic of differentiation that motivates tourism. Anti-tourism—contempt for "the others"—is not an analytical reflection on tourism, but "part of the problem" (10–11).

So the rehabilitation of the tourist is also achieved by suggesting that the tourist may, through his interpretive labor, have an experience of something *like* "authenticity." Unlike Paul Fussell's tourist, MacCannell's doesn't find his motels and sights and souvenir shops to be "pseudo," but enjoys them and keeps on going. He helps to sustain "a collective agreement that reality and truth exist somewhere in society, and that we ought to be trying to find them and refine them" (155). He is, in his way, a social theorist.

It is only at the last step that van den Abbeele parts company with MacCannell. He places much greater stress on differentiation as "the marking process" in tourism—which he radicalizes, in a formalist move, as the *"actual production"* of social differences, rather than the ritual performance of them (10). He also points out that MacCannell's concept of "social structural differentiation" does nothing to modify the totalizing impulse of theory (or tourism), since "nothing is so totalising as a concept of differentiation—nor so apt to be undermined by the very play of differences it attempts to name and de-limit" (13).

For van den Abbeele, the tourist never attains an approximation, or even an intimation, of authenticity, but rather produces social reality as a kind of "figural displacement." It follows that a "radical politics" of tourism will actively affirm the "supplemental play" of the "inauthentic" marker, rather than trying to grasp the Sight or to insist on difference. That is to say, the radical tourist will not struggle for transcendence and the refinement of social realities, but will deconstruct his theoretical practice as tourist.

At first sight, it seems that van den Abbeele's move should lead to a deconstructing of the figure of modern-man-in-general (Man). In fact, something different happens. MacCannell's Man acts out the logic of social structural differentiation to which, and of which, he is Subject. That is, "he" is always already socially differentiated (by sex, race, age, lifestyle, etc.) as a cultural producer, and may be uncomfortable about it. His Manhood, then, is both a grammatical fiction and an unachievable ideal. Van den Abbeele's tourist is actually an indifferent producer of social reality *as* differentiation: his discomforts emerge not from his own social positioning in difference, but from his philosophical mistakes (seeking authenticity, difference). His Manhood, then, is not an object of struggle—something to be achieved— but a presupposition. It still remains the *a priori* of the voyage.

Theory/Tourism

If the tourist, for MacCannell, is a social theorist, he is a "primitive" one. He is "mystified" about his role in constructing modernity, and his work historically precedes that of the social theorist: "Our first apprehension of modern civilization . . . emerges in the mind of the tourist" (1). But he has a responsive potential, because of his own discontent. So for MacCannell, some resolution of the problems posed by tourism may be achieved by social theorists' rethinking and developing it as a mode of "community planning."

Van den Abbeele recoils from both the prospect of "planning" and MacCannell's claim that his theory of tourism can serve as a theory of social totality. Reasonably, he points out that it is really a theory of travel, a theory of modernity seen as "a perpetual narrative of adventure," and he turns instead to question the politics of producing such an "all-encompassing" theory. For van den Abbeele, what is finally at stake is "less the ideology of tourism than the ideological function of theory" (11).

He takes issue with what he sees as MacCannell's eventual reassertion of the "superiority" of the social theorist over the tourist. By giving up his radical "sympathy" for tourism, MacCannell not only reasserts the power of his own position as theorist, but repeats the very *gestures* of mystified tourism. Both tourist and theorist attempt to ambush Presence. But the theorist has the greater pretension. He wants to be not just a sightseer, but a *seer*—a prophet, in possession of knowledge superior to that of "the others." The circle closes: for van den Abbeele the theorist, even more than the tourist, is "part of the problem."

But whose problem? MacCannell's critique of anti-tourism is based not only on sympathy for the tourist (rejection of elitism) but on a concern for the social consequences of modernity's "adventure" for places and people *toured*.[32] This is why MacCannell returns to the question of planning. His final position is not simply one of theorist differentiated *from* tourist but of theorist potentially working *with* particular communities toured. His position as "seer," then, is more limited in its pretensions than van den Abbeele can allow.

The "toured" in fact disappear from van den Abbeele's account as soon as he introduces his critique of the concept of *totality*. Oddly enough, this happens just as he points out that "not everyone has either the political right or the economic means to travel" (11), and that MacCannell's theory therefore only deals strictly with the "leisure class" rather than with Society. Van den Abbeele then suggests that if travel is "relatively restricted, it must be because of some danger it poses to society's integrity." This is consistent with his own desire to argue that the excess of the voyage can constitute a threat to the *domus*. But surely one might draw the opposite conclusion: if for some societies travel is relatively *unrestricted* for large numbers of people, it is because for the "home" society it does *not* pose much of a danger to its integrity.[33] These societies would be, of course, precisely the developed capitalist countries from which the Tourist (like the Theorist) emerges. This is in fact MacCannell's argument: the tourist as a missionary of modernity has a "totalizing" political *force* and this is exactly why MacCannell sees the "international middle class" as a problem in the first place.

For van den Abbeele, however, sympathy for the tourist combined with a philosophically principled critique of totality implies only a general transformation of theoretical practice. He proposes a politics of theory in which the excess of the theoretical voyage would not be restrained, and in which the process of theorizing would not attempt to refer back to a fixed "theorist's" place in a fixed society. So it is the very presupposition of a fixed position, or *domus*, that must be questioned.

This familiar, indeed "domestic" conclusion to a deconstructive analysis of the politics of theory then generates a figure to supplant both the Tourist as realist/empiricist/metaphysician of Presence, and the Theorist as totalizing Seer. This is the Nomad, who "renders impertinent" any opposition between rest and motion, between home and travel (13). Invoking Deleuze to insist that the nomad isn't necessarily in-motion but can travel "*sur place*," van den Abbeele speculates that nomadic theory would "travel from inauthentic marker to inauthentic marker without feeling the need to possess the authentic sight by totalizing the markers into a universal and unmediated vision" (14).

It is a satisfying conclusion. The trouble is that where MacCannell's totalizing concept of modernity does allow for a critique of "present" social differentiation, and for a disarticulation of Man-in-general itself by modernity's Others at home and abroad (precisely because Difference *is* so "apt to be undermined" by the play it attempts to delimit), van den Abbeele's philosophically more sensitive trajectory has the opposite result. It erases social, political, and perhaps theoretical conflict altogether.

In "Feminist Politics: What's Home Got to Do with It?" Biddy Martin and Chandra Talpade Mohanty argue that there can be political limitations to "vigilante attacks on humanist beliefs in 'man' and Absolute Knowledge wherever they appear," if these deny the critic's own situatedness in the social, and in an institutional "home."[34] Something like this has happened in "Sightseers: The Tourist as Theorist" when, at the end of the road, we are ambushed by a figure who, erasing both the *domus* and difference (therefore becoming, in a sense, auto-genetic), and marking a positive denial of situatedness in the social, might effectively be a model for Postmodern-Man-in-general.

'Tis Misconception All.

A PHILOSOPHER said, "All the world is mad, I
am the only sane man in it."

"'Tis misconception all. The world is mad,
And I alone am sane." Such the words
Of England's living sage, he rightly proud
Of wisdom in the courts of wisdom.

An unit in that full and flowing crowd
Of miserable maniacs, I, like them,
Was too intent to win the happiness
And worth of life, to value high the search
For possibilities, convertible,
It might be, to the probable. Too full,
Within the limits of a biassed mind,
Of the sweet claims of many clinging friends,
And the dear wisdom of kind deeds,
The daily earnestness of common life,
To yield, unquestioned, that high-voiced demand
Of all-engrossing sanity. Wise, thought I,
Mothers who bend o'er the helpless babes;
And wise the husbandman, who brings

From God's right hand our daily bread;
And wise the toiler 'midst the clang
Of mighty engines for the world's behoof;
And wise, most humbly wise, the innocent,
If ignorant, who bend the knee
And bow the heart to learn of God.
Thus, tho' yet in love with wisdom, I
Shrank back with thoughts akin to hate or scorn,
And called the wise man—egotist.

—MENIE PARKES[35]

(It's a bit hard to like Menie Parkes, although she is the brilliant daughter effaced by the father's Legend. She had a sad life, and found ferocious consolations in religion. She was Parkes's companion and counsellor, made money writing romances, and married a clergyman who soon died in a fall from a horse. Her own book of poetry was printed privately, as a Christmas gift to her father.)[36]

Detective/Nomad

In "Maps for the Metropolis: A Possible Guide to the Present," Iain Chambers discusses traveling in quite different terms from Georges van den Abbeele. However, Chambers also suggests a figure of the modern intellectual, though one with more limited scope for movement, and more focused pursuits, than the Nomad—the "humble detective."[37]

If the detective himself is humble, he works a grandiose territory. He cruises through everyday life in a place subsuming both the voyage and the *domus*—the city or, more accurately, the Metropolis (for Chambers, "the modern world"). Not surprisingly, then, he travels a lot: "A critical intelligence adequate to the fluid complexity of the present is forced to fly regularly," although eventually, "we also go home" (5).

The privileged metaphor for Chambers's argument is not the voyage but the *map*. Critical movement is defined not in relation to the temporal "lag" that fascinates van den Abbeele, but to spatial shifts between "perspectives." There are two major and apparently conflicting ways of mapping the modern world: the *overview* (the theoretical view from the airplane—rarefied atmosphere, vast generalization, flat earth as disappearing referent, possible implosion under pressure) and the *close-up* (the view on the ground—"down-to-earth" observation, local detail, stubborn and violent materiality of terrain, an overwhelming mess of complexities). A working mediation of these two perspectives is possible, however, on the "giant *screen*" of the contemporary city. There, the streaming images of everyday life provide a fluid space of "immediacy" between the extraterrestrial perspectives of postmodernism and the terrestrial prospects of lived popular culture, while maintaining a tension between the two in "the semiotic blur" of the Present.

So where van den Abbeele's deconstruction of the temporal paradoxes of the travel story finally restructures his map of space (no more tour, no more *domus*), Chambers's mapping of perspectives for remapping space eventually generates a "guide" to *time*—the empire of the Now, the Contemporary, the Present.

These two projects diverge in a number of ways that make it difficult for a detective to compare them. One is about tourism, the other about everyday life (though with their discussions of travel and flight, they overlap). One is situated institutionally by literary theory, the other by cultural studies: while one uses the Aristotelian plot as a trope to define its object, the other refers to punk. One situates itself historically by invoking a "global" European tradition (the "metaphorics of the voyage"); the other situates itself in a history of postwar British subcultures. One is an academic reading of a reading, relentlessly contemplative, and so emerges from what Chambers would call "official culture." The other scans a mixture of materials with the casual attention characteristic, for Chambers, of "popular epistemology" (13). Here is another difference: van den Abbeele's text does not make this kind of upstairs/downstairs class distinction, and so provides no counter-accusation to situate Chambers's project.

In the casually contemplative spirit fostered by a room in a quiet motel, it's also fair to say that while one is very hard going, the other is an irresistibly amusing read. Both texts are serious, but one is arduous, like homework, the other fun, like a magazine. It's not just a matter of marking different desires for audience. Van den Abbeele does not, and of course cannot, attempt the "theorising without theory" he dreams of for the Nomad. He is searching for the possible, convertible—*it might be*—to the probable. Chambers's detective has no time for postponing the conversion: he writes of the daily earnestness and pleasure of common life, in the now codified pop-theory style that has become a contemporary, informal equivalent of traditional socialist realism.

So it seems in overview. In close-up, there are some interesting points of convergence in the trajectories of the Nomad and the Detective.

Both van den Abbeele and Chambers establish their topics *territorially*, by a move of metonymic expansion. For the former, the ordinary tourist as social practitioner becomes The Tourist/Theorist as exemplary interpreter, before being transfigured and redeemed as the Nomad. In Chambers's text, expansion operates at the level of a field of action, rather than that of the actor's competence: postwar British (sub)culture becomes "popular culture" which occupies the Metropolis which becomes co-extensive with "the modern world," and thence with the Present. It's not a bad achievement for two moves toward affirming a logic of the local, the limited, the partial, the heterogeneous.

At the same time, both texts insist that the point of departure for such expansion *anticipates*, as well as preceding in practice, its conclusion. Van den Abbeele reclaims MacCannell's thesis of "the tourist's anteriority to the social theorist" (12) in order to make the Tourist prefigure the Nomad by providing the structure of the dilemma that the latter must displace. Chambers overtly claims that the metropolitan cultures of the last twenty years have "fundamentally anticipated" the "intellectualizing" of postmodernism (6–7). So in each case, it is the terrain of everyday life (lived tourist "theorizing," for van den Abbeele, cultural "mixing" for Chambers) that anticipates a general theoretical program and its actantial "hero" (Nomad, Detective).

That is to say, the social in each case is inscribed as prophetic of the theoretical conclusion to which each of these texts will come. And in each case, that conclusion will assert the displacement of the intellectual as "prophet." As the Nomad displaces the seer, so for Chambers the Detective replaces the intellectual "as a dispenser of the Law and Authority, the Romantic poet-priest-prophet" (20).

At this point, it appears that a point of departure is emerging not from the messy complexity of metropolitan culture or the prophetic space of lived theorizing *en voyage*, but from a bibliography of critical writings from the past twenty years—a point of departure retrieved as the ambush of conclusion, recycled, for ritual revisiting, as a *destination* inevitable, like the Eiffel Tower, on a tour of present possibilities (or politico-theoretical *markers*). Like Anne Zahalka's photographer in her series of images "The Tourist as Theorist 1: (Theory Takes a Holiday),"[38] we begin our planning from brochures and conclude with a review of our personalized images of the sights we set out to see.

When "theory takes a holiday," however, the interesting thing is not the reiterations of narrative structure but the reemergence of a form of personification allegory to articulate that structure. For both Chambers and van den Abbeele (unlike Zahalka), "Theory" not only becomes the subject of the story of flight and transformation, but divides *in the end* into two figures. The story is remotivated for future development by the splitting (and doubling) of Theory into good and bad characters—the Nomad vs. the Seer, the Detective vs. the Poet-Priest-Prophet.

In his classic study *Allegory: The Theory of a Symbolic Mode*, Angus Fletcher argued that the hero of personification allegory is above all a "generator of other secondary personalities, which are partial aspects of himself."[39] The traveler is a "natural" conceptual hero for such allegory, because he is "plausibly led into numerous fresh situations, where it seems likely that new aspects of himself may be turned up" (36–37). Following this, the *tourist* would be a likely hero today precisely because he is plausibly led into *familiar* situations, where old aspects of himself may turn up for renewed recycling. Either way, the point for Fletcher is that the splitting-off of "chips of composite character" is part of a progressive process of reduction that he calls "*daemonic constriction in thematic actions*" (38). The Daemons of ancient myth share with allegorical agents, says Fletcher, the characteristic of *compartmentalizing function* (40).

Thus as the Theorist splits into the Nomad and the Seer, the Intellectual into the Detective and the Poet-Prophet-Priest, two diverging daemonic programs emerge for further adventures by Theory. As the field of action of the hero expands (the nomad universe, the "modern world"), so, correspondingly, his semantic function is reduced, condensed, and sealed off from that of his necessary Alter Ego.

If this is an odd outcome from what starts out in each case as an affirmation of the priority of complex social experience over totalizing theoretical activity, it is particularly odd as an outcome for Iain Chambers, for whom *"the metaphysical adventure is over"* (20). This is the claim that enables his displacement of the metaphorics of the voyage with that of the map. If the detective is certainly still an adventurer, he is, as ten thousand screen stories in the naked city have taught us, nothing if not pragmatic about the process of getting results and the places he goes to get them. The mystery in this case is why, if the metaphysical adventure really *is* over, the streetwise intellectual should begin his practice so strictly positioned in a constitutive opposition to "the Other." Particularly since Chambers, like MacCannell, sees a weak sense of detailed differences (the "others") replacing singular opposition.

But a binary value-system is probably as indispensable to the rhetoric of populism as the construction of emblematic tableaux of Personae performing the functions that define them is to its social portraiture. Menie Parkes's scenes of mother with child, husbandman with bread, or toiler with engine can easily be read as prefigurations of Chambers's post-Rasta black Britons with Italian tracksuits, and male gender-benders with falsettos—with the difference that Parkes's tableau assumes an eternal congruence of person and persona, while populism today predicates its pedagogy on their radical dissociation. In this sense, and in spite of its anti-academic or anti-"official" stance, populism may well be one political trajectory for which the metaphysical adventure can *never* be over.

One could conclude that if the rhetoric of touristic anti-tourism defines "part of the problem" rather than a critical perspective, then in a comparable way an academic anti-academicism defines not a transformed politics of theory but a "part of the problem." However, this formulation is misleading in that it assumes (like the allegory it analyzes) that anywhere and everywhere the problem of "Theory" is the same. Not the least of the little imperialisms performed by these exercises is to place "the modern world" as having-been or still-being under the sway of an intellectual Prophet-Despot who sounds for all the world like an elderly Humanities professor in a venerable but declining European university.

"The problem" for me is the function performed by the figure of the Prophet ("the Other") not in the history of the world, but in Iain

Chambers's argument. Its main role seems to be to eliminate the difficulties raised fleetingly by Chambers as "the relationship between . . . the machinery of capital, commerce and industry and ART or CULTURE" (17).

Chambers reasonably points out that these distinctions are highly artificial, promoting complacent myths of critical exteriority to culture, and that the "struggle for sense" occurs inside the powers of the field mutually constructed by "commerce," and (in his example) music. He argues for situating struggle in the complex "immediate mishmash of the everyday," rather than in relation to a singular *or* "free-floating" first cause. However, in a move that is foundational for some versions of cultural studies, Chambers immediately retreats from extending the complexity principle *to* analysis of relations between the (global) "machinery of capital" and (local) cultural machinations. Instead of entering the "field" constructed "mutually" by industry and culture, the former simply drops out of play. Put baldly, the result is that "the immediate mishmash of the everyday" in this account does not include rapidly changing experiences of the workplace, the home, family life, or mechanisms of state—because it does not include these as "everyday" at all. Nor does it extend to the relations between high-tech culture and the increasingly globalized division of labor that Richard Gordon has called the "homework economy."[40]

Instead, as an account based on the emblematic street experience of un- or underemployed males in European or American cities (or what then becomes its echoes elsewhere), it *restricts* the scope of inquiry to what may well be, in a grim sense, one of the "growth" areas of that economy, but which does not necessarily thereby serve as a useful synecdoche from which general principles of "culture" in "the modern world" may be composed. Perhaps this is one reason why women, in postsubcultural accounts, still appear in apologetic parentheses or as "catching up" on the streets when they're not left looking out the window.[41] The ways in which the economic and technological changes of "the 1980s" (in Chambers's phrase) transformed women's lives simply cannot be considered—leaving women not so much neglected as anachronistically misplaced.

Left as a restricted account of local developments, Chambers's "possible guide" would have a different, more "modest" force. It is the allegorical expansion that gives the lie, like the myth of the Metropolis, to the rhetoric of the local in Chambers's text, and to accounts of popular culture that take the collapse of old dichotomies (production/consumption, industry/culture) as an occasion for simply effacing the first term and expanding the second along with most of its traditional content—pleasure, leisure, play, resistance. Yet it is a difficult reading to argue against, because the imaginary figure of the Enlightenment Intellectual—prophet of Truth, poet of Totality, priest of General Theory, and so on—is still so powerful in debate about culture that the Oedipal effort against him automatically resumes in response to suggestions that relations of production and reproduction, too, are now transformed and transforming in the mishmash of the everyday.

This is how, and why, the figure of the Prophet appears in "Maps for the Metropolis." After raising the question of relations between industry and culture, and stressing the ambiguities and multiplicities of the "mix," Chambers immediately rephrases the issue as one of intellectual "hostility" to popular culture. Like van den Abbeele reducing the problem of tourism to sympathy for or against, Chambers shrinks (and moralizes) any critique of capitalism to "talk of commerce and *corruption*" (20, my emphasis)—and discovers that behind intellectual "distaste" for popular culture there is "a deeper drama. A certain intellectual formation is discovering that it is losing its grip on the world."

This seems to me to be a retreat, not least from the possibility of imagining that the "deep" drama of anybody's anxieties today may have more generous and urgent resonances than a fear of loss of "grip" (the Intellectual as Egotist). It is a retreat from the difficulties that follow once criticism of popular culture is already based on complex experiences of *taste* rather than distaste, of *involvement* rather than distance, so that a strategic "siding" for or against the "popular" becomes a pointless maneuver. Above all, it is a retreat from asking whether the humanist formation exemplified by the Romantic Prophet has not long ago lost out anyway to the quite different formation that Donna Haraway calls "the informatics of domination":[42] of which the privileged figure might be (to maintain the allegorical imperative) that exemplary localist, the Stress Management Consultant—from whose "daemonic" program it is not always so easy to differentiate one's-own as other.

Installed in the assiduously stress-free environment of a family-theme motel, the Unprotected Female Tourist tidies her papers, stares at other people's children tumbling past the window on their way to the pool, and wonders whether the woman changing the bedclothes was a girl she went to school with. A feminist, she thinks uncomfortably, should really begin her "voyage" from these familiar social markers on the map of everyday life—rather than by chasing, like some raddled detective, the traces of their effacement from the itineraries of "the others."

But that's the trouble with travel-stories written as Voyages and Maps. They relentlessly generate models of the proper use of place and time—where to begin, where to go, what to become in between. Among the most prescriptive of genres in the canon of modern realism (including journalism and "speculative fiction"), the travel-story seems strongly resistant to precisely the effort of transformation that "Sightseers: The Tourist as Theorist" and "Maps for the Metropolis" desire to see accomplished.

In Frank Moorhouse's *Room Service*, a useful counter-text to Shepard's

Motel Chronicles, a story called "The Anti-Art of Travel" demonstrates the difficulty of overcoming generic models of teleological drive. Francois Blase—a journalist and tourist who likes to "rove the world in an inconclusive state"—is confronted in the bar of the Albuquerque Holiday Inn by one of his literary "others," the Systematic Traveler. In the course of a chat, Blase is harassed by the S.T. for an account of his theory of travel. Blase resists, but cannot avoid altogether the ambush of reaching a conclusion:

> "But how do you get a picture of the places you've been to?" the S.T. said, harriedly.
> "I don't," I said glumly, "I just don't. I can't generalize, that's my problem. I can't wrap up my observations in a dazzling conclusive verbal sachet. After all, travel is a damned expensive way to arrive at inconclusiveness. . . . "[43]

He hurries on past, however—eventually to end in mid-sentence, muttering inconclusive comments about Boswell and street crime, to a politely bored bar.

III. BILLBOARDS

> *It was some 180 metres from the site of*
> *this Motor Inn on the 24th October 1889*
> *that Sir Henry Parkes whilst Colonial Secretary*
> *and Past Member for Tenterfield*
> *made his famous and historic federation speech*
> *resulting in the formation of the Commonwealth of*
> *Australia.*
>
> *The Sydney Mail of the time*
> *quoted Sir Henry Parkes as*
> *Australia's most far sighted statesman.*
>
> *This Motor Inn is therefore named*
> *The Henry Parkes*
> *In Honour of this great statesman*
> *A man to whom all Australians*
> *should be proudly thankful*
> *For the birth of a nation*
> *In its own right.*
>
> *A COLONY FOR A NATION AND A NATION FOR A COLONY.*
>
> —RESTAURANT PLAQUE, HENRY PARKES MOTOR INN.

Legend

There was a legend still circulating in town when I was a child that the Tenterfield Oration was a myth. The Clerk of Petty Sessions, a man then old enough to have witnessed the event as a boy, would swear that Henry Parkes had merely ridden down the main street of Tenterfield, hopped off his horse, relieved himself around the back of the pub, then headed straight out for Sydney.

When locals laughed at the efforts of booster families to mark out their patch as a Place of far-reaching significance, they made a joke with antecedents. In 1882 Parkes, returning from an exhausting voyage to America, Britain, and Europe to face turmoil over land reforms, lost the poll in East Sydney. The candidate for Tenterfield, a Mr. Edward Reeves Whereat J.P., immediately stood aside and offered Parkes his seat. Elected unopposed, Parkes was baptized by his opponents "The Member for *Whereat.*"

But the joke wasn't really on the Tenterfield boosters. Making an equation between progress for the town and rhetorical contiguity to a prominent figure, the *Tenterfield Star* celebrated Parkes's election by noting that it would assure its future as a transit-town: "with regard to the Clarence and New England Railway, the return of Henry Parkes must necessarily make him a firm adherent to the Tenterfield route. . . . "[44]

To be traversed and attract traversals, for far-flung communities dependent on transport for economic survival and growth, was obviously a means to, and not an end of, the process of settling "place." The railway here didn't blur the landscape, but made it visible, legible, and livable to whites—cutting "culture" into the bush.[45] This dependence, though, is one reason why country towns never really acquired organic "roots," or sentimental "Main Street," connotations in Australian popular culture. The pomposities of civic pride remain defensive against the more powerful mythic pull of the routes for comings and goings.

Whether or not Parkes's "adherence" to the route contributed to Tenterfield's success in becoming a transit-town, his name was firmly established as a patron saint of *passage.* In the circular production of "prominence" that organized regional politics long before the arrival of media and regimes of simulation, the Tenterfield landowners, dignitaries, and small business families dined out on his story for decades.[46] Modern tourism finds in their story-telling its basic semiotic strategy.

Place and Space

In *The Practice of Everyday Life*, Michel de Certeau makes an interesting distinction between "place" and "space." A *place* delimits a field: it is ruled by the law of the "proper," by an orderly contiguity of elements in the location it defines, and as an instantaneous configuration of positions it implies an "indication of stability."[47]

A *space* is not the substance of a place, but the product of its transformation. It exists only in relation to vectors of direction, velocities, and time variables. Space "occurs": composed of intersections of mobile elements, it is *actuated* by the ensemble of movements deployed within it. With none of the univocity or stability of the "proper," it is produced by the operations that make it function in "a polyvalent unity of conflictual programs or contractual proximities."

"In short," says de Certeau, "space is a *practised place.*" The street defined by urban planning is transformed into a space by walkers; and in the same way, an act of reading is a space produced by a practice of a written text (a "place constituted by a system of signs").

One useful consequence of this definition is that no distinction can be made between authentic and "inauthentic" places. At the same time, it avoids any move to predetermine the kind or the *tempo* of spatial (reading, walking . . .) practices deemed "appropriate" to particular places. A written text on a motel wall or restaurant plaque may be spatially practiced in ways, in directions, and at velocities as various as any street, or literary text. By definition, no one spatial practice can correspond to a "proper" use of place, and there are no exemplary users. Nor is there a simple disjunction between the place and its use as space. For de Certeau, stories act as a means of transportation (*metaphorai*) in the shuttling that "constantly transforms places into spaces or spaces into places."

There are two sorts of determinations in stories. One works to found the law of place by the *"being-there* of something dead"—a pebble, a cadaver, perhaps the record of a speech. The other works to specify spaces by the *actions* of historical subjects—stones, trees, or a political rogue in a hurry. There are passages back and forth between them: for example, in a story of the putting to death, or putting into a landscape, of heroes who have transgressed the law of the place, and make restoration with their tombs (or their epitaphs on motels).

That is, both determinations can be at work in any one legend or story. So the memorializing of events occurring at a site cannot simply be divided into, say, bad petit-bourgeois fabrication (myths of place, sacralization) and good popular contestation (semiotics of displacement, debunking). As an activity, memorializing is itself a complex spatial-story practice. Struggles (conflictual programs) occur in the shuttling between stories, and between competing determinations *in* stories. Thus the rival versions of the Tenterfield Oration—say, "Call to the Nation" vs. "Call of Nature"—both commemorate a local event and invest a site with meaning, but the second *enlivens* the first, as well as marking its enshrinement of a something-dead as a socially placed aspiration rather than a "national" event.

This distinction can be useful in dismantling those lingering equations between the place and the *domus,* displacement and the voyage, which in recent years have made the projects of feminist history so fraught, despite the rhetoric of the local, with general-theoretical anxiety—particularly since de

Certeau's concept of story operates at the level of minute phrases and tiny events as well as larger narrative structures. His insistence that "every story is a travel story—a spatial practice" (115) refers to sentences, footsteps, or scraps of TV news rather than to vast developmental schemes for ordering and narrating human life.

Thus he differentiates between "tours" and "maps," not in terms of teleological narrative drives in the one case and fixations of the Present in the other, but as competing modalities *in* a process of narrative description (118–20). In "oral descriptions of places, narrations concerning the home, stories about the streets," for example, indicators of the "map" type ("There is a historic site 180 metres down the road") present tableaux (*seeing* as "the knowledge of an order of places") while those of the "tour" type ("You go down to the School of Arts") organize movements (*going* as "spatializing actions"). In narration, one form may be dominant but be punctuated by the other: tours postulate maps, while maps condition and presuppose tours. It is their combination in a narrative chain of spatializing operations that defines for de Certeau the structure of the travel story: "stories of journeys and actions are marked out by the 'citation' of the places that result from them or authorize them" (120).

The travel story, therefore, does not consist of process contained and directed by origin and destination, nor does it oscillate between "perspectives" on reality. It is itself a movement organized, like any spatial story, between both prospective and retrospective mappings of place, *and* the practices that transform them.

Foundation Stone

Various foundation stories wander around the *Henry Parkes* (on brochures, cards, and a menu in all the rooms) as well as up and down the streets. The front wall Legend, with its war-memorial layout and assertive historical statement, transmutes on a restaurant plaque into the visual form of a poem. In this text, events are elegically distanced by a *tournure* of romance. It emphasizes the emergence of place in time past ("It was some 180 metres . . . " vs. "On the 24th October . . . "), and an archaizing syntax creating "history-effect" combines with a proprietorial enunciative trace in a discourse of obligation ("all Australians should be proudly thankful"). This produces an aura of special importance, like saying grace before the meal. But it also makes the restaurant plaque a declaration of personal commitment rather than a simple touristic seduction.[48]

The plaque has another touch, however, that marks it off from the other stories and yet defines the type of movement that regulates them all. It ends with a kind of slogan: *"a colony for a nation and a nation for a colony."* This is a resonant and memorable phrase. But when you stop to think, it doesn't make sense—or rather, it maps an imaginary place. It works for a world in which New South Wales alone became "Australia," or in which the whole of the Australian continent was occupied by one vast colony. Either way, the whole process of federating six distinct and mutually suspicious colonies into one nation would have been, like the Tenterfield Oration, quite unnecessary.

It could be called a misquotation. The original slogan, attributed to Edmund Barton (later, Australia's first Prime Minister), was "For the first time in history, we have *a nation for a continent and a continent for a nation.*" This production of congruence between natural and political places occurred in a public speech. It begins its course of citation and recitation in historiography not as a text certified by its author but as a reported "memorable impromptu" made at a meeting. In his memoirs, Robert Randolph Garran claimed to have been its first inscriber: it "would have been unrecorded if I had not happened to write it down."[49]

What matters in this story is not a myth of the primacy of the spoken word, but the movement (in this case, of hearsay) that runs between citings of the text, and that in one place of its migration, a plaque on a dining-room wall, transforms it from place-founding slogan to the "score" of a lilting rhythm—a trill, a whistle, a jingle, a musical spatial story.

Memorabilia

If you follow the story down the street and go on a tour of the town, several maps of the present and stories of the past begin to intersect. There's discord about it, not just a codified diversity-and-difference.

The School of Arts enshrines the site of Parkes's speech. It is disconcerting to enter with any sense of anticipation, for the inside turns out to be an everyday lending library. As Dean MacCannell points out, the most difficult sights to sacralize are places where something once happened (battles, speech-events) but there is nothing left to see. All that remains here is a lovely but still walked-on wooden floor.

Down one end, however, there is a roped-off tiny museum of Henry Parkes memorabilia. Apart from a 1915 bust, and a portrait of Parkes in his favorite pose as a late Victorian Moses, most of the objects (wheelbarrow, dog collar, watch) seem to have been collected on the basis of having been *touched* by Parkes, or persons in his vicinity. They are those objects most confusing and emotionally opaque to a media sensibility—genuine relics. But even this image of sanctum is jarred by pieces that seem to have nothing personal to do with Parkes—a modern book on *Georgian Architecture*, local histories of distant places, bits of twentieth-century pottery with a nationalistic theme. It's a museum dedicated not to the remains of a person, but to an old school of history—an inventory of unrelated, age-encrusted, national *faits divers.*

A few blocks away, a rival foundation-place offers something more familiar. It's a showbiz monument—an old shop restored as the home of the "Tenterfield Saddler." Built in the 1860s, it was created a few years ago from a song by the late Peter Allen, an American-based entertainer, commemorating a family connection. The Saddlery is an impeccable third-order simulacrum: even though the building is now "in its original condition," it reproduces an image of a reality with no previous claim to existence. People treat it respectfully as a forebear of Tenterfield's modernity.

The Centenary Cottage museum tries for something completely different. It has long been in transition between an old house crammed with junk, and a "restored pioneer home." An incipient program is readable: the highway-oriented, universalizing pedagogy of simulation hovers as a possibility. But even in the rooms already most organized toward this ideal, the period-effect is overwhelmed by local genealogies. In a clear case of what MacCannell calls "obliteration by the markers," each item is cluttered by the history of its donation: a bed is presented by A, handmade by B from a silky oak cut on property C located at D in 1881, and restored by Mr. and Mrs. E. This museum is unreadable to outsiders. It refuses to efface the gestures of labor, ownership, and gift in the manner essential to catching transient interests—not because it has a deep-rooted, organic sense of "reality" but because it has no idea of its own obscurity. This is a *dynastic* museum— a "who's who *here*" display—and despite its touristic ambitions it primarily lectures the town.

Nothing much here means anything to me. But in the more disorganized parts of the Cottage, two objects immediately provoke what is usually called "nostalgia." One is in the yard, past an old weighing machine stranded in the grass and some singed-looking ferns by a drain. It is an old laundry copper, "historic," but intimately stifling: hot, heavy, stubborn loads of washing to be stirred, potstick circling round boiling water, in a misery of blazing heat every endless Saturday morning. The other is in the chaos of junk inside. Next to a 1921 income tax receipt are the "Last Reservation Tickets for the Lyric Theatre." My own first cinema memory rushes up from the 1950s. But it has nothing to do with hurtling through space, zooming through time, or an aesthetics of disappearance.

It's about *placement*, a memory of anxiety in the picture theater about where to sit, just the same as in the schoolroom. A tension map of proximities for good little white girls to avoid: town Aborigines (all right, really); white West End louts (worse); and worst, in a front row tacitly off-limits to everyone else, the Aboriginal and white-trash families from just out of town on the Common.

Proximities

If within a few blocks it is possible to tour an archaic mode of pedagogy, a parochial display of current class and caste distinctions, and a piece of postmodern aesthetics, then it is partly because tourism here is as yet barely organized. Apart from National Parks and National Trust (historic buildings) activity, tourism operates as a local response to economic distress.[50] It is also relatively innocuous—though there's something devastating about the blatancy of a leaflet available round town called *The Bluff Rock Massacre.* "We punished them severely, and proved our superiority to them," cites the local historian, Ken Halliday, blending geological details of the rock with the tale of a "tribe" being thrown from the top in retaliation for the murder of a shepherd on Bolivia Station in 1844. A more sophisticated tourist operation would obliterate that immediately.[51]

But if their haphazard efforts make country towns eccentric to the global tourist economy, they also suggest a general difficulty in constructing guides to the Present, or theories of the tourist homing instinct. It isn't just that they are obdurately *there*, waiting in ambush like the suburbs on the edge of the Metropolis, with their own "declarations of reality."[52] It's rather that even in the smallest places, where the production of space involves a limited number of "conflictual programs and contractual proximities," in de Certeau's phrase, the operative *simultaneity* of programs and proximities makes the effort to take any one as exemplary (either of the Now, or of a "domestication" of history in myth), only one of the more aggressively territorial programs competing to found its place.

Thousands of miles away, Jean Baudrillard writes in *America*: "Why should I go and decentralize myself in France, in the ethnic and the local, among the scraps and remains of centrality?"[53] He wants to become ex-centered in the center of the world. Fair enough. But when he gets there he finds, like a postmodern mystic, the universe in a Burger King crumb, or a Studebaker, or an empty motel. His America is a "gigantic hologram, in the sense that information concerning the whole is contained in each of its elements" (29). I do know what he means by this. Even in an Australian country town—a vestige of failed decentralization rather than a residue of centrality—I can learn something of All Australia in the Saddlery, or the becoming–Burger King of the old Greek and Chinese cafes down the road.

But the point about holograms (like simulacra) is that they volatilize, rather than replace, other models of signifying practice (spatial stories). In fact, a hologram is one of the visual events least able to admit of *relations in contiguity*: it is defined (in Baudrillard's description) by self-containment. It really doesn't recognize the difficult logic of the *next*—hologram here, cinema next door, painting over there—that activates spaces in contemporary culture and makes philosophies of grounding so difficult to sustain. It is a traffic in negotiable proximities, temporal as well as spatial, between conflicting practices that follows from the decentering of a Renaissance "perspective" on life—and not the restoration of hierarchy by a controlling reference-point that marginalizes the "rest."

A motel is a good place to consider the question of traffic, precisely because it is consecrated to proximity and circulation. It is neither the car nor the highway nor the house nor the voyage nor the home, but a space of movements between all of them. It punctuates traveling with resting and being-there with action. It represents neither arrival nor departure, but operates passages from one to the other in the *metaphorai* of the pause. Motel-time is a syncopation of different speeds in varied degrees of duration.

But it is not an emblematic site, precisely because it exists only transitionally, in any usage, between other possibilities. It provides an operational link not only between practices but between institutions. In countless fictional motels, gangsters, lovers, psychopaths, drifters, and defaulters come to motels to be killed, seized, abandoned, or imprisoned as well as to hide, to escape, to recover—in transit between many kinds of prison, and many attempts at release. So despite its resonance for highway romance, the motel may always, in the end, affirm the being-there of the place and the modalities of the map—but it creates the possibility of the tour.

Mattering Maps

Lawrence Grossberg has used the model of the roadside billboard to pose problems about interpreting events in popular culture and the politics of everyday life.[54] Billboards for Grossberg are "markers," neither authentic nor inauthentic, that are there to be driven by. They don't tell us where we are going but they mark, and comprise, boundaries; they *are* outside, inside, and the limits of the town that they announce, and that we are passing through. They advertise, yet we drive past without attending to what they say because we already know, or it doesn't matter. Yet they do tell us what road we are on, and reaffirm that we are actually moving. They are not there to be "read": yet they are a space in which different discourses appear, so they are sites of struggle. However, an *individual* billboard is indifferent. It is "neither built upon a radical sense of textual difference, nor does it erase all difference" (32).

So Grossberg suggests that interpreting the politics and effects of popular culture is less like reading a book than like driving by billboards; not because the street is the only reality, but because billboards belong simultaneously to the orders of local detail and national structure, and connect to places off the road (factories, jails, houses). Billboards are also like the bric-a-brac in Centenary Cottage—apparently meaningless "signposts" which, for all the irrelevance and seeming uselessness of their specific inscriptions, are sites of investment and empowerment (not necessarily benevolent). For Grossberg, such signposts make it possible to continue struggling to *make* a difference by devising "mattering maps."[55]

So if billboards are dominated (unlike the motel) by the operationality of space and the modality of the tour, by "going" rather than "seeing," they enable in turn the making of maps, the citing and seeing of places. This image is all the more useful if we remember that as well as driving by billboards anywhere, people sometimes stop near particular billboards *somewhere*. People live near billboards, photograph them, picnic and read books beside them, deface them, or even, near Tenterfield, shoot at them.

For most of the 1980s, Tenterfield's limits were marked on the three main roads by *National: The Big Entertainer* billboards. They ringed the town with images of Peter Allen at the piano, declaring that he "Still Called Australia Home," and that Tenterfield was the Home of the Tenterfield Saddler. These routine, concentric productions of Place from the figure of Allen (Saddler/Tenterfield/Australia) were in perfect conformity with the older myth of Henry Parkes (Motel/Tenterfield/Australia). In 1986 they were replaced by billboards advertising a nearby natural wonder, Bald Rock ("Australia's Largest Granite Rock"), each handpainted in the perfect image of its postcard by two women artists, Lou Potter and Jean Braid, from Tenterfield.[56] For a while, these three serialized "individual" billboards will figure on local mattering maps, not as indifferent signposts enabling the making of difference but as signs (for those to whom it matters) of a difference *made*. That they may revert, in time, to indifference makes no difference to the spatial story.

Trajectories

Once out at the billboards, the tourist could go home to the *Henry Parkes* motel, home to her mother's place nearby, or head home on the road to Sydney. Each ending might define a different kind of domesticity: formalist (return to first principles), feminist (return to a maternal space), or postmodernist (Blase admits the transience of her interest in small towns, and reclaims her intellectual mobility). All of these resolutions are perfectly realistic.

In any case, I can leave still thinking about Henry Parkes, of whom I've had very little to say. My interest has been in the disjunctions between, on the one hand, the rhetorics of movement, displacement, and rapidity in debates about popular genres of cultural practice (touring, home-making, mapping, detecting), and, on the other, the feminist insistence on recognizing place and variable *pace* in everyday life. If so, it is because there is a particular stake for feminism in the awkward relations between them.

The problem might be summed up by Prato and Travero's claim in "The Spectacle of Travel" that transport ceased to be a metaphor of Progress when *mobility* came to characterize everyday life more than the image of "home and family"; transport became, instead, "the primary activity of existence."[57] Feminism has no need whatsoever to claim the history of home-and-family as its special preserve, but it does imply a degree of discretion about proclaiming its marginalization.

It is important to remember that in Australia, as in many places, the mobility/*domus* distinction is at best historically doubtful. In settler and immigrant societies, it is mobility as a *means* of endlessly making prospects (or "progress") for home-and-family that becomes, for many people, the primary activity of existence. As the prior condition of such progress, colonization is precisely a mode of movement, practiced *as* an occupation of other people's homelands as well as a destruction of their families and homes, that transgresses limits and borders. In and after colonialism, a European voyage/*domus* distinction loses its oppositional structure—and thus its value for announcing the displacement of one by the other in the course of History.

Yet the sort of claim being made by Prato and Travero does not seek its grounding in historical truth, even the truth of approximation, and thus makes feminist criticism more difficult. It is meant, perhaps, to be a billboard, a marker in a certain landscape. It marks a recognizable trajectory along which it becomes possible not only for some to think of their lives as a trip on a "road to nowhere,"[58] but for others to think of home-and-family as a comfortable, "empowering" vehicle.

So rather than retreating to the invidious position of trying to contradict a billboard, feminist criticism might make its own. I have two in mind, two textual places that might be transformed by a shuttle between them producing a spatial story. As individual billboards, they don't tell me anything in particular—not how to read the history of families, tourism, or Australian politics, and certainly not how to read the relations between cultural change and the persistent vagrancy of clichés. But together, they mark out space for considering convergence and overlap, rather than divergence and distinction, between the rhetoric of mobility and the politics of placement, the mapping of the voyage and the "metaphorics of *home.*"

One is a quotation from Henry Parkes—self-made man, traveler, family man, Premier, modernizer, philosopher, and Father of Federation—who spoke of the political reforms of the 1860s in these terms:

> Our business being to colonize the country, there was only one way to do it—by spreading over it all the associations and connections of family life.[59]

The other is a media anecdote from the *Sydney Morning Herald* in 1987 entitled "Great Moments in Philosophy."[60] Federal Treasurer Paul Keating—self-made man, traveler, family man, future Prime Minister, modernizer, philosopher, republican—refuted accusations that he was using his traveling allowance to purchase antique clocks. Asked why he claimed travel refunds when he lived in Canberra with his home-and-family, he replied on the steps of Parliament House:

> *We are wayfarers on one long road. Mere wayfarers.*

THINGS TO DO WITH SHOPPING CENTERS

The story of everyday practice begins, says Michel de Certeau, "on ground level, with footsteps."[1] To come down from an urban tower and walk away from the panorama-city is to walk toward time and eventfulness, action and eccentricity, spaces of anecdote, discrete locales. In the infinite diversity of the ways in which pedestrians "operate" their city-system, de Certeau finds resistances that elude yet inhabit the disciplined field of spectacular space. Like speaking, walking is a referential activity: with every step, the walker creates a near and a far, a *here* and a *there*, a *now* and a *then*, thus predicating worlds of mobile positions and relations. At least, this is one interpretation of the analogy. De Certeau himself prefers to highlight the contact-oriented aspects of walking, those that set up, maintain or interrupt material flows of communication, like "hello" or "hmmm" in speech: "walking, which alternately follows a path and has followers, creates a mobile organicity in the environment, a sequence of phatic *topoi*" (99).

De Certeau's descent from observation deck to footpath creates a volatile drama of "up" and "down," system and process, planning and living, theory and practice, synchrony and history. The analytical force of this schema weakens, however, with distance from the base of the tower and the crowded streets around it. To keep on walking is to find, in Australian urban contexts, that tower and busy street merge, back there, in the singular vagueness of "town" (downtown); to travel "away from town" is to head toward zones of vastness and *sparseness* where space is neither panoptic nor intimately pedestrian in organization. As Venturi, Scott Brown, and Izenour insisted,[2] suburban space is automobile space; in the car-zones, "up" and "down" are less distinctively "practices" of space than relative *moments* along a trajectory.

The spatial distribution of functions that supports de Certeau's city (looking/moving, observing/doing, mapping/operating) cannot easily be used to segment suburbia,[3] or the patchy straggle of an Australian country town, in terms of theories here, stories there, structure here, history there—even if we aim to follow de Certeau by asking how theories and stories may interact in practice. Another approach is needed to grasp the differences between apparently similar sites; one of the most persistent myths of Australian "suburbanality"[4] projects a bland continuum of interchangeable allotments, each reproducing the cultural whole of which it is a part. If a regional shopping center[5] is not the "other" of an urban tower (any more than down-to-earth living is "the" other of an urban planner's dreams), neither is it simply a self-identical form repeated endlessly in various towns and suburbs as though the latter had no history that might modify the form.

Yet footsteps can still be a way to start. In comparison with the U.S. freeway-billboard spaces classically described by Venturi and his associates, Australian towns and suburbs preserve the habit of walking and treat it with some respect. Nevertheless, there is a hierarchy—as any vulnerable pedestrian knows. Pedestrians abroad in sparse landscapes beyond the city center are not so much out of scale or place as *at risk* in an environment where roads link specialized exercise-enclosures (home, backyard, pool, gym, sports oval, supermarket) with the drive-in bottle shops and liquor barns that fuel potentially predatory cars.[6]

For a female, black, queer, foreign, "funny-looking," or just plain unlucky pedestrian, de Certeau's phatic aspect of walking gains an uncomfortable intensity here. The tactics of inviting and avoiding "followers," as he puts it, are basic to the art of communication across suburban space. There is the hitchhiker, attempting not only to appear desirable as a passenger to an approaching car, but to be desirable in the right way to the right sort of driver. Here is a walker striding along, head down, posture repellent, on the wrong side of the road for an easy lift, hoping to deflect the attention of hostile vehicles. If walking for pleasure or convenience in this landscape is a risky practice, it is safer when phrased (by, say, a track-suit) as "cardiovascular."

If the history of suburban space is to some extent a history of pedestrian displacement, then walking, because of its tense, disproportionate relationship to suburban cultural forms, is a useful way to think about how to do something, as a feminist cultural critic, with those forms. Away from town, walking is understood as slow motion, and a "loiterly" pace (to borrow a wonderful word from Ross Chambers)[7] can help a critic, struggling with massive signs of contemporaneity fashioned for faster-moving eyes than her own, to pick up details lying in a landscape like litter beside the billboards, or the abandoned shopping trolleys sprawling in a culvert, bedecked with flowers and cans.

MANAGING CHANGE

The first thing I want to do is to cite an old definition of modernity. It comes not from feminist theory or cultural studies, but from a paper on "development in the retail scene" given in Perth in 1981 by John Lennen of Myer Shopping Centres. To begin his address to a seminar organized by the Australian Institute of Urban Studies, Lennen told this fable:

> As Adam and Eve were leaving the Garden of Eden, Adam turned to Eve and said, "Do not be distressed my dear, we live in times of change."[8]

After quoting Adam, Lennen went on to say, "Cities live in times of change. We must not be discouraged by change, but rather we must learn to manage change." He meant that the role of shopping centers was changing rapidly from what it had been in the 1970s, and that retailers left struggling with the consequences—planning restrictions, postboom economic conditions, new forms of competition—should not be discouraged, but should change their practices accordingly.

Shopping for me is an anxious business,[9] and for the first part of this chapter I fret about some methodological issues recurrently raised for feminist cultural studies by the management of change in places involving practices regularly, if not exclusively, carried out by women—shopping, driving, organizing leisure activities. Like most fretting, this discussion has an obsessive theme; I worry about "Edenic" or redemptive allegories of consumerism drawn out of literary theory, then used to *frame* analyses of those laborious and anxious activities.[10] However, my argument takes the form of a rambling response to two questions that I've often been asked by women with whom I've discussed these issues.

DIFFERENCE AND IDENTITY

One question comes up almost invariably for academic women with whom I've discussed the topic of shopping centers. They say: "Yes, you do semiotics

. . . are you looking at how malls are all the same everywhere? laid out sys-
tematically, everyone can read them?" They don't ask about shopping centers and change, or about a semiotics of the management of change.

My emphasis is rather the opposite. It is true that at one level of analysis
(and of our "practice" of shopping centers) layout and design principles try
to ensure that all centers are *minimally* readable to anyone literate in their
use. This readability may be minimal indeed: most malls purposely alter-
nate surprise and confusion with familiarity and harmony, and in different
parts of any one center, clarity and opacity will occur in differing degrees
of intensity for different users. To a newcomer, the major supermarket in an
unfamiliar center is usually more difficult to read than the spatial relations
between the specialty food shops and the boutiques. Nevertheless, there are
always some basic rules of contiguity and association at work to assist you to
select shops as well as products.[11]

However, I am more interested in the differences between shopping centers themselves, how they produce and maintain what Neville Quarry calls
"a unique sense of place"—in other terms, a spatial myth of identity.[12] Looking at this involves predicating a more complex and localized *affective* relation to shopping spaces, and to their links with other sites of domestic and
familial labor, than does the scenario of the cruising grammarian reading
similarity from place to place. In one way, all shoppers are cruising gram-
marians. I do not need to deny this, however, in order to concentrate on
how particular centers strive to become special, for better or worse, in the
everyday lives of women in local communities.[13] Men, of course, may have
a special affective relation to *a* particular shopping center, too.

Obviously, shopping centers produce a sense of place for economic,
"come-hither" reasons, and sometimes also because architects and planners
are committed, these days, to an aesthetics or even a politics of the local.
However, we cannot ground analysis of their function, or people's responses
to them, solely on this economic rationale; "going shopping" and actually
spending money are two separate activities. Besides, shopping center identities are not consistent or permanent. Shopping centers do get face-lifts,
and change their image—increasingly so as the great classic structures in
any region begin to age, fade, and date.

However, the cost of renovating them, especially the larger ones, means
that the identity-effect produced by any one center's spatial play in time is
not only complex, highly nuanced, and variable in detail, but also simple,
massive, and relatively enduring overall, and over time, in space. At every
possible level of analysis (and there are many with such a diverse and
continuous social event) shopping centers are overwhelmingly and constitutively paradoxical. This is one of the things that makes it hard to differentiate them. On the one hand, they are so monolithically Present—solid,
monumental, indisputably part of the landscape, and in our lives. On the
other hand, when you try to dispute with them, they dissolve at any one

point into an indeterminacy that might suit any philosopher's delirium of abstract femininity. This is partly because the shopping center "experience" at any one point *includes* the experience of crowds of people (or of their relative absence), and so of all the varied responses and uses that the center provokes and contains.

To complicate matters, this *dual* quality is very much a part of shopping center strategies of appeal, their planned "seductiveness," and also of their management of change. The stirring tension between the massive stability of the structure, and the continually shifting, ceaseless spectacle within and around the "center," is one of the things that people who like shopping centers really *love* about shopping centers. At the same time, shopping center management methods (and contracts) are directed toward organizing and unifying—at the level of administrative control, if not of achieved aesthetic effect—as much of this spectacle as possible by regulating tenant mix, signing and advertising styles, common space decor, festivities, and so on. This does not mean, however, that they succeed in "managing" either the total spectacle or the responses it provokes (including what people do with what they provide).

So analyzing shopping centers partly involves, on the one hand, exploring the sensations, perceptions, and emotional states (negative as well as delirious) that they arouse, and, on the other, suspending those perceptions and states in order to make a space from which to speak other than that of the enthusiastic describer standing "outside" the spectacle *qua* ethnographer, recommending it to others and extracting ethical lessons from it, or, in a pose that seems to me to amount to much the same thing, ostentatiously absorbed in her own absorption *qua* celebrant of popular culture.

If the former mode of description is found in much sociology of consumerism or leisure, the latter mode has had persuasive defenders in cultural studies. Iain Chambers, for example, has argued strongly that in order to appreciate the democratic potential of the way that people live through, not "alongside," culture, appropriating and transforming everyday life, we must first pursue the "wide-eyed presentation of actualities" that Adorno disapproved in some of Benjamin's work on Baudelaire.[14] I still agree with this as a general orientation. But if we look closely at the terms of Adorno's objection, it is possible to read into them a good description of shopping center *mystique*: "your study is located at the crossroads of magic and positivism. That spot is bewitched."[15] With a confidence that feminist philosophers have taught us to question, Adorno continues that "Only theory could break the spell . . . " (meaning Benjamin's style of theoretical practice, not theory-in-general).

For me, neither a strategy of "wide-eyed presentation" nor a faith in whatever style of theory as the Exorcist is quite adequate to dealing with the problems posed for feminism by the analysis of everyday life. If we locate our own studies at that "crossroads of magic and positivism" to be found in the grand central court of any large regional mall, then social experiences more complex than wonder or bewitchment are sure to occur, and to elicit, for a feminist, a more critical response than "presentation" requires. If it is now routine to reject the philosophical mythology of Adorno's scenario (theory breaking the witch's spell), and yet also to refuse critiques of "consumption" as false consciousness (bewitchment by the mall), then it is perhaps not so easy any more to question the "wide-eyed" pose of critical amazement at the performance of the everyday.

At the very least, a feminist analysis of shopping centers will insist initially upon ambivalence about its objects rather than astonishment before them. Ambivalence allows a thinking of relations between contradictory states: it is also a pose, but one that is perhaps more flexible in its own relation to everyday practices of, say, using the same shopping centers often, and for different reasons, rather than visiting several occasionally, but intensely, in order to see the sights. Ambivalence does not eliminate the moment of everyday *discontent*—of anger, frustration, sorrow, irritation, hatred, boredom, fatigue. Feminism is minimally a movement *of* discontent with "the everyday," and with wide-eyed definitions of the everyday as "the way things are." While feminism, too, may proceed by "staring hard at the realities of the contemporary world we all inhabit," as Chambers puts it, feminism also allows the possibility of rejecting what we see, and refusing to take it as given. Like effective shopping, feminist criticism includes moments of sharpened focus, narrowed gaze, and skeptical assessment.

AN ORDINARY WOMAN

Feminist theory has now produced a great many tools for any critical study of identity and difference, and of place in everyday life.[16] Taking these to shopping centers, however, I encounter an awkwardness, a rhetorical one this time, with resonances of interdisciplinary conflict; the difficulty of what seems to be a lack, or lapse, of appropriateness between my discourse as an intellectual, and my objects of study.

Isn't there something really *off* about using the tools of an elite, possibly still fashionable but definitely unpopular theoretical discourse to examine a major element in the lived culture of "ordinary women," to whom that discourse is as irrelevant as the stray copy of a Roland Barthes book I once saw decorating a simulated chic apartment displayed at a "FREEDOM" furniture showroom? Wouldn't it be "off" in a way that it isn't off to use those tools to reread Gertrude Stein or other women modernists, or to write devalued and non-modernist texts by women into the literary canon?

Of course, these are not questions that any academic, even feminist, is obliged to answer. One can simply define one's object strategically, in the limited way appropriate to a determined disciplinary and institutional context. They are questions impossible to answer without challenging their terms; by pointing out, for example, that relevance and appropriateness both depend, insofar as they can be "planned" for at all, as much on the "from where" and the "to whom" of any discourse as on relationships to an "about." Over the years, I have found the pertinence or even the good taste of using semiotic or aesthetic vocabularies to discuss "ordinary" issues questioned more severely by sociologists and historians than by non-academic women, who have variously been curious, indifferent, or amused.

Nevertheless, feminist intellectuals do ask each other such questions, and will no doubt continue to do so as long as we retain some sense of a wider social context, and political import, for our work. So let me try out an answer by going back to basics and examining the function of the *"the ordinary woman"* as a figure in feminist polemics. It is a truism that as a feminist I cannot wish the image, or the reality, of other women away. It is also a truism that a semiotician or an aesthete must notice that "images" of other women—such as the one I've just produced of "sociologists and historians"—*are*, in fact, images.

What happens if I bring these truisms to bear on a visual image (fig. 2.1) of an ordinary woman walking through a shopping center? Some image like this is perhaps what many Australian feminists have in mind when we invoke the social gap between a cultural critic's discourse on shopping centers and her "object of study." This image was originally published in an Australian government report on *The Shopping Centre as a Community Leisure Resource.*[17] It was taken without its subject's knowledge by a sociological surveillance camera at Sydney's Blacktown Westpoint shopping center in 1977 or 1978. Framed as a still image, it proclaims its realist status: the candid-camera effect of capturing an iconic moment of spontaneity and joy is reinforced by bits of accessory reality protruding casually into the frame (stroller, vertical section of a "companion").

These details help us to imagine that we *know what is happening here*: a young mother is strolling the mall, enjoying herself in its ambience and sharing her pleasure with a friend. Unnamed and socially abstracted except for her maternity (for this is an icon of Woman as reproducer of consumption), she is made representative of the leisure-resource potential of "the" shopping center for indeterminately working-class women. "The shopping center," too, is abstracted as representative, since all we see of it here is the speckled floor to be found, twenty years ago, in any downmarket center anywhere. But of course, we know what is happening only *in the image.* We don't know where she came from, what her background might be, how (or even whether) she would describe her class or her ethnicity. She might be white, she might identify as Aboriginal; the image cannot tell us. We don't know why she is there, what she is laughing at, how she felt about her com-

2.1 Mother and child at Blacktown Westpoint, 1977 or 1978.

panion or the child (is it really hers?) at that instant, what her expression was like two seconds before and after the moment she passed the camera, or what her ideas that day about shopping centers, or Blacktown Westpoint in particular, might have been.

This image of an ordinary woman, then, is not a glimpse of her reality, but a polemical declaration *about* reality mobilized between the authors (or better, the authority) of a government report and its professional readership. I can deduce little about that woman at Blacktown, let alone about "women" in "shopping centers," from it. Nor can I pretend that my discourse, my camera, or even my questionnaire, if I had the real woman here to talk to now, would give me unmediated access to her thoughts and feelings about shopping at Blacktown Westpoint twenty years ago, or now. In other words, I cannot look through this image of a woman to my imaginary Ordinary Woman and ask her, *"what does shopping woman want?"*

One possible step away from being off, then, would be to construct my initial object of study as neither "that woman," nor her image, but rather the *institutional* image of shopping-woman framed as illustration to the sociological text (fig. 2.2). Any study of shopping centers today is part of a history of the positioning of women as objects of knowledges, indeed as targets for the maneuvers of retailers, planners, developers, sociologists, market researchers, and so on. There is a lot of research on this targeting, especially in relation to fashion and the history of department stores, and there is research, too, about how the target *moves*, the object evades: this is the study of women's creativity and cultural "production" as a practice of transforming imposed constraints.[18]

Another step away from being off, and also away from trying to be *on* target with/about women (as the Blacktown Westpoint image attempts to be), would be to rethink the terms of the initial question about the gap between my theoretical speech and its object. For, having said that the text-image relation (fig. 2.2) could be my object, the gap too soon narrows to a purely professional dispute, for example, a quarrel between textual critique and sociological constructions of the real, magic, and positivism (again); such disputes are stable in their form and immensely repetitive in their rhetorical flourishes. My difficulty with shopping centers is thus not simply my own relationship as intellectual to the culture I'm speaking about, but *to whom* I will imagine that I will be speaking. Whatever the answer in different contexts,[19] it cannot be to the imaginary Ordinary Woman that professional feminisms do keep projecting.

PEDESTRIAN NOTES ON MODERNITY

The second question I've discussed with other women is often posed with a bracing skepticism: "What's the point of distinguishing shopping centers? So what if they're not all the same?"

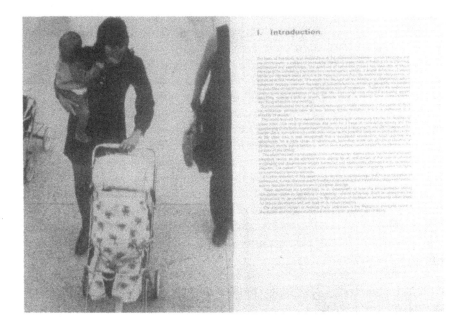

2.2 Mother and child as sociological text. Source: Department of Environment, Housing and Community Development, *The Shopping Centre as a Community Leisure Resource* (Canberra: Australian Government Publishing Service, 1978).

Here, I want to sidestep to make two points about method. The first is that if these reflections on "things to do with shopping centers" could have a subtitle, it would be *"pedestrian notes on modernity."* I still agree with Alice Jardine's fruitful argument in her book *Gynesis* that feminist criticism has a lot to gain from debates about modernity.[20] These remain important not only because of the much-discussed ways in which images of "Woman" have signified a *problem* of power-knowledge, but because of their relation to women's histories as objects of power-knowledge in the terms I described above. I also agree that as well as looking at how "woman" or "femininity" came to function as a fulcrum metaphor in those debates, we need more empirical histories of women's modernisms.[21] However I don't think that there has ever been a risk of women coming in any way to resemble "that profoundly archaic silhouette," as Jardine puts it, "poet and mad-woman—who finally took a peek at modernity and then quickly closed the door" (49).

If the broad impact of modernization in culture is seen as lying beyond the door, not just aesthetic and philosophical modern*ism* (a distinction Jardine is careful to make), then most women have had to go through that door—or rather, different doors—a long time ago. Since the home has been one of the major experimental sites of modernization, for consumerism as well as colonialism, then modernity has rather come through women's doors whether they wished it so or not;[22] and if any archaic silhouette is peeking and hovering at a door, it is perhaps a literary theorist looking back longingly at aesthetic and philosophical dilemmas you can find on remainder at shoppingtown any old day of the week.

This is one context of differentiation in which I'd claim the word "pedestrian." Just like studying women modernists, thinking about shopping centers should be a way to contest the idea that you can find, for example, at moments in the work of Julia Kristeva, that the cultural production of "actual women" has historically fallen short of a modernity understood as, or in terms derived from, the critical construction of modern*ism*.[23] I prefer to study in detail particular instances of the everyday, the so-called banal, the supposedly un- or non-experimental, asking not, "why does this fall short of modernism?" but, "how do classical theories of modernism fall short of women's modernity?"

Secondly, the figure of the pedestrian gives me a way of imaging a method for analyzing shopping centers that doesn't fall unequivocally for the lure of using classical images of the Imaginary, in the psychoanalytic sense, to mirror the shoppingtown spectacle. Such images are very common in the literature about shopping centers, especially big, enclosed, enveloping, "spectacular" centers like Indooroopilly Shoppingtown (fig. 2.3). Like department stores before them, shopping centers are described as palaces of dreams, halls of mirrors, galleries of illusion . . . and the fascinated analyst becomes a theater critic, reviewing the spectacle, herself in the spectacle, and the spectacle in herself. This rhetoric is closely related to the vision of shoppingtown as Eden or paradise: the shopping center becomes a mirror to a special utopian desire, the refined desire of fallen creatures nostalgic for the primal garden, yet aware that paradise is a lost illusion.

The pedestrian, or the woman walker, doesn't escape this dreamy ambivalence. Indeed, sociological studies suggest that women who don't come in cars to shopping centers spend much more time in them than those that do. The slow, evaluative, appreciatively critical relation is not enjoyed to the same extent by women who hit the carpark, grab the goods, and head on out as fast as possible. Different women do both at various times. However, if walking around for a long time creates absorption in the spectacle, then one sure way to at least *begin* from a sharply defined sense of critical estrangement is to arrive at a drive-in center on foot and have to find a way to walk in. Most women non-drivers don't, of course, arrive on foot, especially not with children, but by public transport (which can, at least in Australian cities, also produce an acutely estranging effect).

Allegorical figures such as "the woman walker" lose their tutelary func-

2.3 Postcard, Indooroopilly Shoppingtown, Brisbane, 1985.
Source: International Colour Productions Pty Ltd.

tion, however, if they are confused with an "empirical social user" of shopping centers. It is a futile exercise to try to make generalizations about the users of shopping centers at any particular time, even in terms of class, race, age, or gender. Certainly, it is true that where you find a center in a socially homogenized area—common in some but not all suburban regions of most Australian cities—you do find a high incidence of regular use by specific social groups contributing strongly to the center's identity-effect. Nevertheless, at many centers this is not the case. Even where it is, cars, public transport, visiting and tourist practices (shopping centers are used for sight-seeing), and day-trip patterns of movement, all mean that centers cannot be relied upon to "reflect" the composition of their immediate social environment (or "catchment area").

Different practices of use will intersect in one center on any given day; it is a complex, continuously varying zone of "experience." Some people are there for the one and only time in their lives; occasional visitors pick *that* center instead of *this*, on that day, for esoteric or arbitrary reasons; people may shop at one place but go to another to socialize or hang around. The use of centers as meeting-places, and for warmth, cool, and shelter, by young people, pensioners, the unemployed, and the homeless is a familiar part of their social function, one often planned for by center management through the distribution of benches, video games, and security guards. Many of a center's fans may not live in its vicinity; others, hating it, may have no choice but to go there.

Shopping centers show why you can't usefully treat a public at a cultural event as directly *expressive* of social groups and classes, or their supposed sensibility.[24] Publics are not stable, homogenous entities, and polemical claims that they are tell us little beyond the position being claimed by the speaker. Shopping center designers know this very well. In the early 1980s, retailing theory began to talk explicitly about the need to break down the model of a "vast monolithic middle-class market" for shopping center "product" that had characterized the 1960s and 1970s.[25] The marketing philosophy of the 1980s promoted spectacles of "diversity and market segmentation": that is, images of class, ethnic, age, and gender *differentiation* in particular centers. The point was not that a Vietnamized center would "express" the target culture and better serve local Vietnamese (though it might well do so, since retail theorists seem to have taken the idea partly from the forms of community politics), but that the display of difference would increase a center's tourist appeal to others from elsewhere.[26]

This was, of course, a response to the disintegration of the postwar "middle class" and the ever-growing disparity in the developed nations between rich and poor. The disparity was a threat to suburban shopping centers, and a differential thematization of "shoppers" and centers to serve them was one attempt to manage the change. In 1983, one theorist imagined the future as a proliferating series of shopper-*genres*: "centres will be designed specifically to meet demands of the *economic* shopper, the *recreational* shopper, or the *pragmatic* shopper, and so on."[27] His scenario has been realized to some extent, although once again this does not mean that as shoppers we do in fact conform to, let alone identify with, the proffered generic images of our demands.[28]

That much said about difference, I want to make another point about pedestrian leisureliness and critical time. One thing that *recognizing* their difference allows us to do with particular centers is to write them a history. This can be both difficult and time-consuming. The shopping center "form" itself, often described as "one of the few new building types created in our time,"[29] has had its histories written, often in heroic and expansive terms. However, I have found in practice that while local residents love to tell stories about a development and its effects on their lives, people who manage Australian centers are commonly disconcerted at the suggestion that *their* center has a history. There are several reasons for this: short-term employment patterns, employee and even managerial indifference to the workplace, ideologies about what counts as a "proper" topic for history, hostility to uncontrolled publicity, and, in many cases, a feeling that the history is better forgotten. Building Indooroopilly Shoppingtown, for example, required the blitzing of a huge chunk of old residential Indooroopilly.

A parallel elision of local shopping center histories has shaped much of the literature on centers, except for those that figure as pioneers in the history of development, like Southdale Mall or Faneuil Hall Marketplace in the United States and Roselands in Australia. Critical writing has often drifted either toward autobiography, in which the shopping place becomes a metaphorical site for a literary practice of reminiscence, or the formal analysis of structures found in architectural criticism. Walter Benjamin's "A Berlin Chronicle" (for older market forms) and Donald Horne's remembrance of the site of Sydney's Miranda Fair in *Money Made Us* are examples of the first practice, while Neville Quarry's reviews of The Jam Factory and Knox City Shopping Centre are an example of the second.[30]

More recently, journalistic writers have begun to negotiate this gap in a more exploratory social criticism of the *media* ecology in which malls and other cultural forms and practices (most obviously, television) are linked,[31] and urban activists working in the experience-oriented tradition opened up by Jane Jacobs in the 1960s have turned their attention to analyzing mall-driven development and the ruthless politics of shopping in small towns.[32] However, the genre gap between reminiscence and formal description, experience, and analysis, was inscribed in so-called "Man-Environment" studies by Amos Rapoport's influential book, *The Meaning of the Built Environment* (1982), with its opposition between "users' meanings" and "designers' meanings,"[33] and continues to organize in cultural studies disputes about "consumption" and "production."

A feminist study ought to be able occupy this user-designer, consumption-production gap, not to "close" or to "bridge" it but to move *outside* the repetitive terms of the disciplinary polemics it imposes. A shopping center, after all, is a place combining an extreme project of planning competence (efforts at total unification, total management) with an intense degree of aberrance and diversity in local performance. It is also a place consecrated, famously, to timelessness and stasis (no clocks, perfect weather), yet also lived and celebrated, lived and loathed, in intimately *historic* terms: for some, as a ruptural event in the social experience of a community, for others, as the enduring scene (as the cinema once was, and the home still may be) of the changes, fluctuations, and repetitions of everyday life.[34] This is one reason I think it useful to write a history of particular shopping centers. It is one way in which the clash of *actual* programs both for the management of change, and for resisting, accepting, or modifying "management," can better be understood.

Such a history is useful in other ways. In researching the history of a particular "sense" of place, one has to consider how it works in real social circumstances that inflect, in turn, its workings, and to learn from that place, make discoveries, change the drift of one's analysis, rather than use it as a site of theory rehearsal. Second, such a history can assume that if centers and their myths are transformed by "users," then the history itself must count as a use that involves engaging with other women's ideas about shopping centers over *time*. I've discussed the problems that can arise in this context from such procedures as sampling "representative" shoppers, targeting "user groups," and framing exemplary figures, whether of shopping-Woman, ordinariness, or even "otherness." This doesn't mean that I go to the extreme of thinking sociology pointless, or claiming that knowledge is only produced from personal experience. That would preclude me from asking what it's like to work in a mall for years.

I am simply interested in something a little more pedestrian than either a literary-theoretical reverie or a sociological study. For a third-term rendering sociable my relation to Shopping World, I prefer impromptu shopping center encounters: chit-chat, with women I meet in and around and because of these centers, family friends or total strangers. Collecting chit-chat *in situ* is, of course, a pedestrian professional practice: journalism. Practicing and analyzing journalism is, I would argue, a way of going outside that polemical space contested between users and designers, the social and the aesthetic, in order to ask how shopping centers are produced as well as consumed in particular places.

SHOPPING CENTER GENRES

Before looking in detail at one shopping center history, I'll describe its place in a set of three. I chose this set initially for personal reasons: three familiar shopping centers, one of which my family used and two of which I had often used as a tourist; two of which I loved, and one of which I hated. However, the set itself conforms to a system of formal distinctions used historically by the people who build and manage shopping centers.[35] These are planners' terms, "designers' meanings." However, most people who live in Australian towns and cities are intimately familiar with, even bodily attuned to, these distinctions, and some cities, like Canberra, are built around them.

Until recently, a more or less universally accepted classification system recognized three main types of center: the "neighborhood" center, the "community" center, and the "regional" center. Some writers add extra categories like the "super-regional," a huge and now mostly uneconomic dinosaur, rare in Australia, but common in more populous countries, with four to six full-line department stores. With the aging of the classic suburban form, and the burgeoning of many rival retail formats better adapted to current economic conditions—discount chains, hypermarkets, "theme" environments, history-precincts, specialty malls (an old shopping center renovated, or a new center built, to offer 150 shoe shops rather than the old total lifestyle mix), multiuse centers, simulated street markets (often enfolded in mall-supermarkets to sell "fresh produce"), strip revival, and urban mega-structures—the old schema is losing its reality-productive power. However, it remains solidly operative and unspectacularly dominant in the mundane shopping life of suburbs and country towns.

The classic triad—neighborhood/community/regional—is not defined in terms of catchment-area size, or type of public attracted, or acreage oc-cupied. It depends on the major store that a center offers to "anchor" its specialty shops. Neighborhood stores have only a supermarket, while com-munity centers have a supermarket and either a discount house or a chain store. Regional centers have both of these plus at least one full depart-ment store. The anchor store, usually placed at the end of the central shop-ping strip, is also called the *magnet*; it regulates the attraction, circulation, and expulsion of people, commodities, and cars.

Indooroopilly Shoppingtown in Brisbane (fig. 2.3) is a canonical, post-war regional shopping center. It is also an aristocrat, a "Westfield." As Aus-tralia's leading shopping center developer, Westfield for a time achieved the ultimate goal of operating in the United States and buying into the movie business; in its glory days of the mid-1980s, Westfield celebrated its own norm-setting status in an art corridor at Sydney's Miranda Fair, where you could view full-color photographs of all the other major Westfields in Aus-tralia, including Indooroopilly. Indooroopilly Shoppingtown is an instance of the model form celebrated in the heroic histories I mentioned above; expansionist stories of the centrifugal movement of cars and people away from old city-centers because of "urban congestion" (a euphemism for often racialized class conflict) in American and Australian cases, and war damage as well as congestion in European towns and cities.[36]

Ideally these centers, according to the histories, are so-called "green-field" developments on the edge of or outside towns, in that ever-receding transformation zone where the country becomes the city as suburbia. Of course, they have often been the product of suburb-blitzing, not suburb-creating processes, though the blitzing of one may often help to create an-other on the city's periphery. So strong has been the force of the centrifu-gal imaginary that in the case of the Brisbane *Courier-Mail*'s coverage of the building of Indooroopilly Shoppingtown, the houses being moved to make way for it were represented as flying off happily out, like pioneers, to the far frontiers of the city.[37] The postwar regional center, then, is represented as the "revolutionary," explosive suburban form.

At the opposite end of the spectrum, Fortitude Valley Plaza (fig. 2.4), again in Brisbane, is an example of a neighborhood center as it was in the mid-1980s. "Neighborhood" may summon cosy, friendly images of intimacy, but this center is at a major urban transit point, over a railway station, in a high-density area and on one of the most polluted roads in Australia. The

2.4 Fortitude Valley Plaza Walkway, Brisbane, 1985.

Valley Plaza was an early example not of greenfield nor blitzing development but of the "in-fill" or "twilight zone" development that became popular in the central shopping districts of country towns and old suburbs during the 1970s and early 1980s. "In-fill" means that bits of shopping center and arcade snake around to swallow the "gaps" between existing structures. This practice was important in the downtown revivals that, along with the energy crisis, succeeded the heroic age of the regional shopping center.

Again, the *Courier-Mail*'s coverage was metaphorically apt. Because there had been an old open railway line on the site, the Valley Plaza was said to be resourcefully filling in the "previously-useless airspace" wasted by the earlier structure.[38] It was promoted as a thrifty, even ecologically sound solution to a problem of resources. It is also an example of a center that has undergone a drastic identity change. When I first studied it in 1984, it was dank and dated—vintage pop futurist in style, with plenty of original but pollution-blackened 1960s orange and geometrical trimmings. A few years later it was painted jade green and Chinatownified, with Chinese characters replacing the old op-art effects, to blend in with the ethnic repackaging of Fortitude Valley as a whole—presaging "urban renewal" and displacement of the Valley's traditional street life and communities.

Finally, Green Hills (fig. 2.5) is an example of the mediating category, a community center in East Maitland—a coalfields town near the industrial city of Newcastle north of Sydney in New South Wales. Green Hills is a Woolworths[39] center, with a supermarket and a "Big W" Discount House. Unlike the other two centers, it began as an open-air mall and it is oddly difficult to photograph: not just because it is long and careless of external display (although it once had a coherent inner design as a village square) but because it is *formally* blurry and hard to see from a passing car. The center is badly signed and bordered, as well as mostly hidden from view in relation to the major highway that runs alongside. Whatever the considerations or accidents behind this design, its effect is to secure an introverted identity. Like a lot of cultural activity in Australian country towns, you have to know where it is to find it.

Yet Green Hills was, for many years, very successful. Generically a small community center, it had a regional function; the Big W Discount magnet pulled in people from all over the Hunter Valley who might once have gone through to Newcastle. People didn't come to East Maitland, they "went to Green Hills." So if, in this particular triad, Indooroopilly was explosive and the Valley Plaza was thrifty in the local rhetorics of space, Green Hills was represented in the terms of a go-ahead conservatism—extending and renewing the old town of Maitland, while acting to help maintain the town's economic and cultural independence.

In the short history of Green Hills I've been able to construct, it is clear that allusions to the other shopping center forms played a complex role, first, in Woolworths' strategic presentation to the town of the project to *build* Green Hills, and, second, in the promotional rhetoric used to specify an ideal public to whom the center would appeal—the "loyal citizens" of Maitland.

However, I must make two qualifications about what sort of history this is, and why. First, it is primarily derived from the local newspaper, *The Maitland Mercury*. Other sources generate other stories. This version is concerned with the rhetorical collusion between the local media and the interests of Woolworths, and the ways this relationship cut across two preexisting, but at this point contradictory, collusions of interest between the media and the Council, on the one hand, and the media and local small business interests on the other. Close relations between these parties—Council, media, small busi-

2.5 Entrance to Green Hills, East Maitland, 1985.

ness—are common today in country newspapers, defining "the town's in-terests" very much in terms of the doings of civic fathers and local enter-prise. Sport and the cycle of family life are two major popular cultural sites on which those doings are played out. However, civic fathers and local busi-ness were bitterly divided over Green Hills in a conflict shaped as a debate about the meaning of community. To describe this conflict briefly, I give it the form of an overcoherent or paranoid story.

Second this version focuses on planners' programs; as a long-term if spo-radic user of Green Hills, I was interested in what I didn't already know about it or hadn't noticed when it was happening. In my "experience," this *thing* had simply appeared where once there was a scrubby borderland that in the 1960s divided the joy of leaving town from the ambivalence of coming home, and in earlier decades had been a field of the illicit *outside* town. However, if the production/consumption relation is not just a designer/ user opposition writ large (since relations of production cannot be reduced to "people planning things"), it doesn't follow that images of a development project circulated for a public that is also the development's target "clientele" can be slotted away as production history. I'm not sure that media practices are ever usefully placed on either side of such a dichotomy. To assume that production and consumption are parallel or diverging realities allows another assumption, made more dubious every day by technological change, that we *know enough* now about production and can move to the "other" side—as though production, somehow, stays put.

A SHORT HISTORY OF GREEN HILLS

The story of Green Hills is, in a way, an allegory about a culture of staying put, and it begins, paranoiacally, not with the first obvious appearance of a sign staking out a site (fig. 2.6)[40] but behind the scenes, with an article in the NSW State Planning Authority journal *SPAN* in January 1969, and a report about it published in the *Newcastle Morning Herald* (24 January 1969). The *Herald*'s story had the provocative title "Will Maitland Retain Its Entity or Become a Newcastle Suburb?"

Several general problems were facing Maitland, and many small towns in Eastern Australia, at this time: population drift, shrinking local employment prospects, declining or anachronistic community facilities, "nothing to do" syndrome. Maitland also had regional problems as a former rural service center and coalfields capital en route to becoming a dormitory suburb menaced by residential creep toward Newcastle—then about twenty miles away and getting closer. The town had also suffered physical fragmentation after ruinous floods in 1949 and 1955, newsreel footage of which may be seen in Phillip Noyce's film *Newsfront* (1978). The floods devastated the old commercial center and the inner residential areas: houses were shifted out and away in response to a "natural" blitzing.[41] Rezoning followed: the houses that stayed put (like my family home, submerged up to the rooftop in 1955) gradually became isolated in the middle of panel-beating works and light industrial sheds.

In these inauspicious conditions, the threat of annexation uttered by the *Newcastle Herald* produced an outraged response in that afternoon's *Maitland Mercury* from the Maitland mayor who, in spurning these "dismal prophecies," mentioned the "hope" that Woolworths would soon name the day for a development at East Maitland. From this moment on, and during all the conflicts that followed, Woolworths never figured in the Council discourse as a national chain just setting up a store in a likely spot, but as a gallant and caring savior come to make Maitland whole again—to stop the

2.6 Green Hills sign, 1985.

gap, restore definition, contain the creeping and seeping and save Our Town's "Entity." In actual fact, and following a well-known law of development, Green Hills was built on the town fringe nearest Newcastle; growth around it took the town kilometers closer to Newcastle, and helped to fragment further the old city center.

Four months after the *SPAN* and *Herald* incidents, the *Mercury* published a photo of an anonymous man staring at a mystery sign behind wire in the bush, saying "This site has been selected for another all Australian development by Woolworths" (16 June 1969). The "site" was at that time still a ragged border wasteland, across the hill from a notorious old "slum" called Eastville.[42] The *Mercury* photo initiated a long-running mystery story about the conversion of an indefinite bush-border into a site, the site into a place, and the place into a suburb, in a process of territorialization that I'll call the fabrication of a place name.

To summarize the episodes briefly: first, the mystery sign turned out to be not just a bait to initiate interest but a legal loophole that allowed Woolworths to claim, when challenged by local business firms, that it had fulfilled the terms of a 1965 agreement to develop the site by a certain date (*MM*, 25 June 1969). The sign itself could count as a developmental structure, and it had appeared just in time. Second, the first sign was replaced by another, a board at first adorned only by the letter "G." Maitland "citizens" were to participate in a guessing competition to find the name of the place, and a new letter was added each week until the full place-name, and the name of a lucky winner, emerged. This happened on 22 October 1969; and on the following Remembrance Day, 11 November, the City Council abolished the name of the slum across the highway, Eastville. Eastville's name was to be forgotten, said the *Mercury*, in order to "unify the area with East Maitland" ("Eastville to Go West," *MM*, 12 November 1969).

The basic Green Hills complex—at this stage, a neighborhood center with a supermarket only—was opened in February 1972. The ceremony included ritual displays of crowd hysteria, with frenzied women fainting and making off with 5,000 pairs of eight-cent pantyhose in the first five minutes (*MM*, 10 February 1972). This rite of baptism, or of public consent to the place-name, was repeated even more fervently in November 1977 when the Big W Discount House was added to make Green Hills a community center. This time, women came *wearing* signs of Green Hills identity: said the *Mercury*, "A sea of green mums flooded in. . . . The mums dressed in sea green, celery green, grass green, olive green, green florals—every green imaginable—to take advantage of a 2NX offer of free dinner tickets for women dressed in that colour" (*MM*, 14 November 1977).

That wasn't the end of it. The process known as "metro-nucleation" had begun. In 1972, a company associated with Woolworths began a 100-home subdivision behind the center. The area then acquired more parking, a pub, a motel, light industry, an old people's home, more specialty shops at the center itself in 1980, and then, in 1983, a Community Health Centre. This Centre, said the *Mercury*—forgetting that the forgetting of Eastville had been to unify East Maitland—would serve "to service people living in the Beresfield, Maitland, Bolwarra, East Maitland *and* Green Hills areas" (*MM*, 14 November 1983). Maitland's "entity" at this stage was still a mess, but Green Hill's identity was established, its status as a place-name secure. Presented rhetorically as a gesture of community unification, it had been, in effect, suburban-explosive in function.

The story continues, of course. I shan't follow it further, except to note that after this decade of expansion (a decade of acute economic distress for Maitland, and Hunter Valley coal towns in general), the popularity of Green

Hills declined in the late 1980s. Woolworths got into trouble nationally and their Big W discount stores failed to keep pace with newer retail styles. Green Hills in particular faced stiff competition when a few blocks of the old city center were torn down for a Coles-Myer Super K semi-hypermarket, and rapid in-fill development brought the twilight zone to town. Even residents hostile to these changes transferred their interest to them: one said, "It's awesome how many places they think we can use just to buy our few pounds of mince."

THINGS TO DO WITH HISTORY

This story contains a number of standardized elements. For example, oceanic and hysterical crowd behavior in which the crowd itself becomes a decorative feature of the shopping center's performance is a traditional motif, and the *Mercury* in the late 1960s had run pedagogical news features on how people were behaving at shopping centers in Sydney and the United States;[43] like news features today about advanced uses of the Internet and the information superhighway, these stories were little etiquette guides telling their readers how to behave when they had an opportunity. More generally, the process of development was impeccably ordinary.

Yet in looking at local instances of these general models, the well-known things that shopping centers do, one is also studying the practical inflections, or rewritings, of those models that can account for, and found, a regional "sense of place." In the case of Green Hills, the Woolworths success story was produced by the media as a local response to preexisting discourses on Maitland's "very own" problems of identity and unity. In this sense, Woolworths' success was precisely to *efface* the similarity between what was happening in Maitland and what was going on elsewhere. The exploitation of a sense of "difference" in public culture can be quite as complex as the construction and deconstruction of imaginary identities.

In a critique of the work of Jean Baudrillard, Andrew Wernick writes:

> The sales aim of commodity semiosis is to differentiate the product as a valid, or at least resonant, social totem, and this would be impossible without being able to appeal to taken-for-granted systems of cultural reference.[44]

In the Green Hills case, Woolworths' strategy in selling the center to the town was to appeal to the rivalrous sense of difference taken for granted in the traditional "booster" culture of country towns—towns that have long been losing their old reasons for being and their economic underpinning, and so their sense of the meaning of their history. Donald Horne has defined the principles of Australian boosterism as 1) getting bigger and 2) making it last[45]—in other words, keeping it up.

If space in the reference-system of some feminist theories today is still thematized as feminine (in the ways that Alice Jardine studied in *Gynesis*), and if commodity "appeal" is also sometimes theorized as feminine (as in Baudrillard's *Seduction*, for example), I think that feminists should also keep looking at rhetorics of space and commerce that are, *as* systems of cultural reference, overtly and polemically masculine. Sometimes, these systems seem too crude to merit serious critical attention; like the rhetoric of the feminine itself, they have been denounced and deconstructed so often that it hardly seems worth the effort.

Academic criticism of a public rhetoric does not make it go away, and should never be expected to do so. However, it is a way of understanding *exoterically* what the culture one is criticizing takes for granted. I find the angry ebullience of development hype described rather well in *Gynesis*, when Jardine discusses "male paranoia" in the psychoanalytic sense:

> Male paranoia involves, fundamentally, the fear of the loss either of all boundaries or of those boundaries becoming too painfully constricting. And this encounter with boundaries is almost always described by men as an encounter with what is called "God"—that being who has no boundaries. (98)

She is talking about President Schreber. In boosterism, the being without boundaries is the very *spirit* of Development, as it bounces back expansively after every new disaster; for boosters, ever more Development is seen, paradoxically, to protect against both loss of Entity and the fearfully constricting condition that town councils still call, well into the era of limits, "lack of growth."

I am not at all suggesting that capital imperatives—development, growth, accumulation—are the same as or reducible to some psychology of "masculinity."[46] I only want to suggest that a rhetoric *of* maleness can provide development projects with a reference-system vital, in the propaganda phase, to securing their more substantial means of realization (glorifying "the tough decisions," for example, admits no dispute that the "decisions" in question must be made); and that this rhetoric is in many domains of social life still active, effective, destructive, and utterly impervious to the crisis of Reason so often said, in the name of the "feminine" or "the other," to be engulfing it.[47]

However, reference to "male paranoia" might nonetheless be a brittle joke unless I add two more things to the Green Hills story. One is that part of Woolworths' campaign against local small business interests was precisely to claim that the town might be saved from suburbanization by Newcastle (that is, from loss of boundaries) only if Maitland could further suburban-ize itself internally—burst its outside borders, diversify, and come to "rival" Newcastle. The claim to rivalry was usually mediated by comparisons be-tween an ideal of what Green Hills would become, and Newcastle's proud and historic Jesmond Big W—a structure in fact quite unlike Green Hills, but quite like Indooroopilly Shoppingtown. In a cruel twist, therefore, local business people were positioned not only as losers, but as unpatriotic for even trying to win—traitors to (imaginary) home-town desires, that could better be satisfied by Woolworths.

The other comment is that a claim to rivalry materialized at Green Hills in a suburbanizing decor (fig. 2.7) that gave it that hallucinatory resem-blance to shoppingtowns everywhere else, plus a little *frisson* of distinction, a shivery edge of identity. The taken-for-granted cultural reference-system that unified Green Hills in its heyday was a suburban "garden furniture" aesthetic that not only makes all middling shopping centers seem the same, but, through a play of echoing spatial analogy, makes shopping centers seem like a range of other sites consecrated to the performance of ordinary family life, and to women's work, emotional as well as physical, in leisure: shoppingtown, beer garden, picnic spot, used-car yard with bunting, scenic lookout, town garden, public park, suburban backyard.

Along with colored rubbish cones, neatly rustic borders, foliage, plant-ers, and well-spaced saplings, the brightly colored benches of Green Hills were direct descendants of what Robin Boyd in 1960 called the "desperately picturesque accoutrements" then just bursting out brightly as "features" in Australian beauty-spots.[48] There is nothing desperate about their pictur-esqueness now, although they may mean desperation to some users as well as cheer and comfort to others (those who remember the unforgiv-ing discomforts of seatless, as well as featureless, "authentic" country-town streets). Today, they are saturated in a sense of *longue durée*. Familiar and traditional, they produce that aura of "setting" that gives a powerful coher-ence to public space in Australia, or, more precisely, *cohesiveness* to a "life-style" space declaring the dissolution of boundaries between public and private space, between public domains of work and private spheres of lei-sure.

Janet Wolff has argued that the emergence of the distinction between public and private "spheres" in the nineteenth century made impossible a female *flâneur*, a female strolling heroine "botanizing on the asphalt" as Benjamin put it in his study of Baudelaire.[49] I would argue that the pro-claimed dissolution of public and private on the botanized asphalt of shop-pingtown makes possible, not a *flâneuse*, since that term is anachronistic, but an experience of "modernity" for women in which it is vital not to begin by identifying heroines and victims (even of conflicts with male paranoia), but rather a profound ambivalence about shifting roles.

2.7 Garden furniture with bunting, Green Hills, 1985.

Yet here again, I want to discriminate. At places "like" Green Hills, the function of hallucinatory spatial resemblance and recall is not, as it might be in an urban road-romance, a thinning out of significance through space such that one place ends up like any other. Nor is it, as it might be in a big city, a move in a fast-paced, competitive game where one space says of its nearby rivals, "We Do All the Same Things Better." Green Hills appeals instead to a dream of plenitude, and of a paradoxically absolute yet expansive self-sufficiency: a country town "paranoia" seeking reassurance that *nothing is lacking* in this one spot. It is a motherland dream of "staying home," staying put: as an uncle said to me on a stray visit to Green Hills made simply to be sociable, waving round at the benches and the glass facade of Big W, "why go elsewhere when you've got it all here?" (Two years later, he sent me by myself to buy cut-price T-shirts from Super K in town, a place where everyone wants to shop but no one cares to visit).

SHOPPING FOR REPETITION

Having arrived at the Big W magnet, I conclude with a comment on a text that seems to me to be a critical equivalent of the Eden fable by Myer's John Lennen with which I began. It is a passage from Terry Eagleton's book *Walter Benjamin, or Towards a Revolutionary Criticism* that is also, obliquely, a parable of modernity that depends on figuring consumption as a seductively fallen state.

Paraphrasing and developing Benjamin's study of the *flâneur*, Eagleton writes:

> . . . the commodity disports itself with all comers without its halo slipping, promises permanent possession to everyone in the market without abandoning its secretive isolation. Serializing its consumers it nevertheless makes intimate *ad hominem* address to each.[50]

Now if this is not, as in Lennen's story, a matter of Adam comforting Eve with a note on the postmodern condition, it is matter of Adam comforting himself with an ambivalent fantasy about Eve. It's a luscious, self-seducingly *risqué* fantasy that Adam has, a commodity-thought, rather like the exquisite bottle of perfume or the pure wool jumper in the import shop, nestling deep in an upmarket neoarcade, its ambience aglow with neon pastels or, since that is now overdone, cooled by marbloid Italianate tiling.

But its pertinence to retailing, commodity semiosis, and shopping practices today is questionable, not least because forms like the neoarcade, or the fantastically revamped pre-war elegance of certain city department stores, developed in response to the shopping center forms I've been discussing: a response (now, it seems, a failed one) that offered redoubled *signs* of old-fashioned commodity fetishism precisely because Australian "suburban" shopping centers *don't do so.*[51] Part of my argument has been that in suburban and country town retail environments it isn't necessarily the objects consumed that count in the process of consumption but rather that "unique sense of place"; for this reason, while their "death" has often been predicted they may prove surprisingly resilient as shopping for commodities gives way to shopping for services and experiences. Beyond that, however, I think that the Benjamin-Eagleton style of boudoir-talk about commodities is doubly misleading.

First, I would ask—what is the sound of an intimate *ad hominem* address from a raincoat at Big W? where the secretive isolation of the thongs in a pile at Super-K? The commodities in a Discount House boast no halo, no aura. On the contrary, they promote a lived aesthetic of the serial, the machinic, the mass-reproduced, the "thrifty":[52] as one pair of thongs wears out it is replaced by an identical pair, the same sweatshirt is bought (to "get it over with for a few years") in four different colors, or two different and two the same; a macramé planter defies all middle-class whole-earth naturalness connotations in its dyes of lurid chemical mustard and killer neon pink.

Second, commodity boudoir-talk gathers up into the single and class-specific image of the elite courtesan a number of different relations people may invent to commodities *and* to the changing discursive frames (like shopping centers) that give buying, trafficking with, or ignoring commodities, variable local meanings. Attracted by beautiful theories, critics fall a little easily for the classic image of European bourgeois luxury when looking for a model of commodity exchange. If I were, for the sake of argument, to make up a cranky feminist fable of Adam and Eve and the fall into modernity, I wouldn't have my Eve taking comfort from modernist explanation (as she does from Lennen's Adam), and I wouldn't have her flattering him as she does for Eagleton's "comers." I'd have her as a pedestrian, laughing at both of them, walking on past, saying "you sound like the snake."

Of course, that's not good enough. The Eden story itself is the problem, and the fable of the management of change is wrong with its images of the garden, the snake, the couple, the Fall, and the terms this story imposes no matter how or by whom it's rewritten. Like feminist film theory when it becomes obsessed with the lugubrious and plush seductiveness of white Woman in film noir, feminist cultural studies, too, can find an appealing image of its own concerns, perhaps even of its "identity" as a site of intellectual work, in a breathlessly high-art melodrama of sexual commodification.

A film about these matters and elite courtesans, *Seduction: The Cruel Woman* by Elfi Mikesch and Monika Treut, was shown in 1986 at the first feminist cultural studies conference I attended.[53] Having come to the conference with shopping centers on my mind, this stylish and clever film interested me in its luxuriant difference from the world of an essay I've always wanted to write about country town familial sado-masochism, called "Maitland S&M."

This imaginary text is about the orchestration of modes of domestic repetition, the going back over of the same stories, the same terrains, the same sore spots, that I think a center like Green Hills successfully incorporated and mobilized in its fabrication of a myth of staying put at home. If this sounds like feminist paranoia, I should say that one of the fascinating things about Big W aesthetics is the way that the store provides a set of managerial props for the performance of inventive scenarios in a drama that circulates endlessly between home and the pub and the carpark and Green Hills and back again to home. One can emerge for a good session of ritualized pain and sorrow (as well as, of course, more pedestrian experiences) dressed in nothing more ferocious or costly than a fluffy pink top and a sweet floral skirt.

Insofar as I have myself used the story of Green Hills as an allegory, I have done so to argue that if it's crucial, and fun, to keep on rewriting the given stories of culture, we should also consider that with some stories in some places we can become cruelly bound by repetition, confined by the terms that we are contesting. Then, feminist criticism ties its own hands and finds itself, again and again, bound back home for the same old story.

ON THE BEACH

On the Beach: A Bicentennial Poem
2
(after Juan Davila)

      astonished
trade union delegates
watch a man behead a chicken
in Martin Place—isn't there
a poem about this
& the shimmering ideal
of just walking down the street?
not being religious
we bet on how many full circles
the headless chook will complete
& won't this do for a formal
model of Australia, not
too far-fetched, not too cute?

—JOHN FORBES, *THE STUNNED MULLET* (1988)[1]

On an Australian beach on a hot summer day people
doze in the sun or shoot the breakers like Hawaiian
princes on pre-missionary Waikiki. The symbol is too far
fetched for Australian taste. The image of Australia is of
a man in an open-necked shirt solemnly enjoying an ice-
cream. His kiddy is beside him.

—DONALD HORNE, *THE LUCKY COUNTRY* (1964)[2]

HOME

Some images die hard. By the mid-1960s—when it was still possible for a
white social critic unself-consciously to compare postimperial Australians to

"premissionary" Hawaiians, then fix as the image of the nation a portrait of "a man" with child—the habit of keeping (and killing) chickens was beginning to disappear from the everyday domestic life of most less-than-princely Australians. Today, Donald Horne's "symbols" seem as remote and quaint as the cock crows that can sometimes still be heard in the middle of inner-city Sydney. Yet today, a problem of nationality can still be framed as a scene of white, male Ordinariness; still today, a subject in a state of confusion may dispassionately be described as "running round like a headless chook."

In the preceding chapters, I examined modes of historical persistence at work in unspectacular mediated culture; narrative, rhetorical, and generic modes that I also take to be *practices* of change. Here, I want to frame an account of some problems of history persisting for me in cultural studies by reading back and forth between two quite different texts that make a spectacle of the historic national Ordinary.

In the process, the relations I construct between a passage of *The Lucky Country* and a poem published a quarter of a century later may be far-fetched, but not altogether forced. Both texts are *generically* marked as beach scenes, although it is important that "Martin Place" in Sydney is a downtown pedestrian mall. Both imagine Australia as a womanless, colorless space: "Hawaiian" for Horne in 1964 means "suntanned" and, if a group of trade union delegates in 1988 might well be as mixed as a crowd on the beach, gender and race are unmarked by Forbes as they were ignored by Horne. But both texts offer little allegories of Democracy: each composes a model and then deals critically with it (Horne by correcting himself, Forbes by faking questions), and it is important that what Horne finds "too far fetched" about his own simile is not really its exoticism, still less the displacement of "Aboriginal" that "Hawaiian" effects and represses, but the romantic anachronism, "*princes*." This is the political figure that he replaces with "a man in an open-necked shirt"; this is the kind of *rhetorical* extravagance that John Forbes's poem, more sardonically, aspires to avoid. Both texts, then, are concerned with "taste," and with limits and limitations in a dominant—not marginal—popular aesthetic.

Both *The Lucky Country* and Forbes's poem "2 *(after Juan Davila)*" are also involved in social *narratives* of foundation, and I must now establish some differences between them. Published during the Australian Bicentenary in 1988,[3] *The Stunned Mullet & Other Poems* could easily be described as a "critique" of the national myths of white Australian culture. It may be more precise to think of it as a collection of puzzling little scenes—domestic, political, artistic, and economic as well as historical—connecting up in a discourse on a vast, multimedia public enterprise of narration. Monumental national histories appeared to mark the Bicentenary; media organizations funded reenactments, mini-series, documentaries galore; communities and individuals created a boom in diverse forms of family, local, regional, and ethnic history. In a way, *The Stunned Mullet* is a survival guide for living in the midst of *all that speech.*

Literally a fish knocked semi-conscious (the title poem begins "lips bruised blue / from the impact of the shore"), "The Stunned Mullet" is a phrase alluding to a vernacular myth about speech and stupefaction. It usually occurs in the simile "*like* a stunned mullet"; an unflattering description of the appearance of someone else, or of oneself positioned as other, in a story. It means to be struck "dumb" (in every sense) by some little shock of history—to fall right out of ordinary speech. This is an experience of liminality, but a modest one: it isn't tragic, like Lyotard's "*différend,*" or heroic, like Deleuzian "stammering"; it is not a question of incommensurability between discourses, nor of using a major language in a revolutionary minor mode, but just a matter of momentarily *losing* it (and nothing of major significance is expected to follow from this; it is not a "subversive" moment, but an interruptive one). In Forbes's book, however, the mullet aspires to eloquence; the poems "form words you applaud / because, after all, a fish is speaking."

"2 *(after Juan Davila)*" is from *On the Beach: A Bicentennial Poem,* a sequence of six texts in which the male Anglo-Celtic poet succeeds in failing his national "vocation" to speak in honor of the occasion; the first line of "1" is, "Your vocation calls" (65).[4] He works through various "models" of Australia and of a Laureate enunciative posture—taken from pop-historical images, paintings, tourist spectacles, TV shows, incidents in the street—and only in the last poem, "6," is a "blank, cut-up sense of what your vocation is going to be" glimpsed as *emergent* in the half-light of a beach pub lounge, an originary space "where you first dreamt up / this model of the Ocean / & watched it slide, slowly at first / down the beach & into the surf." The cultural landscape of *On the Beach* is, like colonial history, neither womanless nor "white"; the *scene* considered by poem "2" is, and I will return to it later.

If John Forbes's text is troubled about a white male poet's public role at a festival of origins, Donald Horne is comfortably regarded by many Australians as an ideal model of a "public intellectual," and *The Lucky Country* has been canonized by some as a founding text of cultural studies.[5] In retrospect, it seems to present itself as such ("I came back from a trip to the Far East early in 1963 and decided that Australia was worth a book" [13]), and while *Money Made Us* (1976) in fact gave more emphasis to what we now call cultural practices ("systems of honour, rhetoric, life-styles, cults, entertainments etc"),[6] *The Lucky Country*'s success at analyzing these in a best-selling *social* critique of institutions and protocols of conduct has made it an influential work long after the society it criticized has disappeared. The phrase "the lucky country" has passed as cliché into public rhetoric, losing the biting irony that Horne himself intended—and which "Lucky Country," a scathing song by Midnight Oil, naively later restored.

Yet I know few people (to be honest, no one) now poring over *The Lucky Country* with the same intensity that others accord to rereading Raymond Williams's *Culture and Society*. Horne's *practice* is made canonical, rather than his theses: seeing culture as a field of action, he has worked as a mainstream tabloid journalist, a powerful newspaper and magazine editor, a literary autobiographer, essayist, and novelist, a historian, an academic, and, in recent years, as a prominent cultural policy-maker. Of course, Horne did not found the possibility of his own practice; something about Australian society made his model of action both practicable and influential, and he is not the only eminent intellectual to operate in this way. But *The Lucky Country* as a myth of origins for Cultural Studies 1990 is not an arbitrary choice. Part of its interest now is that it was written as a critical document for a better *future* in which "it might be of interest to know what the huge continent was like in those early days in the nineteen sixties before it was peopled from all over Asia" (13).

Forbes's poem and Horne's book do not have the same kind of relationship to foundation narratives (*On the Beach* is about one such narrative—*The Lucky Country* is a pretext for another), any more than they have a common posture about the terms of their own participation in Australian public life. Horne is an affirmative and canny populist, or a "middlebrow" in the special, positive sense that Andrew Ross has given that term.[7] Reading a Forbes poem is like sharing the secret thoughts of an edgy, skeptical citizen whom canny populism addresses, and sometimes claims to represent.

At the same time, it would be a mistake to exaggerate these differences. Both writers are inventors of imaginary countries; both work in the "future perfect," in Jane Gallop's sense.[8] Both are also masters of one of the dominant registers of public rhetoric in Australia, "irony" (a term that in an American context does not seem to convey either the rich emotional modulations this register can be used to create, or the density of popular suspicion toward discourses of belief and identity that its use by Australians can assume). Both men could therefore be described as working within a national "great tradition" of cultural criticism. So rather than resolve their differences formally as an opposition, I want to accept the tension between them as *productive*. Like the debate in cultural studies over "policy" and "aesthetics"—a model of which I shall also derive by reading Horne and Forbes—this tension in fact creates a space in which I can place my work.

It is tempting to say, *the* space. I'm well aware that the methodological refusal to choose that I've just performed also resonates for me with broader and deeper influences: I see myself as a rhetorical critic, *The Stunned Mullet* as a model text; I, too, idealize Donald Horne's practice, and *The Lucky Country* was one of the great revelations of my early adolescence—the "origin" (it would be easy to say) of a desire that was later to become my interest in cultural studies.

But I do mean "*a* space." I use these texts here to create what Deleuze and Guattari call a *home*. In their sense of the term, "home does not pre-exist"; it is the product of an effort "to organize a *limited space*,"[9] and the limit involved is not a figure of containment but of provisional or "working" definition. This kind of home is always made of mixed components, and the interior space it creates is a filter or a *sieve* rather than a sealed-in consistency; it is not a place of origin, but an "aspect" of a process that it enables ("as though the circle tended on its own to open onto a future, as a function of the working forces it shelters") but does not precede—and so it is not an enclosure, but a way of going outside.

FAMILY ROMANCE

Why put forward *The Lucky Country* (in however cagey a manner) as a text of comparable historical importance to that of *Culture and Society* for "others"? If this is a gesture of reactive nationalism, or even just a shorthand way of insisting on the complex historical parameters of specific conditions for action, then any one of a number of institutionally honored texts might conceivably serve the same purpose—Phillips's *The Australian Tradition: Studies in a Colonial Culture* (1958), Russel Ward's *The Australian Legend* (1958), the essays of Ian Turner or even the conservative symposium edited by Peter Coleman, *Australian Civilization* (1962). I could justify my choice—only Horne's text unequivocally looks forward to that ambiguous ideology of State that we now call multiculturalism[10]—but it is the purpose that I want to consider.

At an international conference held in 1990 at the University of Western Sydney, there was a discussion about why so many people working in quite different contexts had all begun "inventing histories" for cultural studies—often by reifying quite dispersed fields ("Birmingham," "Frankfurt," "Radical Nationalism") or by (de)sanctifying the works of various founding *fathers* ("Williams," "Gramsci," "Horne," "Innis"). Those who stressed the idea of invention felt that, whatever the dangers of myth-making this kind of history entailed, it was an important way in which new projects in cultural studies, and "new" subjects of history, could polemically be defined. For others, it ran the risk of reproducing the worst idealist forms of the History of Ideas, or of substituting History of Theory for empirical studies of culture, or else of performing relentlessly Oedipal disavowals of the most useful work of the past.

It was left to Dipesh Chakrabarty, a professional historian, to suggest that the real problem may be that the genre in which "histories" are being invented for cultural studies often leads people into positing a *single* origin for their practice—something those same people would never do in any other context.[11]

Thinking about my own sporadic impulses to claim some looming historical precedent authorizing me to speak, it occurred to me that for the

Euro-centered tradition of cultural studies from which I *do* speak, this genre has a name—the family romance. The family romance is a type of phantasy in which the subject "imagines that his [sic] relationship to his parents has been modified," usually for the better; for example, that he is adopted or illegitimate, and that his father was actually a prince (perhaps a "Hawaiian prince").[12] In other words, the family romance is a way of "inventing history" that allows us not only to change but to *improve* upon the received and socially sanctioned versions of our beginnings.

The cultural pressure exerted by this genre (that adults rarely practice consciously but which lingers on as a symptomatic archaism) may possibly be felt in the common assumption that any history involving masculine proper names is *necessarily* obsessed with paternity and filiation. In fact, you can write a history of power relations without having a thing about ancestry. The cultural *temptation* of the family romance can certainly be read, however, in attempts to do this by installing a local hero *in the place of* the founding figures already promoted by powerful interests elsewhere; people say that Donald Horne, for example, has always practiced cultural studies in "everything but name." The subsequent move to *name* the "real" (new, improved) Father is not peculiar to intellectuals inventing histories for peripheral national cultures. It is how Frank Lentricchia frames much of his reading of Kenneth Burke against Paul de Man in *Criticism and Social Change*, and it is a strategy that Terry Eagleton uses regularly to redeem for "English" and Marxism selected aspects of poststructuralist critical theory.

Why is this temptation so tempting? In *Roman des origines et origines du roman*—an essentialist study projecting the structure of a Freudian myth onto the history of the European novel—Marthe Robert suggests that for children, the family romance is a response to a moment of grave crisis at the end of the idyll of infancy when social experience brings deflating intimations that other people exist. Glorious plenitude gives way to unflattering comparisons, and the glow of eternity is replaced by the "murky reality" of time.[13] Telling foundling stories is a way of coping by denying the logic of this experience; the family romance is a conservative as well as a nostalgic genre because it allows the child "to mature while refusing to progress." The discovery of sexuality then turns it into an active defence against difference: once uncertain *paternity*, rather than parentage, becomes the object of imaginative work, a new opposition between the feminine (the child's "intimate and trivial" world) and the masculine ("distant and noble") then opens up the possibility of "romanesque" adventure.

In spite of the problems with this account, in which "the child" is really an allegory of certain aspects of imperialism, it has some resonance with the dilemmas of practicing cultural studies in an international frame, though strictly a resonance only; a discipline (if this is in fact what cultural studies has become) is not a personality. But for practitioners, some of whom remember cultural studies as a "project" on a much more intimate scale, the family-romantic genre can indeed provide a defense against the "difference" introduced by even a limited degree of internationalization—a process that not only brings to bear certain "global" market pressures, but also brings into *contact* groups who may inhabit the same nation but never ordinarily meet. Many cultural studies conferences create a landscape of astonishment like a John Forbes poem, where bizarre non-encounters between incommensurable identities are made meaningful only by an effort to *do* something with the startling fact that they can occupy the same space.

I feel at home in a John Forbes landscape, and yet I want to ask whether there is always something wrong with a defensive response to its tensions. I find the family romance tempting at times. It *works*, transnationally, as a shorthand or metonymic way of claiming a difference to be constructed; precisely because of its currency, I can more easily envisage using it to present a critical reading of *The Lucky Country* than I could face embarking in a foreign context on an analysis (with every second word requiring an elaborate gloss, or leading into labyrinths of explanation where I might be the first to lose sight of the point of my beginning) of the intricate debates of Australian social criticism in the 1950s and 1960s—and the struggles for political and institutional power in which these were enmeshed.

Yet without some reference to those distant struggles *then*—without the bitter battles over mass non-"British" immigration that helped to double the population, without the slow dying of the White Australia policy, without the reemergence of demands for Aboriginal citizenship rights, without the conflict between parents with a fading allegiance to Britain or Ireland, and children born, like myself, under the constraints and cultural incentives of the American Alliance, without the class, ethnic, and religious Cold War between proponents of Rome and Moscow that tore the Labor Party apart while critics from all sides attacked the culture being created (in fibro or red brick houses each on a quarter acre block, perhaps a chookyard still down the back) by the rurally based affluence of the suburban working class—it is hard to make sense of the political context of cultural studies in an altered Australia *now*. General invocations of class-race-gender as "global" universals are not, in the end, transnationally sufficient for much more than making gestures of good will.

Then again, Graeme Turner has pointed out that there can be good reasons for defensiveness in an *economic* landscape of "internationalisation."[14] In material conditions where only a couple of publishers vaguely interested in the field survived the corporate mergers and take-overs of the 1980s, the word "international" comes to work in cultural studies as it does in the film and record industries—as a euphemism for a process of streamlining work to be "interesting" to American and European audiences according to a commercial judgment of what those interests are. "Imperialism" is at once too strong and too vague as a name for this process; our governments gladly espouse it as an export strategy for the arts as well as research, and it is consistent with the broader drift of national policy-making in Australia as in other countries. It is also a *new* development insofar as it no longer blocks the circulation of Australian work as "too specific" for readers elsewhere. Instead, it moves to influence what we should be producing *here.*[15]

For those who maintain an activist view of their practice this is a troubling tendency, especially for work on gender, race, and class: after all, this is the "internationalism" that gave us Tina Turner instead of Justine Saunders as queen of the Outback in *Mad Max Beyond Thunderdome,* and that may foster the "strategic" adoption in cultural studies of saleable rhetorics with tenuous links indeed to Australian social conditions. British assumptions about class have played this role in the past, and American constructions of race and "identity" are doing so at present. The interesting question for the future, then, is how to act in this situation without inventing less a history than a new nostalgia for an unchanging, introverted (and imaginary) national culture.

There are two corollaries of this shift in the *realpolitik* of cultural studies. One is that the text/ethnography debate has actually intensified a drift *away* from the concrete values that ethnographers like to invoke; as Graeme Turner remarks, in practice "the current unfashionableness of historicized textual readings of specific instances of Australian media production has resulted in a net reduction of useful work on Australian texts, . . . practices and . . . ideological formations" (7). The other is that a particular *kind* of "Theory" is privileged; working from a core of American and European references, liberally employing metonyms of wider debates ("difference," "pleasure," "resistance") that will signify the text's cross-cultural intelligibility, it may do its real work obliquely, drifting casually in and out of dehistoricized "local" contexts. Other practices are then pushed for *methodological* reasons into the dead zone of the "too specific," or else are obliged to make a home in more cosmopolitan disciplines—History, Comparative Literature, Cinema Studies, English.

Since these pressures on intellectual production do not evenly apply to Australian society at large, their first consequence for cultural studies is, Turner suggests, "a real danger of becoming academically entrenched but socially and politically irrelevant" (7). It is not that the academy poses a threat to some pristine radicality, but rather that the conditions in which academics now operate will shape their work in particular, and in this case limiting, ways. These are the conditions in which a defensive response to "difference" (in fact, to economic inequalities and power imbalances) can be quite reasonable, and in which a project of inventing history by creating an alternative myth of origins for cultural studies "in one country" can sometimes seem to be a locally empowering option.

However the trouble with the family romance is precisely, as Chakrabarty points out, its structural need to inscribe an emblematic *singularity*—"one" country, therefore one *origin*—as the source of its cultural authority. I have mentioned only the Anglo-Celtic masculine possibilities dear to nationalist thinking; it would theoretically be possible to produce "alternative" alternatives, foregrounding figures suppressed by our once dominant radical tradition but crucial to Koori, feminist, and immigrant constructions of Australian history. It is unlikely, however, that even separatist versions of such histories could effectively be written in the form of family romance (and so this is not the context to offer some examples). For only from a position of violent nostalgia for an imaginary British country predating World War Two is it possible to ignore the plurality and mixity of origins that constitutes the nation.[16]

In the repertoire of canonical images of Australia there is a famous painting by Charles Meere called *Australian Beach Pattern* (1938–40). It is a family scene, and while it models its images of strong, healthy, carefree Ordinary Australians in the late 1930s on the heroic postures of European Classicism rather than tourist dreams of a vanished Hawaii, it is also an allegory of Democracy. The value of analyzing the forms in which cultural histories have been composed was emphasized in a 1988 photograph by Anne Zahalka, that "redid" *Australian Beach Pattern* by substituting for its figures representatives of all the peoples that have long inhabited Australia (and enjoyed themselves at the beach). With this simple gesture, something often unremarked about Meere's painting became apparent.[17] His noble, athletic Australians were not "European" gods and goddesses. They were *Aryan*.

OBVIOUS BEACH

One of the most genuinely "popular" forms of cultural studies in Australia is the kind of myth analysis that favors making paradigms of national cultural *topoi*. Books about national culture are often criticized for essentialism, and for nostalgic sentimentality. They are also often best-sellers, and are very widely read.

In this kind of cultural studies, "the beach" has figured often enough to earn a disclaimer in an essay prefacing a recent book in the genre by a British immigrant, Stephen Knight's *The Selling of the Australian Mind*. Knight's tale of arrival and culture shock begins with two other such *topoi*, "the airport" and "the pub," but he quickly removes from his frame of future reference "those obvious things like sport, the beach, the car, the clothes, tourist sites and sounds"; his themes will be derived from his own urban middle-class life "in the business of education and literature."[18] His book is an alternative to the pub-beach-barbecue paradigm explored by a text that Knight does not mention, *Myths of Oz* by John Fiske, Bob Hodge, and Graeme Turner.

Knight's essays are delightful and persuasive. Instead of rehearsing the given features of a "lifestyle" ideology, he organizes his studies of places and practices around *problems* that are commonly discussed in the mainstream

media: the "determinedly secular" ethos of Australian society; the deep refusal of patriotism that sometimes prompts our governments to sponsor
corrective campaigns; the politics of literacy; the greed of the 1980s; "the
growing confrontation with race, history, possession and power" (9). In this
way, Knight treats critical activity as an *aspect* of the culture that he criticizes, and as a part of the everyday lives of the public whom he addresses.
This allows him to overcome that anxiety of critical "position" endemic to
topical myth analysis, described by Barthes in *Mythologies* (1957) as an ago-
nized alienation but which is now more often resolved by an act of identification between the critic and "the people."

Knight is not content, however, to exclude those things that play no part
in his own experience. He dismisses sport-beach-car-clothes-tourism as, in
his view, *superficial* (without "much significance in the deep-laid realities of
life in this country"), and as *external*—"part of a carapace of materialism
which any vertebrate structure of analysis and culture needs to crack open
for the life inside" (7). His mistrust of materialism aligns him here with past
critics of Australian hedonism like Ronald Conway (*The Great Australian Stupor*, 1971; *Land of the Long Weekend*, 1978), although he does not share their
conservatism, and it leads him to ignore the constructive projects of the
1960s that, like *The Lucky Country*, sought to analyze, rather than celebrate,
popular materialism as the *basis* for a new democratic model of social and
political life.[19] It also makes his book indirectly a polemic against *Myths of
Oz*, that presents the beach as both "a national institution" and a myth complex enough not only to negotiate "the deep biblical opposition between
land and sea, or the basic anthropological one between culture and nature,"
but to offer, via "the politics of pleasure" and "overflowing meanings," the
possibility of "subversive" surf.[20]

I have no great sympathy for the idea that going surfing is *subversive*. Yet
I think there is a problem with dismissing "obvious things" if we take them
to be, as Knight does, *inessential*. I must admit to a bias here. The beach for
me has always been a "deep-laid," and thus ambiguous, reality of life, and
my own disinterest in subcultures is probably due to a youth spent admiring
my boyfriends' surfboards in an era when girls didn't ride. But when I read
Knight's dedication, "For Margaret, who kept me here," I realize that were
I to make such a tribute I could say, most sincerely, "For the beach." So I am
shocked by Knight's judgment, and I want to argue with it; on the beach,
he might have learned something about spirituality in our "secular" society
(many Australians, I think, are pantheists), and so something more about
the lack of patriotic feeling for anything much besides sport. But, even as
I think these things, I am more uneasy with the myth-*making* mode I slip
into than I am with Knight's view of the beach. This is the usual problem
with myth analyses when they are (as they were not by Barthes) unified by
a strict thematics, like "subculture," or "nation": personal observation soon
becomes imperious generalization.

However, my real problem with Knight's surface/essence, outside/inside metaphysic of cultural "significance" is the question that it begs. Why *is* the beach now such an "obvious thing"? For whom is it obvious, and how? It is plausible to say that the pop-cultural myth of the beach has a fragile importance indeed for other orders of Australian reality; a historian (for whom "the beach," via *Myths of Oz*, meant "cultural studies") once told me irritably that "most Australians don't go to the beach," and for him this simply proved that "people in cultural studies don't do any research." But we still do have to account for its massive, obsessive inscription: tourism, fashion, soft drink and sanitary napkin commercials aside, a vast anthology could be compiled of beach scenes from literature, cinema, photography, painting, theater, television drama and documentary, newspapers and magazines. How is this without "significance"?

In fact, *Myths of Oz* shares with *The Selling of the Australian Mind* the view that there is something misleading about the beach as promoted by the culture industries. For Knight, it belongs with many other things to a postwar ideology of consumerism that did "special damage" in a country where "the ideology of the collective" had been so strong; "it was an overthrow of the material poverty of most of previous Australian life and of the systems of public self-help, which in this austere environment had emerged earlier than in the rest of the world" (5). So the "obvious" beach is at odds with historic *social* values that may still live on under the carapace of materialism. For Fiske, Hodge, and Turner, media images "colonize" the surf by imposing upon it the meanings of a "culturally dominant class." For them the mediated or "suburban" beach is at odds with the resistant force of the subcultural or "surfing" beach—its "closeness to *nature.*" For them, the mythic Nature promoted by the media is different from the surfing "natural" ("physical sensation, and . . . the pleasure that this produces"). In other words, both texts oppose an image to a deeper (Knight) or other (Fiske et al.) *reality.* Cultural studies is then a means of gaining access to that reality.

Epistemological issues aside, there is a complicated problem here about the relation between cultural studies and history, and how self-reflexive we need to be about considering that relation. I suspect that however we may praise or denigrate the beach as a mythic signifier, a sensual/spiritual experience or a complex ethnographic object (surfers, "materialism," men eating ice creams with their children), we certainly do not do so now from a space "outside" a history in which discourse about real and imaginary beaches has an intense significance for Australian *intellectuals*, especially those for whom the popular is an object of study as well as a condition of everyday living. This is a history that in fact has a great deal to do with a "growing confrontation with race, history, possession and power," thus with the position from which "we" speak, and Knight's text, at least, is aware of this; the title of his prefatory essay and the subtitle of his book is "From *First Fleet* to Third Mercedes" (emphasis mine).

It is not tautological or precious here to speak of history confronting history. Many traditional narratives of Australian history would always begin at the beach: until the 1970s, white historians regularly assumed that only when the convicts arrived on "the fatal shore" did time and "history proper" begin in "the timeless land." One of the most important histories we have of the Enlightenment, Bernard Smith's *European Vision and the South Pacific 1768–1850*, is lavishly supplied with beach scenes—traces of a scientific and artistic struggle to confront the radically different and to convert it into "the other." It probably isn't abusive to speak of a *primal* scene: sexuality and violence are often at stake when people wonder about "first contact" between the Eora and the British, or what happened on the beach, when, after months at sea, female convicts were released to share a borderless prison with male convicts, sailors, soldiers; as Paul Carter points out in *The Road to Botany Bay*, the most chaste of narrative historians will write these "scenes" as though there was someone else *there*, looking on.[21]

It was in confrontation with this kind of history that Eric Willmot observed in his 1986 Boyer Lectures for ABC Radio, *Australia: The Last Experiment*, that Botany Bay 1788 is not necessarily the best "marker" of beginnings for a "polygeneric society."[22] The fourth lecture, "Lucky Country Dreaming," suggests that only in Arnhem Land in 1802 was a scene set "for all the actors of Modern Australia." Willmot's scene is not a fantasy of guilty or anxious presence. He speaks simply of history as a book, and of a page with Aboriginal Australians "looking out to sea," a Macassan ship returning "for the season's fishing," and a British ship appearing for the first time in the bay. The Macassans, coming and going for centuries in the cosmopolitan North, were always ignored by an Anglo imaginary mesmerized by its own "fatal" shore; only when they are represented do "the Europeans, the Asians and the Australians all meet on the shores of the Southland." This reminder that at least three peoples could have occupied a given *historical* space "from the beginning" does not deny tragedy, violence, and conflict. It does try to change what the history of that space may be in future.

My point is certainly not that we cannot write about beach culture without taking all this on board, although I do think that there are often involuntary resonances when people imagine the beach in Australia to offer utopian potential for a naturally natural "nature." My point is that Willmot's use of the beach as simultaneously a positive cultural value and a historical image that is *already* involved in critical debates and political conflicts may point to a more complex project for cultural studies than the elaboration of paradigmatically "given" (sub)cultural or national topics—without denying the value of these, or indeed their cultural power.

In this spirit, it may be more useful to think of the beach as a chronotope rather than as a *topos* or myth. Bakhtin's famous "unit of analysis" based on variable time-space ratios can carry its own essentialist charge, but it does allow us to deal with the density and volatility of cultural reference systems without *either* bringing an impossible totality relentlessly to bear on every single occasion (each stray beach postcard a guilty symptom of colonialism) *or* creating those spatialized paradigms of popular practice that so idealize and purify an atomized present (sport/beach/car) that they may function as defensive guarantees of perfect historical innocence. The beauty of the concept of chronotope is to enable us think about the cultural interdependence of spatial and temporal categories in terms of *variable* relations.[23]

One of the most powerful beach scenes I know works directly on "the beach" in this way. In my reading, it also explains why the beach may be one of the deepest-laid "realities of life" in Australia, one in terms of which the danger of dissociating the pleasures of popular culture from the political conflicts of history—as well as a desire to do so—is lived in the everyday.

Mudrooroo Nyoongah's "Beached Party"—an occasional text for Australia Day (January 26) 1991—could be called an elegy.[24] It is certainly a mourning poem, but only in the first few lines is there a distinction between the present of the oration ("We all, all of us must have a beginning, a birth day") and the historic past ("I, we died a thousand, thousand, / When Governor Phillip carried to terror nullus / His ill cargo: 'I suffer, suffer— / Why exile me here?'"). These lines already complicate the relations between a general human "we," an Aboriginal "I, we," a cited white "I," and the signature "Nyoongah": the rest of the poem shifts and stretches those relations back and forth in a crowded, flickering time-space rather like a party, where nothing so neat as a "split" subjectivity is sustained, where the mood swings wildly between benevolence, sarcasm, pity, and sorrow, and where the pasts and presents of radically different temporalities spill and crash into each other.

The beached party is a mess, but it isn't chaotic. There is a logic that holds together the "cliché" present of staged political consensus and national reconciliation, the "eternal" present of TV, tourism, beach holidays, and real estate sales, and the recurring present of Aboriginal mourning, just as there is a logic able to blur but not efface the differences between the Koori, Australian, human, and Nyoongah identities assumed by Mudrooroo's text.[25] You could call it Modernity, the legacy of Enlightenment, or even just one of those contradictions abounding in popular culture. You could also call it "the environment," or "the hole in the ozone layer." Toward the end of the poem, the party scene clears for a "historical re-enactment" that is also (for "I, we") the present reality of a sacrificial scene: Governor Phillip holds "the shattered body of a Koori in his white arms slowly turning brown," while "I finger the scars of my sorrows and smile at the droppings of my tears," holding the boat steady as Phillip proffers his gifts; then as the musket speaks, "our new nation in mourning each and every year on this date" can salute the birth of its future under the deadly mid-summer sun:

As indifferent skins blister with cancerous growths
And my voice whispers a hopeful, happy birthday, Australia
While daubing sunscreen cream over the worst lesions
                                                    of my past.

"On the beach" (a tag made famous by a novel and a film about the end
of the world at the ends of the earth in Australia) is an old expression meaning *beached*: shipwrecked, destitute, bankrupt, abandoned, washed up. "On
the beach" is also the name of a cultural framework for addressing "the state
of the nation" (also the world, the human condition, public affairs, perhaps
an intimate, even trivial, situation). This is why John Forbes can set part of
his "On the Beach" in a crowded city street, and why Mudrooroo Nyoongah's "Beached Party" can include glimpses of the wood-chipping industry
and struggles over foreign investment. In Marxian criticism, such an address is often assumed to be *essentially* essentialist, as well as pessimistic, and
there can be good reason for this; if "Nyoongah"'s Black mourner/cele-
brant in anti-UV cream defines, in more ways than one, a new kind of historical subject, Forbes's bystanders casually gambling on the outcome of a
certainty as though its grimness does not concern them are ancestral figures from a legend of stoic white working-class "character"—hard, cynical,
soulless—largely invented, in fascination, by intellectuals.

Yet "on the beach" is one of those phrases that can undermine itself:
simply because it is used by someone who still lives to tell a tale, it may refute
its own declaration of a pathetic or hopeless finality. Projected as a narrative
framework, this kind of enunciative irony generates stories of encounter
rather than closure, in time as well as in space. This is how Mudrooroo's
appropriation of the "fatal shore" mode of Australia Day meditation involves the global human future in a recurring Koori past-present. This is
also why John Forbes's "On the Beach" implies that the answer to the question of its own small urban scenario—"won't this do for a formal model of
Australia?"—will eventually have to be, "no."

EPIPHANY IN MARTIN PLACE

A comic cultural encounter is already going on in John Forbes's street
scene. We don't need to know exactly what it is in order to know that it is
happening; something is marked by the effort of memory in the middle of
the text—"isn't there a poem about this & the shimmering ideal of just
walking down the street?"—and by the coding of the poem as a formal imi-
tation "after Juan Davila."

There *is* another poem about this, or something like "this"—a famous
poem by Les Murray called "An Absolutely Ordinary Rainbow." It is not
about trade union delegates watching a man behead a chicken in the street
(just possibly a religious rite, probably an attempt at Art, but certainly a

social transgression). It is about an epiphany transfiguring an anonymous man in Martin Place with a fit of cosmic weeping. His weeping brings the city to a halt; when it is over, "he simply walks" through the crowd and away.[26] Les Murray is a Catholic, a celebrated poet (almost a *de facto* Laureate), and a conservative populist thinker in the Anglo-Celtic tradition; his collection of *Poems 1961–1983* is called *The Vernacular Republic.*

Juan Davila is a gay Chilean-Australian artist, and Forbes's text is a tribute to his work, especially his 1982–83 history painting *Fable of Australian Art,* the first panel of which includes a blank canvas marked "A Republic for Australia." In the past, Davila has used transfigured Christian-colonial iconography to study sexual and cultural difference in the political economy of modernism. Some of his work in the 1980s combined the sometimes transvestite, often male Pieta with defaced Art History "signature" scenes, comic-book characters, pop icons, and figures from Tom of Finland pornography in readings of psychoanalysis; his paintings have sometimes been seized on the request of fundamentalist Christian groups. In 1982 his *Stupid as a Painter,* implicating Michelangelo's *Pietà* in a narrative called "Kiss of Spider-woman," incurred charges of obscenity; in 1988, his image *Bivouac* for a book of critical essays about the Bicentenary was censored lest its treatment of Governor Phillip prompt charges of lese majesty.[27]

While the media may frame him as inverting ordinary values, Davila is not beheading chickens to shock our sacred institutions, and his art is not being framed by Forbes as a "transgression" of Les Murray's. Writing "after Juan Davila" is precisely a matter of framing itself: the metonymic flipping over of an image ("behead a chicken"/"headless chook") from one context to another in which its first meaning is not "negated" but transformed in such a way that all the relationships resulting are *questioned.* The principle is familiar enough to contemporary critical theory. What I may need to stress here is that this questioning comes to bear not on, say, Catholic religious beliefs (Murray's poem is just a vague trace in Forbes's) but on "the shimmering ideal of just walking down the street"—that sacred, secular value of the Absolutely Ordinary.

This is a complicated question. Davila's work in part belongs to a broad critical movement created internationally over at least the past twenty years by people challenging the sexual, racial, ethnic, and class exclusions and defacements that constitute the Ordinary. In that sense, it is inscribed in opposition to Les Murray's aesthetics (although this poem is the only instance I know of a direct contact between them). The relationship of Forbes's poem to "An Absolutely Ordinary Rainbow" is a little more involved: there is a bit of "Murray" in "Forbes" (the wry turn in the phrase "*not being religious*" echoes the spirit as well as the syntax of Murray's marvelous last line about the weeper after his epiphany: "*Evading believers,* he hurries off down Pitt Street"); and while the ideal of beatified ordinariness is treated ruthlessly indeed, an aura still hangs there, "shimmering."

This is not surprising; what shimmers is a powerful mirage. For at least a century in Australia since the heyday of Henry Lawson, theologians of social democracy have seen the white male working-class Ordinary as the luminous truth of the Popular that shines through the Everyday. From D. H. Lawrence in his 1923 novel *Kangaroo* ("this place is meant for all one dead level sort of people") to Donald Horne in *The Lucky Country* ("A society whose predecessors pioneered a whole continent now appears to shun anything that is at all out of the ordinary. The trouble is that, by Australian standards, almost everything that is now important is out of the ordinary"), critics of that democracy have reified the Ordinary as a crippling normalization—almost a repressive *regime*.[28] But as these two quotations suggest, the recurring critique of the Ordinary as a political culture (Lawrence accurately predicted the form that fascism here would take) and as a social philosophy (Horne predicted Australia's economic decline in an age of new technology) has not always required thinking through those exclusions on which it depends.

Cultural studies has much to learn from these not quite resolved encounters. There are always gaps and incommensurables in play between the materials of cultural critique, and it may be in working with those that critical affect is most at stake. What often interests me now is a gap between historic discourses on Australian culture (almost a second language for me, so foreign can they seem) and the transnational critical and political discourses—feminism, Marxism, poststructuralism—that have worked for me as a composite mother tongue. Both are used in public culture today, the former much more widely than the latter; the work most useful to me now in cultural studies increasingly mixes them up. So I am also aware of a gap between the Australian institutional *conditions* that Graeme Turner has discussed and the institutional *assumptions* that often mark transnational criticism (absolutist distributions of the relation of theory to practice, "local" American and British methodology debates—text vs. ethnos, the literary vs. the popular—raised to the status of global human dilemmas). These experiences are productive: "gaps" do not conceal an elusive truth for the critic to pursue, but they do help to define the *social* conditions for inventing a critical practice.

This is not a rarefied issue. Practical problems are at stake about the politics of cultural studies in a particular social formation. In recent years, for example, we have had some discussion of the problems that follow from what Turner, reflecting back on *Myths of Oz*, calls the "*theoretical* weakness . . . of wheeling in British subcultural theory to analyse mainstream Australian popular culture."[29] Not quite so much attention has yet been paid to the problems that follow from wheeling in the abstract aesthetic vocabulary of European modernism to theorize in Australia what that modernism (as Marshall Berman has shown) has always taken to be "the practice of everyday life" and that was historically invested here with once radical, now reactionary, *nationalist* populist values.[30] In 1990, students graduating from high schools throughout New South Wales took an English exam containing a question that I quote from memory: " 'Les Murray makes the ordinary extraordinary and the extraordinary ordinary': Discuss."

This is also not exactly a "specific" Australian issue. If there is a local irony about learning the principle of "making strange" as part of a basic training in the Great Australian Ordinary, there is a broader irony about the reluctance widespread in cultural studies to question rigorously the aesthetic inheritance of frameworks now used to analyze popular culture—a reluctance that can be most intense in schools of media study that wouldn't for the world get involved in any talk of "art" or "literature" or in overly theoretical speculation.[31] Yet Ian Hunter in *Culture and Government* has shown, for example, just how powerful an unscrutinized Leavisite pedagogy of mutual recognition through the text ("this *is* so, isn't it?") has remained for a cultural studies that claims not only to discard canons, but to go "beyond" texts to study *practices*.

THE ORDINARY AUSTRALIAN

The point of Ian Hunter's questioning, like Juan Davila's, is not to reveal a historic complicity that requires denunciation, but to ask what follows in *practice* from certain "shimmering" ideals, and what might also follow from working in a different way. I want to give an example of a problem I have with an ideal of my own that Hunter's work has helped me to clarify, without, however, providing me with a solution I can accept. It arises in a two-way "gap" (for want of a better word) between the history of the Ordinary in Australian social criticism, and the concept of the everyday in European philosophy. This gap, as usual, is material as well as conceptual: the "everyday" is already a complex and well-defined problem for a huge archive of texts;[32] the history of the Ordinary exists only as a scattering of documents put together by "everyday know-how." My terms, necessarily, are caught up in the problem that they try to define. I can only gesture at my problem, and say why I think it matters.

Fortunately, an American critic provides me with an oblique but sound way of beginning. In "An Ontology of Everyday Distraction," Margaret Morse criticizes the anachronism of transferring to the study of U.S. consumer culture today the model of everyday "praxis as enunciation" developed by Michel de Certeau in *The Practice of Everyday Life*.[33] This model is only one version, I think, of one of the most powerful "modernist" themes regularly assumed by cultural studies, the "excess" of process over structure. It is not arbitrary or inconsequential that Henri Lefebvre began *Everyday Life in the Modern World* with a few dense pages in praise of James

Joyce's *Ulysses*, and the "great river of Heraclitean becoming" in which, for Lefebvre, Joyce had redeemed the urban and linguistic quotidian that it helped bring into discourse.[34]

Like most critics following on from Lefebvre's work, de Certeau wanted to transcend the limits of a "critique of graphic representations" that merely looks "from the shores of legibility toward an inaccessible beyond." In the "beyond" of those limits there had to be a way to read non-graphic social practices directly, yet not naively.[35] So in "Walking in the City," de Certeau proposed to "access" that beyond with his model of the pedestrian speech-act. Walking could be considered as *"a space of enunciation"*; "walking is to the urban system what the speech act is to language [*langue*] or to the statements uttered [*énoncés proférés*]." In other words, people's actions in using the city could not be predicted or constrained by a formal power's systematic plan. With this dodgy urban/spatial projection of a linguistic/temporal concept (enunciation), that "shimmering ideal of just walking down the street" became a model of popular practice—and critical process—in administered societies.

In one form or another this, along with the closely related strategy/tactics distinction, has been one of the most influential models for cultural studies in recent years.[36] Morse wonders, however, whether de Certeau could ever have imagined, "as he wrote on walking as an evasive strategy of self-empowerment, that there would one day be video cassettes that demonstrate how to 'power' walk." She suggests that "praxis as enunciation" has dubious value as a "vision of liberation" once processes for gaining access to a beyond (in her terms, an *elsewhere*) have been fully "designed into the geometries of everyday life" with malls, freeways, and television, and now that de Certeau's "figurative practices of enunciation ('making do,' 'walking in the city,' or 'reading as poaching') are *modeled in representation itself*" (195). In the particular time-space economy that Morse calls "everyday distraction," designer process blocks, rather than exceeds, a process/structure dynamic. There is no "escape" in designer escape, or to put it another way, nothing exceeds like designer excess.

Now, in an abstract and quite fundamental way, I doubt that I could think without a concept of enunciative praxis, and while I recognize the environment Morse describes, it is still for me a tourist experience, someone else's elsewhere, and not my everyday life. De Certeau did not think of praxis *only* as enunciation, a term that functions in his texts as an allegory of, and an adjunct to, other kinds of social action. But as Morse points out, de Certeau often does translate enunciation as *evasion*, and this is the problem; at these moments of his text, the "fugitive" nature of the speech act concerns him more than its cohesive, dialogic, or referential powers.[37] In these moments, his work looks forward to a cultural studies that celebrates "resistance" as a programmed feature of capitalist culture rather than toward that process (cohesive, dialogic, referential) by which, as Morse puts it in her own wise

vision of criticism's role in social change, "alternative values and their constituencies have labored to *mark themselves* in discourse" (215).

The evasive/enunciative model of the everyday, moreover, was not
unique or original to Michel de Certeau. It is already at work in Lefebvre's
Everyday Life in the Modern World, and the most extended elaboration of it
that I know is in Maurice Blanchot's wonderful essay on "the man in the
street" from 1959, "Everyday Speech." Writing about Lefebvre's earlier *Critique de la vie quotidienne* (1947–62), Blanchot sets out with miraculous brev-
ity all the elements for a theoretical myth of the Evasive Everyday. In the
intricate dialectic of his text, owing little to Lefebvre's historical materialism, these elements are held together by one refrain: *"the everyday escapes."*[38]
"That is its definition": it escapes all "forms or structures," all "means of
communication," all "dialectical recovery," all "authority, whether it be political, moral or religious," all division between true and false. It is pure
process in excess, and it is always, like "the man in the street," *potentially*
political. For this reason the structural "other" to the excess of everyday
speech is for Blanchot, as it was for Lefebvre, a double figure: the philosopher, the man of "metalanguage" in Lefebvre's phrase, and the *bureaucrat,*
the "man of government," in Blanchot's. For de Certeau, too, the "pedestrian speaker" confronted and evaded a twin: on the one hand, the cultural
theorist; on the other, the urban *planner.*

This is an intense discourse of desire, and it could be analyzed historically in terms of philosophical debates about the question of "the other"
in postwar France. Among the texts still used in cultural studies today,
the symbolic bearer of evasive everydayness shifts easily from Blanchot's
"man in the street," to "the woman in the home" (Lefebvre), to de Certeau's
walker, of whom the mythic projection in his text is "Man Friday on
the beach." In each case, this bearer is marked as discursively other to
"metalanguage"—as female literalness (Lefebvre), as popular rumor, a discourse "without a subject" (Blanchot), or as a "savage" trace of orality in
writing (de Certeau)—while the subject marking it as such shifts between
"the philosopher" in Lefebvre's formal dialogues, the speculative thinker
who also lives in the everyday (Blanchot), and the professional scholar in a
research institution (de Certeau).

This recurring inscription of the historic subject of metalanguage—indeed, of cultural studies—as a white European middle-class male ("Robinson Crusoe" in de Certeau's terms) helps to explain why Wlad Godzich can
argue persuasively in his preface to de Certeau's *Heterologies* that "this other
which forces discourses to take the meandering appearance that they have is not a
magical or a transcendental entity; it is the discourse's mode of relation to
its own historicity in the moment of its utterance."[39] This is also why the
"critique of everyday life" is a discourse of critical *involvement,* and this is also
why this involvement has to take the form of an enunciative praxis.

The interesting thing for me, however, is that for *all* these texts this process must not extend to involvement with the one figure who in fact remains, for all three writers, indomitably "other"—the bureaucrat. Prior to any instance of enunciative praxis, the subject of metalanguage is already split, by this discourse, between theoretical and "administrative" functions, process, and structure: the latter terms are negatively valued, and the semantic attribute "political" migrates toward the former.

Here I must mark a first gap in my discourse, and between the materials I work with. I turn, once more, to Donald Horne's "man in an open-necked shirt." He doesn't say much as he enjoys his ice cream on the beach; according to legend, he is enunciatively "laconic." In spite of his setting, he is much closer to Blanchot's man in the street than he is to de Certeau's Man Friday, who hovers in his memory as some sort of exotic prince; he is totally oblivious to the woman in the home. In a way, he fits the series. But he isn't at all *evasive*: his only everyday praxis is a modest material consumption, and he dislikes symbolic excesses ("too far fetched"). He is the Ordinary Australian: retired now, worried about his pension and "the Asians taking over the country"; even his old trade union mates have just wasted rank and file money on a twenty-page liftout for *Cleo*, that yuppie female fashion magazine. In his prime, he aroused few philosophers to discourse (that would *really* be a bit much). But he was, and he still is, an object of intense desire for many a man of government.

On the other side of this gap, in *Culture and Government*, and an associated essay on "Setting Limits to Culture," Ian Hunter gives a rare defense of a bureaucratic practice.[40] Hunter's critical object is not the Everyday, but Culture in the emergence of English literary education. Nevertheless, his harsh account of "the gigantic ethical pincers of the dialectic" in British cultural studies has a direct bearing on the French tradition. Hunter argues that cultural studies has underestimated its debt, via Marxism, to Romantic aesthetics, to Schiller and Hegel, and in so doing it has misrecognized its place in a history of criticism deployed in schools as an exemplary *ethical* practice, aimed at "forming the self." While cultural studies may claim to offer a materialist analysis of culture, and to politicize the critical process, the dialectic really functions as a virtuoso technique of "ethical athleticism"—in fact, as "a technique for *withdrawing* from the discursive and institutional spheres in which cultural attributes are actually specified and formulated."[41] Such spheres are primarily administrative and bureaucratic; these are the spheres of the "properly" political.

Like the related work of Tony Bennett and other theorists of policy,[42] this argument raises some awkward questions about the "critique of everyday life." Its vulnerability to Hunter's polemic only begins with the way it has so often defined its own processes as well as its objects as *necessarily* "evasive," even as precluded *by definition* from occupying those "spheres" of planning and administration. In the light of Hunter's history, critical "praxis as enunciation" can suddenly look like ethical consent to the *status quo*. This confirms the disquiets of my own experience by showing how and *why* the Romantic inheritance in cultural studies works to create a "fraught space" of ethical grandiloquence in which massive, world-historical problems are histrionically debated on such a level of generality that they cannot possibly be solved, and posed in ways that do not, will not, and cannot ever connect to agencies by which actual social futures may be given a "definite shape." In the name of politics, this praxis enunciates a spiral from, as Tony Bennett puts it, "big debate to big debate": always swinging between activist desire and angst about its own effects, it has the form of precisely the doomed circularity that is known in everyday language as running round like a headless chook.

I have deep reservations about this thesis. Yet one of many things that attracts me to it is its compatibility both with recent feminist work that rethinks "praxis as enunciation" precisely through a pre-Kantian concept of ethics as, in Moira Gatens's phrase, "crucially concerned with the specificity of one's embodiment,"[43] and with the value that radical pedagogies have always attached, both in and out of school, to a "virtuoso" *collective* praxis aimed precisely at "(re)forming the self." Rather than dismissing these, Hunter's argument simply cautions some "ethical modesty" about what they can achieve.[44] But then I am not sure how much is to be gained by depoliticizing as "ethical" whole areas of intellectual practice where people are routinely confronting relations and structures of power; whether culture in media societies can be considered "rare" in the sense that Hunter assumes; whether any "self" can be so singular and orderly that its functions are neatly separable, ethics here, politics there; and whether enunciation in a discourse-*administered* society can ever be restricted to an "ethical" technique.

Now I want to look back across that gap, where uncanny memories are stirring with no immediate justification. In some of our debates about policy and aesthetics, the thematics of process presents itself in an inverted form; cultural theorists desiring to identify more closely with trade union delegates than with poets or painters or pop stars are defending administrative agencies against a presumed "semiotic" excess. This time, we aesthetes are astonished (are they talking about *transgression?*), but not surprised when one or two start hailing, as the object of their desire, that ordinary soul "the Citizen."[45] After all, there is a text about this and the shimmering ideal of just getting on with the job; it is a vision from *The Lucky Country*, by no means unique to that book, in which the white male Ordinary Australian is dreaming, in 1964, a better future for his (br)others:

> The pragmatic, sceptical Australian can walk through the rhetoric of Asia like a blind man avoiding bullets. There they are, out there in Asia, advising on pest control, credit policies, irrigation, language teaching, some of the thousand and one little things that help civilizations survive the radia-

tions of their own bombast. . . . Their ability not to generalize, simply to get on with the job can open the hearts of practical-minded Asians. (229)

Policy theorists would not say this, or would not use such rhetoric to say this, today. (Nor, I imagine, would Donald Horne.) But this rhetoric, and this theory of rhetoric, along with the erasures, desires, and projections that Horne's text inscribes, is part of their history and of the history of the cultural studies I practice in Australia today.

It is part of *my* history, not least because I find myself doing cultural studies in a society where the dominant *political* discourse still sees "rhetoric" as an exotic bombast avoided by the ordinary (everyday life + government), and I often do this using a theoretical discourse that wants to find in the everyday a rhetorical escape from the *metalinguistic* (philosophy + government). The former will not admit of any difference in discourse, and that, in a sense, is its politics. The latter does find it hard, I think, to make a political difference.

CHANGING THE CULTURE

I want to conclude with an informal description of the immediate context for my own view of cultural studies. If my work is influenced more by concepts of everyday life than by debates about popular culture, this is partly a result of the way that feminism leads me to think about practice; I am less interested in music or TV than I am in how these cut across and organize the various time/spaces in which the labor, as well as the pleasure, of everyday living is carried out by Australian women. This is why I do not think of "tourist sites and sounds" as insignificant, like Stephen Knight, but also why I do not think of them *primarily*, like *Myths of Oz*, as settings for reading the popular in terms of signifying practice (although I am an ardent reader). I think of them in the first place as cultural combat zones.

Take a tussle over a hypothetical tourist resort on a beach in the 1990s. It is a site where Aboriginal land claimants, Japanese or Malaysian developers, white racists, entrepreneurs of many ethnicities who will be pro-Japanese but may be anti-Aboriginal, environmentalists, surfers, and a broader community mixed in every respect and divided about development, will all have to fight, unequally, over a space where the "deep biblical opposition between land and sea" is administered by a government committed to sustainable development while trying to stave off bankruptcy. I say "hypothetical" to keep things simple: in reality, there will be Aboriginal supporters of development, racists who are not white racists, deep ecologists confronting Green-vote power brokers. . . .

In this context, culture is one medium of a power struggle in which most participants, at some stage or another, will passionately invoke on their own behalf the interests of "Ordinary Australians." This struggle is represented in the everyday as profoundly economic. Most public discussions of "culture" in the past fifteen years, whether on chat shows, in newspapers, or in pubs, have not been directly to do with TV or poetry or surfing. They have been about the impact of the deregulation of much of the economy on our social structure and ethical systems; about the Uruguay Round of the GATT talks, and the threat of a U.S.-imposed "free trade" model to local culture *industries*; about the pros and cons of APEC; about the emergent division of the world into three rival trading empires with no clear place for "us"; about the conflict between national-economic, global-environmental, and local "quality of life" imperatives. These are all potentially frightening "futures" occurring for us now as media scenarios.

At the same time, culture is now an export industry thought more in relation to debt management than to concepts of a "whole way of life." In the past, the administration of our English departments relegated almost all Australian literature to the unstudied field of the "popular."[46] Today, English departments teach many forms of international popular culture, while "Australian Literature" (including criticism and theory) is a funding category conceptually on a par with opera, rock music, restoring old trade union banners, and financing Aboriginal arts.

In the field of this insistently economic representation of "culture," it is clearly one of the concerns of cultural studies to open up this field to experiences, and critical expressions, of race, gender, sexuality, and class. However, policy-makers in Australia have been, like the teaching professions, comparatively well attuned to such expressions; the media, more erratically so. So it is not always clear that a criticism primarily referring to a North American bibliography in cultural studies has, however heated its claims to politicalness, much practical advice to offer. The thematics of popular evasion, for example, can lead us to ignore that remarkable development in recent years whereby business, the media, and many of Ian Hunter's "administrative intellectuals" have themselves been construing the everyday life of Ordinary Australians as something like an evasive object.

During the 1980s, the word "culture" began to be used by the media in a rather peculiar sense. In 1990, a week after the worst company crashes in Australian history had ended a decade of financial mismanagement and deregulated corporate crime, a groveling TV current affairs show host asked Rupert Murdoch (back home to shut down a couple of newspapers) what "we" could do to save "our" economy. Murdoch replied: "Oh, you know— change the culture." The host did know what he meant, although he nudged Murdoch to clarify that you can't have greenies wrecking the economy "to save some fish or wombats or something." What Murdoch "meant" was a media commonplace that Australia's biggest economic problem is the lazy, hedonist, uncompetitive, beach-bound, lotus-eating ethos of the Ordinary people.[47] So pervasively was this judgment repeated throughout the 1980s that, by the end of the decade, corporate leaders, bureaucrats, politicians, and opinion-makers were sounding like Maoists:

> Changing the culture is not a quick process in something as old and as large as ARC.

> A cultural shift must be made while there is still time. . . .

> Professor [Helen] Hughes . . . said Australians had relied on the "lucky country" attitude for too long. . . . "We have got to cultivate an export culture."

> We are, nearly all of us, bludgers. That is the reason the country is in a mess and it will not get out of that mess until the national bludging culture has been reversed.

These slogans are from, respectively, a chief executive of Smorgon ARC, Australia's largest producer of concrete reinforcing steel; a past president of the Business Council of Australia introducing a planned "debt conference"; a financial journalist reviewing a speech by an academic economist; an editor of the *Australian Financial Review* in his other role as columnist in the nation's biggest-selling Sunday tabloid.[48]

In this context, "changing the culture" primarily means "getting people to do more work for less money." But it is assumed, in the logic of corporate and administrative desire, that this will also mean changing the minutiae of conduct at the workplace ("work practices") and thus the values and expectations of home and family life; liberalizing working-class attitudes to gender, sexual preferences (now constituting "market segments"), and race; *increasing* class consciousness (that is, making social and economic inequality more acceptable to Australians); and thus changing the meaning of some of the enduring myths of white Australian history. During the 1980s, those discourses of desire known as government reports were promoted in the media as part of a *doctrine* of "changing the culture," culture being taken to be malleable, or "calculable," in Ian Hunter's sense. These are complex and ambiguous developments. An example of the "desire" factor is the Garnaut Report, *Australia and the North-East Asian Ascendancy*, that recommended as part of a single strategy the removal of all tariffs by the year 2000 and compulsory teaching of an Asian Language in all Australian primary schools.[49] It did not consider how an overloaded and underfunded state education system might be able to achieve this.

The distinction between popular culture and everyday life becomes tenuous indeed in the mediated policy field. Some people still fear that cultural studies will "aestheticize" politics. I think that cultural studies has to confront the aestheticization of "politics" in the governmental process. For example, an image on the front page of the *Sydney Morning Herald* in 1988, captioned "The Band that Makes You Bop": four figures framed in cliché rock-promo style, half-vanishing in shadows as they tried to look tough and sexy. "Bop" was a pun on "BoP," Balance of Payments. The "stars" were accountants—clerks who had prepared that month's statement on our balance of payments crisis—and the text was a human interest story. The logic of aestheticization was followed right through to modernist self-reference and postmodern obsolescence: by 1990, a cartoon has huge boulders hitting zombies on the head, BOP!—as the Treasurer (Paul Keating) says to the Prime Minister (Bob Hawke), "they get anaesthetized after a while."

It is an article of faith in cultural studies that most people are not zombies. You could say that "changing the culture" is a myth already being appropriated and revised by the people at whom it is directed. A few nights after Rupert Murdoch did his bit for national salvation, an airport fire brigade chief talked on the same show (*The 7.30 Report*) about disaster stress, and the therapy he'd needed after cleaning up a fatal accident. He said he was interested in "changing our work culture"; by "our," he meant men—making it all right for men to admit to emotional distress and seek help to do something about it. This, I think, is "subversive": not perhaps in relation to a political economy that now needs its workers to be more "flexible" than in the past but in relation to the political myth of the Ordinary, past and present, in Australian everyday life—and the attacks that some of its *virtues* are now, in the name of economy, sustaining.

By "changing the culture," this man meant something *ethical* in Ian Hunter's sense. It seems to me that administrative and political, aesthetic and ethical modes of practice may not be so easily or even usefully distinguished once "everyday life" has become, in the name of "culture," an object of bureaucratic fantasy, policy desire, and media hype, as well as a subject of seemingly unlimited cultural production. However it is certainly not useful either to pose problems as though in studying "the everyday" one is always directly involved in a mortal combat with the history of Western philosophy.

In this context, I would like to think of cultural studies as a discipline capable of thinking the relations between local, regional, national, and international frames of action and experience (assuming that these frames necessarily involve many politics of race, gender, sexuality, and class). There could be two consequences of this. First, projects in cultural studies could be oriented a little less toward the big debates galvanizing the discipline worldwide and lot more toward the "ethical" and policy issues being debated in public media in the contexts that we take to concern us. For example, the Garnaut Report might provide a better starting point for discussing, say, "elitism" in Australia than the burden of the Literary in Britain or the United States. Second, I would like to see cultural studies more informed than it has been in the past by debates in political economy and in geopolitics.

I say this, however, as a "textual" critic rather than an amateur social scientist. The question of mediation, materially distinct from the policy process itself, is ignored by most policy polemics. Yet in my opinion, it is at least as appropriate for cultural studies to concern itself with this as it is to aspire to intervene directly in bureaucratic and business spheres. Recognizing that the media instance of the policy process may have a certain autonomy, randomness, productivity, and "citizen input" can make it more difficult to mobilize the oppositions between politics and aesthetics that have marked this debate so far.

For this reason, my own alternative to a family romance of Australian cultural studies would not be to "invent" a history for the field, but to argue the importance *for* its history of reading, for example, Eric Michaels's work on Warlpiri television; Tom O'Regan on the "space-binding" function of new communications policy; Sneja Gunew on critical multiculturalism, migrant women's writing, and feminist critical theory; Stephen Muecke on Aboriginal story-telling and postmodern travel writing; Yuki Tanaka on the Japanese political-construction (as opposed to military-industrial) complex, and Helen Grace on the folklore of finance capitalism and its modes of masculinity.[50] These projects are all engaged in some way with contesting *images* of policy: not simply images of what "policy" is or ought to be, but with its failures and absurdities; with how people live with its operations and unforeseen consequences, and then with multiple mediations and refractions of their own responses; with how they formulate initiatives of their own; with how all this living "exceeds" (to wheel in a useful term) the demands and the desires of the policy imaginary. So they are all concerned with culture and government in a very broad sense.

For this reason, too, my favorite "founding text" for my own version of cultural studies is Sylvia Lawson's great critical biography of a nineteenth-century white male populist magazine editor, *The Archibald Paradox: A Strange Case of Authorship.*[51] A theorization of media work as political practice, it is also one of the most subtle accounts we have of the dilemmas of a "colonial" intellectual (to use the term appropriate to Archibald's time), and of the paradoxical conditions of his political effectivity. More broadly, it is a major reading of the 1890s: the very period in Australian cultural history that saw, partly thanks to Archibald, the apotheosis of the Ordinary in all its sexist, racist, social democratic glory; the very period that saw, partly thanks to *The Bulletin*, the formalization of an aesthetic doctrine forbidding the "too far fetched"; and also the very period in our economic and political history that is figuring in our media now as the model, if not the source, for our problems in the present.

Lawson's is a major reading because it makes these legends problematic:

she shows the radicalism and the idealism mixed up with the worst of the Ordinary; she shows the complexity produced as well as repressed by stereotypes in popular cultural thinking; obliquely, her work shows us why the posing of white male Ordinariness today as an object of cultural "restructuring" may involve, paradoxically, an attack on some social values that may well be, like the uncompetitive and unpatriotic beach, worth defending. In this way, *the Archibald Paradox* for me is an exemplary history of the present.

Fortunately, it would be too far-fetched for anyone romantically to claim Sylvia Lawson as their new, improved Father—academic, journalist, fiction writer, film-maker, and policy lobbyist that she is. One reason is that her achievement in *The Archibald Paradox* was already to show that there never was anything "singular," and certainly nothing perfect, about the period supposed to be at the "origin" of modern Australian culture; we do not look back at the mythic white male 1890s from the plurality and mixity of our society today; that mixity was there, from the beginning.[52]

John Forbes reminds us that knowing this can be a modest survival guide for living with *all that speech* as it circulates endlessly in paranoiac space. His imagery, like everyday speech, can sometimes sound violent, a bit brutal and inhuman—all those stunned mullets and headless chooks, mute victims of a history that mistook itself for a war between Man and Nature. So, too, his discovery of the truth about the stunned mullet when it comes up for air after its burst of eloquence may seem "inhuman" or "impersonal"; in fact, it's rather tender and optimistic:

> *up close*
>
> *the scales are false*
> *in fact a cunning mechanical contrivance,*
> *like Bob Hawke's hair—*
> *they glitter, exposed to the atmosphere*
> *instead of dying, being alloy not flesh.*
>
> —THE STUNNED MULLET

PART TWO

■ ■ ■ ■ ■ ■ ■ ■ ■ ■ ■

MEDIA
TIME

GREAT MOMENTS IN SOCIAL CLIMBING

. . . the fact that many philosophies (including tendencies in Marxism) have imagined themselves to be metanarratives does not make the fantasy true. As Marx once quipped, "One does not judge an individual by what he thinks about himself." There is not now nor has there ever been a metanarrative or a transcendental space. Theory exists everywhere in a practical state.

—Warren Montag[1]

In the work of Michel de Certeau, the urban tower is a favored location for the "erotics of knowledge" called *theory* ("this lust to be a viewpoint and nothing more").[2] However, theory does not have to be imagined only as a "vertical" perspective allowing us to contemplate the world. To this extent like an urban tower, the theoretical is also produced in "horizontal" networks of circulation that are not always fully visible from any given place, and in lateral mobilizations (of money, resources, credit, and information) that are *involved* in the world, not separated from it. A tower does have spots from which we can contemplate, momentarily, "a bustling city" (93), but every inch of it is active in an economy; to this extent like the practice of theory, an urban tower operates in time.

In this chapter, I analyze some popular and scholarly genres interpreting (or, in de Certeau's terms, "practising") urban towers. So let me begin with a few remarks in overview to clarify my argument's structure. This chapter has three parts. The first briefly discusses two uses of "the tower" as *metaphor*, one corporate-populist, the other academic; rather than developing a thematics of the gaze, I am concerned with summits and climaxes. This introduces an analysis of public *events* involving actual towers. The second and third parts of the chapter examine the media narration of two incidents that occurred in downtown Sydney during the huge real estate boom of the late 1980s: a "King Kong" theme promotion of expensive office space in a renovated building, and a "stunt" in which a man dressed as the Human Fly climbed the tallest building in the city, Sydney Tower.

In spite of public nature of both events (and the popularity of *King Kong* jokes), I argue that only the second of these events counts as "popular" culture in the sense that I prefer to use, de Certeau's notion of the popular as a *modus operandi* defined by an art of *timing* rather than a topological relation to some other "zone" (whether "high," or "élite," or "mass") of cultural space. However I read both events, both moments of social climbing, as engaging two different concepts of simulation (one taken from Jean Baudrillard, the other from Gilles Deleuze), and as entailing different models of critical practice.

If this sounds allegorical, I must admit straight away that it is. Allegory is a way of using these two events to frame a critique of a narrowly metonymic argument common in cultural studies today, whereby a singular form ("*the*" tower) is transfigured, by inflation and conflation, as emblematic not only of a condition of culture in general but also of a historic intellectual place of enunciation (deemed "Faustian") that an "advanced" theory would then require that we renounce. I suggest that a gestural renunciation of altitude, overview, and the phantasmal position of "totalizing master-planning" is inadequate to critical practice in the places and times that I, at least, inhabit.

Let me reiterate here what I mean by "space." Again following de Certeau, I assume that space is not a prior condition of something else ("place"), but an outcome, the product of an activity, and so it has a temporal dimension. Reversing the customary notion that "place" is a structured space, "space," says de Certeau, "is a *practised place*" (117). However, I am more concerned with actual spatial practices than with the place/space distinction itself. Examining places produced for a tourist-consumption economy, I have been less interested in a morphology of such places ("the" motel, "the" mall, "the" beach, "the" tower) than in those individuating intensities (*this* motel, *this* mall, and, since I count stories, genres, and readings as spatial practices, *these* beach scenes) that Deleuze and Guattari call "haecceities."[3] However, the historical "stake" of these analyses does involve a turning of the *home/voyage* opposition that has worked so hard, in the nation-building practices of white Australia, to gender the relations between movement (conceptualized as masculine, when related by colonial ideologies of development to linear models of time), and location (thereby rendered feminine, and related to static or cyclic temporalities).[4]

To clarify my concern with gender and space, I should make it explicit that my argument is organized by a shift, but not an opposition, between a *penis/phallus* relation predicated by the corporate and academic discourses that I discuss, and a *face/faciality* relation that I predicate myself. "Faciality" is a term taken from Deleuze and Guattari's analysis of the figure of White Man or "the typical European" in *A Thousand Plateaus*; it shapes in their work a theory of "majority." A human face can but need not entail "faciality," just as in psychoanalysis the penis can, usually does, but need not represent the phallus. The face can form in any "white wall/black hole" system:[5] it is a binarizing mechanism operating at the intersection of a semiotics of *significance* (a paranoid, despotic regime of interpretation, "never without a white wall upon which it inscribes its signs and redundancies"), and a semiotics of *subjectification* (a passional, or "monomaniac," authoritarian regime of prophecy, "never without a black hole in which it lodges its consciousness, passion and redundancies") (167).[6]

An excellent example of the "social production of face" (181) is the relentlessly redundant and self-signifying corporate architecture represented here (fig. 4.1) by the golden turret on the shaft of Sydney Tower—along with all the hyperbolic interpretive discourse, journalistic as well as academic, that described the "changing face" of the Metropolis throughout the 1980s. It is all the more appropriate to refer the concept of faciality to a tourist-telecommunications monument in that the face for Deleuze and Guattari has, "as a correlate of great importance," the formation of *landscape* (172). With their revolving restaurants and viewing decks, tourist towers not only exist to create a landscape for consumption but also, in their role as must-see *objects* dominating the tourist city, help to "populate" with faces the landscape they create.

The concept of "face" does not necessarily give us a better way of thinking about corporate architecture than the psychoanalytic concepts commonly used in cultural theory; I have no intention of structuring my argument around a rivalry between monumental masculine "faces" on the horizon of modern European thought. In shifting from a penis/phallus analysis to a face/faciality analysis, I merely wish to analyze a critical media act (the making of a film called *A Spire*) that seems to require some such shift if I am to assess its significance in the context in which it occurred.

I do not find it useful to construct an unmediated mirror exchange between a theoretical discourse on the one hand, and an object or practice of popular culture on the other ("Here is a bit of *A Thousand Plateaus*, there is a building, THEY MATCH!"). Just as I prefer historical analysis of tourist space, so I want to begin "in the milieu" (or the middle), as Deleuze and Guattari say, created by *popular* theories that develop in and around tourist places. This does not mean effacing my class position and identifying in fantasy with "the people." It does mean trying to define problems in relation to those locally circulating discourses in which the social significance of my objects of study, and thus the stakes involved in studying them, may be defined. I emphasize "circulating"; the local is not a closed place of con-

4.1 Chris Hilton on the face of Sydney Tower.
Source: *A Spire*, Riverheart Productions, 1988.

tainment but a space produced in movement, and the middle, for Deleuze and Guattari, "is by no means an average; on the contrary, it is where things pick up speed" (25).

So I begin with a quotation from a Sydney-based property developer, John Bond, who said, one day in 1987, through clenched teeth on Sydney radio:

The tower is not an ego thing.
You don't spend a billion dollars on ego.[7]

I. EGO THING

Now, after following the long saga of Donald Trump's activities in New York I have a suspicion that John Bond, in his pugnacious claim to be asserting a universal of capitalist common sense, actually expressed a profoundly un-American assumption. In a culturally comparable milieu of corporate U.S.A., it seems almost to go without saying (as least, it did in the late 1980s) that if you have a billion dollars to spend on ego, you do it in a very big way.

While this kind of casual comparison is dubious cultural analysis, it does raise questions of local resonance, and this is my point. What is John Bond disavowing in Sydney, and why? What is at stake in his refusal to conflate a building form with a concept in pop psychology? One way of approaching these problems is to interrogate more closely the terms of Bond's assertion. My first question, however, is not "what *is* 'the tower,' if it isn't an ego thing?" (he has already replied: an investment), but "what, in that case, is an *ego* thing? what is it that the tower is not?"

One thing that was certainly at stake for John Bond in 1987 was a chance to hit back at critics. In insisting that "ego" was not the prime mover in his plans to put a ninety-seven-story "Skytower" into a patch of high Victoriana still left in the Sydney CBD, Bond was responding to one of the most persistent, reductive, and satisfying insults of urban popular criticism: a big tall building asserts a big male ego; but if he needs to assert it . . . it can't really be *big*.

On this occasion, an aspersion had been cast against the ego things of a whole gang of "cowboy" developers by Andrew Briger, a former Deputy Lord Mayor of Sydney. When Briger said that "there is something to do with personal ego among this new breed that perhaps they think they can swing it,"[8] he was questioning their claims of having the power to break the city's planning codes, rather than the formal thrust of their buildings. Another property boom was beginning: one that turned out to be the biggest yet in Sydney's wildly speculative history, and that would leave city office space, at the end of 1989, the fifth most expensive in the world after Tokyo, London City, London West End, and Hong Kong. Skytower was only one of the megatower projects arousing media attention, and not the largest at that: corporations were dreaming once again of spires equipped with launching pads and airship docking facilities; developers were bragging openly of their intimacies with a sympathetic (Labor) State government. One proposed to build 115 storeys above some two-story working-class houses in the oldest part of the city.[9]

Many developers were under attack. But for John Bond, son of Alan

Bond—since bankrupted, jailed, and disgraced, but in 1987 a beer baron, a media super-mogul, and the owner of a company called BIG (Bond International Gold)—dealing personally with castration threats was a routine PR affair. One Skytower cartoon expressed the desires of many Sydney citizens toward the Bond dynasty by having the father's huge Swan Lager tourist blimp (curse of suburban skies at the time) fly splat into the quivering side of the son's enormous urban protrusion.[10]

Popular mockery of the tower form as a (male) "ego" thing involves some ambiguities. It is vaguely anti-phallic: while it assumes that a tower is a "phallic symbol" (in this code, a penis extension), the force of the insult is that someone's *ego* is also a penis extension: in the vernacular, "that bloke thinks with his dick." (This, presumably, is partly what Bond was denying on his own behalf, rather than that desire can be invested in making a lot of money.) But at the same time, a controlled and controlling "masculinity" is reaffirmed as the norm of public conduct. An ego thing is shameful because too prominent, too visible to others; one is caught, or exposed, at "doing" an ego thing; it's a form of unseemly display, and thus a sign of effeteness (why else should Bond deny it?)—like carrying a poodle, or sporting a personalized number plate on an ostentatious car.

The ambiguities arise with the cultural possibility of those associations, rather than with the theoretically well-grounded feeling that an overt or "unveiled" penile display is something other, and something less, than phallic.[11] On the one hand, such mockery works as a form of reductive magic: tall buildings shrivel to the status of minor social pretensions and personality defects; the awesome corporate power that they represent, and that they generate, is denied significance, in the kind of gesture that Andrew Ross calls "no respect."[12] On the other hand, this popular one-liner also seems to act as a form of bad timing: it misses the point about the role of the "urbanization of capital" in creating economic and social inequities, precisely at a time when its operations in our cities are reaching new heights of intensity and savagery, directly affecting our lives.[13] Among the contributing factors to this particular boom was a huge growth in tourism for the Bicentenary; the eviction of low-income tenants to make way for hotels and luxury accommodation to spectacularize the city for visitors was one of the immediate causes of homelessness in Sydney during this period.[14]

But is it just bad timing? In its Australian usage, the urban comedy of castration relies for its effect not just on phallus jokes (transnational signifiers of a problem of power) but on the codes of an old egalitarian vernacular—one massively mocked by 1980s megatower developments, but fluently and effectively spoken by populist entrepreneurs like the Bonds. For to scorn a tower as the projection of a pretentious personality, you have to accept that showing "ego" is undesirable anyway: having it is one thing, flaunting it, another. You need to be able to find it comic that a subject of wealth and power should presume himself superior to others, and then advertise his position. "Ego," in this context, is an *act* of *exhibiting* an unfortunate subjectivity ("making a spectacle of oneself").

This is, of course, a traditional populist way to miss the point about wealth and power. Egalitarian culture in Australia could always imply a policing of appearances ("leveling") without a politics of reform. If showing one's claim to distinction was a solecism ("sticking out like a sore thumb"), having one might be accepted, like a penis, as a perfectly natural fact. To this day, a hostile term for the act of attacking the rich, the privileged, or the powerful in Australia is "cutting down tall poppies." This metaphor was used in 1989 by Alan Bond himself in a speech at the Australian National Gallery to open an exhibition of six paintings from his collection—including his prize possession, van Gogh's *Irises.* Comparing his own financial and legal troubles with van Gogh's artistic struggles, Bond claimed affinity with the impressionists because both he and they had persisted despite the "criticism and mockery" their respective aspirations had received.[15]

Purity and Mixity

> . . . not all towers are frozen objects of purity;
> not all distance is aesthetic.
>
> —PETER CRYLE[16]

In professional discourses on high-rise towers and the city, there is or should be no question of denying the complexity and heterogeneity of the forces transforming urban skylines, nor of conflating a building form with a putative psychosexual cause. One would expect most critics to share with John Bond some version of Ada Louise Huxtable's basic premise that the tall building form is not only a celebration of modern technology but "a product of zoning and tax law, the real-estate and money markets, code and client requirements, energy and aesthetics, politics and speculation. Not least . . . it is the biggest investment game in town."[17]

Yet some recent cultural theory, not necessarily concerned with the actualities of spatial restructuring in particular places, has also developed a habit of magically shrinking towers. In spite of their manic proliferation in city and regional centers all over the world in the 1980s, some writers found ways to declare the new towers archaic; not simply "old-fashioned," but ontologically *residual,* mere left-overs from an earlier phase of development. Instead of being an "ego" projected in space, the tower form figures as an after-image of a previous moment of collective advance through time—one now left behind in the long march of the commodity through culture.

In any work inspired by Robert Venturi, for example, "the new monumentality" is represented not as "tall and imposing" but as "long and low," following an opposition that privileges those regional landscapes in which, for whatever mix of demographic, economic, historic, and cultural factors, mall-freeway systems prevail over tower-freeway systems (the symbiotic relations of which are ignored). Long-and-lowness then becomes a more "true" expression in space of the *temporal* development of an essential Being of Capital. This is explicit in Jean Baudrillard's *America*, where the "real" America is located not in "vertical" New York, but in the desert (the zero degree of long-and-lowness), and on the freeway. In another version, Paul Virilio provides a much more subtle myth of tower archaism with his notion that all "urban sites" are in themselves a mode of persistence or inertia in face of the shattering impact of advanced technologies. The new monumentality is not long and low but invisible; it can be read only in "the monumental wait for service in front of machinery." The position of overview here is no longer a matter of altitude, but of an opto-electronic interface operating in real time.[18]

Most interestingly, for my purposes, Robert Somol announces (without leaving monumental old Chicago) "that today a new mode of power operates and . . . verticality is its first casualty."[19] In a witty reading of Helmut Jahn's State of Illinois Center as an urban ruin, Somol ironically proclaims verticality "dead" in the sense that the city is now literally made of phantoms, its postmodern towers regressive "time machines" or "stylistic second comings" concerned with replicating time, rather than conquering space, in a process of self-referential "cloning." This logic actually leads Somol's deliberately hypertheoreticist discourse back around to restating that fundamental popular insult: "Jahn's simulacral tower" he says "has nothing to do with verticality and vigor"—it is "a prosthesis, a *dildo*" (100, emphasis mine).

There now seems to be parallel between the arts of populist bad timing, and theoreticist wishful thinking. In both acts of comic reduction (tower to penis, tower to dildo), the critical discourse affirms its own performative powers ("saying makes it so"). Somol, furthermore, uses a version of Fredric Jameson's familiar thesis on the "collapse of critical distance" under postmodernism in order to claim that in the implosive space of our simulacral cities ("collapsing into their dead centers of rehabilitation"), it is always already impossible to distinguish critique from affirmation. So discourse can be effective only *as* performance—"a subtle ambiguity, a style that will . . . usually go unnoticed" (115).

A problem arises, however, in the form of a difference over "style" between simulacral and popular criticism. From the latter's perspective, it is not at all clear that a dildo would have "nothing to do" with verticality or vigor. Indeed, a dildo might well be considered the ideal form of both: while any object can of course be diverted to other uses, being vertical and vigorous is pretty much what dildos are for in a first instance, and prostheses are often treated as comic in popular culture because of their unequivocality compared to the ambiguities, and the frailties, of flesh. A dildo in this context represents purity of function and singularity of purpose, unlike the penis, which is mixed, and multiple. To mock a tower-phallus as "really" a penis is thus to emphasize the vulnerability of the penis. To mock a tower-phallus as "really" a *dildo* is to predicate, on the contrary, the greater power of the (absent) penis as the ideal phallic form. Somol's joke assumes that a dildo can be only a "phantom" substitute for "the real thing," the penis-phallus: it depends on the organicist "depth" nostalgia shared by Baudrillard's theory of simulation and Jameson's concept of critical distance, and in this it is quite distinct from a populist emphasis on controlling surface appearance.

Finally, I note that towers are in disfavor nowadays as representing the privileged place of annunciation not only of "Faustian" modernity in general, but also of totalizing theory and "meta-narrative" in particular.[20] In a gesture repeatedly cited today, de Certeau described coming down from the top of the World Trade Center as an act of leaving the solitary, voyeuristic, stasis-imposing position of Master-planning, in order to walk into a bustling, tactile space of practice, eventfulness, and creativity, the street.[21] This is also a story about walking away from a facializing "vision" of structuralism.

Yet de Certeau's move from summit to street reinscribes a theory-practice opposition, semantically projected as "*high*" vs. "*low*" ("elite" vs. "popular") "*static*" vs. "*dynamic*" ("structure" vs. "history") "*seeing*" vs. "*doing*" ("control" vs. "creativity," and ultimately, "power" vs. "know-how"), that actually blocks the possibility of walking away at all.[22] In fact, de Certeau's visit to the World Trade Center is a way of revisiting a history, as well as a place, mapping all over again the "grid" of binary oppositions within which so much debate about structuralism was conducted (by Sartre and Lévi-Strauss, among others). "The tower" here is an allegory of the structural necessity for a politics of resistance based on a bipolar model of power to maintain the imaginary position of mastery it must then endlessly disclaim.[23]

My problem has more to do with town planning than with structuralism. Reading de Certeau's text, along with the others I've mentioned, I experience a revulsion of common sense, an urge to retort that in the overdeveloped world we are not now living in a great age of "master" planning (nor, for that matter, of general theory in cultural criticism), and that this should make a difference to the terms we're going to use, and the "spatial stories" we tell. Whatever else one might want to say about it, the entrepreneurial city of the 1980s was not *la ville radieuse*.[24] Indeed, de Certeau himself made the move "down" from the symbolic position of Planning precisely in order to note that "the Concept-city is decaying" (95).

So I want to turn now to some spatial stories from my own entrepreneurial city, and some discourses about towers that were also active during the real estate boom, but did not involve either a populist reduction ("cutting things down to size") or an intellectual ritual of renouncing the heights ("getting down"). The first of these involves the classic figure in which myths of altitude, property, and archaism may converge.

II. KING KONG

> *Contrary to popular belief, King Kong did not die during that embarrassing incident on New York's Empire State Building. Instead, with assistance from Fay Gray [sic] . . . he migrated to Sydney, Australia. However, they had not anticipated on one thing. . . .*
> "KONG, YOU'RE NOT SAFE HERE, SPIRAL-LING RENTALS OUT OF CONTROL, INFLA-TION, WHERE WILL YOU STAY? . . . "
>
> —"KING KONG: THE MOMENT OF FINAL DECISION"[25]

In June 1989, the "PM Advertising" agency launched a King Kong theme promotion of office space for sale in a building in the Sydney CBD. PM declared that the concept was "perfect for the AWA Building since it shares a lot in common . . . with New York's Empire State Building." The concept was also ambitious. Built in 1939, a mildly ornate office block with a vague reminiscence of the Eiffel Tower on top (a radio tower that better resembles the RKO Pictures logo), the Amalgamated Wireless (Australasia) Ltd. Building—once, it is true, Sydney's tallest—is thirteen stories high (fig. 4.2).

The Kong campaign was an elaborate affair. One columnist saw in its extravagance a sign that the crash was coming: for "In the Know" (*Weekend Australian* 24–25 June), such "bizarre" efforts to publicize space worth $7,000 per square meter meant the panic of pending downturn, not the frenzy of a boom. A huge advertisement spilled across the investment pages of every major newspaper in the country. Its main feature was "King Kong: The Moment of Final Decision," a comic strip printed over two consecutive right-hand pages to heighten the narrative tension. On the first page, the comic was framed by two photographs and two simulated news reports— one about the King Kong theme's success in attracting investor attention, the other about the "increasing demand" for owner-occupier space, as rentals in the CBD reached $1,000 per square meter. A close reading of the text couldn't miss its rigid binary structure. Its overelaboration was also a little bit puzzling; the design was very messy, the ad poorly differentiated from unrelated copy occupying the rest of the page. But on scanning the comic across both pages, the clutter of pairs on the first page eventually made sense.

The comic begins with the famous couple in Sydney. Clinging to the top

4.2 AWA Building, Sydney. Source: *Building* 24 October 1939, 16.

of the AWA tower, Kong and Fay consider their options. Fay has a conservative view of real estate and a nostalgic image of Kong. She wants to run away
from the city and take him Back to Nature ("a BIG ROCK not too far
away"). Her dream home is Uluru (Ayers Rock) in the central desert. But
Kong is a natural real estate animal ("this building looks even better than
the other one with a tower"); with one glance at the quality finish and fabulous views of his prime CBD location, he knows he's sitting on a good investment. So Fay, ever faint-hearted, issues an ultimatum from the bottom
right-hand corner of the page: "Well KONG. It's the AWA Building or me.
What's it going to be? . . . " And when we turn over, King Kong's "natural"
decision is:

KING KONG DROPS FAY GRAY

In fact, the plunging lines of the drawing imply that King Kong *throws* Fay
Gray; a reading confirmed in one of the vertical blocks of fine-print filler
("Poor Fay, thrown over for a more attractive proposition worth really big
bananas in the future") that, by flanking and supporting the central image
of the tower, act visually to enhance its soaring, phallic singularity.

With this clear designer solution to the bothersome clutter of couples,
Kong as corporate beast takes the hard decisions and regains his killer instinct—and when the Beast at last kills Beauty, Fay's domesticated values
of "security" go with her. For Fay is not just a typical tourist seeking, with
Baudrillard et al., authenticity in long and lowness in the desert. Her vision
of making a *home* at Uluru in the "heart" of the continent is a prime suburban fantasy of a stable tradition of meaning. Famous as "solid rock / sacred
ground" in a late 1970s pop song for Aboriginal land rights (but just as
"Solid Rock" in a simultaneously appearing finance company billboard),
"Ayers Rock" is the center of a classic white national imaginary.[26] In rejecting this "suburban" escapist tradition, Kong knows he'll be more at home
in the tough environment of rampant speculation. If his final decision is an
act of passion, rather than reason, then the entrepreneurially "wild" city
really is Kong's natural habitat; and, as the fine print again makes clear, if
push comes to shove, Kong can survive a crisis by trading on his reputation—"all he had to do was sit tight and wait for the movie offers and product endorsements to come in."

The invitation to take this story allegorically is almost irresistible, beginning with the arrival of Kong and Fay as emblems of mobile investment
capital flying around the Pacific Rim. In its brutal explicitness, this ad is a
blaring manifesto for real estate speculation, and the striation of space it
entails—the dividing of city space by enclosure and bordering, the segmen-
ting of populations, a monumental centralizing of corporate wealth and
power ("not to hegemonize the city in the fashion of the great modernist
buildings," as Mike Davis points out, "but rather to polarize it into radically

antagonistic spaces").[27] In more conventional terms, simply by identifying Fay with all the explicit social referents of her image—anxious "housewives," struggling "home-owners,"[28] nostalgic suburban dreamers, even Aboriginal people, all the *inhabitants* of a place—this image of Fay's expulsion from King Kong's urban paradise celebrates the consignment of large numbers of people to the status of "waste products"[29] of spatial restructuring. "The Moment of Final Decision" is a comedy of displacement, eviction, homelessness, the feminization of poverty, and of the end of egalitarianism as a slogan for everyday life.

It is also, though more obliquely, about gentrification and the role of that layer of intellectuals whom Scott Lash and John Urry call, following Pierre Bourdieu, "the new cultural petite-bourgeoisie"—workers in all occupations involving presentation, representation, and the supply of "symbolic" goods and services.[30] For if one were to read "The Moment of Final Decision" allegorically with any honesty, the potential social positioning (and "home-making" practices) of many intellectuals, including feminist theorists, today would be, whatever our commitments and however much our hearts may be with Fay, in fact more like that of the gorilla. However, it is not a matter of noting and perhaps aestheticizing a cynical celebration of our role as the avant-garde of the urban real estate business (recently a subject of criticism from Yvonne Rainer's film *The Man Who Envied Women* to Julie Burchill's novel *Ambition*).[31] The critical question is what *kind* of positioning "The Moment of Final Decision" ascribes to the cultural petite-bourgeoisie.

It is tempting to see it simply as a story of self-interested apes in their rehabbed ivory towers. A great tradition could support this interpretation. In his famous analysis of Goethe's *Faust*, Marshall Berman describes the "tragedy of development" partly as a progression from one place of elevation ("an intellectual's lonely room . . . an abstracted and isolated realm of thought") to another, the "observation tower" from which Faust oversees a world of production and exchange, "ruled by giant corporate bodies and complex organizations."[32] Reductive and parodic as "The Moment of Final Decision" may be, it does draw on this tradition. King Kong flinging Fay from the tower is not only repeating the gesture of Faust's abandonment of Gretchen (destroying the woman who helped make him what he was, and so, destroying his past), but also, in the process, he is transforming his cultural status.

King Kong was classically a victim of Enlightening intellectuals (explorers, film-makers, geologists); in his affinity with savages and women, Kong was the *counter*-Faustian figure of tradition, archaism, and myth. Flipping Fay back into that role (Woman as nature, nostalgia, "home") and then rejecting her appeal has the effect of installing Kong as doubly faithless to his origins. He becomes not only a snob ("happy . . . [to share] the area with some pretty classy neighbours"), and an aesthete ("maybe jungle green walls and carpeting contrasted by a small waterfall near the lifts might be quite relaxing"), but a class traitor—in short, a yuppie.

There is a problem with this, however. While Kong contemplates the city from Faust's special place, the top of the tower, he is not himself in the *position* of the developer. This King Kong is a consumer: a "new" consumer, an active and discriminating reader of advertising images ("well, take a look at this . . . "), a speculator in signs. (This is why Kong, rather than Fay, provides a figure of my own activity inscribed in the image, a *mise-en-abyme* of my reading so far). The solitary Faustian position here has been disseminated into a bustling network of cultural producers, "ideas people"—property developers, real estate agents, marketing experts, advertisers and promoters, city planners, architects, builders, interior designers. Above all, this *text*, rather than the urban situation it operates within (to make a crucial distinction), is not a tragedy but a crazy comedy of boom and bust that, in its material context of grim headlines about imminent property market collapse, said to and of King Kong the new consumer: climb now, crash later.

It may seem fanciful to assimilate a marketing campaign to any discourse on intellectuality. However, there is a minor figure in the Kong assemblage, one invisible in the image but a key player in the story. One of the "news" reports on the first page notes that a special "launch function" was held on a roof-top opposite the AWA Building with Bill Collins, a celebrity "nostalgia buff" film critic. "In the Know" revealed that Collins's task was to "resurrect the story" of King Kong, while a thirteen-meter model was hung from the AWA radio tower. In taking his place in the network of *animateurs* at the PM launch, Collins, the "Golden Years of Hollywood" revivalist, was literally embodying the self-promotional strategy by which Lash and Urry define the "cultural petite-bourgeoisie." Always threatened with downward mobility, they (we) encourage "symbolic rehabilitation projects" that "give (often postmodern) cultural objects new status as part of rehabilitation strategies for their own careers" (295).

Preclusions

> . . . the architecture of redevelopment constructs the built
> environment as a medium, one we literally inhabit, that
> monopolizes popular memory by controlling the representa-
> tion of its own history. It is truly an evicting architecture.

—ROSALYN DEUTSCHE[33]

Having taken an allegorical reading of a postmodern "cultural" object to the point where it can only question its social function, I now want to ask whether "rehabilitation" and "resurrection" really describe what we're dealing with in "The Moment of Final Decision," and whether these terms are sufficient to whatever it is about "postmodern objects" that we are deal-

ing with when confronting commercial rhetorics so explicit about their social, as well as economic, function. It is too easily assumed that once "images
rather than products have become the central objects of consumption"[34]
then a reality once ontologically distinct from the image has undergone
some kind of death—and that the language of necromancy is more apt to
deal with the results than cultural history or political activism.

Robert Somol's necromantic reading of the State of Illinois Center is a
case in point: its terms lead to the conclusion that "we must . . . abandon
the language of struggle (and the concomitant notion of liberation) which
only tightens the tourniquet of power (and futility) around us" (115). The
only response left is "style," a mode of aestheticized knowingness. But as
Rosalyn Deutsche points out, the architecture of redevelopment is precisely
about struggle, and *displacement.* Other versions of popular memory, other
representations of history, other "styles" of experiencing the built environment are violently expelled by the forces of redevelopment as part of the
process of excluding and impoverishing people, of colonizing and "abstract-
ing" urban space.

It is crucial to choose carefully the terms we use to conceptualize the
semiotic aspect of that process. Serious consequences follow for cultural
politics: if one phantom city seems much like any another, if each instance
of redevelopment is made interchangeable with every other, social criticism
and political opposition alike are soon caught up, by this logic, in a cir-
cuit of redundancy, and reduced to routine gestures useful only for the theory market. One problem with the necromantic model of simulation so
popular in the 1980s is an incapacity to make distinctions that "ghosts,"
albeit parodically, the process of abstraction it describes. I want to argue
this briefly by entering the permanently present citational network within
which PM Advertising was operating. King Kong is a useful figure for considering the question of cultural reproduction, precisely because in *cinema*
history he has "died" (and been reborn in his own image, the ideal simulacrum) in so many places and times.

For example, at the end of his 1977 essay "Touche pas à la femme
blanche," Yann Lardeau agrees with PM Advertising that King Kong survived his fall from the Empire State Building.[35] Kong's "real" death probably occurred on the footpaths of Paris, during the publicity campaign to
launch John Guillermin's 1976 remake of *King Kong* in France. A sixteen-
meter, six-and-a-half-tonne King Kong model was assembled by thirty tech-
nicians, animated by electronic wiring and hydraulic pumps, and laid out
flat on the Champs-Elysées for passersby to file past on a platform above.

For Lardeau, this scene of banalized tourist vision and technologically
programmed dreaming (the scene of the simulacrum) is funereal. What lay
on the footpath was something material and "verifiable" that contradicted
the "life" represented by the primal cinematic *King Kong* made by Schoedsack and Cooper in 1933. In that film—so powerful a myth that all later

versions refer to it as their origin—Kong was a force of mystery, terror, and above all, monstrous uncertainty. Neither man nor beast, Kong *was* the ambivalence of the border between Past and Present, Nature and Culture (and therefore, a figure of incest). Kong is drastically changed, Lardeau argues, by the ecologically conscious farce of Guillermin's Oil Crisis remake. Merely a big, vegetarian gorilla hopelessly in love, Kong in 1976 was no longer a border figure (or, like some of his descendants in *Son of Kong, Super Kong, Baby Kong*, etc., a parody of one), but a "site" of confrontation between ecologists and an oil company, between a science of conservation (zoology) and a science of development (geology). This Kong dies by default, not necessity—he should have been put in the zoo.

The Champs-Elysées robot is just an extension of the technical credits of Guillermin's film. So Lardeau wonders if King Kong is still the subject of *King Kong*: pretextual rather than prehistoric, emptied of all ambivalence, he may now be just an occasion for displaying the power of technological expertise. This fits with the cardinal difference between the original and the remake, the shift from the Empire State Building to the World Trade Center (where Kong dies in 1976). For Lardeau, the latter "corresponds to a new phase of capitalist development, in which a bipolar power is redoubled on itself, referring only to itself in a space beyond all content" (123); leaping between the twin towers, Kong is caught in the play of feedback, and so is already finished as a primal force long before he falls.

What could this argument make of 1987 Rehab Kong hanging from a renovated Sydney office block that was only ever a degraded copy of a New York skyscraper? Nothing much, I suspect, or nothing specific (although PM Kong could easily be made to reflect a "third" phase of capitalism in which the postwar system of bipolar power has now been replaced by a multi-centered system representable not by any one monument but by the flows of information that constitute the ad). In fact, the bipolar structure of Lardeau's own frame of reference—original/remake, image/reproduction, reality/technique—can say surprisingly little about the comic positivity of Oil Crisis Kong, except to inscribe in him, as a *non sequitur*, the loss of an older cinema. Lardeau offers an illuminating and poignant reading of Schoedsack and Cooper's film, but his is a structure of comparison that in the end can operate only to generate signs of lack in the present, and to find the present lacking.[36]

Given such a framework, it is correspondingly hard to imagine what to *make* of the diverse King Kongs circulating now in popular culture except to reduce them, improbably, to examples of the Same: a pop-art Kong in a subway T-shirt wanders past the Empire State Building, while a bored "Fay," brushing her hair, holds a mirror as he holds her; a richly colored "Ethnic Arts" card (Mola, Cuna Indians, San Blas Islands, Panama) has KINGON, arms curving round Fay like butterfly wings, surrounded by leaves and flowers; a postcard from a small midwestern town stamps on a *King Kong* panorama of 1933 New York, GREETINGS FROM CHAMPAIGN-URBANA. What can nostalgia for the origin make of a scene from the film *King Kong No Gyakushu* (1967) in which the "real" King Kong does battle with his own simulacrum, a mining-company robot, in front of the Eiffel Tower?[37]

Japanese King Kong has a history about which I know very little. For my reading here, however, the image of King Kong confronting "Mechni-Kong" offers a useful alternative to the original/remake (and "real thing"/dildo) schemata I've discussed so far. I think that the status of the (second-degree) "original" King Kong in *King Kong No Gyakushu* can be defined quite differently from that of the (original) "original" King Kong for Yann Lardeau. The titans blitzing each other near Eiffel's Tower in 1967 do not represent Nature (organic Kong) and Culture (Mechni-Kong), nor the problem of the border between them, but rather a conflict between *mixity* (the hair-covered King Kong model as cyborg), and *purity* (the smoothly unequivocal robot, the dildo). The heroic stature of "mixity" within the terms of this opposition may explain why King Kong, with his ambivalent relationship to power, is most persistently a penis, and not a phallus, myth; hence the proliferation of an arcane literature about the size of King Kong's organ.[38]

An inability to specify such images as potential events—in other words, to read them productively—inhibits the possibility of theorizing cultural practice. An ability to read them repetitively as signs of an Absent Image precludes the thought of "practice" altogether. It is curious, then, that Baudrillard's concept of simulation (death of difference, reference, history, and the real in commodification) remains most influential today through the writings of Marxists like Fredric Jameson and David Harvey, who use it to describe aspects of postmodern culture while discarding its political quietism. Yet this concept precisely depends on a theory of intertextuality that cannot imagine *change*: it recognizes only apocalyptic, thus singular, rupture, and that only in the form of its impossibility as present or future event. For this reason, it is a theory most ill-equipped to come to terms with that *form* of change that Jacques Attali describes in *Noise* as "the minor modification of a precedent"—in other words, with the technique specific to contemporary semiotic economies of serial recurrence.[39]

But if we turn instead to Judith Mayne's 1976 essay on "King Kong and the Ideology of Spectacle"—in its own way an "Oil Crisis" text, discussing the appeal of *King Kong* to American audiences during the Depression—it is possible to see a real difference, a historical change, in King Kong mythology effected by PM's "Moment of Final Decision."[40] In her fine analysis of the workings of sexism and racism in Schoedsack and Cooper's film, Mayne argues that the figure of the Other in the text is defined as an object of spectacle. The white woman, the island natives, and King Kong himself are not only constructed as "other" in ways specific to the conventions of 1930s Hollywood cinema, they are also brought into narrative equivalence as creatures to be *filmed* ("*King Kong* is a film about . . . the making of a film that never is finished") by Carl Denham, the director and "petit-bourgeois entrepreneur."

As a result, socio-economic class comes to function as "the unrepresentable as such" in this imperial economy of spectacle. In Mayne's account, the problem outside the wall or beyond the border in *King Kong* is not to do with incest or impossible congress or with an "untouchable" white female sex: "race and sex are convenient means . . . of forgetting—or repressing— what class is all about" (379). When the petit-bourgeois "cultural" entrepreneur rescues Ann Darrow (Fay Wray) from poverty in New York, a narrative displacement occurs from the scene of the American Depression to a spectacle of exotic sex. The closing scenes of King Kong rampaging through a glittering, prosperous New York (a city as "other" in its way to American Depression audiences, Mayne argues, as the woman, the natives, and Kong) conclude this process of displacement by showing what happens when the entrepreneur loses control of the spectacle: the "laws of representation" are broken down by "this brute reality—so gigantesque that it is unreality itself—that is Kong." But this is not the return of social class to the scene of representation. On the contrary, it "reflects the most fundamental process of displacement operative in *King Kong*." The urban crisis appears, like the Depression for most economists at the time, as something "not fashioned by human beings, but the raw force of nature itself" (384).

Apart from its interest, and its force as a reminder that a "new" cultural class did not pop up overnight, Mayne's reading gives me a basis for defining what *doesn't* happen in 1989 when "KING KONG DROPS FAY GRAY." First, the "corporate beast" now has no need to "naturalize" his actions by opposing savage predation to (economic) reason: the joke is that we know they're the same. Second, "The Moment of Final Decision" is, as the trade critics sensed, a prediction of imminent crisis, not an imaginary resolution of one: the "crash" is accepted, not denied, as intrinsic to the logic of finance capitalism. Third, "The Moment of Final Decision" is a representation of, as well as an exercise in, the process of displacement: by rejecting the "exotic" appeal of "spectacles" of sex and race (Fay Gray's Uluru dreaming), it classifies them as distractions from the real thrills of class conflict and economic passion. Fourth, King Kong now is Carl Denham: there is no crisis *of* representation for the cultural entrepreneur, only crisis *in* representation as he waits for the "movie offers and product endorsements" to secure his shaky future. This is, of course, his big mistake and the biggest joke of the story: the fact that only "image" *is* capital for Kong (and Kong's only capital) is why he will crash, sooner or later, and why the "*cultural* petite bourgeoisie" is the subject of the narrative and the author of the text—but not the addressee of the sales pitch.

PM Advertising's exercise in "simulation" brings the figure of King Kong into the rhetorical and ethical field constituted by a privileged trope of

1980s entrepreneurial or bull market culture that I would call "the *brutal truth.*" This was an ideology of spectacle that rested on the claim that there *is* no "unrepresentable"—no limit now beyond which one cannot go, no desire requiring repression, no conduct, no matter how predatory, that needs to be disavowed. The mock-shock effect of the slogan "KING KONG DROPS FAY GRAY" is thus in Australian terms not only the "brutal truth" that it tells about class, but the way it makes a mockery of the codes still requiring our society to maintain a "classless" appearance. *Wall Street's* Gordon Gekko was perhaps in his heyday the most famous practitioner of the art of brutal truth ("Greed is good. Greed is right. Greed works. Greed clarifies, cuts through and captures the essence of the evolutionary spirit"). In the small world of cultural theory, the rococo writing of Baudrillard— dependent as it was on that formula of perpetual inflation, "ever more *x* than *x*"—functioned not so much in complicity with such neo-Darwinian plain speaking as in counter-point, an elaborate accompanying rhetoric that could only confirm, by its critical helplessness, that bull market "truth" was by nature an incontestable law.

King Kong, however, was not the only cultural entrepreneur dreaming of towers in Sydney at the height of the property boom.

III. THE HUMAN FLY

> *THEY TOLD HIM FROM THE START THAT IT WAS A SUICIDE CLIMB—DANGEROUS ENOUGH DURING THE DAY, EVEN FOR THE MOST EXPERIENCED CLIMBER . . . BUT DEADLY, IMPOSSIBLE AFTER SUNDOWN!*
>
> —THE HUMAN FLY: CASTLE IN THE CLOUDS!

After 1 February 1987, Sydney media were buzzing with reports of a "mystery climber" who had made it to the top of Sydney Tower—and promptly disappeared. TV called him "The Human Fly": newspapers had him dangling 300 meters above "certain death" ("clad in a flame-red climbing suit"), and published dramatic pictures of a tiny figure crawling up the thick cables supporting the Tower's turret. The pictures had come from a "stunned onlooker" who happened to be hanging about with a camera on the roof of a nearby building.

Weeks later, a magazine revealed that the Fly was twenty-six years old, had an engineering degree, worked as a traffic planning consultant and "reckons he's a pretty normal bloke," while "stunned onlooker" evolved into "Glen Kirk," who was "filming a sunrise at the time" that he saw the Fly on the Tower.[41] Then at the beginning of August 1988—just as the property boom in Sydney was nearing its peak—the ABC-TV national network screened *A Spire*, a half-hour documentary by Chris Hilton and Glenn Singleman.

The first film of a series (*I Can't Stop Now*) about people with obsessions, *A Spire* was the story of how and why Chris Hilton had scaled Sydney Tower after six years of planning and preparation; how a mountaineer's fantasy had intensified into an idea of making "a personal statement . . . about the urban environment," and how meeting Glenn Singleman in 1986 had transformed the plan to climb the Tower into a project to make a film about doing it. This project had two components and two goals. One was to ensure that Hilton could climb the Tower without risk of "certain death" for himself or anyone else (Singleman recalls in the film how he had to be convinced it would be "absolutely safe"). The other was making *A Spire* itself.

So this is a double adventure story with two separate happy endings, structured by a time-lapse and a spatial shift between the two (the ascent and the broadcast, the city Tower and the national network). There is a further complication. My object of analysis is actually a text produced during the lapse of time between the two conclusions. *A Spire* exists in two versions, the first of which was a forty-three-minute film made without ABC assistance, but in the hope of persuading a network to buy it. For my second model of social climbing, I want to begin with this "original" version, that can circulate as an independent video.

At this stage, "beginning" isn't easy. *A Spire* is of course impossible to reproduce as accompaniment for an essay. It would also be difficult metonymically to describe "the plot," or to analyze a crucial passage that might "give an idea" of the film, that I must assume most readers won't have seen. However this very problem, familiar to all non-canonical film study and all criticism of temporal arts, allows me to define something unusual about *A Spire* as an adventure story. In contrast to the "punch-line" structure of King Kong's *Moment of Final Decision*—a narrative relentlessly directed, like any one-liner, toward its eventual "singular" outcome—*A Spire* is a narrative of ascent that is neither linear, nor simply "climactic."

Instead, several stories combine in a composite history. Along with footage of the actual climb, there are stories about different people involved, especially Mark Spain, who climbed part of the way up the Tower before deciding to go back down; about the process of researching the Tower's construction, then inventing and testing the climbing tools that might be appropriate to it; about the months of physical and mental preparation in "natural" and urban environments—the Sydney sea-cliffs, a carpark, the tree in an inner-city backyard. These stories drift easily into chat and interview footage: rock-climbers discuss the difference between falling on something "soft," like trees or water, or something "hard," like glass and steel; an Everest climber compares the scaling of Sydney Tower to Christo wrapping an island; various critical responses (from people in the street, a lawyer, an adventurer, a psychiatrist, an architect, a mythologist, an art historian) prolong the *event* of the climb by expanding its significance.

So while *A Spire* is narratively unified by footage from the climb, the extensions and digressions intertwine with it in such a way that the progress of the ascent is constantly interrupted by scenes from other stories, and by others' lines of thought. I say "interrupted," and not "disrupted": a lot of tension builds up in *A Spire*, since most of the footage is from the last, most difficult and least predictable, phase of the climb. What is rather unusual in an "action" adventure is that the tension is not relieved by attaining the obvious goal of the quest (Hilton reaching the top of the Tower), but only with its "anti-climactic" result (once he gets there, nothing happens) and final outcome (he walks away in the street). In fact, the moment of reaching the summit to some extent appears as one "interruption" among others in a fairly smooth process of traveling away from, and then back to, the city streets. I shall return later to the ending of *A Spire*, and to how it represents "overview" not as a position, but as part of a *process*.

First, I want to situate the film in the context of my discussion so far. There is a form of argument influential in cultural studies that would require me now to frame *A Spire* as an allegory of resistance. As a project ongoing throughout the 1987–89 property boom and its attendant social disruptions, the making of *A Spire* (including the "profilmic" event of the climb) inscribes a refusal of entrepreneurial aspirations to dominate and divide up city space. Acting *in* that space, between John Bond's grandiose Skytower dreams and PM Advertising's cynical reason, it should not only bear witness to popular opposition, but provide us with terms of riposte.

Now I think *A Spire* does do this: I do regard it as an act of social criticism and, more strongly, as entailing a practice of opposition and transformation. While there must always be debate about the kind and the scope of political "effectivity" to be claimed for symbolic actions, I do accord them a productive, not a decorative or "aestheticizing," role; I don't mean to flout the expectations that my argument's form has created. However, I also want to learn something from *A Spire*—to respond to, and extend, its productivity. Such learning is one of the purposes of textual analysis, which is not hostile either to generalizing models (on which it depends for its conceptual materials), or to theorization, but rather assumes that the objects we read can provide, through their own material "resistance" to our acts of abstraction,[42] terms for questioning and revising the models we bring to bear. So instead of reading *A Spire* simply as confirming the models of action (resistance, opposition, critique) typically affirmed by cultural studies, I want to read it as inventing a practice for a particular time and place.

Strategy and Tactics

One model of action that immediately seems pertinent to *A Spire* as a critique of entrepreneurial space is de Certeau's powerful distinction in *The Practice of Everyday Life* between strategy and tactics (xi–xx, 34–39). "Strategy" is the name of a mode of action specific to regimes of *place*: it is "the calculus of force-relationships which becomes possible when a subject of will and power (a proprietor, an enterprise, a city, a scientific institution) can be isolated from an 'environment.'" It also requires, and produces, an Other: strategy "assumes a place that can be circumscribed as proper (*propre*) and thus serve as the basis for generating relations with an exterior distinct from it. . . . Political, economic and scientific rationality has been constructed on this model." PM Advertising's image of the spatial and social relations involved in "dropping Fay Gray" is in fact an excellent projection of de Certeau's concept of strategy.

A "tactic," in contrast, is a mode of action determined by *not* having a place of one's own. It is "a calculus which cannot count on a 'proper' (a spatial or institutional localization), nor thus on a border-line distinguishing the other as a visible totality." However this does not imply a dystopian state, or condition, of placelessness; for de Certeau, "the place of a tactic belongs to the other." In other words, as a way of operating available to people displaced and excluded as "Other" by the bordering-actions of strategy, a tactic maintains an *active* relationship to place by means of what he calls an art of "insinuation." Tactics are opportunist: they involve seizing the chance to take what de Certeau calls a "turn" (*un tour*) through the other's terrain, and so depend for their success on a "clever utilization of *time*" (39).

The notion of tactics is not as romantic as it can sound. For one thing, it is parasitic on the notion of strategy: if this means that "tactics" cannot of itself sustain a politics of self-determination for strategically othered people, it also means that it cannot be used to ground an ontology of Otherness, and that individuals cannot be treated, in de Certeau's terms, holistically as full subjects of either strategy or tactics. Furthermore, the distinction itself is not a way of deeming it a privilege to be marginalized, but a way of asking what kinds of action are possible once people historically *have been* marginalized by a specific regime of place. This is why the distinction could underpin, for de Certeau, a theory of popular cultural practice. The popular could be conceptualized as a "way of operating" and an "art of timing" precisely because of its tactical relationship to the so-called consumer society and its strategic installations (motels, supermarkets, television, freeways, high-rise towers . . .).[43]

If we turn to *A Spire* with this distinction in mind, it can help us to read quite closely how the whole project worked. Both the climb and the film were products of an art of very careful "timing." Chris Hilton began what turned out to be a nine-hour climb around midnight on a Saturday, so as to be a long way up the cables around the shaft supporting the turret by sunrise Sunday morning. This meant that the little red Fly could be most advantageously filmed approaching the top of the golden turret with a bright blue sky for backdrop. However, the timing's immediate aim was to avoid alerting the police for as long as possible; hence also the choice of the quietest morning in the week for the "visible" part of the climb.

Scaling a corporate monument without permission is highly illegal ("trespassing, disturbing the peace, public nuisance," smiles Lesley Power, lawyer), and Sydney Tower is fully strategic in de Certeau's sense. Historically one of the inaugural buildings of the "architecture of redevelopment" in Sydney, a tourist tower opened on top of a shopping complex in 1981 to attract people "back to the City to shop,"[44] it is a place entirely proper to the life-assurance company that owns it (Australian Mutual Provident Society), the administration that inhabits it, and the security organizations that police its relation to the "exterior" created by the residents and tourists of Sydney.

So Chris Hilton's "turn" on the Tower involved a risk not only of being arrested at the end, but also of forcible "rescue" half-way up. This has consequences for the narrative tactics of the film. Since so much of the narration insists on the advance elimination of any real danger that Hilton might fall or need to be rescued, thus endangering others, the site of tension is displaced from those images of a tiny figure dangling in vast space that could, and in action adventures usually would, invite us to anticipate death for the hero and still expect a happy ending. While such images in *A Spire* are awesome indeed, there is just as much anxiety about what happens *after* the climb. The tension is stretched across the accumulation in time of delays, hitches, and moments of frustration as the sun rises higher in the sky. The climb takes three hours longer than planned: time to negotiate Mark Spain's descent, time to force a too-tight hanger inch by inch along rusted beams, time to edge around the base of the turret to find an unblocked window-cleaning track—enough time for there to be a guard in the turret looking out as the Fly crawls past the window. This is one reason why the sense of climax overflows the moment of reaching the summit. There is still the problem of getting *away* from the other's terrain.

There is another sense in which *A Spire* can be seen as a tactical response to constraints imposed by "strategy." In a speech to the camera near the beginning, Chris Hilton names the genre problem that the film will have to negotiate: "if this was a tale about climbing a mountain in some wild mountain range of the world, it would be a boys' own adventure story, a tale of survival against all the odds. . . . " These days a rather dismissive term for any bland all-male adventure, the phrase "boys' *own*" points to the formal constraints that not only define the place of the genre in Western action cinema—relative or absolute exclusion of women, isolation of (white) males as "proper" subjects of action, and exteriorization of Nature (and Natives) as "other" to Man—but can also frame in advance expectations of any film in which, as in *A Spire*, a man *does* have an adventure and survive against the odds.

As a way of preempting this response, Hilton claims that shifting the scene from mountain to tower can modify the genre ("this building is in the middle of the city, so it brings to bear a whole lot of other aspects . . . "). Other speakers insist that natural and built environments are continuous, not external to each other, while scenes of men and women rock-climbing make the same point visually when one image includes the spires of the city rising just across the water from the cliffs. More strongly, the boys' own adventure is modified by a series of questions in the film about the distinctions that do exist socially between nature and the city, questions that *follow* from deciding to treat them as the same: "the legal aspects, issues of social responsibility, issues of the built environment and what it's for . . . who owns the outside of a building? is it the public, whose visual space it dominates? or is it the owner of the building?"

In this way, something that may be called a critical difference is introduced to the boys' own adventure. This difference is "critical" in the simple sense that it involves insinuating a space of social analysis into the place of heroic action, but also in the more complicated sense that questioning the proprieties of the climb itself (those "legal aspects") immediately leads the film to question what counts socially as "proper" representation: "is it responsible to climb a building and put your life at risk in front of others? will it encourage young children to climb buildings and put their lives in danger? is that a bad thing? people that come to try and rescue you, will it endanger their lives? will it deface the building? all these sorts of things. . . . " What helps to make this a tactical use of the boys' own adventure, rather than a "critique" from the genre's outside, is Chris Hilton's reluctance throughout to claim the place of the outlaw, propriety's easy opposite: "all these sorts of things are *issues*, because I'm not a criminal and I don't want to break laws and be locked up in jail." Climbing the Tower is never presented as violation or transgression, but as a use of the "place" of the other for purposes alien to it.

Related to this, finally, is the aesthetic practice of the film. If *A Spire* is not a wham-bam action adventure, neither is it an avant-gardist experiment declaring its own deconstructiveness. It presents itself modestly as a fun documentary with talking heads, and amazing scenes. Yet this is why the adventure simply can't be "boy's own." The editing-in of side-stories and interviews casually guarantees a collective production of the whole *A Spire* adventure. A network of "ideas people" figures in the film, some discussing issues of ethics, law, and aesthetics after the event, while others work in advance on the problems of danger and safety; there are a couple of scenes of slide shows, in which a group uses photographs of the Tower to talk through tactics for climbing it. On the level of the film-making adventure, this use of what is now a fairly conservative documentary method with strong links to the great tradition of Australian social realism probably helped to "insinuate" an independent film that cheerfully confesses, theorizes, and depicts a symbolic crime against property into the state-owned broadcasting network.

At this point, it is useful to ask, "so what?" The strategy/tactics distinction can show how a critical practice may bypass various obstacles to succeed "against the odds"; it is pragmatic in the best sense of the term. It also gives me a way of arguing that *A Spire* counts as popular culture while "The Moment of Final Decision" does not; a claim that perhaps risks essentialism, but takes its model of action not from the ethos and practices of postmodern corporate culture but from a critical riposte to them that follows a different logic. This is why I have not presented *A Spire* as a binary opponent to PM Advertising's vision of the city, although that could be done in several ways: grabbing a place vs. reclaiming space, ownership vs. tenancy, eviction vs. infiltration, investment vs. enjoyment, exchange value vs. use value, cynical vanguardism vs. utopian collective practice, brutality and cruelty vs. care and respect for life.

Yet without some way of bringing all this back home to concrete social situations, some way of showing how and why a "different" logic can *matter* and what its local inflections might be, criticism is confined to, at best, rehearsing a list of oppositional values, or at worst, producing pious but empty reassurances that there's something happening somewhere.[45] I'm not sure that the strategy/tactics distinction can always tell us much about what is at stake, or what has been achieved, in a given set of circumstances. What *follows* from reading *A Spire* as a tactical operation of temporarily occupying, rather than territorially claiming, that much contested position at the top of a high-rise tower? What kind of "aspiration" did *A Spire* involve? The title of the film carries overtones of a small business slogan, the enterprise ethos of the "pioneer" school of Outward Bound adventure, or the improving profiles of personal success produced by the Sunday tabloids. So what kind of "popular" critique did *A Spire* produce of the terrain on which it took place?

Rivalry and Simulation

> *I wanted to make a personal statement by climbing it, about the urban environment. I thought it would be a nice image to climb, that people would get a kick out of seeing someone scale down the tallest building in Sydney to a human scale—just one individual, under their own power, bringing down a massive building which sets itself up as being huge, and impenetrable, and intimidating.*
>
> —Chris Hilton

The Human Fly is an unusual superhero. Unlike Spiderman, Batman, et al., he is not a paranoid crime fighter but a "passional monomaniac" (in Deleuze and Guattari's terms) with a social conscience. He just likes to climb and do stunts, but he gets involved in other people's problems and gives the money he makes to charity. This eccentric relation to the Law was always part of his identity as a Marvel Comics creation. In *Castle in the*

Clouds! (3, 1977), readers' letters on the "Fly Papers" page make sure that we don't miss the point: "The Fly is not a neurosis-ridden 'everyman' stumbling into a radioactive accident, thus gaining super-powers. His 'sense of responsibility' doesn't tell him to go out and fight crime as a way of serving humanity. . . . The first issue in which I see the Fly patrolling New York looking for bad guys is the last issue I buy" (Rich Fifield, Monterey, CA).

Reassuring Rich and other readers, editor Archie Goodwin underlines another of the Fly's distinctive features: "we have no plans of turning the Human Fly into a crime-fighter—simply because in *real* life, he *isn't* one!" While carrying the standard disclaimers of similarity intended to any person "living or dead," the Human Fly comics also insist that their hero has as his counterpart a "real-life death-defier" (in fact, "we . . . will see what we can do to have the *real* Human Fly appear in this mag with his two-dimensional *other self*"). Always already double, originally both "model" and "copy," the Human Fly further evolves as simulacrum (a copy of a copy of a copy) in peculiarly unstable ways.

It is not a matter of endless remakes. According to Michael Dean, the Fly does seem to have started out in the 1970s as a real person who had prosthetic surgery after an accident, and then kept on doing stunts, before becoming the Marvel hero who became a media "model" for other real climbers who may, or may not, have known the "original" Fly.[46] A media image of one of these crawling up the Sears Building figures briefly in *A Spire* as a model for Chris Hilton ("I looked in the newspaper and I read an article about a guy who climbed a building in America"). By the time the media in 1987 could shout about SYDNEY'S HUMAN FLY, the question of the original and the copy is academic in the popular sense. All it takes to read that headline is an everyday knowledge that "Human Fly" historically is the name of an action genre in which real people and media images are productively mixed up.

An interesting corollary of the doubled character of the Human Fly is that he is also corporeally "mixed." In name and in physical capacity a man-insect, a hybrid of nature, the Fly is in body a cyborg, a product of science ("Someday I'll have to thank the docs for boosting my skeletal structure with steel . . ."). He cannot be a figure of the dividing-line between "Man" and "Other," like the original, oneiric King Kong. On the contrary, his mixity is often treated as a sign of his human frailty. As soon as the Fly mentally thanks the docs for giving him fingers to dig into cliffs ("and . . . I'm the one who was supposed to be crippled for life!"), he is attacked by a giant condor, a "ROBOT-DRONE." In a clash that recalls the battle scene from *King Kong No Gyakushu*, the Fly's hybrid vulnerability is challenged by the impervious purity of a mechanical bird of prey: "the frail manchild clinging to the ledge . . . is all too human—out of his element—and his metallic attacker is incapable of feeling any pain!"

Images of extraordinary humanoid figures doing battle with metal monsters abounded, of course, in Cold War mass culture, and if it is possible now to redeem them as projecting a "real man's" difference from a relentlessly phallic consistency, it can be argued that they now have a dated air—a vulnerability to the practices of nostalgia that perhaps makes it possible to re-read them in sympathetic ways. From this point of view, the industrial robot has been replaced by the cybernetic replicant; the principle of difference is no longer denied to Man's Other, but made internally constitutive of otherness in such a way, and to such a degree, that Man becomes other to himself, and can no longer be sure what he is. *Blade Runner* is often taken to be a vanguard manifesto of this shift, metonymically representing a new era in history.[47]

However my interest here is again in the modes of living-on effected by older legends (a question of *change* to be addressed by any "historical" approach to culture), and so I want to consider in more detail the Human Fly's original status as hybrid model/copy. A moment ago, I called the simulacrum "a copy of a copy of a copy, . . . " the dots signifying infinite potential for (differential) repetition. They could also signify my elision of the crucial element of closure in the usual definition of the simulacrum as, in Brian Massumi's words, "a copy of a copy whose relation to the model has become so attenuated *that . . . it stands on its own as a copy without a model*."[48] The most influential form of this proposition is Baudrillard's neorealist rewriting of the "*image*" as now bearing "no relation to any reality whatever: it is its own pure simulacrum."[49] The closure here is not simply syntactic, but logical (the differential therefore ceases to operate) and purportedly historical (the era of difference is over, sameness and stasis rule).

Massumi has argued that Gilles Deleuze's essay "Plato and the Simulacrum" offers the beginnings of another way of thinking about mass media simulation, because it takes the inadequacy of the model/copy distinction as a point of departure, not a conclusion. In Massumi's terms, "beyond a certain point, the distinction is no longer one of degree. The simulacrum is less a copy twice removed than a phenomenon of a different nature altogether; it undermines the very distinction between copy and model" (91).

The key phrase here is "*beyond a certain point*." In his reading of the Platonic theory of Ideas, Deleuze suggests that the "infinitely slackened resemblance" implied by the process of copying logically leads to the idea of a "copy" so removed from the original (the Idea) that it is no longer a poor or weak "true" copy, but a *false* copy—a simulacrum, that may externally feign resemblance but is constructed by dissimilarity.[50] The important distinction for Plato, therefore, is not between the model and the copy, but between the copy and the simulacrum. The "false" copy is dangerous because, in its constitutive difference from any model (including the Idea of Difference), it throws into question the validity of the model/copy distinction—and thus the theory of Ideas. The simulacrum is thus the internal enemy, or the "irony," of Platonism; its philosophical figure is the Sophist.

Simulation is not, as it is for Baudrillard, a closure of history (a crisis of hypercopying) but, on the contrary, an *action* (like a productive practice of reading; Deleuze's reading of Plato is "simulated" in this sense). This is why, for Deleuze, the Platonic project depends on a "dialectic of rivalry" (46). True copies compete with false ones; the task of the philosopher is to unmask "false" copies—in order to deny the difference of the simulacrum.

Building on this, Massumi suggests that it is "*masked* difference," and not "manifest resemblance" (however hyperreal), that makes the simulacrum uncanny and gives it productive capacity to "break out of the copy mold." Hence, for Massumi as for others, the allegorical power of *Blade Runner*. The replicant in the end is no longer a "more perfect than perfect" copy-human but a different form of life, capable of entering into new combinations with, if not necessarily subsuming, human beings.

Now, in these terms the King Kong and Human Fly combat scenes I've discussed may belong not only to the "robot" imaginary, but to the Platonic scene of rivalry. In *King Kong No Gyakushu*, a true copy of King Kong fights "Mechni-Kong," the false; even if their confrontation does pit mixity against purity, the penis against the dildo, the basic question once again is simply "who is to be master?" Although the Robot Condor/Human Fly encounter is complicated by a lack of external resemblance (and by a certain "masked difference" that gives the "frail manchild" his edge) the issue of mastery is still at stake. On the other hand, it's hard to say what counts as the Fly's masked difference: is it the steel-bone skeleton, that makes him doubly a false copy, a cyborg disguised as a man who imitates an insect, or is it the organic intelligence that fools his mechanical cousin, a robot disguised as a bird?

I think the significant answer is that it doesn't matter very much. Interrogating the identity of any one media icon may always lead to the scene of rivalry and legitimacy, a choice between true and false, or "truer" and "falser"; at the end of the argument I've just rehearsed, we are merely deciding whether *Blade Runner*'s replicant is more true an "illustration" of Deleuze's model of simulation than the Human Fly of *Castle in the Clouds!* This is not to say, of course, that all opposition, duality or "combat" can be reduced to Platonic rivalry. The aim of Massumi's contrast between two versions of simulation is, like my own, to differentiate them not in terms of their relative legitimacy as "descriptions" of the present, but in terms of their competing political logics, and the outcomes (i.e., the futures) to which they give rise.

In this context, the significant point about the history of the Human Fly is that since his *original* hybridity conforms to the logic of the double and thus to the scene of the robot (the "two-dimensional" figure and his "real life" counterpart), it *therefore* unleashes what Deleuze calls "the positive power which negates both original and copy, both model and reproduction." In other words, "of the at least two divergent series interiorized in the simulacrum, neither can be assigned as original or copy" (Deleuze 53). It follows from this that the Human Fly, interiorizing from the beginning a human climber series and a media image series that pretend to copy each other, only simulates conformity to the logic of the double. This is why trying to assign logical priority or a greater degree of reality to either the series of *human* Human Flies or the series of *media* Human Flies at any stage of their subsequent relationship is—like closing the series by *fiat* or pursuing the long-lost original—an infinitely futile task.

The Deleuzian simulacrum is a process, not a product nor a "state" of affairs, that tends in principle toward infinity. So it implies a kind of limitlessness—"great dimensions, depths, and distances which the observer cannot dominate" (49). Deleuze calls this distance, "vertigo." But this is not the vertigo of Faust, overwhelmed, at the top of a tower, by the endless expanse of territory offered up to boundless ambition. It is the vertigo of Plato, discovering "in the flash of an instant as he leans over its abyss" that the simulacrum, the "other" that his philosophy strategically creates, can destroy his philosophy's foundations. It is the vertigo of a *critical* distance, in which "the privileged point of view has no more existence than does the object held in common by all points of view. There is no possible hierarchy . . . " (53). Because the figure of the observer—Plato leaning over the abyss—is part of the simulacrum, the hierarchy abolished in vertigo is not only that regulating the divisions between the Origin and the first-, second-, third-order copies, determining authenticity. It is also the secular projection of that process in hierarchical myths of space (the top of the tower) and time ("meta"-narrative).

Back in the homelier world of superheroes, it is worth noting that while the Human Fly is no stranger to the ordinary vertigo of cliff tops and ocean depths, he has an unusual allegiance to collective practice. Many heroes have sidekicks and a strong community spirit, but the Fly's "frail manchild" vulnerability demands a lot of interdependence. He isn't invincible, he gets afraid, he needs help. There is a certain elitism of the body involved in his mythology, but no authoritarian structure of command. During stunts, he is surrounded and protected by friends (in planes, on the ground, back at the base) with whom he consults by two-way radio. The Fly is a media creature: he uses radio to orchestrate his stunts, then he constructs his stunts as messages ("giving hope—through example—to thousands of crippled and disabled kids!"). He is a radical, not a rugged, individualist; he expounds the strength of the weak. Far from being a crime-fighter, he is a political performance artist.

A Spire in both its components, climbing and film-making, works with this mythology. It isn't a matter of conscious or unconscious "influence," of quotation, allusion, or copying, but of resonance between the divergent series constructing the simulacrum and of the external effects of resemblance that simulation can produce. For that reason, I don't think it is important to dwell on the many points of "resemblance": the Fly's relationship to the friends and the film crew who made the adventure possible; the importance of the two-way radio, used sensitively in the film to narrate without rancor or rivalry the most awkward moment of the climb, when Mark Spain decides to go down; the didactic packaging of a stunt as a socially responsible action; the formal use of the genre of "personal statement" to further a politics for ordinary people ("I'm so small compared to this monster, this monolith to our civilisation," says Chris Hilton of Sydney Tower). These points can be made, not because anyone set out to imitate a forgotten Marvel comic, and not because someone casually chose a "flame-red climbing suit," but because the myth of Human Fly (as the Sydney media understood) involves a collective production of knowledge.

For me, the important question is what can follow from this. As a visual element in *A Spire*, the Human Fly effect—emphasized by the use of a telescopic lens and the editing of long shots and close-ups—has far from casual consequences. Sydney Tower first appears in the film as the usual postcard "phallus" rearing above the city. Then, as the climb proceeds, slowly but surely the Tower becomes a *face*. After figuring as a distant urban peak, the turret turns into a *surface*, its flat windows and thinly grooved walls becoming an extension of the cliff-face surfaces that were used to prepare for the climb. Precisely because the film's argument is to refuse the cultural construction of difference between natural and built environments, and to defy the prohibition on treating big buildings as fully public space, to speak of the tower becoming a "face" is not just a handy pun, but a response to an actual literalism produced by Chris Hilton's persona on screen.[51] Dressed as the Human Fly, he visibly becomes not a Marvellous superhero who can rival the phallic spire, but (especially in long shot) something quite familiar and "natural" to Australians—an insect crawling on its face (fig. 4.1).

This is one way in which *A Spire* does in the vernacular sense "bring down" Sydney Tower, and mock its forbidding pretensions. It makes the Tower *tangible*; in the interview I quoted above, Chris Hilton speaks of reducing the Tower to "a human scale," not of "cutting it down to size." But is that all there is? By itself, this action need be nothing more than a stylish, daring, but ultimately pointless reassertion of the old egalitarian ethos and its "boys' own" concern with appearances. If so, to make too much of the pun on "face"—to read *A Spire* as simply exposing a social production of faciality by inscribing a sign of the "little man" on a great white Majority wall—would return the film to the dialectic of rivalry. In fact, a whole series of changes follows from this "slight dodge in the real image" (Xavier Audouard's phrase for a perceptual shift pulling in the observer to construct the simulacrum) that has the man becoming an insect while the Tower becomes a face.[52]

As Massumi points out, the concept of "double becoming" in *A Thousand Plateaus* provides a way of theorizing a positive force of simulation without reference to models and copies. The term "becoming," often taken by hasty critics to mean the silly idea that you can do whatever you want, designates a concept with a quite precise structure and a process with specific limitations. First, becoming must always involve at least two terms, not one in isolation, swept up in a process that transforms them both; if a man is becoming-insect, the insect is also changing. Second, double becoming involves an "aparallel evolution," not a specular or dualistic structure, connecting heterogeneous terms;[53] when a man is becoming-insect, the insect is not becoming "man," but something else (to take up one of the unfortunate examples favored by Deleuze and Guattari, while the warrior is becoming-woman, the woman may be becoming-animal).

Third, a man does not become a "real" insect, but becoming is not a fiction that he does; becoming is "real," but what is real is the becoming— the process, or the *medium*, in-between terms. Fourth, this medium of becoming is always minoritarian: "in a way, the subject in a becoming is always Man, but only when he enters a becoming-minoritarian that rends him from his major identity" (291). This is the most important sense in which becoming is double, since there are "two simultaneous movements, one by which a term (the subject) is withdrawn from the majority, and another by which a term (the medium or agent) rises up from the minority."[54] Becoming, then, is by definition an undoing of Man, and an un-making of the Face that is "the form under which man constitutes the majority, or rather the standard on which the majority is based" (292).

Now, I suggested that in *A Spire*, two distinct becomings are produced by the "slight dodge in the real image" of Chris Hilton climbing the turret. In a first phase, a man is becoming-fly as the tower is becoming-face. However, in Deleuze and Guattari's terms, a becoming-Man, and thus a becoming-Face, is impossible. Moreover, the homely Australian face on which a fly crawls (and from which Hilton euphorically calls "I feel totally fucking comfortable! I can't believe it! I feel comfortable!") is no longer the awesome panoptic Face that dominates the corporate landscape. Something happens in between, and it takes a complex form of double becoming: in a second phase, a man is becoming-fly as the fly is becoming-woman, with the Face becoming face as *medium*. One of the satisfying things about this is that, usually, "woman" provides the fertile ground or medium in which another's becoming can be defined. In Massumi's otherwise wonderful analysis of David Cronenberg's remake of *The Fly*, for example, the woman left pregnant after Brundle-Fly's fabulous trajectory passively represents "the powers that be" who "squelch" his hopes for creating a new form of life (94–95). There is no speculation as to whether her reluctance to play madonna to a race of "overmen as superflies" might involve a becoming of her own.

Why speak of a becoming-woman of the Fly in *A Spire* in the first place? The concept of "becoming-woman" does not interest me in the guise of a general Good Thing.[55] However I do think that beyond the "image" of the Fly on the face of Sydney Tower (and sweeping it up in a becoming) there is a narrative process of simulation in *A Spire* by which, as Chris Hilton is becoming the Human Fly, *the Human Fly becomes "Fay Gray"*—that is to say, a figure of "home," but also of displacement; of residency, but also of being evicted; of settlement, but also of fugitive status; in other words, the bearer of an amalgamated Otherness *created* by modern corporate strategy, and supposed to be excluded from its place.[56]

I think this happens toward the end of the climb as the moment of arrival is approaching. Once the Fly starts crawling up the turret, it looks more and more likely that he'll make it ("This is very exposed. . . . I feel strangely calm, though—it's not much higher than a tree"). At the same time, the sound-track shifts our attention to the impropriety of his being there and to the question of his descent: "I wonder if there'll be any people in the observation deck when I get there?" There are people; we see them see him; he whoops, "they're all looking bloody amazed!" and keeps on crawling toward one of the most amazing climaxes to an adventure I have seen. As one stunned onlooker put it to me after watching the video, "boy climbs tower—and falls in."[57]

Hilton heaves himself over the ledge, half-somersaults, kicking wildly in the air—and then can't shake his boots from their straps. In the place of a generically appropriate shot of the conqueror standing upright proudly to possess the view, there is a comically repeated little sequence of two disembodied red legs flailing diagonally against the sky, struggling furiously with floating green ribbons. The legs finally disappear over *into* the top of the Tower, two hands appear on the ledge, and then a head—gazing not out at the landscape, but directly down the ropes still brushing against the turret's face. The camera goes down the rope ("well I'm at the top and there's no-one here to meet me, over . . . "), back up the rope, and then for a brief freeze frame the head at the top of the Tower looks straight down the rope as it drops ("They should be arriving soon, I'd say").

This is not a Faustian moment. There is no overview from the Tower: instead, a wonderful aerial sequence, circling the Tower on a horizontal plane with the turret, celebrates Hilton's achievement (and discreetly shows those unfamiliar with Sydney what its magnitude has been). No one comes to take him away, throw him out of the Tower or punish his appropriation of the heights: "Well, I've been here fifteen minutes now and no-one's come to get me and yet a security guard saw me in there, so I'm just going to go down the stairs now, I've found a way in, so I'll see what happens. . . . " What happens is completely banal: he walks out of the building, his ropes in his bag, and saunters away up the street. An interview ends the story: "So I just walked sort of nonchalantly off, I was feeling quite calm, I wasn't feeling agitated, so I just strolled as if I owned the place and caught a taxi in Pitt St."

Home

I want to make three points in conclusion.

"*I just strolled as if I owned the place*": it would be fun to see the Human Fly's cool, controlled descent as Fay Gray's getaway, a riposte to the proprietorial violence structuring the imaginary of King Kong's *Final Decision*. By appropriating the symbolic high-point of corporate power in the city, the Fly becoming-Fay could assert, with an act of temporary occupation ("*as if* I owned the place"), that residents' action, and a residents' politics, can sometimes succeed "against all the odds."

That would be one of the edifying little tales of resistance with which criticism too often rests content. More pointedly, I think, *A Spire* asserts its residents' politics by redefining the colonial "voyage/home" opposition of which the story of King Kong remains, in all its variants, a classic and haunting expression. In the space of a boys' own adventure, home is a feminized place of stasis that functions as beginning and end; the voyage, a masculinized phase of change and development, is the action in between. On the other hand, Deleuze and Guattari's concept of becoming turns this model inside out. Since "the in-between" of becoming is always a minoritarian process, and since a becoming moves toward another minor term that is also involved in becoming, *Man* is the name of the term that is simply left behind.

PM Advertising's yuppie King Kong follows the boys' own logic when he refuses to make a home with Fay and foreclose his financial adventures. Throwing her off the tower is just his way of saying he isn't ready to settle down. If *A Spire* had followed this logic, the space and time of the "voyage" to the top of the turret should have been clearly distinguished from the worlds of "home" and street. That doesn't happen, but neither are we launched into a process of perpetual transformation. What happens in *A Spire* is more like a polemical expansion of the public space of the street to include the top of the Tower, and an extension of the temporality of "home" to incorporate the voyage. Chris Hilton follows a smooth trajectory—into a bus, up the Tower, down the stairs, into a taxi—that, far from defining a *break* from the setting of everyday life, extends the hours of labor inventing and testing homemade tools, talking with friends, practicing in the backyards, the cliffs, and the carparks available round the city. The logical consequence is that since the concept of home now subsumes "adventure" (dynamism, change, thus time as well as space), it is no longer interiority and enclosure alone, but also exteriority and surface.

Home in this sense does not mean "domesticity," nor does it signify "ownership." It is a version of the active principle that de Certeau calls "practising place." My second point follows from this. Since my analysis is fanciful (a paranoid reading), perhaps nothing as serious as a rethinking of ideologies of home and voyage can really be at stake in a short video about an eccentric and inconsequential episode in the history of the inner city—the story of what one interviewee in *A Spire* calls "just another mad person in Sydney."

Yet the very elements that I've just mentioned were sufficiently serious for the ABC-TV broadcast version of *A Spire* to eliminate them. There are several differences between the independent video I've been discussing, and the broadcast version. Primarily, the series framework *I Can't Stop Now* pulled the story closer to the "passional monomaniac" aspect of the adventure; there was more emphasis on the "black hole" of personal obsession, and less on the "white wall" of inscribing social criticism. The film was shortened by fifteen minutes, chunks of the "digressive" discussion footage removed, and more biographical information provided. This is to be expected with professionalization, and not remarkable in itself.

More interesting is a small step taken in the TV version that is not really required by the codes of broadcast quality. In the first video, there are no significant images of anyone "left at home" while Hilton climbs the tower. There is a quick good-bye at the bus stop, we hear the voices on the two-way radio, but there are so many participant others intercut with the scenes of the Fly on the tower, and they are so dispersed in space and time, that there is no place constructed to be occupied by a singular Other to the Man on the Voyage. The TV version restores that place. Partly because it cuts out several talking heads in order to condense the action, extra emphasis is thrown on two new scenes included for broadcast, involving a quite new figure. A young woman, whom the cultural logic of *narrative* invites us to see as wife or girlfriend or sister, is represented remembering her feelings about the idea of the climb, then sending messages and advice from the climber's home base.

Maria Maley on screen is a woman of great dignity and sangfroid who completely fails to create an impression of "feminine" anxiety. But with this one formal gesture, the man/voyage, woman/home, structure of the boy's own adventure is reimposed on the film, and the spatial hierarchy dividing the top of the Tower from everyday space is reestablished. However I don't think that this spoils the film or distorts or coopts its "message." As a half-hour TV program about the built environment, the broadcast version of *A Spire* still works extremely well. What interests me about the changes is what they suggest about the cultural context in which *A Spire* appeared, and thus its critical point within it.

In spite of its long association in theoretical discourse with a problem of (white) Femininity, it was class that represented the unrepresentable for Judith Mayne in her analysis of 1933, American Depression, *King Kong*. Class was also, if not unrepresentable, then certainly unmentionable in the "popular" culture of Australian egalitarianism—the proprieties of which were so shamelessly flouted in the 1980s by the brutal truths of postmodern corporate culture. Yet, in one gesture of routine editing to brighten *A Spire* for broadcast, there is a very clear definition of something still "unrepresentable," or out of bounds, in Australian public media in 1989. It is neither class, nor the feminine sex, nor any classic figure of the Other, but the possibility of a *non*-climactic and "homely" boys' adventure. What the broadcast version restores to *A Spire* is more than an anchoring image of woman, and a conventional distinction between home and the voyage. It restores what depends on these, a sense of "proper" masculinity. The fabulous Human Fly becoming Fay Gray is more simply and normally Chris Hilton, a man dressed "in a flame-red climbing suit."

Yet my last point is not pessimistic. If the TV version of *A Spire* restored to it some proprieties, this is an indication of the extent to which both films, indeed the whole "adventure," were successful in changing the assumptions about masculinity, spectacle, and city space asserted by John Bond in the quotation from which I began. ABC-TV's revision of the Human Fly's fabulous becoming as Chris Hilton's "personal obsession" was made possible, perhaps necessary, by the degree to which *A Spire* proclaims the Tower "an ego thing"—in the sense that John Bond disavowed.

Chris Hilton made a spectacle of himself, and then helped make a film about it. He produced a social analysis with an act of exhibitionism and then exhibited his analysis in public. In practicing this mode of (very athletic) effeteness, he brought down the Tower not by renouncing the heights, but by reaching them instead. In this way, he invented a form of vernacular criticism that does *not* miss the point about the kind of wealth and power invested in urban towers, but rather, makes a spectacle about that very point.

ECSTASY AND ECONOMICS

Watching the Treasurer

I want to believe the beautiful lies
the past spreads out like a feast.

Television is full of them & inside
their beauty you can act: Paul Keating's

bottom lip trembles then recovers,
like the exchange rate under pressure

buoyed up as the words come out—
elegant apostle of necessity, meaning

what rich Americans want, his world is
like a poem, completing that utopia

no philosopher could argue with, where
what seems, is & what your words describe

you know exists, under a few millimetres
of invisible cosmetic, bathed

in a milky white fluorescent glow.

    —JOHN FORBES, *THE STUNNED MULLET* (1988)[1]

This is a poem about television—in particular, about watching a famous politician perform on Australian TV sometime in the mid-1980s. It is also a poem about glimpsing utopia: it defines a social landscape (a scene of symbolic consumption) and an imaginary space of sorts (televisual); as a means of passage between them it invokes a man's voice, "off." To imagine this voice (not like a voice-off, really, but like watching TV with the sound turned down, an "unheard melodies" effect), you have to know that we are watching Paul Keating, Federal Treasurer[2] (1983–1991) of the Australian Labor government (1983–96), and that he is famed for his suits and his eloquence.[3] The elegance is Italian, the eloquence Australian, and it comes in two main styles, or, as fashion people say, two "stories"—gutter invective (the working-class "boy from Bankstown" story) and policy jargon (the "corporate" story). There are variations and combinations—stirring, visionary speeches, violent, hilarious one-liners—but a basic synthesis of "street-smart" and "high-flyer" modes is what defines, by resolving old class-cultural oppositions, the Keating semantic field.

The poem is about the smooth and ecstatic story rather than the tough and abusive—though that's there, that's part of the ecstasy, trembling in potential along that bottom lip. The press always savored Keating's parliamentary insults (the *Australian* once printed a retrospective, including "sleazebags," "box-heads," "harlots," "sucker," "perfumed gigolo," "criminal garbage," "clowns," and "gutless spiv," while omitting his most famous interpellation of a political opponent, "you stupid foul-mouthed grub"), and relished his often cruel jokes as proverbs. But the Treasurer doing economics live on talk shows was *really* something to be seen. He could mesmerize the camera with those great big burning brown eyes, then move in with a stream of jargon that seemed on the surface unintelligible, and yet let you know, quite simply and profoundly, that really everything would be all right if you just *suffered* a little more, and let him take care of business.

> *That implies—to decode what you're saying—if the exchange rate falls, inflation will rise. But if the government or the country got no benefit from a rising dollar which* should *have had lower inflation, because basically business fattened its margins and profits, surely no-one's arguing now if the exchange rate falls somewhat that that's going to be added to prices. I mean—in a slower economy prices are going to be unwound and inflation will come back. It's as simple as that.*
>
> —PAUL KEATING, 1990[4]

There's an S&M glow about Keating's image as Treasurer. Australians spent the 1980s laughing about the "sex appeal" of Mrs. Thatcher, and at infantile English obsessions with schoolmarms, knickers, and canes, but in the image of this tall, dark, saturnine man there was something, not similar (no elocution lessons for Keating), but comparable—a "Mr. Murdstone" factor, with a softening, comic-romantic touch of Frank Langella's Dracula.[5]

Somehow, too, it was crucial to Keating's aura that he is still a practicing Catholic. Apart from adding a touch of the perverse and fanatic to his Grim Reaper image ("a true believer, in *this* day and age?"), his Catholicism put him in the great tradition of Irish-Australian Labor leaders.[6] This claim as legitimate heir to the "faith" of a mythic, martyred past could sometimes help to counter recurring image problems over whether his policies fitted too well with his yuppified personal tastes: how a "traditional" Labor leader could be a free marketeer and deregulator, buy French antiques and a Sydney mansion instead of "living with the electorate," go pig-shooting with billionaire real estate developers, be "mates" with media magnates and financiers—while redistributing income upward in, he claimed, the interests of the working class.

Yet these image problems were also, like the elegance and the eloquence, constituents *of* his image. Australians spent the decade laughing at an airhead Ronald Reagan, and at bizarre American confusions between history and Hollywood films, but the televisual voice of Keating (articulate, quick on the uptake, smoothly working class) had a power to rouse anxiety about the grounding of *our* sense of history. Questions of history, and a sense of confusion, arose in the gap between how he *sounded* ("traditional Labor"), and what he *said* as "the closest we have had to a right-of-centre Treasurer in this country in the last 50 years."[7] What, now, is tradition?—political analysts asked.[8] What is the difference between "performance" and "policy," when speech *is* action in media? Once, these could be contrasted as the *showy* to the *solid*, the *ephemeral* to the *enduring*; Keating could, and did, "make history" on a celebrity radio talk-back show by frightening financial markets into driving the dollar down.[9] What is happening between folklore and economics, popular memory and political calculation, entertainment and statecraft, national (rhetorical) ideals and global (economic) imperatives—desire and "law"? These questions formed the substance of self-reflective media columns; so placed, they intensified the sense of confusion that such columns, pragmatically, attempt to dissipate.

This is a study of "Watching the Treasurer"—of the poem, and the social experience that the poem *involves* for me. It is not directly about those questions of history that shape its sense of involvement. It is about "Paul Keating" only as a media image, and that only insofar as the poem makes him an allegorical figure of a process of image production, "watching" included, occurring on an interface between economic discourse and television. My portrait is of this figure, and my object of analysis is the media process itself. However, since watching is certainly social, I do say something about the broader context involved. So this portrait is made with mixed materials (including a genre little used in cultural studies, the literary close reading) and framed by certain "mixed feelings" of cross-cultural anxiety.

An enunciative anxiety about split address and cultural noise is endemic to the one-way flow of information between Americans and (among others,

I am sure) Australians.[10] For me, this anxiety is a technical emotion, positive and practical: as Susan Stewart reminds us, to have an indescribable experience is "simply to confirm the ideology of individual subjective consciousness."[11] However, it also involves an exactly descriptive anxiety about context and frame of reference. In Australia I would not need to describe Paul Keating, or explain his significance, as I do in the United States; I would not have to run the risk, therefore, of openly making him up.

> *The unsaid assumption underlying all descriptions is experience beyond lived experience, the experience of the other and of the fiction. In description we articulate the time and space that are absent from the context at hand, the lived experience of the body. Our interest in description may be stated most often as an interest in style, but in fact it is equally an interest in closure. All description is a matter of mapping the unknown onto the known.*
>
> —SUSAN STEWART (26)

In the late 1980s, I came to be aware of feeling an entirely new emotion: adulation of a national leader. I felt it in the comic-ironic mode that is culturally natural to Australians of my general social background (mixed working-class and petit-bourgeois Irish-Australian). I also felt it in the *momentary* mode that can be natural to people whose emotions are media-sensitive. It would overwhelm me on occasions of national solemnity (watching Budget speeches, Special Economic Statements, or election debates on TV), but it could also catch me in the middle of my most basic domestic activities—peeling vegetables, washing up, flipping through theory journals.

When I heard his voice in the house, I was capable of dropping everything to run and fling myself down in front of the television calling out ecstatically "It's him! It's him!" I use "ecstasy" here in the vernacular sense of "a quick rush." But I also felt this emotion *profoundly*; in a punctual economy, duration is not equivalent to intensity or depth. Even when the country went into a recession that Keating probably helped to cause, I always wanted to believe what he said; usually, I did. Yet my attitude to most of the Treasurer's policies wavered from hostile to ambivalent. His attitude to my kind of politics was frankly contemptuous ("basket-weaving").

I say all this in a documentary rather than a confessional mode. This is the kind of experience in which one realizes how powerfully it can be true that "I" *is* an other. And "I" was not alone. When the Treasurer withheld his media presence for weeks, even months, on end, there was wailing and gnashing of teeth in editorials and business columns ("Has Keating Lost It?"); strong men wept on television for the future of our country. The rejoicing when he "returned" was a wonder to behold ("Mr. Keating emerges from his bunker"); headlines shouted that he was picking up reins, handling gears, and pulling levers again; strong men chuckled tenderly at replay footage of his jokes. A feminist study of Keating discourse, mostly but by no means entirely produced by irritably fascinated men, could learn much about the paradoxes of "male homosocial desire" binding our male-dominated, homophobic state culture.[12] My documentary impulse here is more toward exploring the conditions of my own affective *involvement* in this culture. Women produced "Keating discourse" too, and I am not convinced that the feminist concept of "male-identifying" (that does come to mind) is adequate to examining what happened, or what was at stake for *us*, when we did.

Of course, my "entirely new" emotion may well involve something that I have read about precisely in relation to *other* people, in the past and in countries where it is respectable, even normal (as it is not in Australia), to wave flags, cheer parades, and praise the nation. This is known to critical theory as the "aestheticization of politics," and my response to the image of Keating could be said to take its canonical specular form: the constitution of the nation in the image of the body of the leader.[13] If such a mapping of my unfamiliar experience onto a powerful historical precedent (and already available concept) does seem plausible to me, it is, in part, because of the questions that can then arise about its *implausibility*. For on the border between the unknown and the known—or better, in the moment before closure—something can still be said about other historical precedents, and other available concepts.

Philippe Lacoue-Labarthe, for example, supports his account of "the ecstatic identification with a Leader" with a reading of Hans Jurgen Syberberg's *Hitler, a Film from Germany*; concepts of spectacle and identification are crucial to theories of the aestheticization of politics classically understood.[14] But I cannot easily relate my media memories of Hitler at the Nuremberg rallies, or even of Reagan at the L.A. Olympics, to Australian leadership images. It is useful to try, in fact: if to do so is to ignore common sense about a massive disproportion in scale (and differences between cinema and television, not to mention "Hitler" and "Reagan"), it does illuminate imagings of the leadership benignly embodying the nation in our own political history as constitutively white and male, and thus as incarnating the violence of what Carole Pateman has aptly called the fraternal state.[15] Yet disproportion, like difference, matters. Apart from the risk such comparisons run of trivializing Nazism, and of devaluing the violence specific to other regimes, it is important that the leader of a client state is always touched by abjection. He is "unspectacular." However *popular* he may be, his need to grovel on behalf of the nation to its "great and powerful friends" acts as a check on *patriotic* urges to identify closely with him.

Furthermore, the Treasurer is not "a Leader." At best, he can only incarnate burning desire (as Keating did) to have the Prime Minister's position.

The Treasurer's is certainly a powerful office, symbolically as well as politically: his actions massively impact on the lives of ordinary citizens, and thus on the fate of governments; media legend locates the basic passion of the Australian (male) body politic in the so-called "hip pocket nerve." But for this very reason, no Treasurer is capable of effecting, as Lacoue-Labarthe puts it, a "fusion of the community (in festival or war)" (70). Representing work and the management of economic inequality rather than festival or war, the Treasurer *differentiates* a community likely to find "fusion" only in a consensus to blame him for those disasters (drought, other people's wars, commodity price fluctuations) everyone knows he can't control.

There is a related sense in which, if I look for historic Australian models of charismatic leadership, I find no spectacle, and few images at all. "Hitler" still circulates with "Reagan" in my everyday habitat of mixed American, European, Australian, and Asian images; I might see them on television or in magazines at any time. I much more rarely "see" Curtin, Chifley, or Menzies, and, when I do, this rarity defines (as special but "minor") their media significance, as well as the *exceptional* status of the citizenly genres in which they most often appear; historical mini-series,[16] documentary, special-event television. Yet these national figures have not simply been displaced, as a cultural purist might have it, by global icons. They circulate for me, in a low-key way, as *stories*: as clusters of "character" and "event" recalled in media history specials (tragic John Curtin, the alcoholic who "got up from the gutter" to lead the nation at war, then died; saintly Ben Chifley, the railway worker who supervised postwar reconstruction, then died); as other people's memories in family or community contexts; in books that I read for research; as reference points for discussion in late night current affairs shows, or in the quality press. This often aural, sometimes literary discourse is not really popular, now, in portent: more than subcultural or professional (although it is both), it might be described as ethnic.

> *Keating brought to Caucus and machine politics the disciplined infallibility of his Catholicism. Dressed with the smart severity of a Jesuit, he slid along the parliamentary lobbies carrying ambition as an altar boy cradles his missal, reflexes sharpened to strike heretics. Although steeped in Labor tradition personally handed to him by Jack Lang and Rex Connor, Keating was unburdened by the dead hand of the past; he pursued his passion for French antiques at Paddington and cultivated leaders of the financial community at the big end of town. Keating prayed to God and waited on history; he was still to discover a more complex world.*
>
> —PAUL KELLY[17]

In other circumstances, those of the ideal identity between race, *ethnos*, and language community on which the European image of the "nation" has been based, some elements of this discourse might support the totalizing project that Lacoue-Labarthe, following Jean-Luc Nancy, calls "immanentism" (70). But I am "watching the Treasurer" in an immigrant nation, racially and culturally mixed beyond any possibility of dreaming its essence in an aesthetic of purity or "organic" form, and one with limited pretensions to economic and military autonomy. That is, I live in a society constituted—in this respect, unexceptionally—not in immanentism but in *relationality*. So I cannot sensibly oppose a localized aural tradition ("folklore") to a global media culture ("spectacle"). Theoretical problems with such dualisms aside, historically both have formed, and are forming, my "lived experience of the body" (watching, listening, talking), just as each assumes "experience of the other and of fiction."

However, I can make distinctions between my international media culture and my other social knowledges. Only by doing so, in fact, can I say that something unusual about the figure of Keating was its simultaneous availability to me in several affective registers. Widely distributed for many years and, on any given day, over time in diverse networks of cultural production—conversation, newspapers, radio news and talk-back, day-time "women's" TV variety shows, prime-time family news, heavy late-night "analysis" shows, weekend business programs—"Keating" was a constellation of anecdotes accessible to me equally and *convergently* as an appealing capitalized image, a nasty policy paradigm, an enthralling political drama, an unsettling ideological problem, an enigmatic object of analysis and, in terms that Paul Kelly's portrait of Keating serves to suggest, a sentimental folktale.[18]

Of course, many politicians figure widely, if blandly, in the media. When John Forbes wrote "Watching the Treasurer," the Keating *mythos* had been accumulating depth and resonance longer than most; in Federal parliament since 1969, he arrived there already aureoled, at the age of twenty-five, by rumors of ballot rigging. Australian news culture thrives on political intrigue and economic scandal, mostly avoiding, by tacit agreement, harsh exposure of "private lives"; Keating's slightly sinister political reputation, and shockingly virtuous personal life, made him both desirable and legitimate as a popular narrative subject—a mix of hero and villain.[19] Indeed, a well-known folkloric episode (cited by Kelly to frame his portrait) has a Labor Senator in 1977 endowing a journalist with this mission: "You see that man; *watch him* because he's a political killer." Media coverage of Keating was driven by overt myth-making of the most extravagant kind. Kelly's gothic fantasy (1983) of what the young Keating was up to in 1977 is not unusual either for its emotional ambivalence or for the aggravated lyricism, the *literariness* that its subject elicits from a sober and skeptical journalist who (an excellent story-teller) has edited Rupert Murdoch's *Australian*.

For all its extravagance, Keating mythology was intensely and unusually coherent. As in Paul Kelly's text, much of this mythology was organized by precisely those legitimating figures of *reconciliation*—of "Labor" with "the financial community," of "tradition" with a rejection of "the dead hand of the past"—foundational for the consensus rhetoric and corporatist politics of the government in which Keating played only a part, but of which he then came to serve, at least in business and trade union contexts, as a living allegory. Most distinctive, however, was his personal reconciliation of messianic and monetary motifs. In 1988, Edna Carew opened the first chapter ("A Good Catholic Boy") of her romantic biography *Keating* by narrating this portent of his birth: "In July 1944 the International Monetary Fund was born in the town of Bretton Woods, New Hampshire, USA."[20] Spiritual truth is here taking precedence over chronological convention: if the IMF occupies the place most commonly reserved, in biography, for parents or even grandparents, the next paragraph reveals that Keating was in fact born six months earlier than the ancestral figure preceding him in the text.

More routinely, Keating was always being anointed and announced by Labor patriarchs. When not "personally handed" tradition by Lang and Connor, he was, as "the son of a boilermaker" turned small businessman, "breathing it in with his first gasp," or "at his father's knee" (while his mother, in most accounts, ran "a welcoming home").[21] At the same time, he was always upwardly mobile, unburdened by origins, self-educated (leaving school at fifteen), accumulating cultural capital (classical music, Empire furniture, and, in a Taylorist touch, collecting clocks), considering a "Paris option," heading for "the big end of town." The conflict of tradition and experiment, faith and ambition, legitimacy and radical change was often reconciled in Keating folklore by manifestation scenes: Keating lectures the IMF/World Bank dignitaries ("Do something, don't just talk"); Keating berates the venerable Labor Party (officially born in 1891, the first *parliamentary* labor party in the world) as "a bastard of an organization."[22] These scenes could manipulate diverse cultural contents, from provincial "world stage" strutting to esoteric factional hostility. Their *form* was routinely organized by the story of the youthful Jesus sorting out the elders in the temple.

Journalists writing portraits commonly recycle phrases, as well as themes and narrative structures, stored in the clippings archive (and in their aural trade memory). There are technical and contingent as well as culturally determinant reasons for any cluster of "character and event" to assume the shape that it does. But Keating materials are, like the binary structure that contains them, always already "steeped," if not in hagiography, then in historiographical traditions *about* the Labor Party. If Paul Kelly's Keating inhabits many subsequent media texts, his own is shaped stylistically as well as thematically, I suspect, by the anguished moral dualism structuring the great national epic of our postwar liberal culture, Manning Clark's six-volume *A History of Australia* (1962–1987). Kelly's "Keating at prayer" could be a direct descendant of that founder of the labor movement who, in one of Clark's own remarkable portraits, waited on history in the 1880s as one belonging "to that generation of divided men who had been fashioned on the Australian goldfields, men who worshipped two gods: the god of equality and the god of getting on."[23]

For all this romantic legitimation and image saturation, one problem stubbornly remains with subsuming responses to Keating as Treasurer under an "ecstatic identification," as Lacoue-Labarthe puts it, "with a Leader who . . . incarnates, in an immanent fashion, the immanentism of a community" (70). Very few Australians got *ecstatic* about Paul Keating.[24] Even at the peak of his economic charisma in the mid-1980s, polls would still declare that only 4 percent to 7 percent of Australians wanted him for leader—in contrast to an approval rating of over 70 percent accorded to the then most popular Prime Minister in Australian history, R. J. Hawke. Whatever polls may or may not tell us about the distribution of political taste, this comparison ensured that popular *refusal* to identify with Keating was always a constitutive feature *of* his media image.

This raises questions about, once again, relationality rather than "immanence." If, as Michelle Rosaldo has argued, "emotions are about the ways in which the social world is one in which *we* are involved,"[25] then I must certainly restrict the scope of any claims I might make about "ecstasy." It is no revelation to say that, whatever other forms of support he may have enjoyed, Keating was *aestheticized* only by and for a "world" significantly involving intellectuals and media practitioners. By June 1991, when he failed in an early leadership bid that was widely supported by the press, this very thesis was being circulated by journalists thus enabled to reflect on their relations to "the rest" of Australian society in, for once, other than expressive terms. Some debated their relations to Keating in openly *erotic* terms: ABC-TV ran a self-reflexive *Lateline* program on "Seducing the Media," and there was some discussion of Derek Parker's book *The Courtesans*, a formal attack on the press gallery proposing (as its most senior woman member noted) to "throw the trollops out of the court!"[26]

So in order to investigate the non-"immanentist" ecstasy and relational play of identity that I, as an addressee, a consumer, and a citizen-referent of media discourse on the nation, have been calling "Paul Keating," a social restriction does not suffice. I need first to consider more closely some of the discourses of emotion circulating in this "world" that made my own response possible, and marginal.

> The crucial thing to understand about Paul Keating is
> that he is a man of passion.
>
> —CRAIG MCGREGOR[27]

Ecstasy—religious, sexual, political—is, by any definition, an experience out of the ordinary. Greek *ekstasis* comes from *existanai*, to displace, or, as the *Shorter Oxford English Dictionary* has it, to "*put* out of place." Most dictionaries have special entries about poetic frenzy, mystic transport, and divine rapture, states construed as exceptional in a prosaic and secular world. Dictionaries differ, however, in their understanding of that "place" (sometimes a "norm") from which poetry and divinity may either displace or expel us.

For the *Shorter Oxford*, it is the security of a self-identical subject (Man): in ecstasy one is, perhaps unpleasantly, placed "beside oneself" by anxiety or fear as well as "astonishment" and "passion." Some emphasis is given to seventeenth-century "morbid" and nineteenth-century "nervous" states. The *Petit Robert* follows the *Shorter Oxford* through this history of modern pathology. However, it gives the experience of being "comme transportée hors de soi et du monde sensible" a more upbeat inflection of joy, felicity, and wonder: in this semantic world, the idea of being "carried away" more fully contains the possibility of communing with "l'être parfait, l'être infini, Dieu," and the non-ecstatic "place" is broadened to include all ordinary worldly experience. These differences could rashly be schematized by contrasting Protestant and Catholic, even empiricist and Cartesian, theories of subjectivity. They can safely be related as forms of "the ex-stasis, the outside-itself attributed to women by male speculation" that is, for Elizabeth Grosz in her commentary on Lacan's eulogy to St. Teresa, "the phallic refusal to accept an otherness not modeled on the same."[28]

While both dictionaries work with the historical materials of the modern mind/body dichotomy, both define ecstasy as displacement without further specifying the nature of the relationship between the terms thus put in play; neither explicitly divides emotion from intellect, or opposes ecstasy to "reason." The *American Heritage Dictionary* does. Ecstasy is there not only "a state of exalted delight in which normal understanding is felt to be surpassed," but "a state of any emotion so intense that *rational thought and self-control* are obliterated" (my emphasis). This is not a fusional experience blurring the boundaries of the everyday self, but an upheaval internal to the subject; the normal hierarchy of relations between its constitutive parts is overthrown. Instead of being taken "out" to experience the other as infinity and perfection, or even as anxiety, the subject undergoes an inner crisis in which *one* of its capacities (emotion) destroys, by metonymic violence, certain others (rational thought, self-control). By this definition, ecstasy is a violent process with destabilizing effects; in ecstasy, one is radically, if momentarily, unbalanced.

Exactly these oppositional pairings of reason with *control* and emotion with *intensity* structure Craig McGregor's self-titled "social portrait" of Paul Keating. At the outset McGregor, a well-known journalist and critic of popular culture, claims that Keating is less strongly organized by "well-balanced reserve" than "the media people who have labelled him Mister Cool" may suppose. They associate coolness, he suggests, with Keating's *gravitas* and self-possession (control), as well as with such of his attributes as "economic policy," "corporate heavies," and a "monkish jesuitical air"—all metonyms, I think, of "calculation" and thence of an *excessive* rationality. But these are inessential: strip them away and you find a "deep-seated capacity for emotion, anger and diatribe," "warmth and spirit" ("an intensity somewhat akin to the 'fire in the belly' Aneurin Bevan was said to have had"), and again, "fire and conviction." The (real) Keating as a man of passion, then, is opposed to the self-possessed (media) Keating as hot is to cold, and body to mind ("belly"/"monkish"). McGregor interprets this structure in class as well as gender-specific terms: passion is to calculation as the "naked" fighting of "the scrum" (in Rugby League football, traditionally a working-class game) is to the "dark tailored suits" of money and power (78).

A stress on the overwhelming ("fire") and the volatile ("anger," "scrum") tempts McGregor's own discourse here toward ecstasy in a third sense, the "overpowering emotion" and "sudden access of intense feeling" that the *Macquarie Dictionary* casually posits without reference to any boundary or oppositional force, and without any mention of a self. This is ecstasy as pure event, as an *intensity* that "happens," a rush; the *Macquarie* emphasizes the abstract energy that most dictionaries mark as a "surpassing" while spatializing, as *fusion* or *crisis*, its effects. In Jean Baudrillard's theory of media, ecstasy in this sense is an epiphany ("the quality proper to any body that spins until all sense is lost, and then shines forth in its pure and empty form") in which a term may "obliterate" others only because it spins free from binary structures: a term in ecstasy ceases to be "relative to its opposite" (thus annihilating its value), becoming "superlative, positively sublime, as if it had *absorbed all the energy* of its opposite."[29] Some of the more absorbed press portraits of Keating constructed him as sublime in just this way: "We're no match for him," fumed a ravished Alan Ramsey, spinning out on a cricket metaphor: "[not] another one like him in the Parliament . . . the master with both ball and bat . . . the complete political player . . . the Bradman of politics."[30]

In McGregor's text, however, there is a social complication—a referential catch that keeps his discourse hooked back into a binary value system (and a realist practice of character analysis). Australian culture includes a strong tradition of dividing "reason" by associating intelligence with emotion and opposing both to intellectuality; an old mythology of the practical (renewed in clichés about the Man-of-few-words from the school-of-hard-knocks) positively values, *especially in men*, inarticulate empathy and intuitiveness as signs of real smarts; women err on the side of the sensible, the plodding, even the calculating side of reason. Bob Hawke owed much of his popularity (which he called his "love affair with the Australian people") to a myth of his passionate nature: his tears on television, his public temper tantrums, his chaotically twisted sentences and snappish little replies, his legendary drinking and philandering, his hard sacrifice of these to power. Hazel, his equally popular wife, was sensible. So by making passion *crucial* to our understanding of Keating, McGregor is contradicting a common view that in the 1980s we were governed not only by "divided men," but by a living binary opposition: the warm, intelligent Prime Minister and the cold, intellectual Treasurer, the all-round practical man and the "narrow" economic theorist.

So McGregor "humanizes" Keating by taking him out of the cold zone of excessive rationality. However he then intensifies Keating in the *warm* zone, destabilizing him again, while securing his own position as "balanced." McGregor concludes that Keating really *is* narrow, not because he is a theorist but because, in his "bloody-minded" pragmatism and "intolerance," he isn't. Keating lacks in intellectuality, and here this is not a virtue: "he has little political theory to back him up, few general ideas, scorns the intellectual content of politics, relies on his instincts and trusts to his ferocity of purpose to get him through" (84)—just another passionate man. His "political fire" reduced in an ecstasy of "bile" to the "white ash of the personal," Keating is all affect and no ideology—and "anger without ideology breeds reaction."

Moderation is a great virtue in Australian political mythology:[31] to say that "theory" might help to supply it is to try to reconcile intelligence with intellectuality. However McGregor's faith in the restraining force of ideology—taken as belief creatively organized by a coherent set of ideas—already excludes his discourse from the mainstream of public rhetoric, where "ideology" now means a *rigid adherence to* "theory," and thence an extremist impracticality held to characterize both "the Left" and "far Right" of politics: ideology is the place of the other, and the other is always immoderate. Thus Julian Disney, then president of the Australian Council of Social Services, found Keating narrow for reasons opposed to McGregor's. On behalf of "hundreds of thousands of Australians now paying a heavy price," Disney attacked Keating's policy regime for its "economic *dogma*," its "simplistic and extremist *theories*," its "obsession with *ideological* machismo."[32]

> *I'm over forty, I've got four kids, I think it's time to put the cue on the rack.*
>
> —PAUL KEATING, ON BEING VOTED IN A 1990 RADIO POLL "THE SEXIEST MAN IN AUSTRALIA"

Narrowness is a formal topic in Keating portraiture.[33] Whatever value is attributed to the figure of the man himself (in this case, as lacking and as overembodying "theory"), the *topic* permits a discussion not only of the qualities composing an ideal national leader (a political discourse of desire), but also of the proper distribution of thought to feeling, belief to action, doctrine to experience, and theory to practice in the matrix of a white-male-dominated, democratic public sphere (a philosophical discourse of management). Thus McGregor's "Keating" is at once an individualizing analysis of a man with a fatal flaw, and an idealizing expression of McGregor's own messianic yearning for the perfectly balanced Man that his subject ("all mouth and no ears") had failed to become—a *complete* intellectual who could, blending passion and theory, realize the "great humane ideals of the Labor movement." Disney's interest-group rhetoric is not concerned with charismatic leadership. His Keating is merely a figure head for a reductive economic agenda ("machismo") forcing itself, at a terrible cost, on an obdurately complex society; he wants less ideology, and more compassion, in policy rather than persons.

However McGregor's plea for more, not less, ideology does resonate with the terms, if not always the values, of some recent international debates about so-called postmodern politics. In this vicinity of my social world, McGregor's "essential Keating paradox" may seem less idiosyncratic, more entangled, in its troubling (dis)similarity, with other discourses exploring an instability to do with emotion in international media culture. In significantly different ways, several critics have suggested that a general shift is occurring in the relations between "affect" and "ideology" in mediated societies. As they try to define this shift, the term "ideology" pulls back from its Marxist-psychoanalytic entanglement with language and subjectivity, reverting to an older use in naming the object of a social capacity for something like "belief."[34]

For example, in *It's a Sin: Postmodernism, Politics and Culture*, Lawrence Grossberg finds a series of *gaps* opening up "between affect and ideology, between fans and fanatics," between "mattering" and "meaning" in postwar American culture.[35] Carefully distinguishing "the specificity of American hegemony" under Reagan from Thatcherism in Britain, he argues that the New Right's project in the United States has worked most powerfully through a war of affect waged in and as popular culture, rather than by (as in Britain) the State. This war aims to reconstruct an American national-popular by divorcing "common sense" from faith, and from emotional investment: "Reaganism seems to have been built upon the increasingly generally shared mistrust of common sense which renders *ideological* differences less important than the *passion* of one's commitment" (32, my emphasis). So the affect/ideology "gap" is also a "frontier" where the New Right is constructing America as "a powerful affectively charged but ideologically empty identity" (38).

Grossberg's analysis of this gap/frontier is historical, self-reflexive, and irreducibly culture-specific. By making me aware of inhabiting another country and a different social world, it usefully enables comparison. I could not easily separate the state from the popular-cultural strategies of the Hawke-Keating regime. The hegemonic force of its tripartite corporatist alliance (government/business/unions) depended on mobilizing affect through a *masculine*-popular culture—referring not, as in Grossberg's America, to rock and roll, TV and youth, but to gambling, pubs, and sport—saturated in the very "mateship" values that it aimed, ideologically, to reconstruct; simply put, *worker solidarity* was to be reconstituted as *national economic competitiveness*.[36] Affectively drawn into this alliance by family tradition and ethnic background, I was excluded less by gender than by a professional class formation that now leads me, ideologically, to privilege gender and race in a "leftist" way.

So there is much in Grossberg's account of postmodern affect that I can recognize as "mine." With his "increasingly unbridgeable chiasma which leaves us standing on the border of our affective relations, unable to anchor ourselves ideologically" (38), I am at no great distance from exactly the cultural space in which Australian commentators claim that economic rationalism (a philosophy shared since the 1980s by all the major parliamentary parties) has reconstructed "Labor" as an ideologically empty identity—with, however, a *fading* affective charge.[37] At the same time, I am distanced by feminism, as well as nationality, from aspects of Grossberg's account: the negotiation of a "gap" between mattering and meaning is not only foundational for feminism, but may, as Patricia Mellencamp has argued, characterize the historical experience of modernity for women;[38] indeed, what was quite new about this period for me was the way my own "affect" began to channel *toward* an "ideological" mattering of national government. So when Grossberg writes of a postwar "dissolution of what we might call the 'anchoring effect' that articulates meaning and affect" (40), I am aware of a different past (of no such anchoring) as well as another present.

These differences can emerge for me because Grossberg's text is explicitly, in part, a self-portrait. This means that his claims about past and present are framed, and limited in their generalizing force, by a discourse of social memory, and thus a practice of description that resists its own necessary closure; working between known and unknown selves as well as between past and present, he opens up the gaps he describes. Closure of a different kind is produced by those externalizing, as well as generalizing, accounts of postmodern politics that, by positing (as Grossberg does not) a universal model of mass mediation, have sought to *periodize*, on others' behalf, an ideology/affect split. This is really a way of mapping the difference of "television" onto the cinematic terms of "spectacle" and "identification" classically defining aestheticized politics. In the process, a pre-postmodern "past" becomes the object of a stabilizing description of "the way things used to be" before electronic mediation. Instead of opening a series of gaps, this kind of analysis *produces* the foreclosure of ideology that mediation is then said, "historically," to have caused.

Thus for Jochen Schulte-Sasse, a "sentimento*logic*" is now displacing "ideo*logic*" in its ideological role of ensuring socio-cultural reproduction. In "Electronic Media and Cultural Politics in the Reagan Era," he reads the U.S. raid on Libya and the "Hands Across America" megaevent of 1986 as signaling a whole series of drastic shifts: we go from a "linear narration" of human living space, to "synaesthetic fragmentation"; from a subject under the command of a "strong super-ego" ("agonistic, competitive individuals with clearly delimited, ideological identities") to a "narcissistically diffuse" identity under the sway of "the id"; from the "armed" psyche of modern nationalism, its "historical perspective" shaped by localizing, time-lagged technologies (rallies, radio, cinema), to a "feelgood," postmodern national-ism fostered by electronic media now able to aestheticize politics "intensely" on a truly massive scale.[39]

A fusional model of ecstasy is activated here: where, for Grossberg, fissures open across the shifting terrain of a social subjectivity, for Schulte-Sasse the boundaries of an old, hard-edged self are blurred by a surge of indistinctness, in a "paradoxical experience of both identity and dissolu-tion" (147); immanentist nationalism gives way to the softly circular rela-tionality of mass narcissism. This is a version of an old argument in me-dia studies. Adopting what Philip Hayward calls the "gratingly familiar" assumption that "TV and video are characterized above all by their (meta-textual) 'flow' . . . [even though] the most basic level of audience research reveals viewing patterns that disrupt this rigidly simplistic characteriza-tion,"[40] Schulte-Sasse projects this "flow" onto another familiar binary grid opposing fragment to structure, fluid to solid, blur to line, dispersiveness to decisiveness, passivity to activity, absorption to commitment—a grid dependent for its coherence on an elided image/story of asymmetry: sexual difference.

In the context of discussing nationalism, this elision allows Schulte-Sasse to renovate "spectacle" by once again representing television as *not*-linguis-tic, but as "visual and acoustical," in its operations (127). This in turn makes it possible to conserve the concept of identification by projecting onto the "mass" an Oedipal narrative of regression and "identity" loss.[41] His analysis can then avoid the complication of Althusser's concept of ideology, as well as its feminist uses to theorize what Rey Chow calls "the experience of con-sumption and reception . . . that store of elusive elements that, *apart from* 'wages' and 'surplus value,' enable people to buy, accept, and enjoy what is available in their culture."[42]

A lucid or discriminating "sentimental" pleasure will not register for Shulte-Sasse's model of mediation, any more than the television *talk* show can figure for his theory of an alinguistic postmodern mass subjectivity. With so much American experience of television excluded from the study of American national feeling, the prospect of an auratic Australian politi-cian passionately lecturing in economics to a TV audience including at least some appalled but adoring fans watching him in between reruns of *Miami*

Vice and *LA Law* (for Shulte-Sasse, emblematic postmodern shows) can only count as eccentric.

> *I walk on that stage, some performances might be better than others, but they will all be up there trying to stream the economics and the politics together. Out there on the stage doing the Placido Domingo.*
>
> —PAUL KEATING TO THE CANBERRA PRESS CLUB, 7 DECEMBER 1990[43]

However it is only in an avoidance of thinking TV *language* as well as everyday social *disjunction* (marked in Rey Chow's subtle "apart from") and cultural *mixity* ("store"), that the myth of mass culture as Woman can sustain its political form as an elegy on the death of Public Man.[44] I think that any theoretical discourse in which a private/public boundary figures as the vanishing locus of an apocalyptic event, rather than as an unstable object, product and site of social contestation, is a traumatized discourse on the conceptual impossibility *and* the historical actuality of "female" suffrage.[45] Like TV as a private/public medium of the *language* of personal/political "talk," Woman as citizen makes sense for this discourse only as the blur abolishing the line that historically once "clearly delimited" (in Schulte-Sasse's phrase) "ideological" Public Man from his disenfranchised, "sentimentological" others.

Yet there is also something closed about my criticism here, routinely taking its distance on familiar, if necessary, feminist grounds. Schulte-Sasse's objects differ from mine: he theorizes the enabling conditions of *singular* massifying events (prime-time bombing-raids, mass-participation spectacles), while I am concerned with an everyday, low-level process that can organize a mediated *partisan* feeling. Moreover, as part of my experience of that process I find myself consuming much self-reflexive Australian media discourse that, in its gendering of debate about communication and citizen-subjectivity, does not differ greatly in its basic assumptions from Schulte-Sasse's. This raises the question of how cultural and political differentiation may work through the apparently general framework of a discourse of sexual sameness.

Keating certainly provoked gender trouble, but sex was rarely at stake. On the one hand, he was famous for displays of what Gloria-Jean Masciarotte calls "muscular orality" or "voiced muscle."[46] Formal parliamentary boxing aside, he often pulverized media decorum codes with blasts of well-timed misplaced humor: his sensationally vulgar response on Sydney breakfast radio in 1990 to being elected (for the second time) "the sexiest man in Australia" was celebrated with much hilarity on the *Midday Show* by a gift of libidinally restorative black silk pajamas—while "time to put the cue on the rack" passed into the lexicon of phrases used by journalists to add vernacularity to their prose.[47]

In the more specialized media context of an address to the National Press Club, Keating himself gave the voice/muscle theme an operatic frame of reference in his notorious "Placido Domingo speech." This throwaway self-description inspired the media to repeat for months that Keating could turn economics into high art and popularize the outcome. But the joke was widely read as pugilistic. Since the speech also argued that Australia has never had "a real leader," reporters claimed that Keating saw himself as the man of real talent performing in the shadow of a more popular, but less able, Pavarotti. This was a projection of *media* desires and perceptions; Keating had merely described his way of promoting economic policy as "doing the Placido Domingo." However, he was widely quoted as having declared himself "the Placido Domingo *of politics*." From this moment, the Hawke-Keating partnership publicly began to disintegrate.

On the other hand, Keating's eroticized status as an object of media desire ("he seduces us all from time to time, just as he seduces the government and he seduces the Caucus and he seduces the Cabinet")[48] entailed explicit feminization, not because "he" was seductive—the culture of mateship admits this as an unmarked characteristic—but because he could seduce with the fluency of a *speech* (to journalist Peter Hartcher, a "siren-song"), that was also widely mistrusted ("so beguiling that, like Ulysses' seamen, [journalists] deliberately close their ears").[49] He was, in short, a recognized rhetorician, and rhetoric can be construed not only as a "feminine" orality (Voice) but as intellectually feminizing ("plainly short on matter"). Hartcher even called on Edward de Bono to endorse his suspicion of Keating as posing that special threat to Australian masculinity, an "*intelligence trap*": "the more intelligent you are, the more readily you can argue any proposition that you happen upon."

This is exactly the accusation to which journalists themselves are always subject. No matter how loudly they may invoke the greater reality and truth of hard-nosed practical action, their own practice of voice, word, and image must remain, by these criteria, hopelessly rhetorical. In this context, Derek Parker's use of the term "courtesans" to name a special erotic-economic complicity between the government and the press gallery was no casually sexist gesture, but a theory of a mode of governance, "pornocracy," dominated by the corrupting wiles of female rhetoricians: "they thrive on rumour, gossip, and the labyrinthine intrigues of the party system. To the Courtesans, the game is all."[50] Perhaps more significant, then, than the charges of femininity and intellectuality routinely exchanged as insults by powerful men is the shared anxiety, and the longing this banter articulates for a certain something—ideology, solid "matter," a responsible use of power—deemed to be missing from the mediated public sphere (sentimental, rhetorical, formalist) that these same men, effectively, dominate.

In this context, Keating's narrowness was emblematic of a "something" that aroused intense ambivalence. One "How to Pick the Real Paul Keating" cartoon projected the structure of media obsession with Keating as an impossible object (perfectly benevolent, totally destructive) in terms of a *masculine* ambivocality. "Voice" in this structure is not opposed to language, writing, or law, but internally divided. Two identical visual images are verbally differentiated as "The Real Paul!" (Prime Ministerial pretender), and "The Evil Twin!" (cause of the recession); the Evil Twin has a "tongue foul enough to make a wharfie blush" while the Real Paul has a "lovely silky baritone, sings like Sinatra only without his threatening and elitist talent."[51] Like "foul tongue," "language" is an old-fashioned euphemism for swearing: between language and music, profanity and sanctity, muscularity and silk, foul tongue and singing, a problem of identity circulates in the oscillation of love and hostility that constitutes ambivalence, and thus the oscillation that constitutes the question.

A psychoanalytic reading could no doubt further explain the process whereby journalists developed a "Keating thing" as a symptom of their own enduringly ambivalent relations to political power and to sentimental/rhetorical performance.[52] Consumer ecstasy doesn't quite work the same way, involving as it does a basic *failure* of hostility (thus suspending identity as problem), nor does comic criticism: the cartoon solves the problem by implying a third term, a Really Evil Paul Keating who obviously orchestrates ("without talent"), from another position, the production of his voices and images.

For the "matter" melancholics of the media, this solution is itself the problem posed by a political leader who "has it" by openly having only the *form* of having it. In a media economy (the logic goes), a self-promoting image man with the rhetorical force and the legitimacy to promote himself as a self-*made* man, with real old-fashioned policies, may actually offer a leadership-effect, and so generate Being by Seeming. An anxious dream (recurrent in the history of realism, insistent in the "Keating for PM" editorials that appeared with greater frequency as the recession of the late 1980s intensified) takes shape as a hope that nostalgia for political substance may be overcome by a cynical belief in the Image. In such a moment, "Keating" became the name of a utopian discourse in which journalists imagined an ideal "real" political power to be formed in the image of their real "rhetorical" power.[53]

> For sheer entertainment value, Paul Keating was the best treasurer we've had for years. By his panache and style, Keating made economics sexy. A verbal spell-binder, his ability to coin a phrase to describe problems afflicting the economy would leave lesser mortals groping for words. Keating has popularized economics—we now

*breathe economics, speak economics and feast on econom-
ics. The monthly balance of payments figures are received
like the latest cricket score. From the shop-floor to the dance-
floor, everyone is squawking about micro-economic reform.*

—ALEX MILLMOW[54]

Yet cynicism is generally held to characterize now the space of national
politics. There is nothing distinctive about it: cynicism is rather taken to be
a social norm ("the common coin of politics everywhere")[55] against which
any *ecstatic* response may now be defined as aberrant. Thus Slavoj Žižek,
writing from experience of a communist regime, endorses Peter Sloterdijk's
claim that "the cynical subject is quite aware of the distance between the
ideological mask and the social reality, but he none the less insists upon the
mask."[56] No ecstatic fusion or crisis can occur across this distance: cynicism
is merely confronted from the other side by *kynicism*, a "popular, plebeian
rejection of the official culture by means of irony and sarcasm." As a pragmatic, *ad hominem* procedure, kynicism "subverts the official proposition by
confronting it with the situation of its enunciation"—for example, by exposing the personal gain that a politician who preaches the duty of sacrifice
is making "from the sacrifice of others."

"Insisting upon the mask" is a good description of many of the rituals of
Australian politics. But Sloterdijk's cynicism, with its spatialized opposition
of "socially real" *versus* semiotic functions, is too neat a concept for thinking
the messy relations between masks and *other* realities in a pragmatic media
democracy where kynical techniques (exposé narratives, satire, scandaliza-
tion of the political process, aura-enhancing profiles, merciless analysis of
the personal profit motive) are always already part of the media production
of "official" political culture. For example, Bob Hawke was often called "the
great communicator." The allusion to Reagan was kynical (Hawke has a
grating voice, Hawke had delusions of grandeur) but also translative.
Hawke's "image" as an immensely popular leader was neither visual nor vo-
cal but *tactile*, his medium "the common touch": he visited schools and shopping malls, "pressed the flesh" in retirement homes, went touring to *feel* the
People; an idealization of Hawke as embodying a distinctively Australian
version of "great communication" was thus, along with his delusiveness, asserted, enhanced—and communicated.

In a similar way, Alex Millmow's breezy review of Keating's performance
as Treasurer has a kynical panache, prefacing as it does a judgment that "his
constituency, the ordinary folk, paid the price for this economic experiment with . . . their jobs." It also has something of that capacity for making
an "absolutely real and totally ironic" investment of taste in an image that
Grossberg calls, not cynicism or kynicism, but "authentic inauthenticity"
(43, 61). However Millmow's is a subcultural-professional, not a national-

popular, "everyone": easily taking its critical distance ("sheer entertainment") from Keating's image, it claims no distance from the breathing/speaking/feasting/squawking "we" that is animated by his speech. This is a real and ironic investment in a use of *language*, not an image or a mask. It produces identification ("we") not with Keating as specular image (he is reviewed as a speaking subject, indeed, a cultural practitioner), nor with an immanent communal identity or a diffuse collective narcissism, but with the power of an enunciative practice that can ("popularizing," "spell-binding," "sexy") create a specialized "we" that is openly engaged, not in aestheticizing politics (a horizon taken as given), but in *eroticizing economics*.

Here, there is nothing to be revealed about the enunciative situation of "official" economic discourse, since the object of "everyone's" desire is to be *in* a situation to have the power and panache to talk like Keating. This suggests circumstances in which affect and ideology may be, for that limited "everyone," powerfully, if momentarily, convergent. So, too, does the appearance of a "showbiz" profile of Keating by an economics lecturer and a former Treasury officer in a magazine, *Australian Left Review*, that was once a Communist Party of Australia publication and still included former communists among its editors. While technically mediated, these circumstances are not those of an ecstasy of communication in which, as Baudrillard would have it, "we have passed alive into the models."[57] They are those, densely historical, of a social moment in which a passion for *using* a particular descriptive model could pass "from the shop-floor to the dance-floor," and from the bureaucracy to the academy to the Labor Party to the old Far Left to the gentle reader, without, in fact, abolishing differences between existing social spaces—for Millmow, the factory/nightclub opposition is in fact ironically savored—while overriding old political codes assigning specific kinds of speech as proper to particular *places*.

The differences between working and dancing, national accounting and sport, are not threatened by "sexy" economics, any more than is the system of social discriminations excluding from the category "everyone" precisely anyone unable to switch smoothly between practices and positions. What does collapse in this new petit-bourgeois scenario of a lateral social mobility is any expectation of manifest difference between unionist, corporate, parliamentary, "revolutionary," and street-chic ways of *describing* the social world. On this reading, people under the spell of Millmow's Keating do not "pass alive" into an ecstasy of economics. We consume (breathe/feast) and we parrot (speak/squawk)[58] a strictly utopian common language that reproduces sameness across a range of social sites, not by facilitating "communication" between formally differentiated social positions or technical relay points, but, on the contrary, by enabling a sense of *communion* with (the discourse of) the other.

An ability to spread across customary social borders is more often associated with fashion than with the dismal science and, as recession deepened in the early 1990s, some began to distance themselves from "80s economic fashions." But as it circulated through once-antagonistic spaces of Australian political life, the dream of an economic common language had more to do with mysticism than with cynicism or fashion. Millmow does not exaggerate the bodily effect that being, as it were, *liberated* into a world of infinitely free marketeering could have on those Keating fans who, twenty, even ten, years earlier, were thundering from shop-floor to dance-floor about class struggle, social justice, and bourgeois ideology. I saw men on television (trade-union stars, Cabinet Ministers, left-wing think-tank advisers) visibly hystericized by talking economics: eyes would glaze, shoulders hunch, lips tremble in a sensual paroxysm of "letting the market decide," "making the hard decisions," "levelling the playing field," "improving productivity," and "changing the culture." Minds *melted*, rather than closed: those who queried the wisdom of floating the exchange rate, deregulating the banks, or phasing out industry protection were less ignored than *washed away* in the intoxicating rush of "living in a competitive world" and "joining the global economy."

Critics were hystericized, too. Proponents may say calmly that economic rationalism is just a belief that "markets usually allocate productive resources better than planners"[59]—on the surface, a simple post-Keynesian proposition. But for all of its modern history, Australia has been governed by the opposite assumption: "laborism," a social contract upheld in various forms since 1904, exchanged trade protection and currency controls for a state-regulated wage-fixing system and compulsory arbitration; as a capital/labor deal for redistributing national income primarily between white men, laborism was sustained by a massive immigration policy legitimated and administered on racist principles until the 1960s, but by versions of multiculturalism thereafter. So the process of internationalizing the economy had a devastating intellectual (affective, ideological) as well as social effect. As the political alignments of a century slowly began to shatter, even those "new social movements" most critical of laborism—feminism, anti-racism, environmentalism—found themselves recast by its decline as "entrenched" and "vested" interests obstructing *radical* change.

Poorly grasped in its implications at the beginning of the 1980s, the "rationalist revolution"—in fact, an ideological program to justify the effects in the West of the global restructuring of capitalism—often figured in the Australian media as a mix of "Thatcherite" and "Reaganite" slogans confusingly sponsored by Labor. Invasive metaphors soon demonized the new philosophy as an all-devouring alien, formally echoing old war-time caricatures of the German-Japanese menace, not to mention the "Yellow Peril." One cartoon depicted a snake-oil apocalypse ("Once upon a time, people used to talk about **issues** and have fun. Then someone invented the economy. . . . the economy grew and grew! It took over everything and no-one could escape!") in which a horrible, noisy fluid ("HEY WHAT'S THIS BORING

BLACK STUFF!") swamps all human discourse ("I . . . I DON'T KNOW! BUT . . . MY BRAIN! IT'S . . . IT'S ROTTING!") with its gurgling deficit-speak.[60] On the academic side, the sociologist Michael Pusey began a Habermasian study of *Economic Rationalism in Canberra* by defining his object as a "locust strike" delivering our social democracy into "the unfriendly grip of ideas . . . from Britain and the United States—the two great 'stateless societies.'"[61] A senior vice-president of Kemper Financial Services (Chicago) could then urbanely invoke in support of rationalist policies "the intellectual upheaval now occurring in Third World political centres such as Mexico City, New Delhi, Jakarta, and Buenos Aires."[62]

For those unwilling to resort to a paranoid national rhetoric, Keating made economics sexy by acting as a great *describer* in Susan Stewart's sense. He was eloquent, not hysterical or paranoid, and lyrical, not communicative, in promoting economic reform. He used TV to outline a vision of a future "time and space" of plenitude (ever-receding from the lived experience of most Australians) that would follow from a bargained, consensual process of deregulation, contrasting it graphically with the "banana republic" purgatory awaiting a stagnant, closed economy—and with the cruel, truly "Thatcherite" revolution promised by the right-wing Opposition parties. An interest in Keating's style (language, voice) is thus an interest in a *particular kind* of closure, one that may be called "ideological" because it does involve belief as well as affect. Any Treasurer can promise that *economic* discourse has a magic power of "closing the gap that separates language from the experience it encodes,"[63] in order to satisfy longing; such closure is an aim of policy. However the "gap" between Keating's hypercoded Labor vocality and his managerial vocabulary paradoxically also promised that *his* discourse could magically bridge the gulf between the social values (egalitarian, solidary, compassionate) mythically upheld as national ideals in white working-class popular memory, and *realpolitik* of economic rationalism—elitist, divisive, competitive.

> Dream and norm are but twin aspects of the neoconservative vision. The abstract models elaborated by the Chicago School propose a pragmatic, positive political project designed for the aftermath of the present economic crisis. However these models also reveal neoconservative economics to be truly utopian: like all utopias, it is first and foremost haunted by lack, ceaselessly filling within economics and by means of economics what it perceives to be lacking.
>
> —ANNIE L. COT[64]

Donald Horne has suggested that the peculiarly intense imaginary of truth that Australians call economic rationalism might better be described as economic *fundamentalism*. It is not just that variable mix of policies, adopted during the 1980s, in diverse forms, by all the "English-speaking" economies, that aims to reduce the regulatory powers and the social responsibilities of government while increasing the state's efficiency in further distributing wealth to the wealthy, and poverty to the poor.[65] Nor is it just a belief that neoclassical economics offers the most, perhaps now the *only*, rational guide to state action in democratic countries today. Economic fundamentalism also involves an inversion whereby, as Pusey puts it, "society [is] recast as the *object* of politics (rather than, at least in the norms of the earlier discourses, as the *subject* of politics)" and thus as "some sort of stubbornly resisting sludge"—even as "an idealized *opponent* of 'the economy'" (10, my emphases).

For Pusey, this inversion redefines "culture" as merely the malleable, consumable environment of economic action (18), a move familiar to students of the tourist-leisure-lifestyle-art-and-architecture complex that transformed the social landscape of our cities and towns in the boom of the 1980s. But both Horne and Pusey note the back-from-the-dead effect that this new economic determinism has also had in Australia on what Horne bluntly calls "Stalinism," and Pusey "orthodox Marxism." Indeed, Pusey claims that a *market* determinism politically projected as an enduring administrative system is capable of reaching an accommodation "with almost anyone . . . *except liberals*"—who persist in claiming primacy for concepts of community and civil society, and whom the traditional Left and the Right have always agreed to despise (194).

This helps make sense of the panache with which some of yesterday's Althusserians could become econocrats cavorting to the sound of Keating-speak on Alex Millmow's dance-floor. The fundamentalist inversion allows for a moment in which a professional subject of politics—a loose alliance of bureaucrats, advisers, managers, experts, and, more fantasmally, journalists and policy theorists identifying with the forms of power exercised by these—can project as its proper object of action, not "society" in general, but particular cultures in need of "restructuring" for their own economic good. Vintage forms of vanguardism find a new mission in this; there is no need for socialist or modernist nostalgia when the new avant-garde can trade the cell for the committee, write reports instead of manifestos, and leave the garret for the corridors of power.

As well as highlighting the anti-democratic implications of a philosophy that treats society as a by-product ("sludge") of market forces tempered *only* by the actions of an elite caste of experts, the term "economic fundamentalism" is useful for sidestepping that space of media polemic in which opposition is disqualified as "economically *ir*rational." In doing so, it allows us to see this space as one in which a duel of "reason" with "emotion" is being staged with quite desperate intensity. It is a curious conflict, not because "emotion" is here, like "theory," a sign exchanged between adversaries equally claiming rationality, but because this exchange so explicitly occurs between moderate ("pragmatic") and pure ("principled") exponents of the same belief that *the market* is a rational agent. Perhaps because there is no pretense at confronting a significantly different other, the debate has a desperate intensity in that the "rationalist" move on both sides is no longer to impose as universal a particular mode of logic, but rather to displace the argumentative procedures of reasoning with a *furious rhetoric* of Reason—as though the very act of pronouncing the other irrational can magically install the speaker as the guaranteed subject of an intrinsically rational discourse (and thus as a master of "market logic").

In this spirit, a serious journalist such as Peter Robinson can assert in a wonderful othering move that critics of economic rationalism must logically favor irrationalism but, "since no-one is prepared to admit to this openly," will deviously "cloak" their irrationality in "economic *sentimentalism*."[66] By portraying the unemployed as "innocent victims" of "faceless bureaucrats with economics degrees," these unscrupulous "irrational sentimentalists" will then cruelly "assault . . . the emotions through a ruthless appeal to pity and patriotism." Robinson is primarily referring here to people in public life (including Labor politicians) who wanted to respond with old-fashioned "'pump-priming' schemes, 'job-creating' policies, and 'industry assistance' hand-outs" to the severe recession that, by 1991, had overtaken those economies—Australia, New Zealand, Canada, the United States, and Britain—in which the elements of economic rationalism most dominated policy thinking and administrative practice throughout the 1980s. Robinson describes such responses as a "cruel hoax," and as "ruthless" in their sentimentality, because he does not believe they can work.

But the strident illogic of his own polemic makes it painfully clear that Robinson himself has no idea of what *will* work. When he goes on to proclaim "the truth of the matter," that industry policy cannot be "turned on and off like a tap," truth is a revelation that our position in the global economy is now hopelessly mired in lack: on the one hand, Australia "lacks the economic power" to demand that other nations turn their assistance tap *off* in the interests in free trade; on the other, it "lacks the cohesive authoritarian [cultural] tradition" to which Robinson imputes the success of those Asian economies that have thrived on "government interventionism at home." In the end, Robinson's rationalism is fundamentally a *faith*, not in Man or in the powers of human reason, but in the Law of a jealous God: "ultimately," he concludes, "economic reality cannot be mocked any more than cultural reality can."[67]

Of course, this authoritarian fatalism is most sensibly ascribed to a realistic recognition that no deeply indebted trading nation, having handed control of its currency's value to the global financial markets, can hope to solve its trouble by following the will of its people or the whim of its politicians in an "immanentist" isolation. At this level, by affirming *economic* Reason as the transcendent principle that, as John Forbes puts it, "no philosopher could argue with," Robinson merely expresses—using clichés culled from the debris of a culture's perhaps once true belief in Reason, God, and Man—his impatience with those who do not see, or cannot afford to admit, that the powers of at least this nation-state really have been much curtailed. What interests me, however, is the intensity with which such a self-styled "rational" discourse will, when confronting the limits of its own powers in the form of the other's lack, turn doctrinaire rather than practical in the very moment *when it says it knows* that pragmatism requires, not universal norms, but a relational thinking of difference.

Robinson is a moderate exponent of economic rationalism because he does say this: like his daring admission that Australia is not the United States or Japan, his reference to "cultural reality" would qualify in turn as "irrational" and "sentimental" for theorists who dream that Australians can and should abandon their sludgy political culture to model a new society on (as one of them puts it) "*ordo* liberalism in post-war Germany and [*sic*] the commitment to the neo-Confucian order in East Asia."[68] For fundamentalists, the solution is not to review what Robinson concedes to be "innumerable mistakes made in the name of economic rationalism," but to replace our entire political system with "a simple order" based on rationalist principles even more relentlessly applied.[69] Logically, a moderate should confront such fierce utopians, as well as "sentimentalists," with the conditions of a rational compromise between economy and culture. Instead, in a move characteristic of much financial journalism, Robinson turns from berating the nostalgia animating others to exalting inactivity in the melancholy name of a chastened acceptance of Fate.

> *A rational person, according to the philosopher Bertrand Russell, is one who gives any proposition that degree of weight which the evidence for the proposition warrants. In common parlance, we describe such a person as clear-thinking, of sound judgment. Apply such judgment to matters economic and you have your "economic rationalist."*
>
> —G. O. GUTMAN[70]

Watching this bizarre debate spill from the financial press into TV news, reshaped as a conflict of principle between the major political parties (Labor, "moderate," Liberal, "pure"), it seemed by 1991 that the opinion-industry in Australia had been taken over by demented white men very publicly losing their marbles. Given the agony and uncertainty of "the worst recession in 60 years" combined with world political change, this effect was unsurprising; few men of power in our culture have much experience of exercising political agency from a disempowered position, and the madness of those who wanted to "Confucianize" Australia because "Thatcherization" had failed was matched by others who, in facing evidence of a disaster created by big business, banks, Keating's use of monetary policy, global trade war, and some strangely hot dry weather, judged responsible for the nation's woes environmentalists, unions, and Aboriginal people irrationally impeding development.

More than a decade ago, however, Annie Cot suggested, in a fascinating argument with the utopianism of Chicago School economics, that the academic project so pervasively influential as a component of the transnational "rationalist revolution" has itself always been driven by a desire to *evade* the real social disorder of the crisis of capitalist restructuring that it claimed to overcome, and that an analysis of fantasy is needed to follow its reasoning. Cot carefully restricts the object of her analysis. Where Pusey risks paranoia by tracing a massive historical movement that embraces the 1975 Trilateral Commission report (*The Crisis of Democracy*),[71] "postmodernism" in social theory (Niklas Luhmann's systems logic), and the training of a generation of administrators in the "technically-oriented neoclassical economics curriculum that swept through the economics departments of Australian universities from about 1947" (6), Cot focuses on the work of Gary Becker in order to examine the disciplinary rhetoric of a single body of theory. Analyzing the invasive logic of its self-representation as a movement to colonize, across the boundaries of economics, an "outside-itself" that is thus denied its difference, she associates this movement of intellectual *ekstasis* with a theoretical politics of "despotism."[72]

Justifying her spatial metaphors historically, in relation to the constitution of modern "standard" economics as a discipline excluding the family (scene of love, not money) from its field, Cot argues that with the emergence in the 1970s of a theory of human capital promising to provide, as Becker puts it, a "unified framework for all behaviour involving scarce resources," economics began to slip *by its own criteria* "outside its terrain." "Delocalised," economics becomes a utopian *totalizing* discourse that affirms "the universality of its reading of human behaviour by transgressing the market boundaries of economics," and a *totalitarian* discourse that declares itself "the sole bearer of the single, universal norm of all forms of social structure, market or nonmarket, past or present, private or public" (293–94).

With this expansive movement, economics seems to "regress to its original meaning; *oikonomia*, the economics of the household" (296). In fact, an inversion is effected, analogically, whereby the family is seen as the reflection of a market society. The result projected in political terms is a "fantasy of an entire society transformed into a factory" (305). Arguing that such an "expanded" market economics must paradoxically negate the neoclassical concept of the market, Cot suggests that a theoretical figure produced by the inversion of economics and *oikonomia* then functions to explain this paradox, as well as to satisfy a "paternalistic nostalgia" induced by the crisis of the welfare state—the "despotic 'head of the family.'" The despot reconciles love *and* money: defined, in theory, neither by sex or age, the neoconservative head of the family is "that member, if there is one, who transfers general purchasing power to all other members because he *cares* about their welfare" (299, my emphasis). In this fantasy of "pure power"—phantasmal, because it denies the horizontal power relations that constitute the family, analogical, because it must disavow difference in order to function—the "natural order of the market" converges with "the genetic order of nature" in the neo-Darwinian household.

However the "rarely acknowledged" stake of this normalizing movement (and the objective, for neoconservatives, of restructuring, including of the marketing of products) is no longer the domination of space that preoccupied earlier liberal utopians, but the conquest of (non-market) *time*: "where Rousseau and Bentham dreamed of panoptic transparency, the Chicago School advocates a panchronic transparency of human activities" (304).[73] In the context of this shift, the ecstatic disciplinary move can be understood as an *evasive* response to crisis. Cot does not simply argue that neoconservative economics tries to subject all social categories to the principles of market regulation, although this was a feature of the economic mysticism by which policy rhetoric was "carried away" in the 1980s.[74] Her major point is that the boundary between market and non-market spaces is traditionally conceptualized by the Left as the dividing line between "necessity and freedom," and thus as "the prerequisite of a nonmarket and pluralistic socialization." The new Right's effort to annihilate any type of boundary to the market implies, however, that both spaces can "*fuse* in a generalized economic tabulation where human time would be the primary element" (307, my emphasis). In this utopia, the market "shines forth," as Baudrillard puts it, in the "pure and empty" form of an eternal, as well as infinite, economic Sublime.

Cot's is a European reading of an American intellectual project and could, in its formalist aspect, easily be accused of ignoring the diverse institutional contexts and real economic conditions in which neoconservative economics came to influence the political agenda in so many countries after the first "oil shock" of the early 1970s. As Pusey points out, while "the rhetoric may be the same everywhere, the structural context is not": in Australia, the enthusiasm for it on both sides of politics after 1975 needs to be understood in terms of the historical crisis of a particular form of protectionism with no equivalent in the United States or Britain, and which was "seen as leading the nation down the Argentine road."[75]

Yet Pusey's institutional study confirms Cot's premise that the problem posed to pluralistic democracy by economic rationalism as a "norm-setting language" (109) is one of "redefining the legitimate bounds of economic behaviour" (13). Pusey locates the real-political threat of this language precisely in its capacity to substitute a purely "formal" rationalism for the practical rationality preserved by previous philosophies of public administration under capitalism. In this respect, the conclusion of his empirically grounded sociology is not only compatible with Cot's analysis of economic representation, but even more depressing in its vision of the consequences. At that "sublime" moment when the limitless logic of an *economic* formalism is unopposed in policy discourse and administrative practice, for Pusey it in fact turns catastrophic: "in its constructions of time and in its incapacity to read or 'obey' the demands of the external environment" (here physical as well as cultural), "economic rationalism as a model for action is the very opposite of an adaptive system." It "resembles instead a model of the self-destroying system" (21).

Taken together, these analyses help to explain a public debate in which, at the very moment when the evidence would seem to cast doubt on the adequacy of economic fundamentalism as a guide to action, the melancholy exponents of paralysis (the "do nothing" theory of government) competed for honors in "clear thinking" with infantile megalomaniacs identifying with a Market force that could, unimpeded, do everything. Pusey ascribes the investment of a generation of intellectuals in perpetuating such discourse to "a trained incapacity to learn from later experience" (6) related to a privileged class background as well as a training in neoclassical economics. However Cot's analysis of rhetorical forms can better explain how speaking subjects may come to identify, so passionately and inadaptably, with the discursive process of one *particular* training. When pure rationalists call for a "leaner" public sector to replace the "welfare state" in Australia, even though by 1988 Australia had the lowest reported welfare spending of all OECD nations, and smaller government than any but Japan and Turkey,[76] their insatiability supports Cot's claim that an analysis of fantasy is needed to understand a program that, in its ecstatic determination to "fill all gaps between the economic and the noneconomic," in the same movement recoils from the complexity of any "'real,' localised market" (304).

Her account is certainly useful as an allegory of the way in which a figure personifying an ecstatic economic discourse could appeal to media intellectuals who value the power of speech. Despite its many differences from Chicago School utopianism, the economics made sexy by Keating owed some of its *resonance* of "pure power" to the movement analyzed by Annie Cot. In the 1980s, political debate collapsed almost entirely into a discourse of economic management:[77] not only did the difference between the parties reduce, for a time, to management styles, but activists on issues once considered "social" and intrinsically important (from racism, the status of women, and human rights, to public education and the arts) had to reconstruct their objects *and their practices* in order to prove them "not *un*-economic."

A social-factory thematics became ubiquitous, like the dream of controlling time: by 1990, "productivity" was a value to be extracted in any activity from manufacturing to aerobics to writing poetry. While the head of the family was not invoked as a legitimizing figure, a craving for something quite like "the despot's tenderness" infused coverage of the leadership's efforts to increase disposable household income while cutting workers' wages. Whether the Treasurer really *cared* about ordinary Australians as he chopped their pay became as contentious as the exact percentages of love exchanged on a monthly basis in Hawke's "affair" with the people.

However, there was also a movement of charisma running back the other way. The "Keating" made sexy by economics owed much of *his* resonance to an inversion of the promise of a neoconservative utopia: in place of a society transformed into a "diffuse factory," Labor could offer a fantasy of Australia transformed into One Big Union. With its emphasis on bargaining, consensus, and a training of constituents, using radio and television, in metadiscourses legitimating the "hard decisions" that affect them, neocorporatism does differ in crucial respects from neoconservatism. The Hawke-Keating program was underpinned by an Accord renegotiated six times with the union movement, an anathema to "true" rationalists. For this reason, an ecstatic/despotic economics could lend its religious aura all the more powerfully to those very figures who wanted to enhance their necessary practice of economic management, but also to *limit* the social destructiveness of neoconservative logic.

For this reason, too, Keating was a reversible, and not a contradictory, political sign. Not only could he pose with perfect consistency as the voice of continuity and the agent of rupture, but, when his achievements as Treasurer appeared to be self-destructing, he could switch smoothly from playing the public face of the *only* "real" rationalist revolution Australia had then experienced into his other role as the only Man of Action capable of saving our social democracy from rationalist revolutionaries—and of talking the markets into letting him do it.[78] When Caucus made Keating Prime Minister at the end of 1991, the man they chose to lead the nation in its hour of need was not only the Evil Twin who had invoked the Law of economic reality in 1990 in order to justify on television "the recession we had to have." They also elected the Keating who had, just a few months earlier, convulsed the media with laughter at the Opposition Leader, John Hewson, for promising Australians that a "whole other world" would follow from *his* economic reforms. Hewson, said Keating (reciting in Parliament the opening stanzas of a popular song), must be "getting his economics from Sam Cooke":

> *Don't know much about history*
> *Don't know much biology . . .*
> *But I do know that I love you*

And I know that if you loved me too
What a wonderful world this would be.

—"MARIE" AND "PJ" SERENADING KEATING,
BERT NEWTON SHOW, NOVEMBER 1989

I read John Forbes's poem as an analysis of how this mediated double movement—convergent, not diffusive, more fervid than cynical or cool—can work for a willing, wanting subject. "Watching the Treasurer" is a marvelous text about television watched intensely and closely, about seeing "the words come out": a text that creates, in its slide toward "that utopia" of identity and belief, relations so intricate between speaking and seeing and hearing that for me it describes the movement involved in a *desire* to describe—and in my desire to believe Paul Keating's descriptions. If hardly anyone watches television like intellectuals who analyze television (journalists and political commentators as well as poets and cultural critics), then the poem is a study of a particular *way* of watching.

"Watching the Treasurer" has only two sentences. The first is a clear, short statement of desire to believe by a definite "I" addressing everyone, no one, itself (and so perhaps the institution of literature). This comfortably social subject contemplates truth ("lies") and beauty—historic food for poetry—in the form of a display that is ambiguously sacred, like the Communion feast, and domestic, like working-class "tea." The scene is homely, cosy, yet also ceremonial: "I" is desirous, like a dinner guest, but also passive, like a couch potato; "the past" hospitably does the spreading out of lies to be admired and consumed. Then something happens across the space between "feast" and "Television":

> I want to believe the beautiful lies
> the past spreads out like a feast.

> Television is full of them & inside
> their beauty you can act:

It's like an eye moving, naturally, from table to TV set (as anyone's eye might do at dinner), but also like a camera making commonplace moves when tracking around a lounge room. My own desire to eat lies is activated, turned into a greed for (words about) the image, and from "inside their beauty you can act" I have the most wonderful, powerful sense of zooming, and being sucked, into the television—greedy to be consumed by it, yes, but gently, not voraciously, to end up "bathed," to be precise, in that "milky white fluorescent glow." But during the long second sentence, there is a complicated splitting of the terms of the opening scene:

Paul Keating's

bottom lip trembles then recovers,
like the exchange rate under pressure

buoyed up as the words come out—
elegant apostle of necessity, meaning

what rich Americans want, his world is
like a poem, completing that utopia

no philosopher could argue with, where

"I" vanishes, never to reappear, in a series of little displacements between "television," "Paul Keating," and two enunciatively blurry "*you*"s. "I" becomes "you" ambiguously as you, me, Paul Keating, one, everybody ("you can act"), and also, more strongly in the second instance ("what your words describe you know exists"), an other "I" somewhere in an elsewhere of the text. But through all the intricate doubling that formally structures the poem (I:you/you; I/television: you/Paul Keating; I want/rich Americans want:his world/your words), there is, in the movement toward "that utopia," an increasing pressure of convergence between the *visual* ("beauty" to "bottom lip" to "elegant"), the *oral* ("feast" to "lip" to "milky") and the *verbal* ("lies" to "exchange rate" to "words come out") toward a scene of fullness ("feast" to "full" to "completing" to "glow") and fluidity ("lip" to "buoyed up" to "bathed" to "milky . . . fluorescent").

There is also a story here, a little narrative of *ekstasis*. Its three main phases are divided by the two ampersands: an initial setting in *place* (down to "*&* inside their beauty"), an image on *screen* as transition (to "*&* what your words describe"), and then closure in "that" utopian *space* of "glow," syntactically hooked to the rest of the text by the single word, "completing," where:

what seems, is & what your words describe
you know exists, under a few millimetres
of invisible cosmetic, bathed

in a milky white fluorescent glow.

Each phase has its own modality: desire ("I want to believe"); empowerment ("you can act"); knowledge ("you know exists"). So the mediating phase of empowerment, at once a portrait of a "bottom lip" and a *mise-en-scène* of speaking, acts as a kind of passage, an event between two scenes: one on "this" side of a television screen, a place of subjectivity and desire; the other, a space of plenitude (with no true "subject" in the glow at the end) that is not on the other *side* of the screen, but simply elsewhere, other, in relation to the first.

The screen implied by the Keating portrait is not a border between comparable places or spaces. No barrier is traversed, except the ampersand "&": with an effortless metonymic somersault "I" is "inside" the lies inside television and *en route* to "you" by the end of the third line of text. At least, inside their *beauty*: TV's other scene is not a "box" (no room-to-womb symmetry here), but a radiance, an aura, an "inside" without an outside. So if the screen phase acts as a means of transport between a "feast" and "that utopia," it also moves toward a space that is a displacement of the homely terms of beginning. Paul Foss calls this kind of space in Australian historiography a "landscape without landscape."[79] Deleuze and Guattari call it "faciality"; "Jesus Christ superstar: he invented the facialization of the entire body and spread it everywhere (the Passion of Joan of Arc, in close-up)."[80]

This is the story of "I." But there is also "the past" to consider; like "I," our host seems to vanish from the scene with the shift from "feast" to "television." Perhaps the past becomes the other scene, in a shift of temporalities as well as from place to space, with "watching" as a process (and Keating as an image) that can mediate between them. In the beginning, the past is an indeterminate allegorical figure of time, but that "milky white" nimbus maternalizes, in retrospect, both "the past" and the scene of consumption. There is a crazy infantilism somewhere here, a thumb-sucking, megalomaniac dream of power and satisfaction (*"you can act"*) that connects in some delicious way to Keating's "bottom lip." But is Keating like child, or mother? Once inside the beauty of television's lies, "You" and "Paul Keating" work, syntactically, as doubles of each other ("you can act: Paul Keating's bottom lip trembles . . . "), but he looms larger pretty quickly: he starts talking up the exchange rate as a delegated instance of "your" power, but as he does so "you" is carried away by the buoyancy of his words.

It doesn't last. Julia Kristeva once wrote that "the symbolic order is assured as soon as there are images which secure unfailing belief, for belief is in itself the image: both arise out of the same procedures and through the same terms: *memory, sight, and love.*"[81] Perhaps the pull toward presence is so strong for me in the middle of the poem because, in the end, unfailing belief is *not* secured in the Keating image. "Watching the Treasurer" isn't *Videodrome*, with Keating as Debbie Harry on the other side demanding "Come to Momma." Here "you" does bump up against something; not a screen but a layer of distance, "a few millimetres of invisible cosmetic," between wanting and believing, describing and being, and what you see *is* in the end all you get: to push the fantasy of being "sucked in" any further is like pushing your nose against the TV screen to get an eyeful of fluorescence.

If there is no true subject in "that utopia" at the end, there is no more ecstasy either. What visibly "exists" there, "bathed" in glow, is merely a "what"—a relative pronoun, a bit of language, that *relation* "your words describe." Writing, rather than memory, sight, or love (and a desire for control, not belief) predominates in this poem: even the ampersands buttoning the narrative in place are vivid signs of Modern Poetry at its most scrupulously *written*. A history of writing also helps to define the problem of "what your words describe," since, from the beginning, Forbes's feast of lies is literary: "Australian history," claimed Mark Twain in a famous fantasy proposition, "is . . . like the most *beautiful lies* . . . but they are all true, they all happened."[82]

Because of this formal institutional framing, his domestic experience of watching the Treasurer intensely is not universalized by Forbes as representative of the power of "television." This poem is not an allegory of postmodern nationalism or of the psychology of a leadership-cult, and it does not suggest that electronic media can colonize "our" sources of identity; in another Forbes poem, "Baby," the language of television is tenderly adult, not phallic-maternal, and companionly rather than mesmerizing ("you think how beautiful she is & the soft TV agrees" [79]). What "Watching the Treasurer" does do, I think, is tell a story about someone using television as a way of becoming "involved," in Michelle Rosaldo's sense, in a "social world." This is not a story of emotional manipulation and involuntary memory, but the story of a critical question. Beginning from a personal longing ("I want to believe"), the changing subject of the poem passes through a moment of interpretive delirium envisaging total control of the image ("you can act") only to arrive, on that fantasy's other side, at a problem: if Paul Keating's world is "like a poem," then what can a poem be like? How *do* you argue with utopia? *how* can you act inside the beauty of a lie?—if not as Keating does, and as a poem (like *this* poem) can?

It would then be true to say that the poem "acts" by matching the Treasurer's performance with one of its own, although this literary-critical truth is probably a beautiful lie that "I" would only like to believe. For me, the critical power of John Forbes's writing about television culture has more to do with the way that a formal poetic "I" in his texts often struggles to articulate something that his vernacular, screen-wise "you" already quite casually knows. This struggle is not, I think, to reconcile a high art/media antagonism, or even to confront an aestheticization of politics with, as Brecht and Benjamin suggested, a "politicization" of art. Forbes is a poet of sociable disjunction, not militant opposition, and his texts do not bridge gaps. But by never disavowing their literary limits, they do model ways in which the ethical and political dilemmas traversing everyday cultural practices—spreading tea, watching television, talking economics—surpass or even confound the *aesthetic* performative closure that his "I," writing poetry, must nonetheless always achieve.

Thus an adequate description is always a socially adequate description. It has articulated no more and no less than is necessary to the membership of the sign. Independent of this social organization of detail, description must threaten infinity, an infinity which stretches beyond the time of speech in a gesture which points to speech's helplessness when bereft of hierarchy.

—SUSAN STEWART (26)

Paul Keating always did, I must say, arouse a peculiar nostalgia in me. Something about his voice, the way that his facial expression on television condenses in his lips, and, especially, his "language," all act uncannily as after-images of stories that my *mother* has told since I was a child about her early life. A union official hostile to Keating once described him with good reason, I think, as "in style and approach . . . a Labor politician of the 1940s," offering "essentially antiquated images" of "macho aggression, hard conflict, and upward mobility into the ruling class" that "no longer strike a chord among ordinary Australians."[83] That sounds right. Yet these comments are also aggressive in their appropriation of a past (those are not words that my mother would use to talk about the 1940s), and they may also miss something vital about the power of mediated public figures now to orchestrate multiple (as well as communal) and strongly *discordant*, as well consonant, desires and "ordinary" memories.[84]

They certainly do not explain why economics should have come to function in the media as a discourse of orchestration. While the work of social critics like Cot and Pusey can articulate the movement of a disciplinary logic of desire and power, and analyze the effects of its deployment in specific governmental institutions, there is still the curious story of media fascination to consider. After all, it is an *esoteric* movement. If the "doctrine" of economic rationalism has occupied for years a "central position in the political thought of the Right" in most English-speaking countries, it has not played in all of them a starring role on prime-time news, nor acquired the emotional resonance of a discourse on national history and identity (as Peter Robinson puts it, on "what we have and who we are").[85] Another way to pose the problem, then, is to ask why a disparate bundle of economic theories, administrative practices, and political policies should have fused here so powerfully *as* a visible and nameable "doctrine."

In my experience, the public pedagogy of neocorporatism had a lot to do with this, and with the special implication, practical and phantasmal, of intellectuals in its procedures. One did not have to share its aims and values to take pleasure in the *form* of intellectuality personified by the Treasurer, and dismissed as "arrogant" in popular opinion polls. Where Grossberg (26–28) sees the projects of Thatcher and Reagan as responding to, respectively, a "sense of national economic crisis" (demanding "sacrifice in return for the imaginary construction of a promised community of prosperity"), and a "problem of national ego" ("often constructed and understood in terms of the changing position of the U.S. in international relations"), I see the "economic literacy" campaigns of the Hawke-Keating regime as promising economic salvation and the redemption of our imagined "compassionate" society by means of an *internationalist* discourse on Australia's weak position in a changing world economy—and on the need for a well-informed citizenry to endorse the modernizing actions taken by the state on our behalf. This was a politics of consent depending not on mass spectacles or massifying events, but on a continual assertion of the magic of expertise: eroticized images of teaching, learning, (controlled) debate, (limited) consultation, and exquisite mastery of data.

However, in spite of its reliance on myths of information and its increasingly narrow appeal to "the new 'cultural' petite bourgeoisie,"[86] I am reluctant to call such a politics "postmodern" if by that I must understand a fading of ideology in the glow of the TV screen, or its swamping in a milky surge of affect. For there is an aspect of my response to Keating's language that, if I do not call it "ideological" in Chow's sense ("that store of elusive elements . . . "), I am helpless to analyze. It is that necessary something-more that could make his pedagogy acceptable and enjoyable to me as to Millmow's class-specific "everyone," stirring a strong, stubborn, irrational, and *inherited*, almost impersonal, conviction that yes, above all else, the national economy matters, because the Economy is the source from which all good and evil flows. It is a something-more I sense in that "kynical" moment of truth in "Watching the Treasurer," when the swell of Keating's rhetoric is interrupted by a subject who says that he *knows* what its buoyancy means ("elegant apostle of necessity, *meaning / what rich Americans want*, his world is / like a poem")—but still resumes his effort at being carried away.

Such moments of sentimental disavowal could be mapped on to Schulte-Sasse's model of postmodern subjectivity. Yet I think that even a basic historical reading of the values accorded to "the economy" in Australian popular culture, and to "economics" in the dreams of intellectuals, could say more about the affect flowing through political discourse on television. Something mythic, at least, is at stake when the same economic credo can be packaged for public consumption not only as a "revolution" or as an "invasion" by both sides of politics, but also as an *inversion* or a *redemption* of the assumptions of a nation's past. Not least as a revision of late nineteenth-century struggles over free trade versus protection, in the context of which the Australian constitution was framed,[87] economic fundamentalism acts as a discourse of continuity that promises to effect a return to imaginary origins. "The economy" is quite homely to white Australians as the scene of an ecstasy of Reason. In 1976, after another period of economic and political crisis, Donald Horne wrote casually that "Australia is one of the most 'economic' nations in the world—*almost from the start* its 'economy' has been one of its main declared purposes for existing and it is characteristic that its political rhetoric should be to a large extent expressed in economic terms."[88]

If Horne simplifies the "purposes" of a nineteenth-century colony of settlement (since other values, after all, were always present), his acerbic critique of the components of a national economic culture is all the more useful as a corrective to current accounts of *media* culture that, by projecting an abstract postmodern subject who mirrors the structures of global capitalism on the one hand, and the formal properties of particular TV programming styles on the other, unduly simplify the historical burden ("experience") of everyday subjectivity. In a very basic way, we who live in a social world where it can be chic to squawk about micro-economic reform do occupy a specific position in a capitalist order, and we are at home in a media culture that does foster intense but temporary investments in fleeting images. We also, just as basically, live in a society where for almost a century the right of all "citizens" (a concept slowly wrested from the proprietorial control of white men) to a decent living wage, and the duty of the state to ensure it, were *imagined* as fundamental;[89] where "the economy" could mythically be construed as a source of sovereignty, and politically conceived as a relational site for otherwise disjunct popular struggles, in short, for affirming agency; and where the translation of public debate as an antisocial economic jargon is at once intelligible, seductive, and a mark of profound dispossession.

If this imaginary scene is Australian, the methodological issue it poses is not: historical understanding is weakened less by media-watching than by a refusal to think about "watching" historically. This is why Rey Chow's reading of feminist work on ideology for her theory of ethnic spectatorship seems so helpful to me. Developing work by Laura Mulvey, Teresa de Lauretis, and Kaja Silverman, she points to the "responsive, performative aspect" of ideology involved in "any reception of culture" (22). Where this aspect is often romantically purified as "resistance," she keeps it open to older readings of ideology as falsehood and illusion ("beautiful lies") insofar as these make it possible to say that "in what we think of as 'falsehood' often lies the chance of continued *survival*, sometimes the only way to come to terms with an existing oppressive condition" (23, my emphasis).

There is a real inappropriateness in too directly linking the media scenes I have described with struggles for survival. Yet it is also vital to see that even Alex Millmow's parrots are confronting something oppressive. In any political culture based on expertise, the limits to acceptable critical speech are as carefully policed as the power to participate in public criticism is restricted. Neocorporatist pedagogy has a nasty way of feeding images and stories to the people, only to reveal, at strategic moments, that *serious* knowledge, *real* power, was always elsewhere: this is its "arrogance," and this is why squawking is a mimicry that defends against being silenced as well as against belief. This is vital, because it helps to define the force of an apparent nostalgia—the "sadness without an object" that for Stewart "wears a distinctly utopian face, a face that turns toward a future-past, a past that has only ideological reality" (23)—that suffused so many public images and stories of economics in the 1980s and continued to pervade the struggles of the 1990s.

Distinct from, yet relaying, the hidden narratives of policy-making and of "real" economic debate, these images and stories shaped, by the very buoyancy of their rhetoric, a complex sense of longing: double-edged, two-faced. On the one hand, nostalgia for "the Economy" as a source of sovereignty and self-determination—a precious myth that proved hard to sustain in the aftermath of financial deregulation—was rampant in the ebulliently macho bombast of politicians identifying their own discourse with the power of market "forces," and denying the social reality of limits to (their mastery of) economic Reason; the government could seem never more securely in control of the nation's future than in the very moment of losing it. On the other hand there was, in all the speculation about the social meaning of "Keating" (his voice, his narrowness, his rhetoric), as it resonated over the decade with *other* images and stories of the decline of the Left and the epic collapse of socialism, a kind of sadness for that utopia, always known to have an "only ideological reality," that McGregor calls "the great humane ideals of the Labor movement."

In knowing its object, however (perpetually demystified by historians and critics and activists from all sides of politics, and so perhaps impossible to lose), this sadness was less strictly a form of nostalgia than the economic ecstasy that shaped it, and, in its feeling for the beautiful lies that help people to act, more like a way of seizing against helplessness a "chance for continued survival."[90] Meditation on the "traditional" virtues of the Treasurer involved a comic version of taking this chance. In the process he became, willy-nilly, a transitional rather than a terminal figure of history—his portrait a study in uncertainty rather than closure.

LUNCHING
FOR THE
REPUBLIC

6

*Howard's government . . . operates in the wake of two in-
tellectual movements in the past 15 years. The first, following the 1970s, was the conclusion that State power,
regulation, high tax and high-spend policies didn't work
with globalisation. The second, following the 1980s, is
that market-oriented policies aren't enough to sustain
democratic governments. This is the conclusion of the
1990s.*

—PAUL KELLY[1]

Feminism is rarely represented as *missing* from public debates in "today's
multicultural Australia." This is a media phrase for a discursive field shaped
by contending models of national culture. Within this field, the fact that
models do contend—in such genres as the interview, the guest column or
personality spot, the talk show, the documentary or drama series, the current affairs program and the formal TV debate—is taken to mark the difference of "today" from the bad or, from another point of view, the good
old days of monocultural national identity.

Feminists using these genres are now confronted by images of feminism's
role in national life that are cheerfully incommensurate. Feminism is simultaneously superseded (by postfeminist concerns, for example), entrenched
and repressive (for anti-"PC" critics), dispersed or diversified (by feminisms
of difference) and too rigidly a white/Anglo-Celtic/middle-class/baby-
boomer/heterosexual movement—while still having "a long way to go" in
securing for women anything like equal empowerment in public institu-

tions, equal representation in parliament, or really equal pay. Feminism is much contested. That is why it is a force in public life.

So when a republican movement reemerged in the early 1990s, with claims to political credibility and rising community support, there was something disconcerting about the speed with which it produced a "woman" problem: by 1993, "where are the women?" was a question assumed to make sense of feminist as well as female positioning in relation to constitutional change. It made sense by denying our involvement; if women weren't *in* there, shaping the future form of a multicultural Australia, then we must be out of it doing something else. Yet this question was most often posed in the media *by* women, in fact, feminist historians, trying to articulate a feminist "republican" problem: what was wrong with the republican imaginary on offer in Australia? why had feminists so far said so little in such a momentous debate? "what," one asked, "do women want?"[2]

Throughout Australia's short history as a constitutional monarchy, republicanism has existed as an often radical tradition and women have always been involved. The launch in 1991 of a carefully diverse and respectable Australian Republican Movement (ARM) was supported by a number of prominent women, including activist writer Faith Bandler (a South Sea Islander descendant), fashion designer Jenny Kee, social policy analyst Mary Kalantzis, novelist Blanche d'Alpuget, politician Franca Arena, and news anchor Mary Kostakidis. It soon became clear, however, that ethnic diversity and age differentiation were more important than gender to those arguing only for a severance of our formal ties with Britain (the "minimalist" approach). In real-political terms, this isn't hard to understand. Republicanism can be *derived from* multiculturalism in Australia, where fear of cultural difference as socially divisive has been commonly (if not correctly) linked in recent years to an Anglocentric, often "elderly," perspective.

In this logic, a republic would give expression to changes already effected by twenty-five years of "official" multiculturalism in immigration and social policy. Since millions of Australians have no links at all with Britain, it is sensible to replace a monarch 12,000 miles away with an Australian as head of state. When the republican goal was endorsed by the federal Labor government of the time, this diversity-*management* argument, typical of domestic multiculturalism since the 1970s, was combined with an "outward-looking" rhetoric of diversity-*promotion* ("Australia is a multicultural nation in the Asian-Pacific region") used to justify deregulatory economic reform in the 1980s. Since more than two-thirds of Australian trade occurs within the region and closer political and military ties are forming with nearby countries (particularly Indonesia), it is practical now to establish an independent identity.

If republicanism cannot be derived from *feminism* in this intensely pragmatic way, the need to bargain for recognition does not usually discourage feminists from participating in any aspect of Australian politics. Second-wave feminism and multiculturalism are about the same age in this country; while the overlaps and tensions between them are not simple, new, or static, both movements have been deeply involved with government.[3] On this occasion, a special invitation to get involved was extended even to those intellectuals critical of the pragmatism of political life under Labor. "A republic needs vision, after all," declared the Prime Minister's speechwriter, Don Watson, in a national newspaper in July 1993: "whatever shape the federal republic of Australia takes, there will be something unstructured, if not deconstructed, about it. I imagine it as aleatory, impressionistic, figurative, eclectic, bebop."[4]

Alas, Watson's own dazzling sketch for "the first post-modern republic" included only one individuated woman, a reporter from the *New York Times* who says of the republic: "But it's not important, is it?" For some mainstream republicans, "women" represent a plodding resistance, even a fink monarchist streak, in our society. Polls have often suggested that women are less inspired than men by the campaign.[5] Australian women are generally said to be more conservative than men in our approach to drastic change, and there is uncertainty, too, about the meaning of the royalty cults beloved of women's magazines, their reach and form of appeal across boundaries of age, class, and ethnicity. The present monarch is a woman, and some speculate that her remoteness and her Englishness may be less important than her gender and family problems to women for whom the national political process is both remote and overbearingly male-dominated.

The question "where are the women?" became a personal one for me when I tried to participate in an academic conference on republicanism, and found that I simply had nothing to say about my topic, "Feminism and Republicanism"—except that where *I* was in the republicanism debate was not accessible from my work as a feminist cultural critic.[6] I take it that the work we do as intellectuals does not necessarily or even responsibly always engage the "totality" of our persons. There may be many good reasons why feminism and republicanism cannot easily be articulated.[7] Clearly, a feminist does not aspire to be a "virtuous property-owning warrior-citizen"[8] on classic civic republican lines, and Helen Irving has analyzed the problems resulting from the persistent soldierly masculinism of the ARM campaign.[9] What is not so clear to me is whether *feminism* can be held to provide a general platform from which all issues of moment must always be addressed.

BEING AND BECOMING REPUBLICAN

First, let me be explicit about my attitude to republicanism. I think it is important. Whatever my doubts, I am not part of that critical community reaffirming itself routinely around a position of exteriority and a posture of skepticism in relation to this debate, as to so many others that extend beyond the academy and involve majority cultures. I find deeply depressing

Chilla Bulbeck's claim that "for women like me, white Anglo-descended, middle class by training if not birth, whether we are a republic or a monarchy hardly matters."[10] After twenty-five years of feminism, I wonder, is that all we have to say? Are white middle-class Anglo women now so passive that they cannot want to make a difference to ensure that a change will matter? When did this happen? Or, to put it another way: how did white middle-class Anglo womanhood come to signify such *indifference* for its self-styled representative ("women like me") intellectuals?

For there is a gap between the "women" and the "me" in Bulbeck's formulation of a likeness. Worrying that only her gender divides her historically from "white nationalism" in Australia, she goes on to say: "I see that the national icons like the bushworker or the lifesaver are male, not that they are white." Yet Bulbeck knows perfectly well that these icons are white. She claims not to "see," but it is she who *writes* "that they are white"; in fact, to emphasize their whiteness, not their maleness, is the function of the sentence. So this "I" who does not see whiteness is a projection of some kind, fuzzily distinct from the writer of the text; perhaps a memory of an earlier self, or a mark of a part of her present self still capable of blindness, but also a sign of identification with all those *other* women who—*unlike* Bulbeck in her writerly role—do *not* see the whiteness of our national icons.

Well, I am like the women of Bulbeck's description, give or take the "Anglo." I am also a feminist intellectual who has heard and read so much about race and ethnicity in recent years that I see whiteness almost before I see maleness, now, when I look at our old national icons. But when Paul Keating made a speech in Parliament in 1992 about Britain selling out Australia in the Second World War, my heart stopped.[11] I was profoundly moved, and in a way that the relentlessly knowing, oh-yeah, negative postures of traditional feminist "critique" can do little to modify and, these days (speaking personally), nothing to match. However, this was not an emotive response to bushworker and lifesaver icons, nor an anti-British feeling stirred by events before I was born. I was moved by a memory from my childhood in the 1950s and 1960s. I heard my father's voice telling stories about the guns of Singapore, about Winston Churchill saying "Australia is expendable" and the great Labor leader John Curtin defying Churchill to bring our troops "*home*" to the Pacific in 1942; and I recalled the political feeling of those stories. I remembered that other time when—back before the Vietnam War, the radicalisms of the late 1960s and then the long, dreary years of conservative recoil—people dreamt of an Australia with its own foreign policy, thus more room for experiment at home, and of an Asian-Pacific, not a White, Australia.

In other words, I was moved by the *recurrence* of a rhetoric of independence that I had never expected to hear in this country again. At some stage, probably around 1975 when the Whitlam Labor government was dismissed by the Governor-General, Sir John Kerr, using his "reserve powers"

as the Queen's representative in Australia, I must have begun to assume
that independence as a goal was for other people—people in Nicaragua,
for example. Nineteen seventy-five had a bitter effect on many Australians,
including those of us who had, just three years earlier, helped to elect the
first federal Labor government since 1949 with the first vote of our lives.
The big-spending, high-wage Whitlam government was dramatically progressive on most issues dear to the "new social movements" of the time.
It also made a serious mess of the economy, and alarmed U.S. agencies
by allowing wild talk about closing U.S. military installations in Australia.[12]
When Whitlam was sacked in an atmosphere of crisis and intrigue, including tales of CIA activity against him,[13] two convictions took hold in popular
political wisdom: any future Labor government must put economic management at the top of its agenda; no future Australian government could
risk offending the United States in defense or foreign policy.

Labor's years back in power under R. J. Hawke (1983–1991) did little
to shake these convictions. So to hear the old rhetoric used again by Keating was extraordinary, as though *anything* might be possible. It was heart-
stopping in the same way as the ending of the *terra nullius* doctrine by the
High Court's *Mabo* decision,[14] and the destruction of the Berlin Wall; and
the revival of that rhetoric was connected to these events. It recurred in
a new national context, an unfamiliar world; it signified change, not nostalgia. Keating's attack on Britain's treatment of its former colony came in a
speech made *for* a time when settler Australians have to renegotiate our own
colonizing history, just as the country's strategic value to the United States
has suddenly declined; a time when nationhood is in question, and "independence," for the first time, a necessity.

Change can be quite shocking for white middle-class Cold War babies.
For all that talk of revolutions, those of us who grew up in Australia did so
under a political settlement of immense and dazing stability and in an ideological climate of seemingly endless fatalism. The "end of history" in cultural theory seems to me a perpetuation of this, and I sometimes think that
the widespread tendency in feminism to know in advance that any event is
just more of the same old story, more of the *same* patriarchy, the *same* racism, the *same* form of class exploitation ("nostalgia for something really
old in something really different, which always [comes] down to the same
old thing"),[15] is in Australia as much a legacy of the Menzies era (1949–66)
as it is a defense against the disappointments of experience. A bitter refusal
to acknowledge our successes, always insisting that nothing has changed,
too easily becomes that old familiar feeling that nothing ever *can* change.

Yet for all that I can, like Chilla Bulbeck, project another "I" that sees
things somewhat differently. When I survey what Elaine Thompson calls a
"shopping list" of reforms, I know exactly what I'd like.[16] For the centenary of Federation in 2001, I'd like a republican constitution involving some
form of recognition of Aboriginal sovereignty; an Australian head of state,

appointed not elected, with a strong ethical aura (as in Ireland) but purely ceremonial powers; an adversarial lower house elected preferentially from single-member constituencies, as at present; and an upper house for "states and minor parties" elected, as at present, by proportional preferential voting, but with a strictly limited role of reviewing legislation—no rejecting of the budget, no blocking of supply (as in 1975), and no way for minor parties to paralyze government. While it is possible to justify these choices from a feminist position, what I'd really like them to bring me is an endless Labor government—an undemocratic and utterly impractical wish.

Here is the fuzzy core of my republican/feminist problem. If my own enthusiasm is not significantly feminist, this is in part because it isn't really republican. I accept that Barry Hindess may be right to suggest that the republican ideal is anachronistic in the world today,[17] and that skeptics who argue that the monarchy has a very low impact here (the "*de facto* republic*" position) have a point. For me, the republican ideal is even vaguer and more remote than the British monarchy. With many other people, I watched TV and became a republican overnight; it's a vehement, instant, thing with shallow roots in my education and none in my experience.

However, this enthusiasm distanced me, once again, from those forms of feminism that foster a belief that nothing national or party-political really matters to women's lives. It was also sustained by memories that decreasing numbers of Australians share, and that were shaped by that "stable" society whose basic organization is now so rapidly changing. So I have found media debate about the technical difficulties of becoming a republic more sobering than off-putting, and I am not sure it was altogether a bad thing that an ebbing of wild enthusiasm followed from that discussion. Perhaps there *is* something to be said for a society organized around an absent power symbol, as well as a history of popular resistance to patriotic display anywhere but in sport.

Feminist *cultural* critique, however, is not well-equipped to assess what that "something to be said" might be, let alone to orient debate toward a non-militant form of republicanism. In the many disciplines that intersect now on the broad terrain of culture, we say that academic feminism has moved into affirmative mode; the demonstration of a uniform oppression has long since made way for the study of women's diverse practices, as well as of our differences, conflicts, and complicities as historical agents in a colonial class society. Yet, except on issues of sexuality, most academic feminist input to *public* debate still comes from historians and political or social scientists with a confident grasp of national institutions, adversarial processes, and political structures of feeling little attended to in cultural theory. For all the sophistication we have brought to bear in thinking identity and difference, feminist cultural critics have had little that is constructive to say about the identities, interests, and allegiances (national, economic, generational, regional, state-based, even party-political) that a nationwide movement can mobilize along with, or sometimes *instead of,* those of race, ethnicity, gender, and sexuality.[18]

In this context, the problem with cultural theory is less the "academic" inflection it has given feminist criticism than the narrow model of political culture as primarily psychic, interpersonal, and utopian that a preference for psychoanalysis and philosophy over formal historical and social knowledges can impose. Borrowed from the United States by an odd consensus between right-wing political parties (who want to make Australian civic life more American) and left-wing cultural theorists (who talk as though it already is), this "privatised"[19] model of politics is especially constricting in a country where a mere proposal to *teach* the Constitution in schools could be denounced, in 1994, as a Labor plot to indoctrinate children. People of my age had a colonial school education; many of us know little about those aspects of the political system that cannot be derived from personal experience. This may be one reason why cultural critics of my generation have moved more slowly than historians to extend the affirmative work we do in our disciplines toward a positive feminist account or *version* of cultural history capable of participating in the conflict over national reshaping that is already well underway.

By "positive" I do not mean "patriotic." I mean an account that could sustain what Ann Curthoys and Stephen Muecke call "a provisional reconstructive practice towards nationhood which investigates its rhetorical tactics."[20] Curthoys and Muecke emphasize the discontinuities, as well as the continuities, between earlier radical nationalisms and what they call "the newer post-nationalism, a sense of nation informed by intense and cross-cutting multiplicities":

> If the earlier nationalisms were predicated on *unity* (of race), *exclusion* (of Others), and on white exploitation of the land, then the post-national varieties can be predicated on *difference* (both internally and externally), *inclusion* (a multiculturalism not confined to the European) and a *re-legitimation* of Aboriginal sovereignty over the land.(179)

"Post-nationalism" may not be the right term for these developments in a society where racism persists, as Curthoys and Muecke say, "with strength," and the popular appeal of a rhetoric of unity remains strong.[21] Even in the Keating version that Curthoys and Muecke describe, it was unclear how, or in whose interests, a relegitimation of Aboriginal sovereignty as endorsed by white settler institutions would combine with a multiculturalism administering "difference" on Anglo-Celtic terms. Keating transposed our nation-founding military myth from Gallipoli in Turkey, 1914 (a losing imperial battle fought by "Anglos" against "others" in a European war), to the Kokoda Track in Papua, 1942 (a multi-racial victory against Japanese imperialism in the Pacific); any historical discourse organized by a theme of Men at War and an allegory of national economic self-interest remains nationalist in the most traditional way.

In calling for a *reconstructive* practice "toward" nationhood, however, Curthoys and Muecke want to stress the open, unachieved status of Australian republicanism and the opportunities that the radically changing context of national politics provides for new forms of mobilization. Their point is not simply that the massive scale of these changes has left socially privileged practitioners of a hermeneutics of suspicion, muttering on the sidelines of most fields of contestation, open to the charge of indulging a purist politics of self-marginalization. More strongly, Curthoys and Muecke argue for a *re*constructive mode of participation that could promote (and thus protect) the "post-modern, post-colonial and feminist" elements circulating in national politics and the republicanism debate. This would mean working from examples of achievement, such as the political gains of Australian feminism, and the "immense discursive and narrative power" exercised culturally by Aboriginal Australians, in order to make the struggles that enabled these achievements "exemplary" of what nationhood *might* be.[22]

Their strategy exploits the vagueness of the republican ideal by asking what new ideals this new name at our disposal might be used to mobilize: it makes a republican "virtue" of experiment. This even has a resonance with media slogans: in headlines, "post-nationalism" and "non-nationalism" have been used to invoke a blurry but desirable aim.[23] For Curthoys and Muecke, such a strategy has consequences for the kind of history that an Australian republic would require. While national in scale and import, it could not, they stress, be national*ist*: it would have to be grounded in an effort to grasp "the nature of the colonial relationships between indigenous and incoming peoples," and, as Curthoys points out in another context, it would assume that our only shared past as Australians is "an *international* past, a myriad of individual regional and national histories that have been brought together in this place."[24]

It should be easier and more exciting for feminists to develop a republican politics on the basis of these imperatives to work *toward* postcolonialism and to *produce* multiculturalism than to be carried away with old bipolar party enthusiasms. Yet the claims of feminist indifference suggest that matters are not so simple. I think Peter Beilharz identifies something crucial about our unresponsiveness when he argues that we are living through the decline of the model of "industrial citizenship" that laborism put in place in the 1950s. What we need now, he says, is a reinvention of citizenship in the context of a "republicanism beyond labourism."[25] But if this is easier said than done, more readily defined than desired, part of the problem may be that in Australia what Kobena Mercer calls the "not so 'new'" social movements, with their "'race, class, gender' mantra," have not only developed in conflict with laborism but also created positive programs by a practical engagement *with* it.[26]

A certain aphasia can follow from the decline of industrial citizenship. The struggle against the privileging of the white male worker as industrial citizen has shaped feelings and investments, as well as habits of debate, over a long period of time. Without that figure and its derivatives, like the "white middle-class woman," so powerfully *there*, as a centralizing instance making sense of our talk about margins, the value of familiar gestures suddenly becomes uncertain. Declaring feminist indifference is one such familiar gesture. There may be a diffuse expectation in the "margins" of debate that the centralizing role played by industrial citizenship can and will be reinvented from the same old sources of social power (that do continue to exist), and that our choices are therefore limited to adopting a studied cynicism or to making alternative proposals in a strictly minority spirit.

Perhaps this expectation of a reinvented symbolic center is mistaken. I find it encouraging that an aura of buffoonery rapidly enveloped the efforts of Malcolm Turnbull and Thomas Keneally, prominent advocates of republicanism, to masquerade as emblematic citizens. What interests me is less their embodiment of an explicitly masculine patriotism than the way they also implicitly articulated a *class* model of intellectual sociality—how they presented themselves as prompters of a "popular" debate. Of course, Turnbull and Keneally appear on television not as professional intellectuals but as media personalities. Turnbull is the upper-middle-class lawyer and merchant banker as postindustrial citizen (with a family connection to Angela Lansbury). Keneally plays the Irish-Australian popular novelist (author of *Schindler's List*) and organic representative of the petite-bourgeoisie. So they do not voice the interests of "a" class transcending the media world in any simple sense. Rather, their performances predicate the national-popular as an audience for whom their own *personae* are central, and a popular debate as mimetic of their chat. In other words, they assume that public leadership is a function of what our pundits call (in eloquent self-hatred) "the chattering classes."

NOT LUNCHING WITH THOMAS KENEALLY

One of the most remarkable things about ARM literature in the early 1990s was its emphasis on lunching. Both *Our Republic*, Tom Keneally's book of reminiscences, and *The Coming Republic*, a more useful collection of essays orchestrated by Donald Horne, are structured by lunch allegories in which personalities—real celebrities in Keneally's case, imaginary social stereotypes in Horne's—gather around a lavish supply of food and wine to discuss an Australian republic.[27] *Our Republic* is embarrassing in this respect, with its name-dropping and its bottles of Chardonnay; so giddy is the political whirl that, by the end of the book, Keneally has almost lost track of any issues extrinsic to his social calendar and his amazing job opportunity at U.C. Irvine. There is a class as well as a "Sydney" parochialism to this that may explain the book's failure to stir much fervor in the recessionary year of its publication, 1993. I am embarrassed by it, however, because the lunch-burble is all too familiar, in form if not in setting or stellar quality, from my own professional life. *Our Republic* has an awful fascination as a book that sets out to celebrate the white male nationalist heritage (convicts, soldiers, the Irish), only to turn into a book about transnational chattering-class *networking*.

"Lunch" is an old-fashioned way for culturati to network; younger chatterers prefer, on the whole, to keep working the modem. But it has a role in ARM discourse that is more fundamental than its value as an index of shifting subcultural behaviors. "Lunch" is a democratized version of the literary conceit of the bourgeois dinner, that set piece of so many novels, plays, and films in which the conflicts and desires of entire social formations are fought out in exquisite detail in a unified space and time.[28] In republican discourse, a lunch scene stages the ideal of "free and rational debate" that characterizes classical republican thinking and limits its claims to realism. Admittedly, the ideal Australian literary lunch is a boisterous occasion at which people get a little irrational and maybe speak a little too freely. Nonetheless, the use of this conceit elides basic questions about the nature of public debate in a media society.

As a utopian allegory of the social, lunch has its problems. It is basically *mono*cultural in a liberal pluralist mode, questioning neither the forms of European bourgeois sociality nor the resonance of the hospitality trope so often used to assert the dominance of an Anglo-Celtic "home" culture over more tenuously "invited" immigrant cultures (thus erasing our own history as unwelcome guests of indigenous Australia). In this respect, a lunching model of national debate has the same failings as the "better cuisine" model of multiculturalism; the role of exotic elements in both cases is to flavor the mixture, not alter the basics. As Ghassan Hage pointed out in a prescient article, new forms of racism can and do inhabit this state-promulgated tolerance.[29] Like a badly behaved guest at an otherwise convivial lunch, the intolerably different legal citizen of Australia can still be told to "go home."

To be fair, neither *Our Republic* nor *The Coming Republic* invokes hospitality in this way. Both books aim to start discussion for a broad readership already used to debating multiculturalism as a working set of arrangements with supporters as well as critics across all the great divides—indigenous and non-indigenous, black and white, Anglo-Celtic and non-Anglo-Celtic, European and non-European—used to map Australian society. The special difficulty that emerges with Keneally's slide from populism to networking is that neither the literary model of lunching nor the culinary model of multiculturalism can tell us how any conversation about changing the form of the nation can be extended to involve large numbers of diverse people *on* a national basis. This is really another version of the question, "where are the women?"—the question of the historical conditions for democracy today. Neither lunch nor multiculturalism is an intrinsically democratic institution. Official multiculturalism is, first and foremost, a management policy, while any lunch that acts as a media talking-point is an event for social elites, who may or may not impersonate for the occasion particular social identities on behalf of different constituencies.

I have no problem with the idea that the opinion industry works on a loop around which interest groups, most but not all of whom are also social elites, send each other messages about "what's going on."[30] A lucid grasp of the potentials of this process is vital to the mingling of marginal with mainstream politics, as the battle for a Native Title Act showed in 1993. On that occasion, the major participants—the Aboriginal delegates, various factions of the Labor Cabinet, Senate minor parties, state Premiers, the mining and farming lobbies—all used the media not only to pressure and outwit each other in public but to involve a national audience in what became a stirring emotional drama with a cliff-hanger structure; an "underdog" theme that distributed sympathy, for a while, to the Aboriginal position; and a (not undisputed) happy ending by Christmas.[31] At the same time, they all used the media to inform, or misinform, each other and the audience about the significance of each new development. I learned more about law and history, both indigenous and colonial, during those months of watching TV than in all my years of formal education.

By an even subtler, more impersonal pedagogy exercised by the medium of television itself, I also acquired a greater respect for the politics of negotiation to which all of these elites were committed by virtue of taking part. The losers in this battle (if not the war, that may continue for years to come) were the Coalition parties who flatly *opposed* the bill. In doing so, they claimed to represent majority opinion. Perhaps they did. Racist scare campaigns, backed by some mining interests, did their best to persuade non-Aboriginal Australians that our homes were at risk as a result of the government's decision to respond to the *Mabo* judgment with national Native Title legislation. But by shutting themselves out of the *formal* arena of struggle over "what's going on," and with no other site of authority (unlike the bill's Aboriginal critics) from which to enter the discussion, the Coalition parties relegated that opinion to the limbo of the minor and unnewsworthy—in media terms, to the past.

The media past is only temporary, and it is *always* open to revision. Opinions marginalized during those crucial months of 1993 were virulently "mainstream" again by 1996, though with lessened power to completely reverse the effects of the *Mabo* judgment.[32] Whatever long-term results such battles of opinion may have, it is at least clear that they do not operate in the "talking tableau" mode of a literary lunch. In order to facilitate free and rational debate, the Enlightened fine-dining tradition stages a conflict of *ideas* in a voluntarily created, benignly convergent setting in which all participants are fictively equal; as Gary Shapiro points out, "the temporary community and good cheer tend to obscure real differences of power . . . which are likely to influence the outcome of any discussion of matters of taste."[33] Media *opinion* battles, in contrast, do not abstract ideas from social struggles. They activate differences, and at least some of the power imbalances, within as well as between social groups as these diverge and converge on particular issues, by staging their conflict as part of a multifaceted, open-ended, and expansive saga of national life that only ever achieves provisionally its moments of resolution.

In a relatively small and cohesive media system, it is not the content of one's opinions but a willingness and, much harder to achieve, a *capacity* to take part in "the public culture," helping to create that "mirage that can float over a society, purporting to be its national life,"[34] that defines what may count at any given time as a mainstream position. So the idea of professional chatterers prompting a debate about the nation's future is not necessarily ludicrous. Problems arise when its exponents want to deny the specialization of interests that gives people networking power (more precisely, *times* of power) as mediators and mirage-makers on the loop.

This denial may take nationalist, populist, or panicky postmodernist forms, but it thrives on a belief derived from literary culture, and the genteel white middle-class notion of a "general" reading public, that the distinct taste cultures constellated by particular media shows add up to a coherent national public that is sentimentologically *represented*, as well as amused, by media personality discourse. Lurking not too far from the surface here is a class fantasy that cultural workers may "rise" to play the same symbolically central role in future that industrial workers did in the past. However, the media sphere, while powerful, is not *central* to our society (it is not the only public sphere and it interacts erratically with others), and it is used by many political movements and social forces, very few of which are only class defined, struggling to further their own interests in and through that sphere.

Not all intellectuals are chatterers, and not all media chattering is usefully described as intellectual. I do not think that national debates are impossible today, or that intellectuals cannot take part in variable ways. I do question whether a national debate can take the form of a mass festival of opinion and ideas, a kind of mega-lunch to which feminists should, as it were, bring a plate. Obviously, no feminism engaging with republicanism can be a singular force that massively represents "women." As we never tire of saying in other contexts, feminism itself is a mixed discourse and a hybrid political space. Since feminist practices are connected as well as defined by all the involvements that women have as social agents, large numbers of women are *only* likely to engage with any national struggle in a conjunctive mode of "feminism *and . . . and*," where our interests as women will combine with our interests in the labor movement, and/or in the rights of indigenous people, and/or in the needs of differing old and new settler groups, of lesbians and/or working mothers, as intellectuals, and so on.

This is why the formulation "feminism and republicanism," however handy it may be, is misleading. Only in a history of "isms" do these terms confront each other in an unmediated dual relationship; feminist politics are most visible and audible when at least three terms are in play. This does not mean that the concept of feminism is meaningless or that straight white women who identify only as feminists (let alone Anglo-descended women, a goodly chunk of the population) should be invisible or inaudible. It simply means that "the women" may never arrive in one spectacular contingent to seize the floor of republican debate.

TOO SOON, TOO LATE: POSTMODERN "REPUBLICAN NON-NATIONALISM"

If we approach the modalities of women's involvement in this orthodox feminist way, other questions can arise about the broad conditions in which the activist's chronic problem of organizing differences is projected as a nation-*building* issue. What did it mean for middle-class women to be invited in the Keating years to an "aleatory, impressionistic, figurative, eclectic" *unification* movement, and to bring our differences with us? What ideals were being mobilized by *that* republican movement? Before imagining feminist futures, perhaps we need to examine more closely the conflicting political cultures that actually dominate the present. Once multiculturalism has been projected as a model for national identity, however controversially and with whatever degree of hypocrisy, forms of analysis used in the past to affirm a politics of heterogeneity and multiplicity against binary models of political opposition, and to articulate embodied social identities against an abstract form of citizenship, may no longer serve as well as they once did.

Republicanism certainly aims to produce what Homi Bhabha calls the "problematic unity of the nation."[35] Even the sparest forms of minimalism would transform a constitution preoccupied with "difference" as the protection of "states' rights" into one investing national identity in a head of state; with the monarchy goes an externally oriented way of uniting Australia. For this very reason, fears that a republic would stir belligerent passions are not only expressed by "elderly" Anglophiles. A progressive Judge, Michael Kirby, defends the monarchy as a tempering force against nationalism ("I can live quite peacefully with the sombre fact that our head of government attracts only a 19 gun salute"),[36] while migrants from parts of Asia and Europe have spoken as "Australians for Constitutional Monarchy" on the grounds that they came here to get away from nationalist conflicts. Writing as an anti-monarchist, Barry Hindess warns that "the very idea of a modern republic" presents "a misleading and potentially destructive image of a political community endowed with a distinctive common culture."[37]

Voiced as fears, as experiences, or as wagers on a logic of history, these arguments are unanswerable. They invoke powerful precedents from our international past that noone can say with certainty will or will not apply here in future. Another argument points to the genocide and the racist exclusivism that constitute a national past for Anglo-Celtic Australians. What makes *this* precedent uncertain is that our twentieth-century efforts to destroy Aboriginal culture,[38] and our exclusion of "Asians" with the White Australia Policy, were both entangled in a history whereby immigrants from different nations, mainly but not only English, Irish, Scottish, and Welsh, united under the monarchy to become assiduously *British* in Australia. It follows emotionally, if not logically, that to get rid of the British monarchy is to end, not to initiate, a phase of virulent nationalism. Yet this is why Hage can convincingly argue that the "we" of republican discourse implies an Anglo-Celtic identity: despite the thematic centrality accorded to multiculturalism, the "we" refers "to an *old* Anglo-Celtic history and deals with a present Anglo-Celtic problem."[39]

Arguments from historical precedent usefully contest the unity of existing national narratives. They also tend to reiterate old histories, either minimizing the conditions in which what Hage calls "republican nationalism" is taking shape, or maximizing, as Hindess does, the distance between "now" and "then"; to paraphrase Michael Naas, they begin with a politics of which they proceed to give us examples, instead of beginning with examples from which to invent a politics.[40] Like Curthoys and Muecke, I prefer to wager on the second course by asking what proponents actually mean by republican "*non*-nationalism." The old nationalism was a *protectionist* as well as a racist settlement that thrived on Australia's cultural and physical isolation. What sort of unity can be projected for a free-trading nation at the mercy of world economic forces that no government can control? for a society unable effectively to legitimize its norms with reference to a common culture, yet with large numbers of citizens yearning to do so? for a technologically constituted public sphere not only open to global information flows and regional political pressures but providing the first simultaneously *national* image-space in Australian history?

It is an awkward time to ask these questions. They seemed a little easier to pose some years ago, when an "aleatory" multiculturalism had not been rejected as a national model by a multiethnic majority of Australians, and a monarchist Prime Minister, John Howard (Liberal) had not been entrusted with the task of furthering debate about a republic that the polls still say an enlarging majority wants. However, this very awkwardness of "present" time is the core of those questions, as well as a historical condition of their framing.

Graeme Turner has pointed out that the "earlier, racially exclusionary forms of Australian nationalism did not disappear" in the Labor years; "they just fell into disuse."[41] Yet reviving them cannot restore the protected national economy and the Western imperial dominance that once sustained them; as rhetorics *of* nationalist "return," they return too late. Displacing Labor, the Coalition government did express nostalgia for an abstract national unity and an enunciatively empty model of citizenship ("all of us").[42] However, since most Liberals now oppose the regulation of cultural relations, the planning of cultural futures and the very idea of constructing identity, they are hampered in experimenting with new ideas of citizenship, even right-wing ideas. Admirers of the privatized, "personalized" U.S. model of civic life after Reagan, Liberals somehow have to hold the support of rural and working-class voters who want to restore (without paying for them in taxes) the "values" of the semi-socialist Australia that Labor began dismantling, while still attacking the ethically deep-rooted *social* institutions (national health care, public broadcasting, mass higher education) that they promised to maintain in order to win that rural and working-class support.

Instead of a strong "values" politics of individualized citizenship, these contradictory pressures in fact give rise, as they have in other countries, to a scapegoating, populist attack on "cultural elites" represented as infesting those social institutions. While free trading and privatization continue to "diversify" and to render more unequal Australian social and economic life, national unity is mobilized around brittle but passionate and historically potent rhetorics of anti-elitism and anti-intellectualism. Such rhetoric can easily be combined with republicanism, and a color-blind, socially liberal egalitarianism. However, *this* republican nationalism can neither forgo the notion of a common culture nor realize commonality in daily life; unable to overcome its own lateness, it projects a future given over to nostalgia and disappointment.

This does not make it less dangerous. So times are awkward, too, for proponents of republican non-nationalism to elaborate counter-models; it is too soon, once again, for the radical republicanisms that some feminists espouse to make serious political sense. However, I want to review the now *oppositional* mainstream model in order to ask what cultural feminism can learn from its recent "unpopular" history.[43]

It is striking just how minimal most manifestos of the early 1990s are when it comes to republican ideals. Rather than endowing Australians with a "common culture" in any positive sense, they focus on ways of managing differences, on a shareable code rather than a "community," in what they assume can only ever be a problematic national *process*. They offer plans for, not definitions of, republican government, how-to guides that declare no self-evident truths. What makes them mainstream in Australian terms, compared to, say, ideas for a corporation-based democracy or for Swiss and Californian remodelings of the electoral system, is an emphasis on formally effective, not morally redemptive, conciliation procedures that give continuity and stability while securing the conditions for change to keep on being negotiated. Donald Horne, for example, wants a civic *instead of* a national identity, defined by a commitment to act in a certain way (legally, constitutionally, democratically, respecting equality under the law) and, in a major modification of non-Aboriginal tradition, to "custodianship of the land we share."[44]

Don Watson agreed that a postmodern republic "exalts the nation less than the way of life," valuing tolerance, difference, worldliness, and:

> humanist and even some romantic traditions, but not schmaltz, false sentiment and fascism. I have this sense that the pragmatism and dogmatic gradualism which delayed the moment for so long might end up serving us brilliantly.[45]

This is about as close as republican non-nationalism comes to a unifying profession of faith. It has its "Anglo-Celtic" resonances, including the sweetly ironic approach to romanticism ("even some") and the stern attitude to schmaltz. As Jon Stratton and Ien Ang point out, the "way of life" is an old notion vaguely investing cohesion in mundane practices, not identities or ideals.[46] The real-political bite, however, is in the "*dogmatic gradualism.*" This phrase invokes with wonderful exactness a traditional laborist faith, shareable now with Horne's classically liberal civics, in a pragmatism that stubbornly holds the line against revolutionaries, extremists, vanguardists, and disruptively visionary radicals of left *and* right, while slowly, unsensationally securing the popular consent, and the practical means, that enable deep and lasting social change.

Perhaps what makes this dogma postmodern in Watson's invocation is that it has floated free of its anchorage in the dialectical struggles that over a century formed the Labor Party (capital vs. labor, Catholicism vs. communism)[47] to become diffusely available as a *professional* culture, not a partisan ethos. In modern times, the gradualism had an aim called "civilising capitalism,"[48] and its mode of solidarity was exclusionary: non-unionists out of the shop, married women out of the workforce, cheap imports and "cheap labour" out of Australia, Aborigines out of history altogether. In Watson's postmodern times, the aim was to create, in a self-reflexive process of civilizing *pragmatism* ("with . . . even some romantic traditions"), an open and inclusionary national, not white male working-class, movement beyond "tyrannies of all kinds," one among them "the market fetish and greed of the 8os"—something much less absolute than capitalism. Pragmatism won its battle for a free-trade ethos in the 1980s. By 1994, Labor's unifying themes were affirmative action for women in politics,[49] reconciliation between indigenous people and settlers ("Mabo"), and a republicanism based on multiculturalism. This dispersal of the singular adversary allowed the rhetorical shift from exclusion to inclusion to work smoothly: now racism, sexism, homophobia, were all kinds of tyranny, but capitalism was the horizon of the world.

I prefer to call this political culture "corporatist" rather than, as some do, "Anglo-Celtic."[50] One reason is that its resources were mobilized effectively by diverse minority groups, feminists among them, demanding to negotiate their own inclusion in the national process.[51] Another is that few people of any ethnicity could participate in its inclusiveness. Any corporatism has an exclusionary bottom line dividing those who can and do contribute (in this instance, Labor-compatible "players" and their constituencies, including the "disadvantaged") from those who could contribute but do not—such as, to be sure, the loony Left, but also rural and working-class people alienated by professionalized unionism, and an urban, bureaucratic culture of "political correctness."

Any corporatism penalizes the non-"players" in a society. In this instance, punishment was a greater disempowerment—ridicule, irrelevance, moral humiliation—that people were often deemed to have brought upon themselves. To be excluded on this basis was, however, a provisional affair. Since one aim of Labor corporatism is to shut down violent *expressions* of social conflict, no single group was ontologically invested at an official level with outsider status.[52] Behaviors and attitudes, not social identities, were scapegoated, including popular behaviors and attitudes—often (but not only) displayed by recalcitrant "redneck" Anglo-Celtics—that threatened to attack the imagined identities of others. The premise of such action is not that social conflicts are thereby solved or prejudice eradicated, but that these must never *appear* to have legitimacy or to engage majority opinion.

This is the political culture that shaped the reemergence of republican debate in Australia. In its vesting of cohesion in professionalism and an urbane civil society, feminism and multiculturalism had and still have a problem to confront that is not dispatched by invoking scary precedents, or recycling critiques of ethnic or militarist nationalism. While any corporatism has tyrannical potentials, the policing of modes and thresholds of conflict in Australia has for decades been enabled by a "public opinion" network linking (often over lunch) government to the "business community," the media, the professions, the lobby groups, the culture industries, the unions, and the academy. Along with practitioners of all kinds of identity politics, feminists are firmly embedded in this network. We helped to create it, and in our most severely critical as well as cooperative gestures, we refined and expanded its capacities.[53]

Any assessment of Australia's tyranny potential would have to at least consider the popular view that this casual network or "culture" of like-minded souls represents a more immediate threat to liberty and cultural diversity than the prospect of an upsurge of flag-waving patriotism. Certainly, by the mid-1990s there was widespread support for such a view. Yet neither of these precedent-based scenarios, invoking a politically correct "Stalinism" (or "McCarthyism") and fascism respectively, attends to the actual conflicts now shaping Australia's future. These are not *nationalist* conflicts in any ordinary sense. They arise, every day, from the tensions involved in, on the one hand, the transfiguration of what were until quite recently "minor" interests (feminism, Aboriginal self-determination, anti-racism, gay and lesbian rights) as symbolically but not always substantively major national issues, and, on the other, the economic *internationalism*—sometimes expressing a "Pacific Rim" chauvinism, always accepting transnational capitalism as the limit of national policy—that in many ways has enabled both the displacement of the old racist nationalism by multiculturalism, and the emergence of a new, "postmodern," racist nationalism.[54]

A list of such tensions could be very long. It would include the appalling gap between the cultural prestige accorded to "Aboriginality" and the living conditions and prospects of many Aboriginal people; the discrepancy between the high feminist profile of the new labor movement and the effects on women workers of the enterprise bargaining and superannuation schemes supported by that movement; the harsh contrasts between the cosmopolitan richness of urban cultural life, the social wasting of immigrant suburbs by long-term unemployment, and the devastation of rural Australia by bank foreclosures and service "downsizing"; the inconsistency of Australian human rights policies and practices at home and in the region.

One way to frame such a list, however, is to note that a missing term in Watson's vision of tyrannies transcended by postmodern republicanism, and in Labor's historic compromise between identity politics and capitalism, was *colonialism*. Old as well as new colonial processes, "internal," regional, and global in scale, continue to impact, obliquely and directly, on the very communities whose symbolic incorporation in the nation is so eagerly sought, in different ways, on both sides of national politics. Yet the overlaps and discontinuities between the national imperialisms that created modern Australia, and the *corporation*-based colonialisms reshaping our society today, rarely figure in either republican or cultural feminist debate.

The conflicts resulting, however, are the everyday stuff of Australian politics in ways that becoming a republic is in itself unlikely to inflect toward catastrophe *or* redemption. These conflicts block the tendency of even the most gradualist of feminisms to identify with either the state or the networks of influence with which we are involved, and they help to ensure that the nation "can no longer be conceived as a closed container for all that we are . . . or any sort of limit for the directions of feminist thinking":[55] they *regionalize*, within and beyond the borders of the nation, feminist frameworks of thought and action. I believe they also undermine anyone's chances of unifying the people in a swell of singularly national subjectivity. This political culture works with varying degrees of limited difference (*more* limited by the Liberals than by Labor) and with a controlled (Labor) or free-market (Liberal) approach to managing social heterogeneity; within those limits, its models of citizenship can in practice be embodied as diversely as you please.

THE VERY IDEA OF A NATIONAL DEBATE

It seems to me that if a *popular* national debate was underway by the mid-1990s, then Mabo, rather than the monarchy, was its focus.[56] Mabo is so crucial to the conflict of powers and values in Australia that it could sink the republic. Some people claim that, no matter which party holds government, a republic is inevitable sometime soon. It isn't, of course: it has to be accepted at a referendum by a majority of electors *and* a majority of the six states.[57] The result can depend on those states (Western Australia and Queensland) in which significant areas of land may be reclaimed under Mabo, and where white panic is most likely to fuse with an intense anti-centralism historically shared with smaller states such as Tasmania. The state-based identities and passions that republicanism aims to temper will be crucial to the outcome here; Australians usually vote "no" to any proposal enhancing the powers of central government, even when we say we agree with the *content* of a proposal.[58] Land management has been a matter for state, not federal, governments. Mabo changed that: by recognizing the rights of some Aboriginal groups, it has had, as a republic would, a nationalizing force. At the same time, Mabo fragmented white images of a uniform Aboriginality; in reporting the politics of Mabo, the media at last had to recognize differences and conflicts in *Aboriginal* opinion.

Popular debates, in which people in all walks of life talk and argue on an everyday basis about a complex shared concern, are quite rare. Something of the qualitative difference in this respect between "the republic" and "Mabo"—media signifiers both—can be grasped if we try to imagine using a lunch allegory to canvas the politics of Mabo. If the idea seems incongruous it isn't because "lunch" connotes consumption and urban banter (as though no Aboriginal people ever indulge in either) but because the social circulation of Mabo cannot be contained in that way. The republican lunch is a self-referring class figure in a media-centered discourse. There is nothing wrong with that, as long its limits are recognized. Mabo, however, is the name of a vast, intricate mesh of distinct but connected debates: technical matters of land tenure; ongoing political struggles over economic, social, and ethical priorities as well as federal/state relations; philosophical questions about the value of governmental acts of redress; and profoundly emotional conflicts over ways of being attached to one's own land and culture—each of which touches on something fundamental to Australian life.

Moreover, while Mabo as an instance of "the immense narrative and discursive power" achieved by Aboriginal people has had its brilliant media stars, it is not a product of personality politics. Nor was Mabo staged for "the people" universalized as media consumers. In this respect, recent Aboriginal constructions of the public sphere can offer "examples" of a politics capable, even under duress, of going beyond (in Peter Beilharz's phrase) the laborism of the past and the elite networking of the present. While Aboriginal people do not "speak from the hyperluxury of the first world with the reflective thoughts of a well-paid, well-fed, detached scholar,"[59] those of us who do speak from such positions have a great deal to learn from how Aborigines have dealt politically with First World institutions as *specific* intellectuals,[60] while working from the bases in Aboriginal societies and politics that define their organic relationship to their people. The national authority of a Marcia Langton or a Noel Pearson is not media-derived, though it has been media-disseminated; it preceded and has outlasted the promotion of their personal roles in the Native Title negotiations. Such authority is community-based, and it *also* derives from their use, for Aboriginal purposes, of specific professional and symbolic skills.

These skills have included using the media to criticize "the white 'take-me-to-your-leader' syndrome"[61] that animates coverage of Aboriginal activists, and to circulate Aboriginal models of authority and action in other cultural contexts. During the 1980s, a model of cultural *pedagogy* was transferred to national politics; white Australians began to be addressed not as competent oppressors but as young, ignorant people in need of teaching. More recently, Langton has used the model of "a *theatre* of politics in which self-representation has become a sophisticated device" to analyze Aboriginal media practices; and the notion of an "*actual dialogue*," in which all parties test and repeatedly adjust imagined models of each other ("be it at a supermarket check-out or in a film co-production"), to define a working form of intercultural exchange.[62] Another model is *diplomacy*, with the terms "negotiation" and "protocol" being used to enable an ethics of intercultural conduct as well as to assert Aboriginal rights in the political domain.[63] Pearson has argued publicly for a manipulation of middle-class cultural prejudices ("to capture the middle ground . . . you have to win them over by form"),[64] and an orchestration of radical and moderate approaches.[65]

If these practical models exploit the performative dimension and participatory potentials of a mediated public sphere in ways that do translate between at least some of Australia's communities (even as they alarm and anger others), they also extend to the daily news the "investigation of rhetorical tactics" that Curthoys and Muecke seek in a reconstructive movement *toward* "nationhood." However, they make the very idea of the nation provisional in ways that must complicate any contrast between the plurality of indigenous nations and a singular nationalism invested in a monolithic state, or between the divisive present and a more harmonious "non-nationalist" future.

On the one hand, white Australians have been told, contentiously, that our nation-building culture is the object of a reconstructive practice; old euphoric modes of national address have been rendered "touchy" for state occasions, and the late-1980s shift from a rhetoric of guilt to an ethos of responsibility asked us to participate in the reconstruction—a project that carried, for many white people, its own euphoric charge. On the other hand, as the strength of the backlash against these changes suggested, *actual* dialogue and diplomacy demand a much more strenuous and cautious response to the task of articulating what Tim Rowse calls "the plurality of historical experience" in Australia than a happy-families version of diversity can provide.[66]

In 1996, the new Coalition government immediately took a confrontational approach to Aboriginal organizations, reviving long-discredited talk of "integration" and assimilation. Even under Labor, however, it was clear that a singular model of citizenship could not be extracted from "Mabo" as a symbol of corporatist reconciliation. In the media sphere, all viewers are increasingly confronted with images of Aboriginal groups forming international alliances with other indigenous peoples, anti-colonial movements, and agencies such as the World Council of Churches and Amnesty International, to pressure or *bypass* Australian governments in order to fight for basic human rights (water, food, shelter) for their communities. At the same time, the models of diplomacy and protocol are being adopted by transnational corporations seeking to negotiate with the traditional owners of land.[67]

We are also confronted with images of Aboriginal regional self-government movements and distinctively urban voices challenging state-sanctioned Aboriginal organizations; and with a radically undiplomatic politics of critique and protest that continues to be necessary, not least in feminist contexts, to procure the kind of "discursive power" for real people, not a floating cultural abstraction, that translates as social and political empowerment. Discursive power does not mean that Aboriginal interests converge with "the national interest." The same Noel Pearson who once used an inclusionary national rhetoric to accuse the Liberal leader of "urinating on a historic Australian achievement" when he threatened to repeal the Native Title Act, said bluntly in another context, "Mabo is extremely conservative. It is 90 to 95 per cent about protecting existing European interests."[68]

It is often stressed in discussions of multiculturalism that the position of Aborigines is *particular*: the indigenous people cannot be subsumed by a "national" policy that confirms their dispossession. The idea that an exemplary particularity can articulate something general has hovered on the fringes of theory for many years.[69] It is neglected, I think, because of the tenacity of a philosophical assumption that "the" particular (but exemplarists would speak of "a" particular) can only *oppose* or *illustrate* "the" general, resulting in bloody particularism on the one hand and typification, more benignly, on the other.[70] Republican lunching plays on the second possibility. It uses the cultural resources of popular comic realism, casting "the people" as a series of social types, to promote an additive, not a pluralist, model of multicultural nationality—in fact, a colonial "logic of the collection" that, as Hage explains, exhibits the diversity of exotic ethnic life available in Australia.[71] The politics of Mabo have demonstrated the *general* inadequacy of this way of thinking, and they have also shown how challenges to it can sometimes work through national as well as local, regional, and international frameworks.

Bruce Robbins has used the phrase "comparative cosmopolitanism" to add to the inclusiveness and diversity of multiculturalism in the U.S. context an edge of "necessary but difficult normativeness" that "makes room for moments of generalising . . . without offering license for uninhibited universalising."[72] One generality useful to feminist critics that arises from the cosmopolitan example of Aboriginal media practices is that the possible nations we theorize can take shape in struggles to transform an actual nation; in this perspective on practice, the venerable *opposition* between identity politics, with their transversally local and transnational force, and a national politics thought only in terms of closure and containment, is itself of limited and local value. Mabo is not the only issue to have had a nationalizing force while mobilizing incommensurable interests in a transnational frame. The environment, massively, is another; so was an appeal by Tasmanian gay activists to the UN Human Rights Committee that forced the Keating government to introduce federal privacy legislation potentially capable of overriding state laws then effectively prohibiting homosexual acts in Tasmania.[73] These examples are not interchangeable. However, like the long-standing commitment of Australian feminists and multiculturalists to the "regulatory practices and processes of social cohesion-building,"[74] each has involved using the adversarial system to affect the contents and priorities of national politics.

To be *involved*, however, is not the same as being subsumed by, limited to, or identified with a particular process. Something crucial about the abrasive flexibility of what I have loosely called "identity politics" is as easily ignored in a purist withdrawal from the contaminating space of the national as it is by lurid projections of the dangers of a republic. Such politics are not based on an ideal of the common good, and they do not derive their goals and values from a covertly sectarian abstraction of "the" national interest.[75] For this very reason, they can construe both the state and the nation as practical sites of struggle and experiment. Moreover, social movements that collectively produce "experience" are neither motivated nor *organized* to exclude what Rowse calls "more troubling rhetorics"[76] from their own discursive spaces, let alone from the media or any other public sphere. Groups do try, of course; but it is much easier to eject an unwelcome guest from lunch than it is to purge identity politics of unnegotiably troublesome elements. This is not to romanticize the ineffectually "critical" approach to politics that Beatrice Faust dismisses as "expressive" ("happy to let off steam—especially if it can be done in front of a permissive and supportive audience").[77] It is to point to a real, even a pragmatic condition of the kind of democratic practice that Irving envisages as "a process of continuous debate, of continuous attempts to articulate new rights, new institutions and new models of representation."[78]

None of this thinking is alien to feminism, and it puts us in a stronger position to deal in a positive way with republicanism in future. The media-centered logic of republican discourse is not just an anecdotal aspect of its social circulation. One reason why hasty "feminist critiques" of classical republicanism and theories of civil society seemed so far removed from the *realpolitik* of Keating's republic is that the latter so baldly asserted the need for a national *marketing image*.[79] It did not depend on restating the "same old" nationalist mythology precisely because it was intended for economic and political conditions in which the borders of the nation, and the powers of the state to close them, can no longer be taken for granted. Keating's republic was about *international trade*, not civic humanism, and *sales psychology*, not democratic participation; becoming a republic was supposed to make us "feel better," which is good for the economy, and make Australia "look better" to its trading partners. Within the parameters of a managerial discourse, this argument may well be right. However, feminists need neither accept nor reject on principle a republicanism so construed in order to work out how to participate to further our agendas.

The emergence of "locality rights" as a basis for creating a regional, rather than a national, politics for indigenous peoples in Australia and countries in Asia should help to remind us that the marketeers' republic is not a product of European folkish nationalism, though it may arouse and manipulate nationalist feeling.[80] It is a product of a transnational economic and social order that savagely exploits women's labor and makes a mockery, in many places in our region and within Australia, of demagogic talk about citizenship. As trade unionist Pathma Tamby Dorai put it to a conference celebrating the centenary of women's suffrage in South Australia, "fantastic economic growth is being projected for Asia as against Australia, but on whose backs?"[81]

Dorai's question was not simply gestural. Australian feminists could, she suggested, pressure Australian companies to develop a formal code of conduct recognizing the rights of workers in the Asian-Pacific countries in which they are investing (and her demand was itself an act of international pressure). A similar call has been made by a Bombay-based children's rights campaigner, Alpa Vora. Rejecting trade sanctions against Third World goods made by children ("protectionism dressed up as social concern"),[82] she argues for the acceptance of ethical hiring and wage policies by Australian investors; recognition of the growing child labor problems in Australia's own clothing industry; support for campaigns to provide schooling and health care to child workers in particular factories; and more cooperation between Australian aid agencies and anti–child labor groups in Asian countries.

If cultural feminists, too, think "regionally" in this way of the republic as an occasion for an internationally oriented politics that uses the nation as an *open* framework for action, then we are not back in the mythical world of bushworkers and the lifesavers: it is crucial that these were not only "white male" but *protectionist* national icons. We are in a world being reshaped in many ways by the emergence of Asian capitalism and by the harsh mythology of what we call, for convenience, "economic rationalism." This is not unknown territory for feminists. It is the very ground on which our practice of a conjunctive, not additive, pluralist politics—feminism *and* labor relations, feminism *and* anti-racism, feminism *and* immigration policy, feminism *and* human rights, feminism *and* environmentalism, even feminism *and* cultural theory—has been formulated and tested, often quite successfully, for many years.

It is on this ground that we, too, can work to make a difference between the monarchy and a republic. We may not succeed. But if we choose not to try, and in the end there *is* no difference, we will have no one to blame—as we lunch, perhaps, at the Henry Parkes Motel, revamped yet again to commemorate a monarchist Grandfather of the Republic—but ourselves.

EPILOGUE: FUTURE FEAR

> *If the man who wants to do something great has need of the past at all, he appropriates it by means of monumental history; he, on the other hand, who likes to persist in the familiar and the revered of old, tends the past as an antiquarian historian; and only he who is oppressed by a present need, and who wants to throw off this burden at any cost, has need of critical history, that is to say a history that judges and condemns.*
>
> —FRIEDRICH NIETZSCHE (1874)[1]

> *[Howard is] like the old schoolteacher we would never dream of revisiting. . . . He's such a familiar dreariness in our lives that I look forward to the next three years with despair. He's back! He's back!*
>
> —BOB ELLIS (1997)[2]

Around 1990, a strange convergence developed in public between environmentalist doomsaying and a form of white supremacist racism that I had thought extinct in Australian political life. Even the ghost of "White Australia" seemed dead at last in 1987, when the then Opposition Leader, John Howard, sought to differentiate the Coalition from a Labor government that had stolen most of his policies by hinting to an economically stressed electorate that he might restore racial discrimination to immigration policy: "One Australia" was to be the new slogan. Australia lost a fortune in investment from Southeast Asia in about two months. The media declared racism abhorrent, big business agreed, and "One Australia" vanished; a history, it seemed, had ended. Then suddenly, there was talk of something new called a "green and red-neck alliance."

Certainly, the phrase is flippant. Many environmental scientists, activists, and farmers argue without any reference to race that the desperately dry Australian continent, now inhabited by eighteen million people, can viably support only *ten* million people indulging even a modified version of our present majority lifestyle. Given the phenomenal rate of soil degradation, salination, desert expansion, forest destruction, water pollution, and species extinction achieved since 1788, this is not hard to believe. However, when the Bureau for Immigration Research held a conference in 1990 to discuss, among other things, this issue, members of what one journalist awkwardly called "the previously internationalist left-liberal class" claimed that the best way to reduce population would be to eliminate immigrants who "grew up in the crowded cities of other countries, and have yet to appreciate a lifestyle intrinsically related to open space; or . . . have little knowledge, national pride or concern for the unique landscape, flora and fauna in Australia."[3]

At this time in our history, the "crowded cities" envisioned as emptying hordes of environmental vandals into our "open space" are Asian cities. While this coding is not always made explicit, it doesn't need to be. A century ago this same exclusionary logic, invoking class struggle rather than "lifestyle," and wages and conditions for white male workers rather than concern for flora and fauna, made the White Australia policy the linchpin of the Labor and trade union ethos. It is true that in reaction to that history, intimidatory cries of "racism!" have long greeted any effort to debate immigration seriously (with the result that anti-racists with no ideas about the water supply have a fragile credibility on this issue). However, the stamp of supremacism really is clear on this particular logic. It assumes that the other, unlike us, is always the same ("impossible to unionize" becomes "can't relate to nature"), and that we in "our" national difference have a monopoly on knowledge and concern.

Even in the ruthless terms that catastrophism can impose, it seemed fantastic to consider making the same mistake twice in the name of "ecology in one country." Yet the weird historical recurrences shaping a racist environmentalism exceed the old dialectic of "white" and "Asian" in 1890s *fin de siècle* discourse, reaching back another century for sustenance to the primal colonial scene. Relaying conflicts with indigenous people in the United States and Canada,[4] some environmentalists began arguing that what remains of our "unique landscape" after two hundred years of white settlement has to be protected from Aboriginal people—"modern" Aborigines, with guns, jeeps, land rights, and powers to negotiate with multinational mining companies.

A few years later, neither racism nor recurrence was out of the ordinary in Australian public culture. In the person of Prime Minister John Howard—family man, economic rationalist—Donald Horne's 1964 model Ordinary Australian returned as "Mainstream Man."[5] By the end of 1996, when the man in the open-necked shirt spent his first Prime Ministerial summer holidays at the beach, the monumentalism and the political correctness of the Keating era had been swept away: a small town mayor from South Australia had exercised his free speech right to call Australian children "mongrels," and an independent Member of Parliament, Ms. Pauline Hanson (fittingly, for a secular, egalitarian society's version of Pat Buchanan, a hard-working fish-and-chip-shop owner and single mother of three), had dominated media time all year with warnings that "we are in danger of being swamped by Asians," and revelations that Aboriginal people are "privileged" in Australian society.

However, parliament had also, eventually, reiterated (too late, for those bashed and abused in the surge of support for Hanson, and none too soon for the tourist industry) bipartisan opposition to race discrimination and intolerance. More "mainstream," in truth, than Ms. Hanson was the creeping antiquarianism that allowed her apocalyptic white whining to become respectable again after thirty years as disreputable. She spoke of social catastrophe in an old and once revered language of flat equality (black and white should be treated "the same") and economic nationalism ("no more Asians") that really does not deem itself racist ("Aborigines can have the same rights as the rest of us" and "Asians already here can stay").[6] When the overwhelming majority of poor, economically "redundant," and culturally "uncompetitive" people in a nation are white, this language is very easily redeemed as that of the oppressed—white victims of history silenced by the new, cosmopolitan, multicultural elites.

There is a sort of truth in this perception.[7] If few of the conflicts of history I examine in this book are peculiarly Australian (however distinct the political landscape in which they were waged), an eccentric feature of Australian public culture in the period I discuss was indeed the relative power enjoyed by "politically correct" elites with access to the media and to government, fluency in the workings of both, and sometimes class-impervious agendas: there are lessons for the future in the ugliness projected by a "mainstreamed" identity politics that disavows its own class power, or merely confesses it in hand-wringing mode. However, this is a truth about media power and temporal or *momentary* experiences, not deep social structures and spatial distributions of power.

Howard shaped a space and time of recurrence and redeemed the old "white panic" by collapsing these two sorts of truth.[8] Borrowing from George Bush's attacks on political correctness, he successfully conflated the *idea* of "disadvantaged groups"—Aborigines, the unemployed, single mothers, new immigrants—with the *image* of the visibly well-fed and audibly educated "elite" who spoke for those groups on television; as in the United States, tabloid radio became the privileged medium of a rising popular hatred for "elite minority groups." In Australia, this hatred also expressed popular *revolt* against a public culture in which "a majority of the people [did] not appear . . . at all," or felt "presented in some way in which they [did not] recognise themselves."[9]

Howard's triumph, however, was to provide a historical framework that made this new, future-oriented and violently divisive rhetoric seem to be a way of *returning* to a more secure and socially cohesive past. Pundits and academics have often argued that Howard, for whom white Australians have "nothing to be ashamed of" and "much to be proud of," has no historical sense, or a cynical view of Australian history. Nothing could be further from the truth. "Tending with care that which has existed from of old, he wants to preserve for those who shall come into existence after him the conditions under which he himself came into existence": Howard is what Nietzsche called an *antiquarian* historian.[10]

In Bob Ellis's unsympathetic portrait, Howard appears as a "drab little shifty suburban man."[11] He does venerate and seek to preserve only a very little set of drab-white suburban values. Howard has an antiquarian's "extremely restricted field of vision" (Nietzsche, 74); he tends with care only the repressive social ethos ("family values"), cold politics, and parochial, Anglo-Celtic mainstream culture of the 1950s and 1960s. However, when so many rural and working-class people were economically ravaged *and* feeling culturally despised (a mood caught exactly in the angry title of Les Murray's 1996 *Subhuman Redneck Poems*),[12] and when even the overworked and insecurely employed multicultural urban elites were seeing headlines screaming that Sydney had become the "middle class sweatshop" of Asia,[13] his aura of drabness and littleness gave Howard a formidable power to be *historically* "shifty."

He used the media effectively to shift the frame of historical argument away from "the world stage" that Keating was mocked for "strutting," and back to a "home and family" narrowed once again to a heterosexual, nuclear space; and he changed the dominant *genre* for conducting historical debate from Labor's "big picture" saga featuring Great Men and Major Events to an intimate, episodic "battler" story focused, like the radio serials of old,[14] on ordinary men and women with everyday problems, struggling to make ends meet in modest homes and shopping centers around the nation—battlers striving to keep the family together for a day at the beach, or a weekend away in a cheap but friendly motel. In flat, dull, adenoidal tones, Howard talked *small* of a familial, neighborly, tenaciously everyday history. "Here we have lived," he said to white Australians, "for here we are living; and here we shall live, for we are tough and not to be ruined overnight."[15]

Then he shifted public rhetoric back into an "either/or" mode. In an evil retrogression, people were once again cast as Aborigines *or* taxpayers, ethnic *or* Australian, noisy minority *or* silent majority. In this way, social experiments toward an open or outside-oriented inclusiveness ("and . . . and") are translated into the divisive schema whereby an exclusive kind of inclusiveness ("For All of Us," as the slogan went) first projects and then opposes the insider-exclusiveness of the "elites" with their hyphenating talk of "and . . . and." Unsurprisingly, this move was gendered: as he tenderly embraced (in Nietzsche's words) "trivial, circumscribed, decaying and obsolete" social values, Howard was hailed for "appealing to women" and "feminising" national politics.[16]

"Arrogant" Keating was a perfect target for this shifty operation. His own experiments in creating smooth space between home *and* family *and* world, between nationalism *and* multiculturalism *and* cosmopolitanism, were pried away from the dense milieu of contending ideas and social interests that had formed them and were subsumed under one aspect of his personal cult, his love of *monumental* history. The myth of Keating as a "man of deeds and power . . . who fights a great fight, who needs models, teachers, comforters and cannot find them among his contemporaries" (Nietzsche, 67) was a gift to Howard in his twenty-year struggle to translate the alien individualism, religiosity, and moralism of U.S. neoconservative politics into an obdurately communalist and "kynical" social vernacular.[17] In Australia of all places, "the demand that greatness shall be everlasting . . . sparks off the most fearful of struggles" (68). When Labor chose "LEADERSHIP" as its 1996 slogan, Howard found his translation: Paul Keating was "up himself."

It became an advantage for Howard that he often looked embarrassed on TV; that he fluffed his lines on radio, and made mistakes about his policies; that he tripped and fell in front of the cameras at the peak of his campaign. He embodied "the little man's" *stress*. When Howard promised in one of his all-time worst interviews to have Australians feeling "relaxed and comfortable" in time for the 2000 Olympic Games in Sydney and the Centenary of Federation in 2001, people engrossed in the turbulent, significant, nation-making-or-breaking politics of Reconciliation, republicanism, and Asian-Pacific regionalism laughed, and shuddered. Most Australians loved the idea.

Between the catastrophism of the far Right and Left, and the relentless drive of managerial Labor to colonize life in an endless restructuring process, Howard offered hope of a return to the "simple feeling of pleasure and contentment" that antiquarian history "spreads . . . over the modest, rude, even wretched conditions in which a man or a nation lives" (73). Yet anyone with an eye for the history in images could see, in a different, temporally more shallow set of references constellated by a new Treasurer, Peter Costello—abusing his opponents in Parliament, dressing in snappy suits, doing the Macarena on breakfast television—the empty future of that hope. Living conditions were in the hands of a poor or weak true copy (not a simulacrum)[18] of Keating Mark 1, an economic rationalist "revolutionary" who believed, unlike his model, that the poor were deserving of wretchedness and deserved no help from government.

What future, at such a time, for what Nietzsche called "critical" history? I think it can only go on with its work of judging, its effort "to break up and dissolve a part of the past" in the process that Nietzsche described as producing a "second nature" capable of becoming a new first nature (75–77). This is a drab thing to say, and I must admit that the vitality of Nietzsche's text fades for me at this point, encrusted as it is by a history of repeated academic citings—like the wings of Walter Benjamin's poor angel of history, beating sluggishly in the service of a not very lively professionalism.[19] Yet if there is a dullness in this vision of the critical (and a dreadful prefiguration of puritanical PC in Nietzsche's call for a "new, stern discipline [to] combat our inborn heritage and implant in ourselves a new habit" [76]), for me there is a *deadness* in both the cynical and the panic-stricken alternatives available in cultural theory.

Critical energies in cultural studies of popular media are often pulled between two rival but complicit temporal modes I have touched on in this book: chronic stasis ("it's all more of the same, nothing ever changes"), and acute contemporaneity or dynamitis ("that was then, this is now!"). Both prolongations of historicism, the first gives rise to the futilitarianism, to use an old Australian word, of a detached yet insatiable critique; the past already holds the answers to the problems of the present, and only at the end of history will a "real" change occur. Its much more amusing rival thrives on semiotic emergencies and lives an "end of" history *aesthetically* every day; incapable on principle of learning from the past, it gives rise to what Jane Goodall calls, in her careful comparison of late-nineteenth-century talk of neurasthenia with our own preoccupation with stress, "terminal cases of cultural hypochondria."[20]

Both, however, share a political mistrust for "reform" and an intellectual disinterest in *protracted* becomings, activist time: the first, because all time this side of the end of capitalism and patriarchy is mortgaged or "sold out" to cooptation; the second, because immanent apocalypse entails a "complete obsolescence of the experience of effort."[21] Both inhabit a present thick with "fatal prediction,"[22] thin in practical possibility: neither has *time* for the idea that monumental and antiquarian histories contending in public and popular culture might also be active, to good or bad effect, in what Nietzsche called "the service of life." More congenial to both as an approach to mediated politics is Nietzsche's own vision of a time in thrall to "the critic without need, the antiquary without piety, the man who recognizes greatness but cannot himself do great things"—a time that for Nietzsche is also a *space* of environmental disaster in which the species of history, "estranged from their mother soil," proliferate noxiously in emigrating, and degenerate into "weeds" (72).[23]

Of course, time is short for many dedicated, worldly activists as well as for cultural theorists. Catastrophists, for example, will say that environmental imperatives must take immediate precedence over others; that the future depends on the planet's capacity to keep sustaining human life, and it is too late now to work slowly: choices, they say, must be made. I do not wish to decry this sense of urgency. Real dilemmas are emerging, many of which will make it more difficult in future for the old "liberal-left" cultures to maintain their political imaginary by identifying with a spectrum of causes once smoothly construed as coherent. As a citizen whose support for land rights and Aboriginal self-determination is (if I am forced to choose) more inflexible than my opposition to uranium mining or to hunting, I am aware of a hiatus in my thinking at this point.

I can easily believe that massive ecological breakdown is not only probable but imminent. In those moments when I am watching Kuwaiti oilfields burn on television, hearing about a 1,200-kilometer, toxic blue-green algal bloom killing a river system that waters a third of Australia, or just watching my frangipani tree forget to lose its leaves in winter, I fear that most speculation about the future to which I could ever have access is "academic" in the sense that society as I know it will likely collapse, or be transformed unimaginably, within my lifetime. On the other hand, I choose to act on an everyday basis as though my fear has no real value.

As an intellectual, I have several ways of displacing this fear. I can call it "millenarian" and analyze "myths." I can support environmentalists who work to negotiate solutions to disputes and problems. I can help draw attention to the damage done by intensive agricultural methods and tourist resort development (rather than by "immigrants"), and to the efforts of people creating alternative technologies; show how choices are socially structured, historically inflected, and open to change; work to promote more constructive modes of public political debate. Yet the hiatus remains: what good does it do (I wonder at times, observing my frangipani) to write a history of the discourse of "unique landscape" used in our media today? But when I see a man on television fighting a proposal to drain a creek in the desert to bring the grass on a Japanese-owned golf course up to "international" standard, I know what cultural history can aspire to do at the very moment when I hear him veer ("I"m not racist, but . . . "), into ranting about "the Japanese" who are "taking over the country."

I think it important to my work as a cultural critic not to deny my own spasms of drab-white suburban fear, or to displace them by dismissing incorrect emotions about the future, such as helplessness, doubt, or anxiety. Whether Marxist or postmodern in inspiration, whether haunted still by the Five-Year Plan or imposing a disciplined cheerfulness about "resistance" in popular culture, criticism of that sort seems to me to restrict the scope and perhaps the *audience* of its work by defensively ignoring the tensions most people are subject to in forming their own sense of agency. For me, there is something tinny about demands "for" agency that erase a sense of the *messiness* of living and acting in the world today. One broad consequence of what David Harvey has called time-space compression is not, I think, the much-vaunted "fragmenting" of a (European) sense of history that Harvey perceives in postmodernism,[24] but rather a proliferation of heterogeneous and *volatilized* temporalities rendering global a struggle over history that is more intense than ever before.[25]

More than by schematic and sweeping theories, I am encouraged by Ruth Levitas's argument that the difficulty of thinking about the future now results from a concrete problem:

> . . . the difficulty of identifying points of intervention in an increasingly complex social and economic structure, and of identifying the agents and bearers of social transformation. It is difficult, therefore, to imagine and believe in the transition to an imagined better future. The problem about contemporary utopias is not that it is difficult to produce imaginary maps of the future, but that it is difficult to produce adequate maps of the present which permit images of a connected but transformed future.[26]

It is only in the middle of the concrete problems of this temporal in-between—the time of that transition during which, in any narrative, the things that happen, happen—that it becomes meaningful, I think, for cultural critics to make their maps and their modest proposals for action.

Catastrophism tells us *why* we should stake all future time on action in the next few years, but the "how" of such massive action remains (as in any project vaguely entailing an "overthrow" of capitalism) unclear. Pragmatism offers the medium-term temporality of the committee, the report, the grind of international, regional, and local negotiation between competing, even incommensurable economic interests, political programs, and historical visions. As a citizen, I am usually more sympathetic to the relative realism of the latter than the absolute realism of the former, because I think pragmatism is a practice on balance more capable of working its way past *obstacles* to change.

However, I see the temporality of cultural politics in other terms again. Critics work primarily as mediators—writers, readers, image producers, teachers—in a socially as well as theoretically obscure zone of values, opinion, ideology, belief, and emotion. If we can and do become involved in broader social and economic struggles, whatever political effectivity we might claim for *critical* work can be registered, most of the time, only by gradual shifts in what people take to be thinkable and do-able in relation to particular circumstances in time, place, and space. In more settled times, this can be cast by its enthusiasts as an intrinsically splendid endeavor. In fearful or turbulent times, it is easily denounced as trivial. In between, I agree with Margaret Morse when she says that:

Changes in shared fictions, values and beliefs occur over the long term, slowly and incrementally, not merely because once shared values are discredited or may no longer be viable, but because alternative values and their constituencies have labored to mark themselves in discourse. I believe the criticism of television can serve cultural change when it keeps such long-term goals in mind.[27]

To undertake such positive labor, it is necessary to gamble on the *openness* of the future, as well as to make a commitment to creating in the present some sense of continuity and solidarity with those who have labored in the past.

For this reason, I am unmoved by what twenty years of changes in feminism have taught me to think of as bombast about the dire political failings of this or that critical claim or position. I do not believe that much of the future hangs on anything said in an academic book or a conference. On the other hand, I have no time for ritual breast-beating about the futility of it all ("the world is falling apart while we sit around . . . "). Most people with a more than careerist investment in critical practice feel doubt, even anguish, about the purpose and the value of their work, and often this helps us to think. But there is also a time-honored practice of self-lacerating anti-intellectualism that, by fearlessly revealing that someone's paper on popular aesthetics has failed to dismantle the military-entertainment complex, works only to deflate the significance of other people's labor.

I mentioned in a previous chapter Ian Hunter's history of this and other critical rituals, *Culture and Government: The Emergence of Literary Education.*[28] Hunter's criticism of "critique" as an ethos of self-formation is still what Michèle Le Doeuff calls *atopian*,[29] unplaceably unplaced, in relation to most critical debates not directly concerned with cultural or educational policy. However, Hunter perhaps explains this atopianism himself when he argues that since the romantic imperative to reconcile "divided ethical substance" in cultural critique can never be effected, the imperative works repetitively to maintain a fraught space of *crisis* where massive problems are invoked on such a level of generality that they cannot possibly be solved, and in ways that cannot connect to agencies by which actual social futures may be given definite shape.[30]

If we take this, for the sake of argument, as a fair description of the dynamics of cultural studies debates, it follows that critique is not a practice that can shape social futures, but, on the contrary, one that *needs*, even as it multiplies differentiated critical selves, *to fail* to identify what Levitas calls the "points of intervention" enabling effective action. Hunter is not alone in making this argument. In a similar spirit, Tony Bennett suggests that the figures so often called "agents" of social transformation—classes, races, genders, the people—might better be described as "*phantom* agents."[31] Using the example of public museum politics, he suggests that if agents are "entities capable of arriving at decisions and putting them into effect," then:

> One would find neither classes nor "the people"—or, for that matter, races or genders—active as identifiable agents in the sphere of museum politics. What one *would* find, of course, would be claims to *represent* class or popular interests, claims which might be advanced by a whole range of effective social agents—museum critics, sectional pressure groups like WHAM [Women Heritage and Museums], committees of management, teams of designers, curators, sometimes even boards of trustees. (31)

This is not to say that classes, races, and genders do not exist, as the saying goes; for Bennett, these and "similar constructs undoubtedly have a real existence as both the targets of specific political programs and as representations which inform the suasive strategies of social agents." However, "they cannot themselves be such agents" (31–32).

I think that Hunter and Bennett may be right about this. Conceding the point creates problems for cultural theorists and critics only if we do not take seriously, *in* our work, the institutional locations *of* our work as mediators, teachers, and writers, that is, producers of suasive strategies. Irritably, I want to add that feminist theorists and critics of culture have always taken location seriously. Reaching no further than a few texts I often use to think with, I find Michèle Le Doeuff's histories of women and philosophy;[32] the work of Gayatri Spivak, so meticulously clear about the fine pragmatics of discourse, power, and agency in academic contexts;[33] Patricia J. Williams's "alchemy" of race and rights, literature and law, personal and professional knowledges;[34] I find Claire Johnston's untimely essays on women's cinema and film history.

All the same, it does seem hard for cultural studies as, let's say, an ethos, a collectively shaped disposition, to throw off the megalomaniacal idea inherited from "English" that a training in reading can and does form a caste of total subjects (or, as Hunter might say, "whole persons") fit to administer a nation or even the world. Few critics would want to avow such an absurd aspiration. Yet the yearning for total responsibility, with its promise of an ultimate but ever-deferred state of completeness, continues to authorize conduct on those occasions when academic groupuscules gather, in tourist hotels and conference rooms, to denounce each other for "erasing" the agency of an unlimitable number of subjects (classes, races, genders, sexualities, and the popular serving, on these occasions, as only the most general of what Rey Chow calls "*portable oppressions*"),[35] and thence for complicity in multiple historical crimes.

Perhaps the history of "English" also structures our professional imaginary when, as practitioners of a seriously sedentary mode of action (traveling theorists *sit* on planes, as they sit at desks), we dramatize our engagement with a wider world by projecting ourselves discursively as heroes and heroines of mobility: the intellectual as nomad, detective, tourist, pedestrian, social-climbing gorilla. It certainly marks our practice intimately in those moments when we ask of a stirring, imaginative, eloquent, and scholarly critical discourse that has manifestly just inspired and strengthened people, "Yes, but what *else* can this do?"

I suspect that cultural criticism would benefit greatly from understanding better what it is that such a discourse actually does. Hunter and Bennett are not concerned with this question, being interested in, respectively, other modes of intellectual work, and more socially actionable ways to frame research in cultural studies. However, those of us who are committed *by desire* to making "room for maneuver"[36] on the broad terrain of aesthetics do need to consider, along with our questions of affect, the questions of effectiveness that Hunter and Bennett raise.

For Bennett, the issue of agency is best approached "by way of Brecht's remark that it is no use just to write 'the truth'; one has . . . 'to write it *for* and *to* somebody, somebody who can do something with it'" (31). By adding a demand that we be much more socially exact in naming that somebody who "can do," Bennett makes it hard to respond simply by adding (as beleaguered cultural critics are still wont to do) "our students" to the list of phantom agents; not because students are phantoms, but because their very status *as* "our students," what they "can do" in that (temporary) capacity, and any projections we might make about the value of our pedagogy for their lives, are internal to the self-shaping regime of critique that Bennett, like Hunter, is challenging.

Rey Chow, another feminist who writes about the institutional frames of academic work, provides a better way of responding to Bennett in the course of her own criticism of the "moral and/or rhetorical" victories won for phantom agents by "a guilt-tripping discourse along the lines of 'who speaks?'" For Chow, the problem with "who speaks?" is that "the emphasis of the question is always on 'who'" (146). Designed to elicit the answer that those who have power speak, this question disavows the power and the technology that enables it to be put, and simplifies oppression by "trying to understand the world in the form of a coherent narrative grammar, with an identifiable (anthropomorphic) subject for every sentence." To foreground the "multifarious and contradictory" nature of oppression in Hong Kong, Chow begins her own account of Chinese popular music with a different question: "*what plays?*"

Now, by doing this, Chow creates a context for her question. As her essay proceeds, it becomes clear that to ask "what plays?" ("what are the forms of surplus? How does surplus inhabit the emotions? What is the relationship between surplus, the emotions, and the portability of oppression?") in contemporary Chinese popular music is not at all to displace a question of effects with a question of emotion. It is, on the contrary, to ask of this music how emotions can *work*, and what may be *effected*, musically, in a context where an obdurate "inarticulateness" combats "the talking function of the state"; where "who speaks?" is an order-word underlying a forty-year history of political interrogations and purges; where the Romantic critical themes of partiality and excess ("surplus") can describe ways of living with totalitarian rationality; and where the "symphonic effects" of an official culture of collectivity are encountering a *"revolution in listening"* (162) enabled by a particular technology, the Walkman. For Chow, this technology not only gives access to an individualizing "freedom to be deaf to the loudspeakers of history," but also to a different kind of collectivity: "not necessarily an 'other' to be idealised from afar but rather a mundane, mechanical, portable *part* of ourselves" (164).

Except at that vital last point, this is not a context in which I am any kind of social agent. So is there anything that I can *do*, responsibly, with Chow's analysis of Chinese popular music? I think the answer is, yes: the Walkman invites readers to render portable "what plays" for them in the essay,[37] just as it allows the question of the portability of the East Asian street scenes that Chow describes, in the U.S. academic setting of her work of description, to arise as, exactly, a *question*. Perhaps the Walkman itself is a "point of intervention" in this context. For, just as Chow uses music to elaborate historical particularity (for example, how an "openly autistic self" can play against Chinese communism), her use of the Walkman also suggests that this history, this music, is not sealed off from whatever our own may be; what we learn from the essay about individuals and a portable collectivity may not be consigned to a separate and (if we are Western) safely non-Western sphere.

It is the masking of our *use* of technologies that Chow criticizes, not portability itself. So I think it fair to say that, by replacing the "who?" question of identity with "what?" and "how?" questions of practice, and by displacing "questions of linguistics and narratology applied to issues of power" (145) with a question of pragmatics ("plays"), Chow focuses in a more practical way than Bennett does on what he calls "suasive strategies," as well as on the "popular" resistance such strategies may *encounter*. Her approach allows us to ask "what plays?" even in those basic professional activities of speaking and writing, and, when we do ask "who speaks?" (for I think there are times when we must), it reminds us to keep the emphasis on "speaks"—on technologies and techniques of persuasion.

This returns me to the question of cultural criticism and social effectiveness. Brecht, according to Bennett, wrote "to and for somebody" who was in fact the proletariat as phantom agent. Bennett's activist prefers to work pragmatically for social agents who are clearly defined and endowed *as* agents by institutions in which questions like "who speaks?" and "what plays?" have definite answers, and may well entail each other; to know what interests are represented on a committee is often to know what will play.

Chow defines a third possibility. She "lodges" her question of pragmatics in a "realm" of Chinese music that is historically distinct, open to portability, and technologically part of a broader process of circulation (or, as Deleuze and Guattari might say, of "pick-up" rather than "cut-up")[38] in which there is no way of limiting, with any finality, "for and to" whom *anything* plays.

Bennett ignores this third possibility and, by opposing only a broadly managerial mode of activism to the "ineffable complexity" of a socially useless critique, he lodges activism exclusively in a small world of exactly situated somebodies (elite minorities, in fact) who know other somebodies who "can do"; in an orderly world, with a coherent narrative grammar of action that is not only based on efficiency and limitation (for me, this is a great virtue of Bennett's approach), but also strongly founded on closure against the *indefinite* in social life. This means that Bennett's theory cannot take the media, or any technologies of cultural circulation, seriously as forces for social change.

Yet the fact that the most insignificant statements can circulate and be picked up unpredictably is, like the problem of dealing with indefinite interlocutors in uncontrollably porous contexts, routinely confronted by anyone asking "what?" and "how?" questions of suasion, whether in media work or at any of the other points where intellectuals intervene as mediators, speakers, and writers. Effective suasive strategies cannot be derived from the constants of a grammar, any more than Bennett's capable "somebody" can be abstracted as a "subject"; both act in densely social zones of continuous variation in everyday life. The useful polemic in cultural policy studies against the aesthetic illusion that we change the world by exchanging critiques should not lead us to forget (once again) the pragmatic force exerted by emotion, desire, affect, and the audible energy that Rey Chow calls "surplus," in "definitely shaping" social futures. Tabloid radio, after all, once shaped a future that is now a very "definite" part of the present.

In practice, critics have ways of handling indefiniteness and portability in cultural work. We focus on groups whom we know that we address, and agnostically shrug away the rest; we collect anything from testimonials to market research that may serve us as a guide; some of us do stage our subjectivities and histories as research projects; others play ethnographer, studying what particular groups "can do" with materials that come their way. My inclination is to learn from what Hunter calls the "positive sciences" of criticism, rhetoric, and historical philology;[39] I find that these can provide, when they are allowed to include a pragmatic study of genre and narrative, better *technical* guides to action than the mono-generic (and, therefore, socially inflexible) deconstructive practice of critique now often so simply called "theory."[40]

Whatever one thinks of these diverse techniques, all share a recognition that indefiniteness and portability do not render culture ineffable or unusable as a medium of focused endeavor for people who do not make "policy."

However, as portability increases and intensifies, the indignant or grammatic "PC" parochialism of assuming that you *know* the political import of this or that act or practice will not be very helpful in future. At the same time, the intellectual fantasy of control historically invested in vanguardist forms of thinking about the future—the manifesto, the utopian program, that great book to change the course of history—may itself become obsolete.

I quite like that idea. Classical utopian writing depresses me profoundly, and my idea of an empowering vision of the future is the ending of *Terminator 2: Judgment Day*. But I doubt that the future is quite as open as that wonderful film suggests with its affirmation that freedom and responsibility are possible, not only in the fantasy futures by which we dream our opposition to regimes of grim necessity, but as real practices in the present of an indeterminate and unpredictable historical time. In reality, however, the past often now seems more terrifying than the future did under the old Cold War dispensation (and as it was at the end of *The Terminator*). As the sense of a history moving with grim necessity into bloody repetition becomes insistent in global media, I can understand why some critics long for the benign, familiar closure of that stirring manifesto, that singular avant-garde gesture, that great book to initiate a "whole new era."

However, I have more faith in Morse's model of cultural politics because it does not require that we sacrifice to fear and "crisis" the possibility of drawing on a *different past*: not a mythic, idealized or "nativist" past;[41] and not Nietzsche's family-romantic "critical" past "in which one would like to originate in opposition to that in which one did originate" (76) (in other words, a past diametrically opposed to that revered by antiquarians); but an actual past in which real practices of freedom and responsibility become possible *because* "alternative values and their constituencies have labored to mark themselves in discourse."

Sharing neither the immobilizing conviction that practical action is pointless or doomed in the present, nor the panicky belief that immigrants, the Internet, postmodern architecture, and aliens from outer space are terminating history, I think it worth remembering that cultural criticism is necessarily subject to phases of market *boredom* with the "critical" historical sense created by the labor Morse invokes, and with the slow, incremental temporality endured by any struggle with serious designs on the future. My response to such boredom is—that's tough for cultural critics. Alternative values and their constituencies may be obliterated in an apocalyptic event, but they will not disappear by decree of some jaded *culturati*, nor fade to fit the needs of the conference component of the hospitality industry.

On the same basis, however, I disagree with the view put forward by Harvey, among others, that the value-parasitic "cultural mass" collectively tends, because of its class positioning, to "lack the reassuring support of a moral tradition that [we] can call our own"; as I also disagree with the idea that this cultural mass has "internalised" a host of struggles with general significance, such as feminism, under "the banner of postmodernism."[42] I do know what Harvey means by this, and he is not the only one to apply it to academic forms of feminism. However, long before I could be aware of any such thing as a "banner of postmodernism," feminism taught me the value of doing cultural work, not the other way around. Alternative *histories* matter too, and the labor of marking and remarking them in discourse is, it seems, never-ending.

For example, if we must, with Harvey, construct bipolar models to grasp the relations between modern and postmodern ways of conceptualizing place and space, then the present as well as the future of cultural politics could look quite different if we began with a different past. Instead of starting out, once again, from, say, Marx and Heidegger (thus staying firmly rooted in that Black Forest farmhouse of social theory called the Dialectic of Modernity and Tradition), we could stage a debate between Marx and Spinoza, and one between Heidegger and Frantz Fanon; another between Alexandra Kollantai and C. L. R. James, and another between Judah Waten (a Russian-born Jewish Australian Marxist) and Emma Goldman.

My preference would be to abandon the bipolar model. I would like to see a discussion of space, place, and history begin with, say, Jamaica Kincaid's *A Small Place*, an essay on Antigua with plenty to teach about the global economy of tourism, colonial history, and the politics of cultural identity; with Sally Morgan's *My Place*, a text about Morgan's experience of finding at the age of thirty that she was an Aboriginal not an Indian Australian, and what her own history had to with the racial and sexual politics underpinning the success of the cattle industry in Australia; with Cynthia Enloe's *Bananas, Beaches and Bases: Making Feminist Sense of International Politics*, an economic and cultural study of the gender politics of the "place construction" (army bases, embassies, brothels, servants' quarters, homes) indispensable to global military space; and with the late Eric Michaels's book about the cultural politics of television invented by the Warlpiri people in Central Australia, *For a Cultural Future: Francis Jupurrurla Makes TV at Yuendumu*.[43]

In this way, the "cultural mass" might well have access to a political as well a moral tradition that could not be, in the possessive self-identical sense, "our own," but that can powerfully shape and sustain our future labors; making it easier, as Laura Mulvey puts it, "to build from one historical context to another without the endless loss inherent in the 'tradition of the new.'"[44] We could also see that place-based movements need not be parochial or place-bound,[45] and may well provide more concrete ways of historically articulating a politics of space than those sweeping, schematic traditions of theorizing that think themselves universal have so far been able to achieve. One thing such movements can certainly offer is their decades of experience in just how hard it can really be to sustain international movements—and their knowledge that it is, sometimes, possible to do so.

As I try to finish this epilogue, the media distract me, with talk of historic events, from the roar of the tourist-shopper planes flying above my head; quietly, the Labor Party reclaims its faith in car and sugar tariffs, and the *Business Review Weekly* gasps that "Keating Is Dead";[46] spectacularly, more than half a million people (a big crowd for a city of four million, even allowing for tourists) line the streets for the Sydney Gay and Lesbian Mardi Gras, this year starring by popular acclaim a "Pauline Hanson" float escorted by Koori and Asian dancers with big bags of fries on their heads. I turn to Eric Michaels's *Unbecoming: An AIDS Diary*, another text about globalization, place, and the stakes of personal identity.

An essay is included that he probably wrote in 1982 about a moment of decline, as he judged it then, in gay politics. Having spent years learning from the mixed-media, "historical" strategies of traditional, if not especially Heideggerian, Aboriginal societies, Michaels, a Jewish American, wrote this about the future for gay men; and also, I dare say (watching Mainstream Man on television), "for all of us":

> For starters, we need to take some responsibility for our own history, for conveying it to our young. It is not nostalgia. If one is going to go to all the trouble to be gay, one ought to do a more interesting and useful job of it. Models exist in our very recent past. They should be recalled.[47]

NOTES

PREFACE

1. "The Theory of Women's Liberation," in Ann Curthoys, *For and against Feminism* (Sydney: Allen & Unwin, 1988), 11.

2. Gilles Deleuze and Félix Guattari, *A Thousand Plateaus*, trans. Brian Massumi (Minneapolis: University of Minnesota Press, 1987), 81; first published as *Mille Plateaux* (Paris: Minuit, 1980).

3. The main exhibition, *Frames of Reference: Aspects of Feminism and Art*, was in August 1991. *Dissonance*, involving over seventy independent projects in several cities, ran from July to October 1991 and gave rise to the collection *Dissonance: Feminism and the Arts 1970–90*, ed. Catriona Moore (Sydney: Allen & Unwin, 1994).

4. Gough Whitlam and R. J. ("Bob") Hawke were Labor Prime Ministers of Australia, in 1972–75 and 1983–91 respectively. In the 1980s, the content of the opposition organized by their names was, broadly, radicalism (Whitlam) vs. pragmatism (Hawke); confrontational politics vs. corporatism and social consensus; ideological passion vs. cool, competent professionalism.

5. Laura Mulvey, *Visual and Other Pleasures* (Bloomington: Indiana University Press, 1989), 159–76.

6. I owe this formulation, and therefore much else, to Helen Grace.

7. Interest in Deleuze and Foucault in the 1970s was fostered more by debates in Gay Liberation than by those then prevailing in the Australian women's movement. See Paul Foss and Meaghan Morris, eds., *Language, Sexuality and Subversion* (Sydney: Feral Publications, 1978); Meaghan Morris and Paul Patton, eds., *Michel Foucault: Power, Truth, Strategy* (Sydney: Feral Publications, 1979).

8. Deleuze and Guattari, *A Thousand Plateaus*, 97–98; Gilles Deleuze, "He Stuttered," *Gilles Deleuze and the Theater of Philosophy*, ed. Constantin V. Boundas and Dorothea Olkowski (New York and London: Routledge, 1994), 23–29.

9. Lesley Stern, in Lesley Stern, Laleen Jayamanne, and Helen Grace, "Remembering Claire Johnston," *Framework* 35 (1988): 115.

10. She also edited *Notes on Women's Cinema* (1973), *Frank Tashlin* and *Jacques Tourneur* (1973 and 1975, both with Paul Willemen), *Dorothy Arzner—Towards a Feminist Cinema* (1975), and in 1976 she co-edited the legendary *Edinburgh '76 Magazine* (*Psycho-analysis/Cinema/Avant-Garde*), featuring Rosalind Coward, Christian Metz, Geoffrey Nowell-Smith, Stephen Heath, Kari Hanet, Julia Kristeva, and Peter Wollen. An almost complete bibliography is in *Filmnews*, "Remembering Claire Johnston," May 1988, 15.

11. Stern, 115.

12. Stern, 118: "Paranoid discourse sees pattern and purpose in absolutely every-thing, everywhere. The anti-paranoid or hebephrenic, on the other hand, be-lieves that no pattern or interpretation is privileged and so can see no patterns in anything."

13. Jerome Christensen, "From Rhetoric to Corporate Populism: A Romantic Cri-tique of the Academy in an Age of High Gossip," *Critical Inquiry* 16 (Winter 1990): 438–65.

14. Gilles Deleuze and Félix Guattari, *Kafka: Toward a Minor Literature*, trans. Dana Polan (Minneapolis: University of Minnesota Press, 1986), 41; first published as *Kafka: Pour une littérature mineure* (Paris: Minuit, 1975).

15. Patrice Petro, "Feminism and Film History," *Camera Obscura* 22 (January 1990): 144.

16. See *Camera Obscura* 20–21 (May-September 1989), "The Spectatrix."

17. Roland Barthes, *The Rustle of Language*, trans. Richard Howard (Oxford: Blackwell, 1986), 49–55.

18. Ronald Bogue, *Deleuze and Guattari* (New York: Routledge, 1989), 122.

19. See Peter Burger, *Theory of the Avant-Garde*, trans. Michael Shaw (Minneapolis: University of Minnesota Press, 1984).

20. Claire Johnston, "Women's Cinema as Counter-Cinema," in *Notes on Women's Cinema* (London: SEFT, 1973), 31.

21. Deleuze and Guattari, *A Thousand Plateaus*, 106.

22. Burger, *Theory of the Avant-Garde*. See also Andreas Huyssen, *After the Great Divide: Modernism, Mass Culture, Postmodernism* (Bloomington: Indiana University Press, 1986).

23. Deleuze and Guattari, *Kafka*, 17.

24. See Réda Bensmaïa, "On the Concept of Minor Literature: From Kafka to Kateb Yacine," *Gilles Deleuze and the Theater of Philosophy*, ed. Boundas and Olkowski, 213–28.

25. Deleuze and Guattari, *A Thousand Plateaus*, ch. 4 ("November 20, 1923: Postulates of Linguistics") extends *Kafka*'s concept of the minor with a theory of exigency and *timing* ("dates") in language and history, while ch. 10 ("1730: Becoming-Intense, Becoming-Animal, Becoming-Imperceptible . . . ") suggests that the subject of a *becoming*-minor is always a majority.

26. Deleuze and Guattari, *Kafka*, 18: "Kafka's solitude opens up to him every-thing going on in history today."

27. See some of the essays in *New Times: The Changing Face of Politics in the 1990s*, ed. Stuart Hall and Martin Jacques (London: Lawrence & Wishart in association with *Marxism Today*, 1989).

28. Deleuze and Guattari, *A Thousand Plateaus*, 107–108.

29. Ibid., 76. On speech acts, see 77f. The concept of "order-word" is more com-plicated than I can indicate here. While it may refer to classes of statements (im-peratives, slogans, buzzwords, "words for the day," "words from our sponsors"), it is also used by Deleuze and Guattari to identify both the elementary unit of all lan-guage and an imperative force that is *immanent* to language.

30. Johnston, "Women's Cinema as Counter-Cinema," 30–31.

31. Stern, Jayamanne, and Grace, 127.

32. Claire Johnston, "Femininity and the Masquerade: *Anne of the Indies*," (1975), in *Psychoanalysis and Cinema*, ed. E. Ann Kaplan (New York: Routledge, 1990), 68.

33. David Harvey. *The Condition of Postmodernity* (Oxford: Blackwell, 1989). I discuss this further in "The Man in the Mirror: David Harvey's 'Condition' of Postmodernity," *Cultural Theory and Cultural Change*, ed. Mike Featherstone (London, Newbury Park, and New Delhi: Sage, 1992), 253–79.

34. A few examples from different disciplines are Rosalyn Deutsche, *Evictions: Art and Spatial Politics* (Cambridge, MA: The MIT Press, 1996); bell hooks, *Yearning: Race, Gender and Cultural Politics* (Boston: South End Press, 1990); Cindi Katz, "Major/Minor: Theory, Nature, and Politics," *Annals of the Association of American Geographers* 85.1 (March 1995): 164–67; Judith Newton, "History as Usual? Feminism and the 'New Historicism,'" *The New Historicism*, ed. H. Aram Veeser (New York: Routledge, 1989), 152–67; Michele Wallace, *Invisibility Blues: From Pop to Theory* (London: Verso, 1990).

35. For example, a life/writing opposition is precluded by Teresa de Lauretis's sense of "experience" as "an ongoing process by which subjectivity is constructed semiotically and historically"; *Alice Doesn't: Feminism, Semiotics, Cinema* (Bloomington: Indiana University Press, 1984), 182. A critical review of the term is Joan W. Scott, "'Experience,'" *Feminists Theorize the Political*, ed. Judith Butler and Joan W. Scott (New York and London: Routledge, 1992), 22–40.

36. Ann Curthoys, "What Is the Socialism in Socialist Feminism?" *Australian Feminist Studies* 6 (Autumn 1988): 17–24. Replies and responses by Rosemary Pringle, Pauline Johnson, Carol Johnson, Daphne Gollan, Philipa Rothfield, and Judy Lattas follow in issues 6, 7/8, 9.

37. Paul Willemen, "Rotterdam," *Framework* 20 (1983): 44.

INTRODUCTION

1. Carolyn Steedman, "Culture, Cultural Studies, and the Historians," *Cultural Studies*, ed. Lawrence Grossberg, Cary Nelson, and Paula Treichler (New York and London: Routledge, 1992), 621. Further references in parentheses in the text.

2. Lawrence Grossberg, "The Formations of Cultural Studies: An American in Birmingham," *Strategies* 2 (1989): 144.

3. Henri Lefebvre, *Critique de la vie quotidienne I: Introduction* (Paris: Grasset, 1947), followed by *Critique de la vie quotidienne II: Fondement d'une sociologie de la quotidienneté* (Paris: L'Arche, 1962).

4. Henri Lefebvre, *Everyday Life in the Modern World*, trans. Sacha Rabinovitch (New Brunswick: Transaction Books, 1984), 40; first published as *La vie quotidienne dans le monde moderne* (Paris: Gallimard, 1968).

5. Fredric Jameson, *Postmodernism, or, The Cultural Logic of Late Capitalism* (Durham: Duke University Press, 1991).

6. David Harvey, *The Condition of Postmodernity: An Enquiry into the Origins of Cultural Change* (Oxford: Blackwell, 1989). Harvey's title alludes to the account of postmodernism as an *epistemological* condition in Jean-François Lyotard, *The Postmodern Condition: A Report on Knowledge*, trans. Geoff Bennington and Brian Massumi (Minneapolis: University of Minnesota Press, 1984).

7. On the "posthistorical," see Elizabeth Deeds Ermath, *Sequel to History: Postmodernism and the Crisis of Representational Time* (Princeton: Princeton University Press, 1992), and Lutz Niethammer, *Posthistoire: Has History Come to an End?* trans. Patrick Camiller (London: Verso, 1992).

8. O. K. Werckmeister, *Citadel Culture* (Chicago: University of Chicago Press, 1991), 183.

9. Gilles Deleuze and Félix Guattari, *A Thousand Plateaus*, trans. Brian Massumi (Minneapolis: University of Minnesota Press, 1987), 81.

10. Carl Schorske, cited by Steedman, 620.

11. Humphrey McQueen, "The Pineapple of Professional Correctness," *ABC Radio 24 Hours* June 1996, 57. McQueen suggests that a "shying away" from the present by historians has left cultural theorists and literary critics "more alone in that territory" than we should have been.

12. I have in mind the frequency with which Australian media pundits who are not historians pass judgment on the historical value of films, books, and TV shows, debate the history curriculum in schools, and predict the "historical" import of news items. Conflict over political correctness in Australia has been waged most intensely for control of the language of history—for example, whether public museums and school texts should say "invasion" or "settlement" to describe the arrival of the British in 1788—rather than over the literary canon.

13. Marc Augé, *Non-Places: Introduction to an Anthropology of Supermodernity*, trans. John Howe (London: Verso, 1995), 25.

14. See, for example, Tony Swain's history of the impact of Western "time" on the space-based ontologies of Aboriginal Australia, *A Place for Strangers: Towards a History of Australian Aboriginal Being* (Cambridge, New York, and Melbourne: Cambridge University Press, 1993).

15. Steedman (617) follows Dominick LaCapra in conflating the concept of culture with the "culture-concept," thus assuming that *commonality* and *coherence* are always held to characterize *a* "culture" thereby made co-extensive with the history of the European nation-state: in cultural studies, I would argue, this conflation does not hold. See LaCapra, *History and Criticism* (Ithaca: Cornell UP, 1985), 71–94.

16. Dipesh Chakrabarty, "Trafficking in History and Theory: Subaltern Studies," *Beyond the Disciplines: The New Humanities*, ed. K. K. Ruthven (Canberra: Australian Academy of the Humanities, 1993) 101–108. Future references in parentheses in the text.

17. Stephen Muecke, "Experimental History? The 'Space' of History in Recent Histories of Kimberley Colonialism," *The UTS Review* 2.1 (1996): 4.

18. See Chakrabarty's poignant account of the role of theory in "globalising" the project of *Subaltern Studies*; "Trafficking in History and Theory," 101.

19. Serious attempts to theorize the specificity of cultural studies have been rare, in part because of a coyness about staking claims to disciplinarity. Among the exceptions are Tony Bennett, "Coming out of English: A Policy Calculus for Cultural Studies," *Beyond the Disciplines: The New Humanities*, ed. K. K. Ruthven, 33–44; and Lawrence Grossberg, *We Gotta Get out of This Place: Popular Conservatism and Postmodern Culture* (New York and London: Routledge, 1992). Grossberg follows Stuart Hall in defining cultural studies as a particular kind of *practice*. Stuart Hall, "Cultural Studies and Its Theoretical Legacies," Grossberg, Nelson, and Treichler, 277–94. On Hall's practice as a theoretical model *for* cultural studies, see *Stuart Hall: Critical Dialogues in Cultural Studies*, ed. David Morley and Kuan-Hsing Chen (London and New York: Routledge, 1996).

20. Inderpal Grewal and Caren Kaplan, eds., *Scattered Hegemonies: Postmodernity*

and Transnational Feminist Practices (Minneapolis: University of Minnesota Press, 1994), 17.

21. Lawrence Grossberg, "Cultural Studies: What's In a Name?" B. Aubrey Fisher Memorial Lecture, October 1993, published by the Department of Communication, University of Utah, Salt Lake City, Utah, 9.

22. Something like an orthodoxy on this topic was set out for cultural theory in Robert Young, *White Mythologies: Writing, History and the West* (London: Routledge, 1990).

23. "Panorama: The Live, the Dead and the Living," in *Nation, Culture, Text: Australian Cultural and Media Studies*, ed. Graeme Turner (London and New York: Routledge, 1993), 19–58.

24. On the complexities of this belated experience of a "nationalised" image-space, which occurred in the same year that the "internationalisation" of Australia's economy began, see Tom O'Regan, *Australian Television Culture* (Sydney: Allen & Unwin, 1993).

25. A brief glossary for U.S. readers. Founded in 1891, the *Labor Party* is Australia's "grand old" party (see ch. 5 below). Internally organized by a faction system and tight rules of party discipline, it embraces several philosophies. Its "left" wing includes social activists drawn to the left of the British Labour Party; its "right" wing, usually dominant in government, includes admirers of the U.S. Democratic Party. The conservative side of politics in postwar Australia is represented by "*the Coalition*," a sometimes delicate alliance of the business-oriented *Liberal Party* (once comparable to the pre-Thatcher British Tories, now heavily influenced by the right of the U.S. Republican Party), and the rurally based *National Party*—socially conservative, with a dash of "agrarian socialism."

26. Maximilian Walsh, *Poor Little Rich Country: The Path to the Eighties* (Harmondsworth and Ringwood: Penguin, 1979). I am not endorsing this hyperbole. The extreme poverty inflicted on many remote Aboriginal communities is not what economists have in mind when they talk of Australia's "third world" potential, and during this same period surveys based on quality of life criteria placed Australia among the richest countries in the world. In what follows, I am interested in the *force* of these intimidatory discourses of economic pathos, as they draw on popular images and, for some people, memories of imperialism elsewhere to organize support for anti-social economic policies in the present.

27. "Reconstruction" became a government as well as an academic buzzword in this period through an influential Australian Council of Trade Unions report, *Australia Reconstructed: ACTU/TDC Mission to Western Europe* (Canberra: Australian Government Publishing Service, 1987).

28. Donald Horne, *The Public Culture: An Argument with the Future* (London and Boulder: Pluto Press, 1994), vii.

29. The term "Anglo-Celtic" for Australians of mostly British and/or Irish heritage came into wide use in the second half of the 1980s as a way of naming the (by then) largely melded, mutually assimilative culture of Australia's dominant and largest ethnic bloc. It outraged many people, both as an ahistorical and racializing term (unlike the conceivable but impossibly clumsy alternative, "British-Irish-Australian") and an insult to Gaelic Catholics in their struggles with other "Celts" as well as with the English. Accepted in the public culture for a while, it is under challenge again. I have never liked it, yet no other term quite serves the purpose.

30. These shifts were not uniformly effective or socially real. See Ghassan Hage, "Anglo-Celtics Today: Cosmo-Multiculturalism and the Phase of the Fading Phallus," *Communal/Plural* 4 (1994): 41–77.

31. Let me be clear about my attitude to tourism. *Of course*, most people enjoy being tourists. In Australia's relatively benign conditions, many also benefit from the improved services that tourism fosters as well as provides. The question, however, is not whether the tourist industry is "good" or "bad," but how it *works* in particular situations. See Andrew Ross, *The Chicago Gangster Theory of Life: Nature's Debt to Society* (London and New York: Verso, 1994), 21–98.

32. Graeme Turner, *Making It National: Nationalism and Australian Popular Culture* (Sydney: Allen & Unwin, 1994), 111.

33. Jennifer Craik, *Resorting to Tourism: Cultural Policies for Tourist Development in Australia* (Sydney: Allen & Unwin, 1991), 231.

34. Horne, *The Intelligent Tourist*, (McMahon's Point: Margaret Gee Publishing, 1993), 325–33. Michel Picard discusses this model in "Cultural Heritage and Tourist Capital: Cultural Tourism in Bali," *International Tourism: Identity and Change*, ed. Marie-Françoise Lanfant, John B. Allcock, and Edward M. Bruner (London, Thousand Oaks, and New Delhi: Sage, 1995), 44–66.

35. A classic and still useful interpretation of these extraordinarily complex concepts is J. P. Bury, *The Idea of Progress: An inquiry into Its Origin and Growth* (New York: Macmillan, 1932). See also Jeffrey Alexander and Piotr Sztompa, eds., *Rethinking Progress* (London: Unwin Hyman, 1990) and Yi-Fu Tuan, *Morality and Imagination: Paradoxes of Progress* (Madison: University of Wisconsin Press, 1989).

36. Lyotard, *The Postmodern Condition*, xxiv. Often paraphrased as a flat claim that grand narratives are "dead," Lyotard's argument is rather that today we have difficulty in believing them.

37. Theodor W. Adorno, "Progress," *The Philosophical Forum* XV.1–2 (1983–84): 55.

38. W. E. H. Stanner's scathing summary of the driving principles of pastoralism is cited by Noel Pearson, "Mabo and the Humanities: Shifting Frontiers," *The Humanities and a Creative Nation: Jubilee Essays*, ed. Deryck M. Schreuder (Canberra: Australian Academy of the Humanities, 1995), 52.

39. R. W. Connell, *Ruling Class Ruling Culture: Studies of Conflict, Power and Hegemony in Australian Life* (Cambridge: Cambridge University press, 1977), 195.

40. Paul Gilroy, *The Black Atlantic: Modernity and Double Consciousness* (Cambridge, MA: Harvard University Press, 1993), 53, my emphasis. Histories of the effects in Australia of "history as progress" include: Lynette Finch, *The Classing Gaze: Sexuality, Class and Surveillance* (Sydney: Allen & Unwin, 1993); Humphrey McQueen, *A New Britannia* (Ringwood and Harmondsworth: Penguin Books, 1970); Rosemary Pringle, "Octavius Beale and the Ideology of the Birthrate: The Royal Commissions of 1904 and 1905," *Refractory Girl* 3 (Winter 1973): 19–27; Kerreen M. Reiger, *The Disenchantment of the Home: Modernizing the Australian Family 1880–1940* (Melbourne: Oxford University Press, 1985); Henry Reynolds, *The Law of the Land* (Ringwood and Harmondsworth: Penguin Books, 1987).

41. Donald Denoon, *Settler Capitalism: The Dynamics of Dependent Development in the Southern Hemisphere* (Oxford and New York: Oxford University Press, 1983), 207.

42. See my "Panorama: The Live, the Dead and the Living."

43. See Tony Bennett, Patrick Buckridge, David Carter, and Colin Mercer, eds.,

Celebrating the Nation: A Critical Study of Australia's Bicentenary (Sydney: Allen & Unwin, 1992); Turner, *Making It National,* ch. 4.

44. In Australian usage, "minority" is not always a racially coded term, and it is not officially used for that purpose in administration. For the ideology of egalitarianism, it is wrong to attribute "minority" status to any Australians unless they do something to claim it. The word usually refers to any group overtly dissenting or diverging from "mainstream values" as defined, at any given time, by the majority of the Anglo-Celtic majority of the population. This means that in practice it can carry a strong racist, homophobic, and anti-feminist charge.

45. Simon Schama's *Landscape and Memory* appeared when this work was largely completed. Along with the work of Michel de Certeau, the book which most directly prompted me to think about the temporal dimension and commemorative aspects of tourist landscapes was Kevin Lynch, *What Time Is This Place?* (Cambridge, MA: The MIT Press, 1972).

46. A particular focus for this image was the Sydney Gay and Lesbian Mardi Gras; the gay and lesbian tourist trade grew significantly in this period. See Gay Hawkins, *From Nimbin to Mardi Gras: Constructing Community Arts* (Sydney: Allen & Unwin, 1993).

47. Since voting is compulsory for Australian citizens, federal elections do provide some evidence for talking about national trends. In this, the most comprehensive defeat for Labor since 1949, many of those in whose name progressive social activists act deserted the party in droves, along with its multiethnic working-class base. Change on this scale cannot be understood using the very categories of "identity" politics ("whites" and "Anglo-Celtics" versus "others," for example) so resoundingly rejected by the electorate. More salient is the pattern of socio-economic division whereby Labor held, just, the three major urban centers of financial and cultural power (Sydney, Melbourne, Canberra) and lost the rest of the country.

48. R. Goodman, cited in Edward W. Soja, *Postmodern Geographies: The Reassertion of Space in Critical Social Theory* (London and New York: Verso, 1989), 173. Soja glosses "regional war" as "an intensified territorial competition that stretches across the whole hierarchy of spatial locales."

49. David Harvey, "Flexible Accumulation through Urbanization: Reflections on 'Post-Modernism' in the American City," *Antipode* 19/3 (1987): 260–86.

50. In this respect, Sydney Tower simply followed U.S. experiments in mall-driven redevelopment of urban centers. See Bernard J. Frieden and Lynne B. Sagalyn, *Downtown, Inc.: How America Rebuilds Cities* (Cambridge, MA: The MIT Press, 1989).

51. "Sydney Tower," *Island Magazine* 9/10 (March 1982): 53–61.

52. Roland Barthes, *The Eiffel Tower and Other Mythologies,* trans. Richard Howard (New York: Hill & Wang, 1979).

53. "When William van Alen came to design a building for Walter P. Chrysler the brief was clear: 'Make this building higher than the Eiffel Tower'"; Charles Knevitt, "Towers of Power," *Weekend Australian* 2–3 November 1985, 18.

54. Roland Barthes, "Change the Object Itself," *Image-Music-Text,* selected and trans. Stephen Heath (Glasgow: Fontana, 1979), 165–69.

55. Jean Baudrillard, *L'effet beaubourg: implosion et dissuasion* (Paris: Editions Galilée, 1977).

56. Geoffrey Blainey, *The Tyranny of Distance: How Distance Shaped Australia's History* (Melbourne: Sun Books, 1966).

57. See Arthur Kroker's influential analysis of the CN Tower in *Technology and the Canadian Mind: Innis/McLuhan/Grant* (Montreal: New World Perspectives, 1984), 9–10.

58. David Bromfield, "Making the Modern in the Newest City in the World," *Aspects of Perth Modernism 1929–1942* (Perth: Centre for Fine Arts, 1988), 2–8.

59. See *The Pirate's Fiancée: Feminism, Reading, Postmodernism* (London: Verso, 1988), 241–69. The phrase "positive unoriginality" is adapted from a comment made about Australians in 1913 by the U.S. feminist Jessie Ackermann: "They are positively unable to originate. Everything is a copy with some small alteration, usually a disadvantage to the subject" (245).

60. Jacques de Weerdt, "L'espace rural français: vocation touristique ou processus de touristification?" Paper presented to the 1990 World Congress of the International Sociological Association, Madrid.

61. Robert Somol, "' . . . You Put Me in a Happy State': The Singularity of Power in Chicago's Loop," *Copyright* 1 (fall 1987): 98–118. Future references in parentheses in the text.

62. Cultural remodeling for tourism is by no means unequivocally bad in its effects, and I discuss examples in "Panorama: The Live, the Dead and the Living." See Jennifer Craik, *Resorting to Tourism*, and John Urry, *The Tourist Gaze: Leisure and Travel in Contemporary Societies* (London, Newbury Park, and New Delhi: Sage, 1990).

63. On this period, see "Contemporary Aboriginal Art," *Artlink* 10.1/2 (1990); *Postmodernism: A Consideration of the Appropriation of Aboriginal Imagery*, ed. Sue Cramer (Brisbane: Institute of Modern Art, 1989); Henrietta Fourmile, "Aboriginal Heritage Legislation and Self-Determination," *Australian-Canadian Studies* 7.1–2 (1989): 45–61; Adrian Marrie, "Museums and Aborigines: A Case Study in Internal Colonialism," *Australian-Canadian Studies* 7.1–2 (1989): 63–80.

64. Among the most influential in the second half of the 1980s were Diane Bell, *Daughters of the Dreaming* (Melbourne and North Sydney: McPhee Gribble with Allen & Unwin, 1983); Sally Morgan, *My Place* (Fremantle: Fremantle Arts Centre Press, 1987); Henry Reynolds, *The Other Side of the Frontier: Aboriginal Resistance to the European Invasion of Australia* (Ringwood and Harmondsworth: Penguin Books, 1982) and *The Law of the Land* (Ringwood and Harmondsworth: Penguin Books, 1987). For the impact of these accounts on white feminist concepts of history, see Ann Curthoys *For and against Feminism* (Sydney: Allen & Unwin, 1988), 136–49. More recently, testimonials by Aboriginal people forcibly taken as children from their families by the state, up to and including the 1960s, has further eroded the complacency of early feminist discourses on "home": see Coral Edwards and Peter Read, *The Lost Children* (Sydney and New York: Doubleday, 1992); and *Bringing Them Home*, Report of the National Inquiry into the Separation of Aboriginal and Torres Strait Islander Children from Their Families (Commonwealth of Australia, 1997).

65. Margo Huxley and Kate Kerkin, "What Price the Bicentennial? A Political Economy of Darling Harbour," *Transition: Discourse on Architecture*, 26 (Spring 1988): 57–64.

66. Leonie Sandercock, *Cities for Sale: Property, Politics and Urban Planning in Australia* (Melbourne: Melbourne University Press, 1977).

67. See Grossberg, *We Gotta Get out of This Place*.

68. Eric Michaels, *Bad Aboriginal Art: Tradition, Media, and Technological Horizons* (Minneapolis: University of Minnesota Press, 1994), 138–39.

69. Emile Benveniste, *Problèmes de linguistique générale* (Paris: Gallimard, 1966), 237–50.

70. Interdisciplinary feminism is not much help with my doubts about cultural criticism that claims to be "history." Some Australian defenders of traditional history have followed U.S. historians such as Gertrude Himmelfarb in creating panic *about* "violence" done to the discipline by interlopers, including feminists: Keith Windschuttle, *The Killing of History: How a Discipline Is Being Murdered by Literary Critics and Social Theorists* (Sydney; Macleay Press, 1994); Gertrude Himmelfarb, *On Looking into the Abyss: Untimely Thoughts on Culture and Society* (New York: Vintage Books, 1994). However, many Australian feminist historians have shown even less sympathy than their U.S. colleagues for a cultural criticism solemnly said to entail the belief that "there are no real women" and no such thing as truth: Patricia Grimshaw, Marilyn Lake, Ann McGrath, and Marian Quartly, *Creating a Nation* (Ringwood: McPhee Gribble, 1994), 4; see Joyce Appleby, Lynn Hunt, and Margaret Jacob, *Telling the Truth about History* (New York and London: Norton, 1994).

71. Jean Baudrillard, *Simulations*, trans. Paul Foss, Paul Patton, and Philip Beitchman (New York: Semiotext(e), 1983); Jameson, *Postmodernism, or, The Cultural Logic of Late Capitalism*, 21–25.

72. See John Fiske's reading of Chicago's Sears Tower, *Reading the Popular* (London and Boston: 1989), 199–217.

73. On this debate, see John Docker, *Postmodernism and Popular Culture: A Cultural History* (Cambridge: Cambridge University Press, 1994), 90–102.

74. Somol, "' . . . You Put me in a Happy State.'"

75. While aesthetic postmodernism played explicitly with paradoxes of "theory as progress," all "*post*" rhetorics tend to pose this problem; see Anne McClintock, *Imperial Leather: Race, Gender and Sexuality in the Colonial Context* (New York and London: Routledge, 1995), 9–15.

76. See Perry Anderson, "Modernity and Revolution," *Marxism and the Interpretation of Culture*, ed. Cary Nelson and Lawrence Grossberg (Urbana: University of Illinois Press, 1988), 317–38; Marshall Berman, "The Signs in the Street: A Response to Perry Anderson," *New Left Review* 144 (1984): 114–23; Paul Willemen, "Response to Donzelot," *The Apprehension of Time*, ed. Don Barry and Stephen Muecke (Sydney: Local Consumption Publications, 1988), 28–32.

77. The term "textual" flung around cultural studies, often with pejorative intent, seems to me a misnomer based on a conflation of U.S. literary formalist constructions of "the text" with the very concept of textuality. See John Frow and Meaghan Morris, eds., *Australian Cultural Studies: A Reader* (Sydney and Urbana: Allen & Unwin and University of Illinois Press, 1993), xix.

78. For example, Robert Young, *White Mythologies: Writing, History and the West* (London: Routledge, 1990). A good discussion of cultural theory from a historian's point of view is Michael P. Steinberg, "Cultural History and Cultural Studies," *Disciplinarity and Dissent in Cultural Studies*, ed. Cary Nelson and Dilip Parameshwar Gaonkar (New York and London: Routledge, 1996), 103–29.

79. For this reason, I think Anne McClintock is clearly right to question, in her crucial work on British imperialism and popular culture, the value of "inscribing history as a single issue": *Imperial Leather*, 11. However, much the same can be said (as McClintock notes), of any significant social category of analysis. So I should clarify my usage further. For me, the terms "history" and "culture" always inscribe a

multiplicity, indeed, a contradictory and conflict-ridden mass, of issues. Therefore, I write them in the plural ("histories," "cultures") only when there is a practical reason and a clear frame of reference for doing so. Putting an "s" on every noun as a matter of principle can't in itself tell us anything about the terms pluralized (and, thereby, rendered discrete and autonomous) or about the concrete forms of their relationality in particular circumstances.

80. Deleuze and Guattari, *A Thousand Plateaus*, 75–148.

81. William Gibson, *Idoru* (London: Viking, 1996), 14.

82. I discuss tourist narratives in Australian literature and cinema since the 1970s, and their implications for the model of national "identity" as a colonial quest and a white male narrative of becoming, in "Crazy Talk Is Not Enough," *Environment and Planning D: Society and Space* 14.4 (1996): 384–93, and "Life as a Tourist Object in Australia," *International Tourism: Identity and Change*, ed. Marie-Françoise Lanfant, John B. Allcock, and Edward M. Bruner (London: Sage, 1995), 177–91.

83. Noel Pearson, "Mabo and the Humanities: Shifting Frontiers," 43.

84. See my "Afterthoughts on Australianism," *Cultural Studies* 6/3 (1992): 468–75.

85. See John Frow, *Cultural Studies and Cultural Value* (Oxford: Oxford University Press, 1995).

86. Michel de Certeau, *The Practice of Everyday Life*, trans. Steven F. Rendall (Berkeley and London: University of California Press, 1984).

87. Slavoj Žižek, *Tarrying with the Negative: Kant, Hegel and the Critique of Ideology* (Durham: Duke University Press, 1993), 212.

88. In an Australian context, see Catrina Felton and Liz Flanagan, "Institutionalised Feminism: A Tidda's Perspective," *Lilith* 8 (1993): 53–59; Adele Murdolo, "Warmth and Unity with all Women? Historicizing Racism in the Australian Women's Movement," *Feminist Review* 52 (1996): 69–86; and Tikka Jan Wilson, "Feminism and Institutionalized Racism: Inclusion and Exclusion at an Australian Feminist Refuge," *Feminist Review* 52 (1996): 1–26. Colonialism is a framework of historical experience that makes it impossible for white women to abstract their "own" cultural traditions and pleasures from an active relationship *to* what Žižek calls "communities of the other." For this reason, what Catherine Hall calls "the work of remembering empires differently" involves a critical *look* at those traditions and pleasures: "Histories, Empires and the Post-Colonial Moment," *The Post-Colonial Question: Common Skies, Divided Horizons*, ed. Iain Chambers and Lidia Curti (London and New York: Routledge, 1996), 65–77.

89. Directed by Ronald Thompson, Andrew Joshua, Kevin Rogers, Raymond Geoffrey, and Brian Burkett, *Ngukurr: Weya Wi Na* was produced in 1988 by Ngukurr School Council, Ngukurr Adult Education Committee, and Yugul Manggi Media. Thanks to Pat Laughren for introducing me to this film. On Central Australian television, see Eric Michaels, *The Aboriginal Invention of Television in Central Australia 1982–1986* (Canberra: Australian Institute of Aboriginal Studies, 1986).

90. "In this naming of the world, all people who are not indigenous Australians are whitefellas, whatever their skin colour or background": Tikka Jan Wilson, "Feminism and Institutionalized Racism," 5. Wilson discusses this term (and much else) as an African American immigrant to Australia.

91. On the Northern Territory's history as an imaginary site of the Other, see Jon Stratton, "Deconstructing the Territory," *Cultural Studies* 3.1 (1989): 38–57.

92. I owe this observation to James Hay.

93. See Roberta Sykes, *Black Majority* (Hawthorn: Hudson, 1989). Aboriginal people won full citizenship rights only in 1967, following a referendum approving an amendment of the federal Constitution.

94. See Wai-Teng Leong's very different account of tourism policy in Singapore, "Culture and the State: Manufacturing Traditions for Tourism," *Critical Studies in Mass Communication* 6 (1989): 355–75.

95. I refer to Johannes Fabian's famous critique of "allachronism," casting the other into another time; *Time and the Other: How Anthropology Makes Its Object* (New York: Columbia University Press, 1983).

1. AT HENRY PARKES MOTEL

1. Henry Parkes (1815–1896) came with his wife to Australia from Birmingham, England, as an assisted immigrant in 1838–39. He was a penniless artisan, and despite business and journalistic ventures he spent much of his life near or in bankruptcy. He had belonged to the Birmingham Mechanics' Institute and was influenced by the early phases of Chartism. The timing of his emigration left him "for good, a Birmingham man of 1832 rather than of 1839: a radical, but dedicated to middle and working class co-operation as the key to reform and progress"; A. W. Martin, *Henry Parkes* (Melbourne: Melbourne University Press, 1980), 17. He married three times, and fathered the last of seventeen children at the age of seventy-seven. During a political career that lasted from 1848 till his death, he was five times Premier of New South Wales—presiding over the implementation of most of the ideals he had arrived with, as well as of a pro-white, anti-Catholic vision of Australia's destiny. By the 1890s he was an arch-conservative, baffled by the new Labor Party.

Needless to say, Parkes's 1889 speech in Tenterfield did not "cause" Australian Federation. His reasons for making it seem to have been partly opportunistic, and the speech itself had at best a symbolic effect in galvanizing public interest in the matter, particularly in NSW. However, it is still invoked by constitutional reformers: see Kenneth Wiltshire, *Tenterfield Revisited: Reforming Australia's System of Government for 2001* (St. Lucia: University of Queensland Press, 1991). In this usage, as in mine, the figure of Parkes is a motto or an emblem, rather than an object of historical study.

2. Anthony Trollope, *Travelling Sketches* (London: Chapman and Hall, 1866), 29–42.

3. John Urry in *The Tourist Gaze* (London, Newbury Park, and New Delhi: Sage Publications, 1990), 70, gives a useful account of consumer service as "emotional work."

4. On this association in Australian colonial culture, see Sue Rowley, "The Journey's End: Women's Mobility and Confinement," *Australian Cultural History* 10 (1991): 69–83.

5. Iain Chambers, *Popular Culture: The Metropolitan Experience* (London and New York: Methuen, 1986), 12–13. Further references in parentheses in the text. It is unclear in Chambers's model how a sign is rendered "individual" or attention "isolated."

6. Georges van den Abbeele, "Sightseers: The Tourist as Theorist," *Diacritics*, vol. 10, December 1980, 13. Further references in parentheses in the text.

7. Dean MacCannell, *The Tourist: A New Theory of the Leisure Class* (New York: Schocken, 1976). Further references in parentheses in the text. On the concept of "marker," see Jonathan Culler, "Semiotics of Tourism," *The American Journal of Semiotics* 1.1/2 (1981): 127–40.

8. M. M. Bakhtin, *The Dialogic Imagination: Four Essays*, ed. Michael Holquist, trans. Caryl Emerson and Michael Holquist (Austin: University of Texas Press, 1981).

9. Robert Venturi, Denise Scott Brown, and Steven Izenour, *Learning from Las Vegas: The Forgotten Symbolism of Architectural Form* (Cambridge, MA: MIT Press, 1977), 34–35.

10. "Jumbuck" is an old colloquial term for "sheep." Said to be derived from Aboriginal English ("jump up"), it is known to most people today only from the words of "Waltzing Matilda," a traditional popular or "alternative" national anthem based on an 1895 poem by A. B. Paterson.

11. Daniel Boorstin, *The Image: A Guide to Pseudo-Events in America* (New York: Harper and Row, 1961).

12. "Places are odd and call for interpretation. . . . Pseudo-places entice by their familiarity and call for instant recognition." Paul Fussell, *Abroad: British Literary Traveling between the Wars* (New York and Oxford: Oxford University Press, 1980), 43.

13. Jean Baudrillard, *Simulations* (New York: Semiotext(e), 1983), 1–79. Baudrillard acknowledges his reading of Boorstin in *La société de consommation* (Paris: Gallimard, 1970).

14. Paolo Prato and Gianluca Trivero, "The Spectacle of Travel," *The Australian Journal of Cultural Studies* 3.2 (December 1985): 27.

15. Paul Virilio, "Véhiculaire," in *Cause commune: Nomades et vagabonds* (Paris: U.G.E. 10/18), 1975, 52. My translation. On the concept of "non-place," see Marc Augé, *Non-Places: Introduction to an Anthropology of Supermodernity*, trans. John Howe (London: Verso, 1995).

16. Richard Sieburth, "Sentimental Travelling: On the Road (and Off the Wall) with Laurence Sterne," *Scripsi* 4.3, 203.

17. Stories of early or "primitive" audiences fleeing the train rushing toward them on screen are foundational in cinema mythology. However in both Virilio's *Esthétique de la disparition* (Paris: Balland, 1980) and Baudrillard's *America* (London: Verso, 1988), the connection between fast transport and the perceptual shifts effected by cinema is developed in terms of *disappearance*. For Virilio, concerned with movement as militarization rather than tourism, the invention of the camera is also associated with the chrono-photographic rifle and the Gatling gun: *Pure War* (New York: Semiotext(e), 1983), 82–83; *War and Cinema* (London: Verso, 1989); *The Vision Machine* (London and Bloomington: BFI and Indiana University Press, 1994).

18. Virilio, *Speed and Politics*, 8–9. Virilio's term is actually "*implantation*," not "installation." He argues that the strategic implantation of the fixed domicile is more important to the historical formation of bourgeois power than commerce or industrialism.

19. Venturi, Scott Brown, and Izenour, 34–35.

20. See Anthony Giddens, *The Constitution of Society* (Cambridge and Oxford: Polity 1984), 122–26, and MacCannell, *The Tourist*, 91–102.

21. See Ken Halliday, *Call of the Highlands: The Tenterfield Story 1828–1988* (Tenterfield Shire Council and Australian Bicentenary Authority, 1988), 1–2, and the entries for *Bundjalung [Jukambal]*, *Ngarabal*, *Nganyaywana*, and *Southeast Region* in *The Encyclopaedia of Aboriginal Australia* (Canberra: Australian Institute of Aboriginal and Torres Strait Islander Studies, 1994).

22. On country towns and progress, see Donald Horne, *Money Made Us* (Ringwood and Harmondsworth: Penguin Books, 1976).

23. Parkes's "crimson thread of kinship" model of cohesion retains some currency today in versions of a national familialism based not on the racially exclusive consanguinity prized by Parkes but on an "affinity" created by immigration, intermarriage, and shared labor. See Geoffrey Blainey's Foreword to E. Lloyd Sommerlad, *The Migrant Shepherd: Ober-Rosbach to Tenterfield* (Avalon Beach: Clareville Press, 1986), vii; and Wiltshire, 46.

24. Since this argument is sometimes read as a contribution to the literature of "travelling theory," I want to emphasize that my concern here is with *stopping*; with the motel, not with "the road"; with intermittency in time, not smooth motion in space.

25. John Robertson and Charles Cowper, factional leaders in the New South Wales parliament. Nineteenth-century colonial politics was not organized by a party system but around vying personalities.

26. Henry Parkes, *Studies in Rhyme* (Sydney: J. Ferguson, 1870).

27. For other readings of MacCannell, see John Frow, "Tourism and the Semiotics of Nostalgia," *October* 57 (1991): 123–51, and Urry, 8–15.

28. This is one way in which a hierarchical distinction between "travelling" and "tourism" is maintained. For example, in Baudrillard's *America*, "nothing is further from pure travelling than tourism or holiday travel" (9); the tourist, rather than the traveler, is archaic for Baudrillard, precisely because of a presumed touristic quest for meaning, reason, and reality. For a critique of this presumption, see Urry, 100–102.

29. Sam Shepard, *Motel Chronicles* (San Francisco: City Lights Books, 1982), 102.

30. See Angelika Bammer's editorial on the complexities of "home . . . as a moveable concept" in the special issue of *New Formations* 17 (Summer 1992), "The Question of Home."

31. Neither writer pays much attention to the "work" of the leisure industry, or considers domestic labor in relation to either industrial or "post-industrial" production. Doing so might have made the industrial/postindustrial line more difficult to draw. Instead, domestic labor is subsumed, in these analyses, by the shift from "work" to "leisure."

32. See also MacCannell, *Empty Meeting Grounds: The Tourist Papers* (London and New York: Routledge, 1992), 87–113.

33. After the 1987 military coup in Fiji, efforts at economic protest on behalf of the deposed, elected government of Dr. Timoci Bavadra were undermined by the introduction of cut-price airfares from Australia. It is hard to say to what extent touristic imperviousness to a coup in a nearby country does count as a danger to *Australian* "integrity."

34. Biddy Martin and Chandra Talpade Mohanty, "Feminist Politics: What's Home Got to Do with It?" *Feminist Studies/Critical Studies*, ed. Teresa de Lauretis (Bloomington: Indiana University Press, 1986), 193–94.

35. Menie Parkes, *Poems, Printed for Private Circulation* (Sydney: F. Cunninghame, 1867), 15.

36. A. W. Martin, ed., *Letters from Menie: Sir Henry Parkes and His Daughter* (Melbourne: Melbourne University Press, 1983).

37. Iain Chambers, "Maps for the Metropolis: A Possible Guide to the Present," *Cultural Studies* 1.1 (Jan. 1987): 1–21. Further references in parentheses in the text.

38. Anne Zahalka, "The Tourist as Theorist 1: (Theory Takes a Holiday)," *Cultural Studies* 2.1 (January 1987): 17–28.

39. Angus Fletcher, *Allegory: The Theory of a Symbolic Mode* (Ithaca and London: Cornell University Press, 1964), 35. Further references in parentheses in the text.

40. Cited in Donna Haraway, *Simians, Cyborgs and Women: The Reinvention of Nature* (New York: Routledge, 1991), 166.

41. See Angela McRobbie, "Settling Accounts with Subcultures," *Screen Education* 34 (Spring 1980): 37–49; on women at windows, Dick Hebdige, "The Impossible Object: Towards a Sociology of the Sublime," *New Formations* 1 (Spring 1987): 47–76. On the confinement of women to theoretical spaces of consumption, reproduction, and the private in urban studies, see J. K. Gibson-Graham, *The End of Capitalism (as We Knew It)* (Cambridge, MA, and Oxford: Blackwell, 1996), 78–81.

42. Haraway, 161.

43. Frank Moorhouse, *Room Service: Comic Writings of Frank Moorhouse* (Ringwood and Harmondsworth: Penguin Books, 1985), 52.

44. 6 December 1882. Cited in Norman Crawford, *Tenterfield* (Tenterfield District Historical Society, 1949), np.

45. As recently as 1988, a sense of the railway's importance to pioneering suffuses Ken Halliday's celebratory local history, *Call of the Highlands*. Although passenger trains no longer arrived in Tenterfield, and the line itself was closed in the following year ("National Birthplace Goes off the Rails," *Sydney Morning Herald* 23 October 1989), the chapter on the "Coming of the Railway" is one of the longest in the book.

46. See Halliday on "The Federation Speech," 40–43, and Sommerlad, 109.

47. Michel de Certeau, *The Practice of Everyday Life*, trans. Steven F. Rendall (Berkeley and London: University of California Press, 1984), 117f. Further references in parentheses in the text.

48. The motel was built by a couple whose family had known Henry Parkes in his heyday, but before he was knighted. So the motel is named simply the *Henry Parkes* in order to represent the nature of the family connection.

49. R. R. Garran, *Prosper the Commonwealth* (Sydney: Angus & Robertson, 1958), 101.

50. Like many country towns, Tenterfield, faced with decline in agriculture, protests against the timber industry, shrinking demand for wooden railway sleepers, and closure of the local meatworks, talked in the 1970s about the possibility of its own extinction. Natural and historical "resources" began to be mapped for a semiotics of attraction. If the highway brings fewer commercial transports in search of wood and meat, it does bring some urban transients in search of trees, animals, fresh air, and pioneer homes. Nevertheless, many residents depend on welfare to survive.

51. The massacre was duly ignored in Halliday's Bicentennial history, *Call of the Highlands*. However, the two pages on "The First Inhabitants" are indicative of changes in pioneer historiography induced by Aboriginal demands for representation and the pressure of tourist curiosity: on the complexities of the genre, see Julian Thomas, "Heroic and Democratic Histories: Pioneering as a Historical Concept," *The UTS Review* 2.1 (1996): 58–71. During the Bicentenary period, local histories also began to recognize Chinese (Halliday, 32; Sommerlad, 49–50), German (Halliday, 30, Sommerlad, passim) and unspecified "non-English speaking" (Halliday, 144) aspects of pioneering; a precedent was set by Glen Hall's history of the adjoining Clarence River district, *The Road to the River (1839–1939)* (Lismore: Northern Rivers College of Advanced Education, 1975). In 1992, a major popular history of Chinese pioneering appeared: Eric Rolls, *Sojourners: Flowers and the Wide Sea* (St. Lucia: University of Queensland Press, 1992).

52. Donald Horne, *The Great Museum: The Re-Presentation of History* (London and Sydney: Pluto Press, 1984), 1.

53. Baudrillard, *America*, 28. Translation modified.

54. Lawrence Grossberg, "The In-difference of Television," *Screen* 28.2 (spring 1987): 32. Further references in parentheses in the text.

55. "Mattering maps define different forms, quantities and places of energy. They 'tell' people how to use and how to generate energy, how to navigate their way into and through various moods and passions, and how to live within emotional and ideological histories": Grossberg, *We Gotta Get out of This Place* (New York and London: Routledge, 1992), 82. The term "mattering maps" is cited from R. Goldstein, *The Mind-Body Problem* (New York: Laurel, 1983).

56. "Bald Rock Highlight," *Tenterfield Star* 17 November 1986.

57. Prato and Trivero, 40.

58. See Dick Hebdige, *Hiding in the Light* (London and New York: Routledge, 1988), 233–44.

59. N.S.W. Legislative Assembly, 14 August 1866. Cited in Stephen Murray-Smith, ed., *The Dictionary of Australian Quotations* (Melbourne: Heinemann, 1984), 211.

60. "Great Moments in Philosophy," *Sydney Morning Herald* 30 June 1987.

2. THINGS TO DO WITH SHOPPING CENTERS

1. Michel de Certeau, *The Practice of Everyday Life*, trans. Steven F. Rendall (Berkeley and London: University of California Press, 1984), 97. Further references in parentheses in the text.

2. Robert Venturi, Denise Scott Brown, and Steven Izenour, *Learning from Las Vegas: The Forgotten Symbolism of Architectural Form* (Cambridge, MA: The MIT Press, 1977).

3. The Australian concept of suburbia does not always connote affluence or even material comfort. Approximating a unit of municipal government, a "suburb" can be a grouping of inner-city neighborhoods as well as an outer zone of a city. "Inner-city suburbs" are often gentrified and expensive, while outer suburbs, poorly serviced and inhabited largely by diverse new immigrant congregations, can be concentrated sites of poverty and disadvantage. Insofar as "suburbia" and "*the* suburbs" can suggest a stereotype of upwardly mobile family life, they tend to refer to *working- and lower middle-class* lifestyles and aspirations. This is why suburban and country

town images are easily blurred by corporate propaganda in the ways I discuss in this chapter.

4. John Hartley, "Suburbanality (in Cultural Studies)," *Meanjin* 51.3 (1992): 453–64.

5. "Shopping center" is a partial Australian synonym for a mall. While both terms are used, "mall" in Australia tends to refer either to a shopping street closed to traffic or to a large, enclosed *regional* shopping center rather than the "community" and "neighborhood" centers I am primarily concerned with in this chapter. Since "shopping center" is the more comprehensive term, used as such by most of the industry papers I discuss, I have kept it for the sake of exactness.

6. See my "Fear and the Family Sedan," *The Politics of Everyday Fear*, ed. Brian Massumi (Minneapolis: University of Minnesota Press, 1993), 285–305.

7. Ross Chambers, "Strolling, Touring, Cruising: Counter-Disciplinary Narrative and the Loiterature of Travel," *Understanding Narrative*, ed. James Phelan and Peter Rabinowitz (Columbus: Ohio State University Press, 1994), 17–42.

8. *Shopping for a Retail Policy*, A.I.U.S. Publication 99 (Canberra: Australian Institute of Urban Studies, 1982), 3.

9. Anxiety is devoid of neither pleasure nor cognitive rigor. See Patricia Mellencamp, *High Anxiety: Catastrophe, Scandal, Age, and Comedy* (Bloomington and Indianapolis: Indiana University Press, 1992).

10. This is not to say that I "worry" about *consumerism*. My theme in this discussion is not "consumption" in the sociological sense, but the ways in which cultural critics project the popular and write ourselves into landscapes and narratives of cultural change.

11. These rules are subject to interpretation. See the dispute in Kevin Smith's film *Mallrats* (1995) over whether an "upstairs" cookie stand counts as part of the "downstairs" food court (identity through associated commodities) or as "an autonomous unit for mid-mall snacking" (identity as location).

12. Review of The Jam Factory in "A Shopping Guide," unpublished paper. My thanks to Professor Quarry for sharing this with me. Another section of the paper is published as "Knox City Shopping Centre: A Review," *Architecture Australia* 67.5 (November 1978): 68.

13. On the industrial motivations of such striving, see Jon Goss, "The 'Magic of the Mall': An Analysis of Form, Function, and Meaning in the Contemporary Retail Built Environment," *Annals of the Association of American Geographers* 83.1 (1993): 18–47.

14. Iain Chambers, *Popular Culture: The Metropolitan Experience* (New York and London: Methuen, 1986), 13.

15. Theodor Adorno, "Letters to Walter Benjamin," *Aesthetics and Politics*, translation editor Ronald Taylor (London: Verso, 1977), 129.

16. Some of the useful collections providing entry-points to the now vast international literature on this topic are: Erica Carter, James Donald, and Judith Squires, eds., *Space and Place: Theories of Identity and Location* (London: Lawrence and Wishart, 1993); James Duncan and David Ley, eds., *Place/Culture/Representation* (London and New York: Routledge, 1993); Michael Keith and Steve Pile, eds., *Place and the Politics of Identity* (London and New York: Routledge, 1993); Doreen Massey, *Space, Place and Gender* (Cambridge: Polity, 1994); Sophie Watson and Katherine

Gibson, eds., *Postmodern Cities and Spaces* (Oxford and Cambridge, MA: Blackwell, 1995).

17. Department of Environment, Housing and Community Development, *The Shopping Centre as a Community Leisure Resource* (Canberra: Australian Government Publishing Service, 1978).

18. A few examples only: Elaine S. Abelson, *When Ladies Go A-Thieving: Middle-Class Shoplifters in the Victorian Department Store* (New York: Oxford University Press, 1990); Susan Porter Bensen, *Counter Cultures: Saleswomen, Managers, and Customers in American Department Stores 1890–1940* (Urbana and Chicago: University of Illinois Press, 1988); Beverley Kingston, *Basket, Bag and Trolley: A History of Shopping in Australia* (Melbourne: Oxford University Press, 1994); Mica Nava, "Consumerism Reconsidered: Buying and Power," Cultural Studies 5.2 (1991): 157–73; Gail Reekie, *Temptations: Sex, Selling and the Department Store* (Sydney: Allen & Unwin, 1993); Elizabeth Wilson, *Adorned in Dreams: Fashion and Modernity* (London: Virago, 1985).

19. On taking seriously the variability of contexts of address, see "Epilogue: Future Fear."

20. Alice Jardine, *Gynesis: Configurations of Woman and Modernity* (Ithaca and London: Cornell University Press, 1985). Further references in parentheses in the text.

21. Many feminist redefinitions of the historical fields of modernism and modernity have been published since *Gynesis* first appeared, including: Giuliana Bruno, *Streetwalking on a Ruined Map: Cultural Theory and the City Films of Elvira Notari* (Princeton: Princeton University Press, 1993); Rey Chow, *Woman and Chinese Modernity: The Politics of Reading between West and East* (Minneapolis: University of Minnesota Press, 1991); Rita Felski, *The Gender of Modernity* (Cambridge, MA, and London: Harvard University Press, 1995); Patricia Mellencamp, *Indiscretions: Avant-Garde Film, Video, and Feminism* (Bloomington and Indianapolis: Indiana UP, 1990); Patrice Petro, *Joyless Streets: Women and Melodramatic Representation in Weimar Germany* (Princeton: Princeton University Press, 1989); Griselda Pollock, *Vision & Difference: Femininity, Feminism and the Histories of Art* (London and New York: Routledge, 1988); Bonnie Kime Scott, *The Gender of Modernism: A Critical Anthology* (Bloomington and Indianapolis: Indiana University Press, 1990); Hortense J. Spillers, ed., *Comparative American Identities: Race, Sex, and Nationality in the Modern Text* (New York and Routledge, 1991).

22. Forceful modernizations of "home" are discussed in, for example, Stuart Ewen, *Captains of Consciousness: Advertising and the Social Roots of the Consumer Culture* (New York: McGraw-Hill, 1976); Rita Huggins and Jackie Huggins, *Auntie Rita* (Canberra: Aboriginal Studies Press, 1994); Kerreen M. Reiger, *The Disenchantment of the Home: Modernizing the Australian Family 1880–1940* (Melbourne: Oxford University Press, 1985); Henry Reynolds, *With the White People* (Ringwood and Harmondsworth: Penguin, 1990); Ileana Rodriguez, *House/Garden/Nation: Space, Gender and Ethnicity in Postcolonial Latin American Literatures by Women* (Durham and London: Duke University Press, 1994).

23. Françoise van Rossum-Guyon, "Questions à Julia Kristeva—A partir de Polylogue," *Revue des sciences humaines* 168 (1977): 495–501.

24. See John Frow, "Accounting for Tastes: Some Problems in Bourdieu's Sociology of Culture," *Cultural Studies* 1.1 (1987): 59–73.

25. George Sternlieb and James W. Hughes, "Introduction: The Uncertain Future

of Shopping Centers," in Sternlieb and Hughes, eds., *Shopping Centers, U.S.A* (Rutgers, NJ: Center for Urban Policy Research, 1981), 3.

26. On the links between community politics, tourism, and difference-promotion, see Gay Hawkins, *From Nimbin to Mardi Gras: Constructing Community Arts* (Sydney: Allen & Unwin, 1993).

27. John A. Dawson, *Shopping Centre Development* (London and New York: Longman 1983), ch. 7.

28. On the heterogeneity of "contemporary purchasing activities" (and in "the world beyond the mall" in a British context), see Nicky Gregson and Louise Crewe, "The Bargain, the Knowledge, and the Spectacle: Making Sense of Consumption in the Space of the Car-Boot Sale," *Environment and Planning D: Society and Space* 15.1 (1997): 87–112.

29. A much-cited phrase from Victor Gruen and Larry Smith, *Shopping Towns U.S.A.* (New York: Reinhold Publishing, 1960), 11. Gruen is widely regarded as the inventor of the modern enclosed mall, and his book was influential on subsequent accounts, such as Nadine Beddington, *Design for Shopping Centres* (London: Butterworth Scientific, 1982), 22.

30. Walter Benjamin, "A Berlin Chronicle," *One-Way Street and Other Writings*, trans. Edmund Jephcott and Kingsley Shorter (London: New Left Books, 1979), 293–346; Donald Horne, *Money Made Us* (Ringwood and Harmondsworth: Penguin Books, 1976); Quarry, see n.7 above.

31. See William Severini Kowinski's wonderful "odyssey" of U.S. shopping center life, *The Malling of America: An Inside Look at the Great Consumer Paradise* (New York: William Morrow, 1985).

32. For example, Roberta Brandes Gratz, *The Living City* (New York: Simon and Schuster, 1989); Jane Jacobs, *The Death and Life of Great American Cities* (New York: Random House, 1961).

33. Amos Rapoport, *The Meaning of the Built Environment; A Nonverbal Communication Approach* (Beverly Hills: Sage Publications, 1982). For Rapoport: "meanings are in people, not in objects or things. However *things do elicit meanings. . . .* Put differently, the question is how (and, of course, whether) meanings can be encoded in things in such a way that they can be decoded by intended users" (19). In this approach, "meanings" are independently existing variables exchanged, or channeled, between autonomous subjects. So in spite of his stress on "nonverbal communication," Rapoport's concept of meaning corresponds to the conventional conduit model of verbal communication. See Briankle Chang, *Deconstructing Communication* (Minneapolis: University of Minnesota Press, 1996).

34. Alongside a range of "social portraiture" films explicitly set in and around malls, action and horror films often use malls routinely to stage not only the power relations in a community or society (as in the 1993 Cynthia Rothrock film directed by Kevin Hooks, *Irresistible Force*), but also temporal paradoxes and logics of history: George Romero's *Dawn of the Dead* (1979), Peter Hyams's *Time Cop* (1994). On the cinema-shopping nexus, see Anne Friedburg, *Window Shopping: Cinema and the Postmodern* (Berkeley and Los Angeles: University of California Press, 1993).

35. A standard definitional text for the 1970s period is the *Shopping Center Development Handbook* (Washington, DC: Urban Land Institute, 1977).

36. It is well worth consulting the older American and British works on shopping

center development to see this class and race-specific history being written as the "universal" story of a commercial building form: G. Baker and B. Funaro, *Shopping Centers, Design and Operation* (New York: Reinhold Publishing, 1951); Wilfred Burns, *British Shopping Centers* (London: Leonard Hill, 1959); James Hornbeck, *Stores and Shopping Centers* (New York: McGraw-Hill, 1962); Colin S. Jones, *Regional Shopping Centres* (London: Business Books, 1969); Louis G. Redstone, *New Dimensions in Shopping Centers and Stores* (New York: McGraw-Hill, 1973). See also J. M. Freeland, *Architecture in Australia: A History* (Ringwood: Penguin Books, 1972), ch. 14. In Australia, the postwar "flight" from the inner city was in many cases a forced march imposed on long-established, ethnically diverse working-class communities by state policies of urban renewal linked with spiraling real estate values.

37. "From Dust to Shops," *Courier-Mail* 26 February 1969; "Mini-City to Open— July 8," *Courier-Mail* 7 April 1970. In a *Courier-Mail* story on 6 March 1980, Alderman Sallyanne Atkinson, "a campaigner for the preservation of Queensland buildings," claimed that the mobility of Queensland houses was one of their special virtues ("'Many weatherboard homes in Queensland are unique because they can be moved,' she said. 'Many occupy prime real estate sites that are tremendously valuable'"). Alderman Atkinson eventually located her office in Indooroopilly Shoppingtown, and became Mayor of Brisbane.

38. *Courier-Mail* 2 July 1968.

39. Woolworths is an old Australian company, not the U.S. chain of the same name.

40. In view of my claims about the difficulty of spotting Green Hills from the highway, I should stress that this photograph is taken from a peripheral access road.

41. As in so many cases of "natural disaster," these floods were intensified and channeled by economically motivated human engineering. In 1955, levee banks on the Hunter River directed the greatest volume of water away from farms and toward shops and working-class housing.

42. In this context, "slum" means old weatherboard, fibro, or slab housing inhabited mostly by poor white families.

43. For example, *Maitland Mercury* 18 April 1969, on Sydney's Roselands ("it could be Japan, but it's not . . . "); and 23 October 1969, on American children being taken sixteen miles in their pajamas to a twenty-four-hour Foodland "in the middle of the night."

44. Andrew Wernick, "Sign and Commodity: Aspects of the Cultural Dynamic of Advanced Capitalism," *Canadian Journal of Political and Social Theory* 8.1–2 (1984): 31.

45. Horne, ch. 8.

46. My thanks to Louise Johnson for pointing out to me the possibility of this interpretation.

47. See ch. 5, below.

48. Robin Boyd, *The Australian Ugliness* (Ringwood and Harmondsworth: Penguin Books, 1963), 105.

49. Janet Wolff, "The Invisible Flâneuse: Women and the Literature of Modernity," *Theory Culture & Society* 2.3 (1985): 37–46.

50. Terry Eagleton, *Walter Benjamin, or Towards a Revolutionary Criticism* (London: Verso and NLB, 1981), 27.

51. A document of this period is Corrie Perkin, "Store Wars," *Good Weekend* 7 June 1986, 16: "The Big Store Is Big Time Again, More Glamorous than Ever Before."

52. See Gregson and Crewe, 110.

53. The first version of this chapter was given as a paper to the "Feminist Criticism and Cultural Production" conference, Humanities Research Centre, Australian National University, Canberra, 1986. Thanks to Susan Magarey and Susan Sheridan.

3. ON THE BEACH

1. John Forbes, *New and Selected Poems* (Sydney: Angus & Robertson), 65. Further references, in parentheses in the text, are to this edition, which includes a selection from *The Stunned Mullet* (Sydney: Hale & Iremonger, 1988).

2. Donald Horne, *The Lucky Country* (Ringwood: Penguin Books, 1964), 21. Further references in parentheses in the text.

3. Presented as a "national" Bicentenary, this event marked only the invasion of Botany Bay in New South Wales (then Kamay, home of the Eora people) by Britain in 1788. The Bicentenary of the nation of Australia ("Federation") occurs in 2001.

4. On "Anglo-Celtic," see Introduction, note 29.

5. Horne was invited to open the first national Cultural Studies Association of Australia Conference at the University of Western Sydney in 1990.

6. Donald Horne, *Money Made Us* (Ringwood and Harmondsworth: Penguin Books, 1976), 6.

7. Andrew Ross, *No Respect: Intellectuals and Popular Culture* (New York and London: Routledge, 1989), 15–41. One difference between Australian and American "middlebrow" culture as Ross describes it may be that the former has not been subject to either a successful patrician or an effective left-wing backlash.

8. Jane Gallop, *Reading Lacan* (Ithaca and London: Cornell, 1985), 74–92.

9. Gilles Deleuze and Félix Guattari, *A Thousand Plateaus*, trans. Brian Massumi (Minneapolis: University of Minnesota Press, 1987), 311, my emphasis.

10. Few terms create more cross-cultural noise than "multiculturalism." In Australia, this is the name of an official policy that, since the mid-1970s, has grounded national unity *in* the cultural diversity created by immigration. See ch. 6 below; Stephen Castles, Mary Kalantzis, Bill Cope, and Michael Morrissey, *Mistaken Identity: Multiculturalism and the Demise of Nationalism in Australia* (Sydney: Pluto, 1988); Jon Stratton and Ien Ang, "Multicultural Imagined Communities: Cultural Difference and National Identity in Australia and the USA," *Continuum* 8.2 (1994): 124–58.

11. Discussion session on "Australian Cultural Studies: Past, Present and Future," University of Western Sydney, Nepean, December 1990.

12. J. Laplanche and J.-B. Pontalis, *The Language of Psycho-analysis* (London: The Hogarth Press, 1980), 160–61.

13. Marthe Robert, *Roman des origines et origines du roman* (Paris: Gallimard, 1972), 44–50.

14. Graeme Turner, "Dilemmas of a Cultural Critic: Australian Cultural Studies Today," *Australian Journal of Communication* 16 (1989): 1–12. Further references in parentheses in the text. See also "Of Rocks and Hard Places: The Colonized, the National and Australian Cultural Studies," *Cultural Studies* 6.3 (1992): 424–32.

15. This pressure is itself an "internationalising" problem for scholars working in

contexts peripheral to the geography of global publishing in English. See Kuan-Hsing Chen, "Voices from the Outside: Towards a New Internationalist Localism," *Cultural Studies* 6.3 (1992): 476–84.

16. On the implications of admitting mixed origins for national historiography, see Ann Curthoys, "Single White Male," *Arena Magazine* 8 (1993–94): 28, and the discussion of her arguments in ch. 6 below.

17. See Geoffrey Dutton, *Sun, Sea, Surf and Sand—The Myth of the Beach* (Oxford and Melbourne: Oxford University Press, 1985), 84–85. On the "racial ideals" in *Australian Beach Pattern*, see Linda Slutzkin, "Spartans in Speedos" in *Creating Australia: 200 Years of Art 1788–1988*, ed. Daniel Thomas (Adelaide: International Cultural Corporation of Australia Ltd. and Art Gallery Board of South Australia, 1988), 176–77.

18. Stephen Knight, *The Selling of the Australian Mind: From First Fleet to Third Mercedes* (Port Melbourne: William Heinemann Australia, 1990), 1–11. Further references in parentheses in the text.

19. See also Manning Clark's essay from 1963, "The Ruins of the Ideologies," in *The Australian Dream*, ed. Ian Turner (Melbourne: Sun Books, 1968), 348–51.

20. John Fiske, Bob Hodge, and Graeme Turner, *Myths of Oz: Reading Australian Popular Culture* (Sydney, London, Boston: Allen & Unwin, 1987), 71–72.

21. Paul Carter, *The Road to Botany Bay* (London & Boston: Faber and Faber, 1987): see Eleanor Dark, *The Timeless Land* (Sydney: Collins, 1941); Robert Hughes, *The Fatal Shore* (London: Collins Harvill, 1987); Bernard Smith, *European Vision and the South Pacific 1768–1850* (Oxford: Oxford University Press, 1960). For alternative beach scenes: Patricia Grimshaw, Marilyn Lake, Ann McGrath, and Marian Quartly, *Creating a Nation* (Ringwood: McPhee Gribble, 1994); Colin Johnson, *Doctor Wooreddy's Prescription for Enduring the Ending of the World* (Melbourne: Hyland House, 1983); Henry Reynolds, *The Other Side of the Frontier: Aboriginal Resistance to the European Invasion of Australia* (Ringwood and Harmondsworth: Penguin Books, 1982); Anne Summers, *Damned Whores and God's Police: The Colonization of Women in Australia* (Ringwood and Harmondsworth: Penguin Books, 1975); Eric Willmot, *Pemelwuy: The Rainbow Warrior* (Sydney: Weldons, 1987).

22. Eric Willmot, *Australia: The Last Experiment* (Sydney: ABC Enterprises, 1987), 32–33.

23. M. M. Bakhtin, *The Dialogic Imagination*, ed. Michael Holquist, trans. Caryl Emerson and Michael Holquist (Austin: University of Texas Press, 1981). As chronotope, the beach in Australia can be very sinister; see my "Fear and the Family Sedan," *The Politics of Everyday Fear*, ed. Brian Massumi (Minneapolis: University of Minnesota Press, 1993), 285–305.

24. Mudrooroo Nyoongah, "Beached Party," *The Sydney Morning Herald* 19 January 1991. As part of the Sydney Writers' Festival, this poem was commissioned as an occasional piece for Australia Day. Mudrooroo Nyoongah has published novels and criticism under the names Mudrooroo, Mudrooroo Narogin, and Colin Johnson.

25. The poem works on the colonial history of naming and violence underlying the unifying term "Aboriginal," which designates both a reality produced by colonialism and an indigenous people's politics that, as in the poem, ensues. "Koori" means "people" in Southeastern languages, including those spoken by the groups

who witnessed the First Fleet's arrival; it is used today in NSW and Victoria to signify Aboriginal people generally. "Nyoongah" is used by Aboriginal peoples in the Southwest of the continent to identify themselves and their homelands. See *The Encyclopaedia of Aboriginal Australia*, general editor David Horton (Canberra: Australian Institute of Aboriginal and Torres Strait Islander Studies, 1994).

26. Les Murray, *The Vernacular Republic: Poems 1961–1983* (Sydney: Angus & Robertson, 1990), 23–24.

27. See Juan Davila and Paul Foss, *The Mutilated Pieta* (Sydney: Artspace 1985), and *Juan Davila: Hysterical Tears*, ed. Paul Taylor (Melbourne: Greenhouse 1985). *Bivouac* is printed in *Island in the Stream*, ed. Paul Foss.

28. D. H. Lawrence, *Kangaroo* (Ringwood and Harmondsworth: Penguin Books, 1968), 82; Horne, *The Lucky Country*, 24.

29. Graeme Turner, "Return to Oz: Populism, the Academy, and the Future of Australian Studies," *Meanjin* 50/1 (autumn 1991): 20 (my emphasis).

30. Marshall Berman, *All That Is Solid Melts into Air: The Experience of Modernity* (New York: Simon and Schuster, 1982).

31. On the contradictions of this attitude in ethnographic Cultural Studies, see Virginia Nightingale, "What's 'Ethnographic' about Ethnographic Audience Research?" *Australian Cultural Studies: A Reader*, ed. John Frow and Meaghan Morris (Sydney: Allen & Unwin, 1993), 149–61.

32. See Mike Featherstone, "The Heroic Life and Everyday Life," *Cultural Theory and Cultural Change*, ed. Mike Featherstone (London, Newbury Park, and New Delhi: Sage, 1992), 159–82.

33. Margaret Morse, "An Ontology of Everyday Distraction: The Freeway, the Mall, and Television," in *Logics of Television*, ed. Patricia Mellencamp (Bloomington: Indiana University Press, 1990), 193–221. Further references in parentheses in the text.

34. Henri Lefebvre, *Everyday Life in the Modern World*, trans. Sacha Rabinovitch (New Brunswick: Transaction Books, 1984), 1–6. See also Adorno's succinct formulation of what could easily be read as an axiomatic for a modernist cultural studies: "Good is what escapes, finds language, and opens the eye"; "Progress," *The Philosophical Forum* XV.1–2 (1983–84): 59.

35. Michel de Certeau, *The Practice of Everyday Life*, trans. Steven F. Rendall (Berkeley: University of California Press, 1984), 97.

36. On the strategy/tactics distinction, see ch. 4 below and "Banality in Cultural Studies," *Logics of Television*, ed. Patricia Mellencamp (Bloomington: Indiana University Press, 1990), 14–43.

37. A major reworking for cultural theory of enunciation as *both* performative *and* referential is Homi K. Bhabha's *The Location of Culture* (London and New York: Routledge, 1994).

38. Maurice Blanchot, "Everyday Speech," *Yale French Studies* 73 (1987): 12–20.

39. Wlad Godzich, *The Culture of Literacy* (Cambridge, MA, and London: Harvard University Press, 1994), 272, my emphasis. Discussing the relation between the rational subject of humanistic geography and "that Other" which is "the notion of place itself" as unknowable, beyond language, and feminine, Gillian Rose aptly calls this *mode* of relation "aesthetic masculinism": *Feminism and Geography: The Limits of Geographical Knowledge* (Cambridge: Polity, 1993), 60.

40. Ian Hunter, *Culture and Government: The Emergence of Literary Education* (Lon-

don: Macmillan, 1988); "Setting Limits to Culture," *New Formations* 4 (spring 1988): 103–24.

41. Hunter, "Setting Limits to Culture," 110.

42. See "Future Fear," below: Tony Bennett, "Putting Policy into Cultural Studies," *Cultural Studies*, ed. Lawrence Grossberg, Cary Nelson, and Paula Treichler, 23–37; Stuart Cunningham, "The Cultural Policy Debate Revisited," *Meanjin* 51.3 (1992): 533–43, and "Cultural Studies from the Viewpoint of Cultural Policy," *Nation, Culture, Text: Australian Cultural and Media Studies*, ed. Graeme Turner (London and New York: Routledge, 1993), 126–39; Meaghan Morris, "A Gadfly Bites Back," *Meanjin* 51.3 (1992): 545–51; Tom O'Regan, "(Mis)taking Policy: Notes on the Cultural Policy Debate," *Cultural Studies* 6.3 (1992): 409–23.

43. Moira Gatens, "Corporeal Representation in/and the Body Politic," in *Cartographies: Poststructuralism and the Mapping of Bodies and Spaces*, ed. Rosalyn Diprose and Robyn Ferrell (Sydney: Allen & Unwin, 1991), 85.

44. Ian Hunter, *Rethinking the School: Subjectivity, Bureaucracy, Criticism* (Sydney and New York: Allen & Unwin and St. Martins Press, 1994).

45. See the debate between Stuart Cunningham and Elizabeth Jacka, "Cultural Studies in the Light of the Policy Process—A Curate's Egg?" in *Australian Cultural Studies Conference: 1990 Proceedings* (University of Western Sydney, Nepean: Faculty of Humanities & Social Sciences, 1991), 26–56.

46. See "Panorama: The Live, the Dead and the Living."

47. See, for example, the *Far Eastern Economic Review*'s lurid promotion of its cover-story "Australia—Time to Get Serious," on 10 October 1991, with an image of a bunch of beer-swilling white men whooping it up at a mock "regatta" held annually on a dry river bed in Alice Springs.

48. "Swan Steels ARC for Competition," *Sunday Telegraph* 26 November 1989; "Coming to Grips with the Debt Crisis," *Australian Financial Review* 20 November 1989; "Poor Performance 'Shooting Aust [sic] in the Head,'" *Australian Financial Review* 26 October 1989. Peter Robinson, "Fair Go, We're All Bludgers," *Sun-Herald* 18 June 1989.

49. Ross Garnaut, *Australia and the Northeast Asian Ascendancy* (Canberra: Australian Government Publishing Service, 1989).

50. Respectively, Eric Michaels, *Bad Aboriginal Art* (Minneapolis: University of Minnesota Press, 1994), 99–125; Tom O'Regan, *Australian Television Culture* (Sydney: Allen & Unwin, 1993); Sneja Gunew, "Home and Away: Nostalgia in Australian (Migrant) Writing," in *Island in the Stream*, ed. Paul Foss (Sydney: Pluto, 1988), 35–46; Stephen Muecke, *No Road (Bitumen All the Way)* (Fremantle: Fremantle Arts Centre Press, 1997); Yuki Tanaka, "The Japanese Political-Construction Complex," in *Technocratic Dreaming: Of Very Fast Trains and Japanese Designer Cities*, ed. Paul James (Melbourne: Left Book Club, 1990), 71–77; Helen Grace, "Business, Pleasure, Narrative: The Folktale in Our Times," *Cartographies: Postructuralism and the Mapping of Bodies and Spaces*, ed. Rosalyn Diprose and Robyn Ferrell (Sydney: Allen & Unwin, 1991), 113–25, and "A House of Games: Serious Business and the Aesthetics of Logic," *Australian Cultural Studies: A Reader*, ed. John Frow and Meaghan Morris (Sydney and Urbana: Allen & Unwin and University of Illinois Press, 1993), 69–95.

51. Sylvia Lawson, *The Archibald Paradox: A Strange Case of Authorship* (Ringwood and Harmondsworth: Penguin Books, 1983).

52. John Docker, *The Nervous Nineties: Australian Cultural Life in the 1890s* (Melbourne and Oxford: Oxford University Press, 1991).

4. GREAT MOMENTS IN SOCIAL CLIMBING

1. Warren Montag, "What Is at Stake in the Debate on Postmodernism?" in *Postmodernism and Its Discontents: Theories, Practices*, ed. E. Ann Kaplan (London: Verso, 1988), 95–96.

2. Michel de Certeau, *The Practice of Everyday Life*, trans. Steven. F. Rendall (Berkeley and Los Angeles: University of California Press, 1984), 92–93. Further references in parentheses in the text.

3. Gilles Deleuze and Félix Guattari, *A Thousand Plateaus*, trans. Brian Massumi (Minneapolis: University of Minnesota Press, 1987), 260–65. Further references in parentheses in the text.

4. "Movement" is unequivocally masculinized in white Australian narrative traditions *only* when structured as "voyage," that is, as goal-directed and entailing the possibility of "progress." Aboriginal nomadic movement, historically misconceived in this framework as "aimless," is thus assimilated in a Romantic mode to the feminine, the primal, and the timeless. See Ross Gibson, *The Diminishing Paradise: Changing Literary Perceptions of Australia* (Sydney and London: Angus & Robertson, 1984); Kay Schaffer, *Women and the Bush: Forces of Desire in the Australian Cultural Tradition* (Cambridge: Cambridge University Press, 1988).

5. Deleuze and Guattari, ch. 7. The face can also form, they say, in a black blotch/white hole (Rorschach) system, but the dominance of the white wall/black hole image in their account is explained like this:

> The face is not a universal. It is not even that of the white man: it is White Man himself, with his broad white cheeks and the black hole of his eyes. The face is the typical European, what Ezra Pound called the average sensual man. . . . Not a universal, but *facies totius universi.* Jesus Christ superstar: he invented the facialization of the entire body and spread it everywhere (the Passion of Joan of Arc, in close-up). Thus the face is by nature an entirely specific idea, which did not preclude its acquiring and exercising the most general of functions: the function of . . . binarization. (176)

6. See also *A Thousand Plateaus*, ch. 5, especially 120–21.

7. Cited in Michael Laurence, "Now, the Billion-Dollar Game Comes to the Boil," *Sydney Morning Herald* 15 August 1987.

8. Cited in ibid.

9. This proposal was eventually rejected ("Carr Cuts Skyscraper Plans Down," *The Sydney Morning Herald* 31 August 1987). On the history of property speculation in Sydney, see M. T. Daly, *Sydney Boom, Sydney Bust* (Sydney: Allen & Unwin, 1982). On the more recent impact of the Pacific Rim tourist and construction industries, see Abe David and Ted Wheelwright, *The Third Wave: Australia and Asian Capitalism* (Sydney: The Left Book Club, 1989).

10. In fact, Skytower failed to "get up," as journalists say; the site was sold to Bond's Japanese partner and, at the time of writing, remains a hole in the ground pending floorspace transfer negotiations affecting other city sites.

11. Jane Gallop, *Feminism and Psychoanalysis: The Daughter's Seduction* (London: Macmillan, 1982), ch. 3.

12. Andrew Ross, *No Respect: Intellectuals and Popular Culture* (New York: Routledge, 1989).

13. See David Harvey, *The Urbanisation of Capital* (Oxford: Basil Blackwell, 1985).

14. My analysis is not directly concerned with the political economy of the 1987–89 property boom, but with the politics of spectacle that played a small part in that boom. However, the significant economic factors included a huge shift of investment interests to assets acquisition after the 1987 stockmarket crash and the subsequent easing of interest rates, combined with the reintroduction of negative gearing for rental properties in the mid-1980s by the Federal government.

15. See Sylvia Lawson, "Art in Bondage," *Australian Society* 8.8 (August 1989): 52–53, and Stuart Macintyre, "Tall Poppies," *Australian Society* 8.9 (September 1989): 8–9.

16. Peter Cryle, *The Thematics of Commitment: The Tower & The Plain* (Princeton: Princeton University Press, 1985), 9.

17. Ada Louise Huxtable, *The Tall Building Artistically Reconsidered: The Search for a Skyscraper Style* (New York: Pantheon Books, 1984), 8.

18. Jean Baudrillard, *America* (London: Verso, 1989); Paul Virilio, "The Overexposed City," *Zone* 1/2 (nd): 14–31.

19. R. E. Somol, "'. . . You Put Me in a Happy State': The Singularity of Power in Chicago's Loop," *Copyright* 1 (1987): 98–118. Further references in parentheses in the text.

20. The *locus classicus* of this critique of "Faustian" modernity is Nietzsche's scathing portrait of the "overproud European of the nineteenth century" positioning himself "high and proud upon the pyramid of the world-process": *Untimely Meditations*, trans. R. J. Hollingdale (Cambridge and New York: Cambridge University Press, 1983), 107–108.

21. De Certeau, 91–96. On the problem of *extending* this high-density urban model to other social landscapes, see ch. 2 above.

22. While consistent with the critique in *The Practice of Everyday Life* of the work of Michel Foucault—whom in that book de Certeau, like many other commentators, takes for an exponent rather than a critic of the concept of "total" power (62–63)—this pull toward populism is at odds with de Certeau's other work on the historical emergence of "popular culture" as an object of study, and the matrix of power-knowledge relations defining such study today (131–64). See "The Beauty of the Dead: Nisard," and the essays on Foucault, in *Heterologies* (Minneapolis: University of Minnesota Press, 1986).

23. On this issue, see John Frow, "Michel de Certeau and the Practice of Representation," *Cultural Studies* 5.1 (1991): 52–60, and Tony Schirato, "My Space or Yours? De Certeau, Frow and the Meaning of Popular Culture," *Cultural Studies* 7.2 (1993): 282–91.

24. See M. Christine Boyer, "The Return of Aesthetics to City Planning," in *Philosophical Streets: New Approaches to Urbanism*, ed. Dennis Crow (Washington, DC: Maisonneuve Press, 1990), 93–112; Dean MacCannell, *Empty Meeting Grounds: The Tourist Papers* (London and New York: Routledge, 1992), 87–113. However, see also Oren Yiftachel's case study of the uses of planning to repress and disadvantage minorities in developing societies: "The Dark Side of Modernism: Planning as Con-

trol of an Ethnic Minority," *Postmodern Cities and Spaces*, ed. Sophie Watson and Katherine Gibson (Oxford and Cambridge, MA: Blackwell, 1995), 216–42.

25. *Australian Financial Review*, 15 June 1989, 47–49. I assume that "Fay Wray" becomes "Fay Gray" for legal reasons. As always, the interesting thing is the use of the first name of the "original" actress to identify the *role* of King Kong's female other.

26. The power of this imaginary may be deduced from the hysteria surrounding the "Lindy Chamberlain" case of alleged maternal infanticide at the Rock; see Noel Sanders, "Azaria Chamberlain and Popular Culture," *Australian Cultural Studies: A Reader*, ed. John Frow and Meaghan Morris (Sydney: Allen & Unwin, 1993), 86–101; and Fred Schepisi's 1988 film with Meryl Streep, *Evil Angels* (a.k.a. *A Cry in the Dark*). On Uluru as a focus of contemporary Aboriginal as well as white nationalist myth-making, see Ann McGrath, "Travels to a Distant Past: The Mythology of the Outback," *Australian Cultural History* 10 (1991): 113–24.

27. Mike Davis, "Urban Renaissance and the Spirit of Postmodernism," in *Postmodernism and Its Discontents: Theories, Practices*, ed. E. Ann Kaplan (London: Verso 1988), 87.

28. Australians historically have enjoyed high levels of home ownership. Owning a house has been a *working-class* ideal and figures as such in national mythology ("the Australian dream"). So the "struggling home-owner" is not equivalent to the comfortable suburbanite of U.S. urban imagery, but one of the most vulnerable targets of spatial restructuring and economic reform. On the architectural history of home ownership, see Robin Boyd, *Australia's Home* (Harmondsworth: Penguin, 1978).

29. Patricia Mellencamp, *Indiscretions: Avant-Garde Film, Video, and Feminism* (Bloomington and Indianapolis: Indiana University Press, 1990), 142–45.

30. Scott Lash and John Urry, *The End of Organized Capitalism* (Madison: University of Wisconsin Press, 1987), 295f. Further references in parentheses in the text. Lash and Urry are less pessimistic about this "layer" than Bourdieu, preferring to see the "new petit bourgeois" as a member of the lower echelons of the service class. On the implications of these debates about class for cultural studies, see John Frow, *Cultural Studies and Cultural Value* (Oxford: Oxford University Press, 1995).

31. See Sharon Zukin, *Loft Living: Culture and Capital in Urban Change* (Baltimore: Johns Hopkins University Press, 1982).

32. Marshall Berman, *All That Is Solid Melts into Air: The Experience of Modernity* (London: Verso, 1983), 39, 67–68.

33. Rosalyn Deutsche, "Architecture of the Evicted," *Strategies* 3 (1990): 176.

34. Lash and Urry, 290. My emphasis.

35. Yann Lardeau, "Touche pas à la femme blanche," *Traverses* 8 (Mai 1977): 116–24. Translations mine. Further references in parentheses in the text.

36. In contrast, see Donna Haraway's strong analysis of a 1982 Hallmark greeting card ("Getting Even"), featuring a scared little Kong harassed in his bed by a giant blonde woman at his window; *Primate Visions: Gender, Race, and Nature in the World of Modern Science* (New York and London: Routledge, 1989), 160–62. Because Haraway bases her comparison on a culture-specific as well as historical reading of Kong's tragedy in the Schoedsack and Cooper film ("for the white inflamed imagination he was the icon of the captive black man's love for the white woman. Beast and 'primitive,' Kong was lynched"), she is able define the *force* of the contemporary

comic image; "The Cruise missile will not enter this domestic scene to save a black homosexual" (162).

37. See the *Aurum Encyclopaedia of Science Fiction*, ed. Phil Hardy (London: Aurum Press, 1984), 265.

38. This question is insistent in the iconography of Guillermin's *King Kong*, not only in Kong's love-scenes with "Dwan" (Jessica Lange), but also in gross close-ups of a huge bolt closing the village gate. See Robert Anton Wilson, "Project Parameters in Cherry Valley by the Testicles," *Semiotext(e)*, 14, *SF* (1989): 337–43.

39. Jacques Attali, *Noise: The Political Economy of Music* (Minneapolis: University of Minnesota Press, 1985), 109. I discuss Jameson's use of Baudrillard in "Panorama: The Live, the Dead and the Living," *Island in the Stream*, ed. Paul Foss (Sydney: Pluto Press, 1988), 160–87.

40. Judith Mayne, "'King Kong' and the Ideology of Spectacle," *Quarterly Review of Film Studies* 1.4 (1976): 373–87. Further references in parentheses in the text.

41. "Sydney's Human Fly," *Daily Mirror* 2 February 1987; "Exclusive: The Human Fly," *People* 23 March 1987.

42. On the resistance of textual materials, see Anne Freadman, "Sandpaper," *Southern Review* 16.1 (1983): 173.

43. See Marc Augé's useful discussion of de Certeau in *Non-Places: Introduction to an Anthropology of Supermodernity*, trans. John Howe (London: Verso, 1995), 79–85.

44. See the Introduction, above; on the "back to the City" movement, "Sydney Tower," *Island Magazine* 9/10 (1982): 53–61.

45. Susan Ruddick points out that one problem with the strategy/tactics distinction is that "in the long durée tactics disappear from view without a trace"; "Heterotopias of the Homeless: Strategies and Tactics of Placemaking in Los Angeles," *Strategies* 3, (1990): 184–201. While she finds it useful for describing how the homeless make use of "spaces that have been strategically organised by other actors," she suggests it needs to allow for the *relative permanence* in particular places gained by this use of space: "the homeless, simply by their presence in a particular place, change its symbolic meaning" (191).

46. Personal correspondence. Michael Dean gave me *Castle in the Clouds!* thus enabling me to write this chapter.

47. See Eric Alliez and Michel Feher, "Notes on the Sophisticated City," *Zone* 1/2 (nd): 40–55; Guiliana Bruno, "Ramble City: Postmodernism and *Blade Runner*," *October* 41 (1987): 61–74; David Harvey, *The Condition of Postmodernity* (Oxford: Basil Blackwell, 1989), 309–14.

48. Brian Massumi, "Realer than Real: The Simulacrum According to Deleuze and Guattari," *Copyright* 1 (1987): 90–97. Further references in parentheses in the text.

49. Jean Baudrillard, *Simulations*, trans. Paul Foss, Paul Patton, and Philip Beitchman (New York: Semiotext(e), 1983), 11.

50. Gilles Deleuze, "Plato and the Simulacrum," trans. Rosalind Krauss, *October* 27 (1983): 48. Also in Gilles Deleuze, *The Logic of Sense*, trans. Mark Lester with Charles Stivale (New York: Columbia University Press, 1990), 253–66.

51. On literalism, see Paul Willemen, *Looks and Frictions: Essays in Cultural Studies and Film Theory* (London and Bloomington: BFI and Indiana University Press, 1994), 27–55.

52. Cited by Deleuze, "Plato and the Simulacrum," 49. Deleuze develops the im-

portance of this "slight dodge," or *clinamen*, for his theory of simulation in "Lucretius and the Simulacrum," *The Logic of Sense*, 266–79.

53. Deleuze and Guattari, *A Thousand Plateaus*, 10. On becoming, 232–309.

54. See "Too Soon Too Late" above. It is worth repeating that for Deleuze and Guattari, "minoritarian" as becoming or process is distinct from "minority" as an aggregate or state (*A Thousand Plateaus*, 291), and the musical term "minor" is used to think in terms of metamorphosis.

55. For useful feminist discussions of this concept, see Rosi Braidotti, *Nomadic Subjects: Embodiment and Sexual Difference in Contemporary Feminist Theory* (New York: Columbia University Press, 1994), 111–23; Elizabeth Grosz, *Volatile Bodies: Toward a Corporeal Feminism* (Bloomington and Indianapolis: Indiana University Press, 1994), 160–83; Alice Jardine, *Gynesis: Configurations of Woman and Modernity* (Ithaca and London: Cornell University Press, 1985), 208–23.

56. By "including" the Tower/face in this process of double-becoming, filmic narration in *A Spire* itself becomes simulation in Deleuze's sense at the very moment when "it doesn't even work to invoke the model of the Other, because no model resists the vertigo of the simulacrum" (Deleuze, 53).

57. Thanks to James Hay for this observation.

5. ECSTASY AND ECONOMICS

1. John Forbes, *New and Selected Poems* (Sydney: Angus & Robertson, 1992), 61. Further references, in parentheses in the text, are to this edition, which includes a selection from *The Stunned Mullet* (Sydney: Hale & Iremonger, 1988).

2. The Treasurer is something like the Chancellor of Exchequer in Britain and something like the head of the Federal Reserve, several White House committees and the Secretary of the Treasury rolled into one. It is a very powerful office, second in prominence only to that of Prime Minister.

3. My use of the present tense here refers to the fictional moment of the poem. The historical narrative subtending my analysis is more complex. As Federal Treasurer during the boom and bust of the late 1980s, Paul Keating aroused intense media interest in his person as well as his "economic rationalist" policies (freer trade, financial deregulation, and privatization of State assets). In June 1991 he challenged the then Prime Minister, R. J. L. Hawke, for the leadership, decided by the 110 members of Labor Caucus. Hawke won, but Keating challenged again six months later and won by a handful of votes. He was Prime Minister for a little over four years, winning a general election in 1993 but losing to the right-wing Liberal-National Coalition in March 1996.

My focus in this chapter is mostly on 1986–1990 when basic changes were effected in the ways that we conceptualize the role of the State in economic affairs and citizen's lives. Later, Keating reinvented his image: as Prime Minister, he promoted the great themes of "history" and "social justice" considered in the next chapter. Appealing to intellectuals and community activists but unattractive to working-class and rural constituencies who had borne the brunt of his *economic* reforms for a decade, this shift was widely blamed for Labor's defeat in 1996.

4. Keating in preelection debate with the then Leader of the Opposition, John Hewson (Liberal), ABC-TV *Lateline*, March 1990. "Inflation will come back" here means "inflation will go down." It did.

5. Mr. Murdstone is the sadistic stepfather in Charles Dickens's *David Copperfield* (1850). Frank Langella adapted his stage interpretation of Dracula for John Badham's romantic film *Dracula* (1979).

6. On the Labor Party, see Introduction, note 25.

7. Max Walsh, "Now, It's a Question of Pride for Paul," *Sydney Morning Herald* 11 October 1990. Standards have changed since Walsh wrote this. In 1996, Peter Costello (Liberal) was appointed as a true "right-of-centre Treasurer."

8. See Graham Maddox, *The Hawke Government and Labor Tradition* (Ringwood: Penguin Books, 1989) and Dean Jaensch, *The Hawke-Keating Hijack* (Sydney: Allen & Unwin, 1989).

9. In March 1986, Keating told John Laws on air that Australia could easily become a "banana republic." By the end of the show, the $A had reportedly dropped four cents. In the longer term, the remark was canonized by journalists for inaugurating a historic shift away from expectations of continued domestic growth, and toward cutting wages and reducing foreign debt. The tenth anniversary of the remark was solemnly marked by all major newspapers in March 1996, one economics writer going so far as to declare the banana republic "a chilling reality"; Paul Cleary, "Banana Republic Vision Comes True," *Sydney Morning Herald* 14 May 1996. Such hyperbole primarily allows journalists to celebrate their own professional power to create financial "events"; see n. 78.

10. This chapter began as a paper to the *Discourses of the Emotions* conference, organized by Kathleen Woodward, Center for Twentieth Century Studies, University of Wisconsin-Milwaukee, May 1990.

11. Susan Stewart, *On Longing: Narratives of the Miniature, the Gigantic, the Souvenir, the Collection* (Baltimore and London: Johns Hopkins UP, 1984), 26.

12. Eve Kosofsky Sedgwick, *Between Men: English Literature and Male Homosocial Desire* (New York: Columbia, 1985).

13. On the individual as "appendage of a leader figure," see Ansgar Hillach, "The Aesthetics of Politics: Walter Benjamin's 'Theories of German Fascism,'" *New German Critique* 17 (spring 1979): 99–119.

14. Philippe Lacoue-Labarthe, *Heidegger, Art and Politics* (Oxford: Blackwell, 1990), 61–76. Future references in parentheses in the text.

15. Carole Pateman, *The Sexual Contract* (Cambridge: Polity Press, 1988).

16. On the significance of this genre in the 1980s, see Stuart Cunningham, "Style, Form and History in Australian Mini-Series," *Southern Review* 22.3 (1989): 315–33.

17. Paul Kelly, *The Hawke Ascendancy: A Definitive Account of Its Origins and Climax 1975–1983* (Sydney: Angus & Robertson, 1984) 31.

18. See Helen Grace, "Business, Pleasure, Narrative: The Folktale in Our Times," *Cartographies: Poststructuralism and the Mapping of Bodies and Spaces*, ed. Rosalyn Diprose and Robyn Ferrell (Sydney: Allen & Unwin, 1991), 113–25. An example of a discourse of sentimental ethnicity (Irishness) legitimizing the Labor regime is Fia Cumming, *Mates: Five Champions of the Labor Right* (Sydney: Allen & Unwin, 1991).

19. See John Edwards, "Paul Keating: A Lust for Power," *Sydney Morning Herald* 24 September 1988. The same discretion about private life is not usually extended by the media to private citizens.

20. Edna Carew, *Keating: A Biography* (Sydney: Allen & Unwin, 1988), 5. Symptomatic of Keating's distancing of his Prime Ministerial persona from the Treasurer's harsh mission is the way that Carew's updated biography, *Paul Keating: Prime Min-*

ister (Sydney: Allen & Unwin, 1992), began with Keating's own birth: "Paul John Keating was born on 18 January 1944 in the suburb of Bankstown, New South Wales, in Australia, the first child of Matt and Min Keating" (5).

21. Carew, p. 12. See John Lyons, "Our Prime Minister in waiting," *Weekend Australian*, 22–23 August 1987; Phillip Knightley, "The Real Keating Revealed," *Sunday Telegraph* 20 August 1989.

22. Carew, p. 1; Geoff Kitney, "Coarse Keating Put off Course," *Australian Financial Review* 31 December 1987.

23. C. M. H. Clark, *A History of Australia*, vol. V, *The People Make Laws 1888–1915* (Melbourne: Melbourne University Press, 1981), 40–41. I am citing here Clark's portrait of William Guthrie Spence, from which this excerpt may clarify both the political configuration and the metonymic style of discourse I have in mind:

> Thanks to his teachers [Carlyle, Ruskin, Morris, Bellamy, and Blatchford] he, too, could look with fervour to a new world, blessed with plenty, purified by justice and sweetened by brotherly kindness. Yet he laid up for himself modest treasures on earth: he yearned for a block of land and a house in which to foster individualism, and all the petty bourgeois virtues. . . . On women and Aborigines he dropped not a word. He wanted a society in which white Anglo-Saxon men could get on: women could help these men to climb a few rungs on the ladder. He knew nothing of romantic love between man and woman, nothing of the vision splendid on the sunlit plains extended, nothing of the 'dynasty of man.' For him socialism was a question of how many 'bob' [shillings] a man got in a day. He was an Australian trade unionist.

24. Arguably, popular culture in Australia cannot tolerate "ecstatic identification" with any Leader; certainly, Keating's effort to run on the slogan "Leadership" failed badly at the 1996 election (see "Future Fear," below). The point at issue here, however, is not whether this is an Australian peculiarity but whether the theoretical model of "identification" is useful for analyzing television.

25. Michelle Z. Rosaldo, "Toward an Anthropology of Self and Feeling," in *Culture Theory: Essays on Mind, Self and Emotion*, ed. Richard A. Shweder and Robert A. LeVine (Cambridge: Cambridge University Press, 1984), 143.

26. Michelle Grattan, "Ideological Spectacles: Reporting the 'Rat Pack,'" *Media Information Australia* 60 (May 1991): 9.

27. Craig McGregor, *Headliners: Craig McGregor's Social Portraits* (St. Lucia: University of Queensland Press, 1990), 77. Future references in parentheses in the text.

28. Elizabeth Grosz, *Jacques Lacan: A Feminist Introduction* (Boston: Unwin Hyman, 1990), 175. Grosz is glossing here the work of Luce Irigaray.

29. Jean Baudrillard, *Fatal Strategies: Crystal Revenge*, trans. Philip Beitchman and W. G. J. Niesluchowski (New York: Semiotext(e)/Pluto, 1990), 12. My emphasis.

30. Alan Ramsey, "Black, Blue and Deep in the Red," *Sydney Morning Herald* 1 December 1990. Donald Bradman was a legendary Australian cricketer of the 1940s.

31. See Graham Freudenberg, *Cause for Power: The Official History of the New South Wales Branch of the Australian Labor Party* (Sydney: Pluto Press, 1991).

32. "Keating? Welfare Boss Says: No Way," *Sydney Morning Herald* 24 October 1991. My emphases.

33. James McClelland writes of a "narrowly based" erudition, "shallow" learning, and "the narrowness of Keating's economic expertise"; "A Moneybags not a PM," *Sydney Morning Herald* 10 September 1987. In contrast, Peter Robinson sees "a mind that is set on expanding its horizons"; "Take a Good Look at Keating and Co.," *Sun-Herald* 30 August 1987.

34. See Michel de Certeau, *The Practice of Everyday Life* (Berkeley and Los Angeles: University of California Press, 1984), 177–98.

35. Lawrence Grossberg, *It's a Sin: Postmodernism, Politics & Culture* (Sydney: Power Publication, 1988), 38. Future references in parentheses in the text.

36. Thus Alan Bond's victory in the 1986 America's Cup yacht race was construed as a *political* triumph for the Hawke regime; see Doug McEachern, *Business Mates: The Power and Politics of the Hawke Era* (Sydney: Prentice-Hall, 1991); on Bond, see ch. 4 above and Graeme Turner, *Making It National: Nationalism and Australian Popular Culture* (Sydney: Allen & Unwin, 1994), 15–40.

37. David Burchell and Race Matthews, eds., *Labor's Troubled Times* (Sydney: Pluto Press, 1991); Andrew Scott, *Fading Loyalties: The Australian Labor Party and the Working Class* (Sydney: Pluto Press, 1991).

38. Patricia Mellencamp, *High Anxiety: Catastrophe, Scandal, Age and Comedy* (Bloomington: Indiana University Press, 1992).

39. Jochen Schulte-Sasse, "Electronic Media and Cultural Politics in the Reagan Era: The Attack on Libya and *Hands Across America* as Post-modern Events," *Cultural Critique* 8 (winter 1987–88): 138, 126–27, 150–52. Future references in parentheses in the text. Schulte-Sasse sees Nazi aesthetics as prepostmodern in contrast to the archaizing "print culture" emphases of U.S. neoconservatism (125). A similar argument is taken to different conclusions by David Harvey in *The Condition of Postmodernity* (Oxford: Blackwell, 1989). Harvey claims that an image-dominated *aestheticizing* regime is displacing a mode of *ethical* apprehension based in "narrative." Assimilating cinema and photography to television, he posits a "spatial" Image culture fixated on "surface" appearance; his theme of a corresponding loss of "depth" (narrative, history) is consistent with Schulte-Sasse's account of the decline of ideologic's superego-driven subject. But where Harvey demands a return to meta-theory and a search for unity within difference, Schulte-Sasse questions "the very possibility of sustaining forms of cultural politics whose sense of responsibility encompasses the whole of society" (152).

40. Philip Hayward, "Culture, Logic and Criticism," *Media Information Australia* 61 (1991): 72. Hayward is reviewing Fredric Jameson's *Postmodernism or, The Cultural Logic of Late Capitalism.*

41. A strong critique of the value of the concept of identification for analyzing Reagan's use of television is Kenneth Dean and Brian Massumi, *First and Last Emperors: The Absolute State and the Body of the Despot* (Brooklyn: Autonomedia, 1992), ch. 3.

42. Rey Chow, *Woman and Chinese Modernity: The Politics of Reading between West and East* (Minnesota: Minnesota University Press, 1991), 22.

43. Cited in Michael Gordon, *A Question of Leadership: Paul Keating, Political Fighter* (St. Lucia: University of Queensland Press, 1993), 10–11.

44. The classic text giving political "form" to the myth of mass culture in this way is Richard Sennett, *The Fall of Public Man* (New York and London: Norton, 1974).

45. See Pateman, *The Sexual Contract,* and Jean Baudrillard, "The Ecstasy of Com-

munication," in *The Anti-Aesthetic*, ed. Hal Foster (Washington: Bay Press, 1983), 126–34. Famous for its methodology for thinking the postmodern image as "more-visible-than-the-visible," this essay is also a classic articulation of the rhetoric of media flow—invasive, excessive, obscene, solicitous, "a large soft body with many heads" (129)—to a discourse on the death of the citizen.

46. Gloria-Jean Masciarotte, "C'mon Girl: Oprah Winfrey and the Discourse of Feminine Talk," *Genders* 11 (fall 1991): 81–110. In a note to her remarkable essay, Masciarotte uses the phrase "muscular orality" (107) to describe the style of U.S. TV hosts who, like Geraldo Rivera, engage in "the beating up of the *different* speaking subject." Keating did not and politically could not do this: Australian TV has no homegrown equivalent of these shows, although by the mid-1990s many right-wing "tabloid radio" shows were mimicking their sensibility. What Keating as Treasurer did instead was "beat up" on anyone differing from *him* by imposing on all occasions his white masculine "working classness." Keating's own term for his often highly entertaining media mode was "throwing the switch to vaudeville."

47. For example, Peter Robinson, "Time to Rotate the Top Job," *Sun-Herald* 10 November 1991.

48. Alan Ramsey on ABC-TV *Lateline* (*Seducing the Media*) 4 June 1991.

49. Peter Hartcher, "Keating Becomes a Victim of the 'Intelligence Trap,'" *Sydney Morning Herald* 2 November 1991.

50. Derek Parker, *The Courtesans: The Press Gallery in the Hawke Era* (Sydney: Allen & Unwin, 1990), 5.

51. "Colquhoun," *Sydney Morning Herald* 4 November 1991. A "wharfie" is a longshoreman, and a traditional labor icon.

52. For a Lacanian reading of this "thing" as *objet petit a* ("a sublime, evasive body which is a 'thing of nothing,' a pure semblance without substance") functioning in diverse political systems, see Slavoj Žižek, "The King Is a Thing," *New Formations* 13 (1991): 20. A slightly different version of this argument is in *For They Know Not What They Do: Enjoyment as a Political Factor* (London: Verso, 1991), 255.

53. See Mike Seccombe, "From Paul to John, Special Delivery," *Sydney Morning Herald* 25 October 1989: "Some 2,000 years before modern politics . . . Demosthenes was asked what he thought the most important part of rhetoric. He replied: 'delivery, delivery, delivery.' Keating's got it. Hewson hasn't."

54. Alex Millmow, "Profile: Paul Keating," *Australian Left Review* 130 (July 1991): 3.

55. Peter Robinson, "Time to Rotate the Top Job." Robinson is comparing faction politics in Japan and Australia.

56. Slavoj Žižek, *The Sublime Object of Ideology* (London: Verso, 1989), 29, discussing Peter Sloterdijk, *Critique of Cynical Reason* (Minneapolis: University of Minnesota Press, 1987). Žižek continues his own argument by analyzing a more basic operation that he calls "ideological fantasy."

57. Baudrillard, *Fatal Strategies*, 9.

58. Millmow is alluding to a famous joke by Keating (who specialized in *macro*-economic reform): "now in every pet shop in Australia, the resident galah is talking about micro-economic reform." A galah is a pink and grey crested parrot, and a loquaciously stupid person.

59. Robert Garran, cited by "Cassandra" (Senator Peter Walsh, A.L.P.), "Rationalists Winning Some, Losing Some," *Australian Financial Review* 19 November 1991.

60. "Colquhoun," "Once upon a Time . . ." *Sydney Morning Herald* August 21 1989.

61. Michael Pusey, *Economic Rationalism in Canberra: A Nation-Building State Changes Its Mind* (Cambridge: Cambridge University Press, 1991), 1–2. Further references in parentheses in the text. The term "stateless society" is cited from J. P. Nettl. Pusey explains that Australia's "structures are in many essential respects symmetrically opposite to those of the United States (where the state has the full strength of an empire in relation to other foreign states . . .) but which is, as all the literature agrees, the archetype of a weak state in relation to economic interests within." The Australian state has always had a strong "internal authority" while remaining externally weak (15).

62. David D. Hale, "Australia's Economy: Can It Survive Free Trade?" *Weekend Australian* 16–17 November 1991.

63. James Clifford, *The Predicament of Culture* (Cambridge: Harvard University Press, 1988), p. 219. He is discussing Susan Stewart, *On Longing*.

64. Annie L. Cot, "Neoconservative Economics, Utopia and Crisis," *Zone* 1/2 (nd): 293–311. Future references in parentheses in the text.

65. Economic rationalism can also be described as a revival of purist economic liberalism. For Robert Manne, "the stimulus for this revival were [sic] the publicists for the governments of Reagan and Thatcher. Its most influential authorities were von Hayek and Milton Friedman. Proponents of this doctrine sought to achieve rapidly a global regime of universal free trade; the privatisation wherever possible of State-owned enterprises; the rapid deregulation of finances and the national economies; and a return to what was generally called 'small government.'" Robert Manne, "The Future of Conservatism," *Quadrant* (January-February 1992): 49–55.

66. Peter Robinson, "In Search of Elusive Economic Panacea," *Australian Financial Review* 11 December 1991. My emphases.

67. In this kind of journalistic discourse, "economic reality" or "the global economy" works as a Lacanian "big Other" to which reference must be, as Žižek points out, "radically ambivalent" in that "it can function as a calmative and reassuring influence . . . or as a terrifying paranoiac agency." Slavoj Žižek, "The King is a Thing," 28. See also *For They Know Not What They Do: Enjoyment as a Political Factor,* 256–62.

68. Wolfgang Kaspar, "The Revolution We Have to Have," *Weekend Australian* 12–13 October 1991.

69. The phrase "a simple order" is Kaspar's. In fact, while the neo-Confucian model has attracted some in the Labor Party, the Liberals have rather looked to New Zealand for inspiration. However, it is worth noting far from simplifying its *political* form as Kaspar would wish, New Zealand has accompanied its rationalist revolution with a complex new electoral system making it hard for any party to obtain a clear parliamentary majority.

70. G. O. Gutman, "Rational View Needed on the Playing Field," *Australian Financial Review* 23 December 1991. Gutman writes as an investment funds manager.

71. Michel J. Crozier, Samuel P. Huntington, and Joli Watanuki, eds., *The Crisis of Democracy: Report to the Trilateral Commission on the Governability of Democracies* (New York: New York University Press, 1975).

72. Cot's assessment of the ambitions of the Chicago School is shared by Donald

N. McCloskey who calls Becker "the Kipling of the economic empire"; *The Rhetoric of Economics* (Madison: University of Wisconsin Press, 1985), 76. For a feminist account of "new home economics," see Rhonda Sharp and Ray Broomhill, *Short Changed: Women and Economic Policies* (Sydney: Allen & Unwin, 1988), and Marilyn Waring, *Counting for Nothing: What Men Value & What Women Are Worth* (Sydney: Allen & Unwin, 1988).

73. Cot points to the unacknowledged link between "the monetization of non-market time" and "the development of . . . so-called underground, parallel or 'shadow' economics" (306). We can extrapolate from her argument the simultaneous emergence of homelessness as the "extra-social" product of neoconservative utopianism, and of a rhetoric blaming homeless and unemployed people for the personal time-mismanagement held to cause their situation. See Eric Alliez and Michel Feher, "The Luster of Capital," *Zone* 1/2 (nd): 315–59.

74. George Bush's famous description of Reagan's policy imaginary as "voodoo" economics can here be given a Judeo-Christian frame of reference more appropriate to its cultural determinants.

75. Robinson, "In Search of Elusive Economic Panacea." In economic journalism, Argentina is often cited as the nation most like Australia in that they share a past as territorially huge, affluent, agriculturally based and Europe-identifying Southern "settler" democracies, and of trying to secure this position with protectionist economic policies and a populist political culture. To this list, *Le Monde* added in 1992 a "crisis of apathy" called "Argentine Syndrome"; "Aust. 'in Argentine Syndrome,'" *Australian Financial Review* 3 March 1992. A more serious comparison of the two economies is James Levy, "The Error in Argentina's Ways," *Sydney Morning Herald* 19 April 1995.

76. Peter Roberts, "Rich to Get Richer at the Expense of the Poor," *Australian Financial Review* 22 November 1991. Four years later Max Walsh quietly admitted in the business pages that "Australia runs the tightest welfare system of all the advanced economies"; "Menzies Was Right, after All," *Sydney Morning Herald* 21 December 1995.

77. See Michael Keating and Geoff Dixon, *Making Economic Policy in Australia 1983–1988* (Melbourne: Longman Cheshire, 1989); on managerialism in social policy, Christine Jennett and Randal G. Stewart, *Hawke and Australian Public Policy: Consensus and Restructuring* (South Melbourne: Macmillan, 1990).

78. The semiotic sensitivity of financial markets becomes a matter of concern after deregulation, when stray remarks by politicians can trigger excessive economic events. However, the reportage of these often brief events is also structured by media power fantasies. When the $A dropped in January 1992, the *Australian Financial Review* reported with pride that government advisers blamed market reaction on one of its headlines which had inadvisedly used the words, "massive fiscal stimulus" ("$A Fall Tells Keating to Watch His Step," 13 January 1992).

79. Paul Foss, "Landscape without Landscape," in *Island in the Stream: Myths of Place in Australian Culture*, ed. Paul Foss (Sydney: Pluto Press, 1988), 1–3.

80. Gilles Deleuze and Félix Guattari, *A Thousand Plateaus* (Minneapolis: University of Minnesota Press, 1987), 176.

81. Cited in Jacqueline Rose, *Sexuality in the Field of Vision* (London: Verso, 1986), 141.

82. Mark Twain, *Traveling the Equator*, cited by Kylie Tennant, *Australia: Her Story* (1953) (London: Pan Books, 1964), 8.

83. Lindsay Tanner, "Labourism in Retreat," in Burchell and Matthews, *Labor's Troubled Times*, 73–74. Tanner is now a Member of Parliament.

84. Rolando Caputo pointed out to me that a different "Keating" resulted from stressing the Italian-elegant side of his image instead of (as I have) the Irish-eloquent side. The notion of an *orchestrated discordance* specific to the acoustic as well as visual media image also allows us to register the convergent force of those politicians who are, as Keating was, intensely disliked by the electorate. Often called polarizing or divisive, they are in fact more remarkable for their power to attract and absorb media interest to a disproportionate degree, becoming the "centre of attention" at the expense of policy debate and promotion.

85. Robinson, "Search for Elusive Economic Panacea." Robert Manne, a conservative critic of economic rationalism, has noted that "only perhaps in New Zealand have [these doctrines] passed through the body politic with less resistance"; "Conservatism: The Way Ahead."

86. Scott Lash and John Urry, *The End of Organized Capitalism* (Madison: University of Wisconsin Press, 1987), 295.

87. See Graham Freudenberg, *Cause for Power*, and J. A. La Nauze, *The Making of the Australian Constitution* (Melbourne: Melbourne University Press, 1972).

88. Donald Horne, *Money Made Us* (Harmondsworth: Penguin Books, 1976), 12 (my emphasis).

89. See Roberta B. Sykes, *Black Majority* (Hawthorn: Hudson Publishing, 1989), and Sophie Watson, ed., *Playing the State: Australian Feminist Interventions* (Sydney: Allen & Unwin, 1990). Both these texts offer histories of struggles for citizenship by people excluded from the social contract of laborism, and both give accounts of conditions in the present which underscore the *imaginary* aspect of the "rights" I am discussing here.

90. I owe my appreciation of the importance of this distinction to Dipesh Chakrabarty, who has pointed out to me that when cultural critics dismiss "nostalgia," they are often trying to deprive people of the weapons they have to fight with.

6. LUNCHING FOR THE REPUBLIC

1. Paul Kelly, "Howard's Report Card: A Year of Governing Cautiously," *Weekend Australian* 1–2 March 1997. Kelly is discussing the emergence of "values" politics in the United States, United Kingdom and Australia: "it doesn't matter whether you talk to Bill Clinton, Tony Blair or Howard, they are all operating in this environment." John Howard became Liberal Prime Minister of Australia in March 1996.

2. Marilyn Lake, "Sexing the Republic: What Do Women Want?" *Age* 2 December 1993; see also Helen Irving, "Feminists to Turn up Heat on the Republic," *Sydney Morning Herald* 20 August 1993.

3. See Hester Eisenstein, *Inside Agitators: Australian Femocrats and the State* (Philadelphia: Temple University Press, 1996), and n. 53 below.

4. Don Watson, "Birth of a Post-Modern Nation," *Weekend Australian* 24–25 July 1993.

5. A poll in October 1993 had only 41 percent of women in favor of a republic

compared with 56 percent of men (AGB McNair Bulletin Poll, cited in Lake). By June 1995, the figures had risen to 45 percent of women and 59 percent of men; Herald-AGB McNair poll cited in Milton Cockburn, "Voter Support Strong, but Only When They Decide Who Leads," *Sydney Morning Herald* 7 June 1995.

6. A first draft of this argument was presented to a public seminar organized in November 1993 by the Research Centre in Intercommunal Studies, University of Western Sydney, Nepean. Thanks to Ghassan Hage and Lesley Johnson.

7. See Anne Phillips, *Democracy and Difference* (Cambridge: Polity Press, 1993), 75–88.

8. David Burchell, "The Virtuous Citizen and the Commercial Spirit: The Unhappy Prehistory of Citizenship and Modernity," *Communal/Plural* 2 (1993): 17–45.

9. Helen Irving, "Republicanism, Royalty and Tales of Australian Manhood," *Communal/Plural* 2 (1993): 139–51.

10. Chilla Bulbeck, "Republicanism and Post-nationalism," in *The Republicanism Debate*, ed. Wayne Hudson and David Carter (Kensington: New South Wales University Press, 1993), 89.

11. Australian House of Representatives, Daily Hansard 27 February 1992, 373–74.

12. See Desmond Ball, *A Suitable Piece of Real Estate: American Installations in Australia* (Sydney: Hale & Iremonger, 1980); Barrie Dyster and David Meredith, *Australia in the International Economy in the Twentieth Century* (Cambridge: Cambridge University Press, 1990).

13. For a U.S.-oriented version of this story, see John Schlesinger's film, *The Falcon and the Snowman*, 1984.

14. See Henry Reynolds, *The Law of the Land* (Ringwood: Penguin Books, 1987). The constitutional fiction that Australia was a land belonging to "no-one" ("*terra nullius*") at the time of British invasion in 1788 was overturned when the High Court recognized a form of native title in *Mabo v. Queensland* (1992). Subsequently, deciding a case brought by the Wik people of Cape York, the Court in late 1996 judged that native title can co-exist with the pastoral leases that extend over 70 percent of Australia.

15. Jürgen Habermas, *The New Conservatism* (Cambridge: The MIT Press, 1989), 135.

16. Elaine Thompson, "Giving Ourselves Better Government," in Donald Horne et al., *The Coming Republic* (Sydney: Sun Australia, 1992), 148–60.

17. Barry Hindess, "The Very Idea of a Modern Republic," *Communal/Plural* 2 (1993): 1–15.

18. Progressive "race-class-gender" culturalisms have had great difficulty accounting for their own failure to mobilize anything like the huge constituencies appealed to in their rhetorics of identity and difference. However, for a feminist approach to *economic* "difference" that deals creatively with this problem by drawing on cultural theory, see J. K. Gibson-Graham, *The End of Capitalism (as We Knew It): A Feminist Critique of Political Economy* (Cambridge, MA, and Oxford: Blackwell, 1996).

19. I borrow this term from Lauren Berlant, "The Face of America and the State of Emergency," *Disciplinarity and Dissent in Cultural Studies*, ed. Cary Nelson and Dilip Parameshwar Gaonkar (New York and London: Routledge, 1996), 397–439.

20. Ann Curthoys and Stephen Muecke, "Australia, for Example," in Hudson and Carter, *The Republicanism Debate*, 181. Further references in parentheses in the text.

21. In 1996, the Coalition's winning slogan "For All of Us" tacitly claimed that Labor had governed only in the interests of minorities. That racism played a role

in the slogan's success is suggested by the results gained by three white candidates from largely rural states who were rebuked by their own parties for racist remarks; all received "sympathy swings" from voters. One, Ms. Pauline Hanson, was disendorsed by the Liberal Party for discriminatory comments about Aborigines. She stood as an Independent in a hitherto safe Labor seat and won it with a 20 percent swing.

22. Curthoys and Muecke base their notion of the exemplary on Jacques Derrida, *The Other Heading: Reflections on Today's Europe*, trans. Pascale-Anne Brault and Michael B. Naas (Bloomington and Indianapolis: Indiana University Press, 1992). It can be argued that they overstate the cultural authority achieved by Aborigines, given the anger at "special privileges" supposedly enjoyed by indigenous people that broke out in 1996. I disagree. Aboriginal "discursive and narrative" power remains immense now compared to thirty years ago; it is the *struggle* to achieve this that Curthoys and Muecke call "exemplary," and to say there is a backlash against it is to say that this struggle continues.

23. "An Australian Non-Nationalism," *Sydney Morning Herald* 12 February 1994; "National Independence a Far Cry from Virulent Nationalism," *Financial Review* 14 June 1994.

24. Ann Curthoys, "Single White Male," *Arena Magazine* 8 (1993–94): 28. My emphasis.

25. Peter Beilharz, "Republicanism and Citizenship," in Hudson and Carter, *The Republicanism Debate*, 115.

26. Kobena Mercer, "'1968': Periodizing Politics and Identity," *Cultural Studies*, ed. Lawrence Grossberg, Cary Nelson, and Paula Treichler (New York and London: Routledge, 1992), 425.

27. Horne et al., *The Coming Republic;* Tom Keneally, *Our Republic* (Port Melbourne: William Heinemann Australia, 1993).

28. *The Coming Republic* makes use of this antecedent in a comic and deliberate way.

29. Ghassan Hage, "Racism, Multiculturalism and the Gulf War," *Arena* 96 (1991): 8–13.

30. Michel de Certeau, *The Practice of Everyday Life*, trans. Steven F. Rendall (Berkeley: University of California Press, 1984), 177–89.

31. The negotiations involved having the Act passed by the Senate before a deadline imposed by an impending legal challenge to Mabo by the state government of Western Australia.

32. See Rick Farley, "The Political Imperatives of Native Title," *Australian* 15 May 1996.

33. Gary Shapiro, "From the Sublime to the Political: Some Historical Notes," *New Literary History* 16.2 (1985): 213–35.

34. Donald Horne, *The Public Culture: An Argument with the Future* (London and Boulder: Pluto Press, 1994), vii.

35. Homi K. Bhabha, ed., *Nation and Narration* (London and New York: Routledge, 1990), 5.

36. Michael Kirby, "Reflections on Constitutional Monarchy," in Hudson and Carter, *The Republicanism Debate*, 74.

37. Barry Hindess, "The Very Idea of a Modern Republic," 15.

38. See Anna Haebich, *For Their Own Good: Aborigines and Government in the South*

West of Western Australia 1900–1940 (Nedlands: University of Western Australia Press, 1992).

39. Ghassan Hage, "Republicanism, Multiculturalism, Zoology," *Communal/Plural* 2 (1993): 117.

40. Michael B. Naas, "Introduction: For Example," in Jacques Derrida, *The Other Heading*, xxii.

41. Graeme Turner, "Two faces of Australian Nationalism," *Sydney Morning Herald* 25 January 1997.

42. This is a currently dominant *factional* rather than a definitive approach; much of Australia's existing multicultural policy framework was initiated by a previous Liberal Prime Minister, Malcolm Fraser (1975–83).

43. For an academic elaboration of "postmodern" republicanism from a left-wing position, see Paul James, "As Nation and State: A Postmodern Republic Takes Shape," *The State in Question: Transformations of the Australian State*, ed. Paul James (Sydney: Allen & Unwin, 1996).

44. Donald Horne, *How to Be Australia* (Monash University: National Centre for Australian Studies, 1994).

45. Watson, "Birth of a Post-Modern Nation."

46. Jon Stratton and Ien Ang, "Multicultural Imagined Communities: Cultural Difference and National Identity in Australia and the USA," *Continuum* 8.2 (1994): 147.

47. One factor distinguishing the history of the Australian Labor Party from that of the British Labour Party is the former's significant Catholic constituency; see Ross McMullin, *The Light on the Hill: The Australian Labor Party 1891–1991* (Oxford: Oxford University Press, 1991). On the conflict over communism, see Robert Murray, *The Split: Australian Labor in the Fifties* (Melbourne: Cheshire, 1970).

48. Bede Nairn, *Civilising Capitalism: The Beginnings of the Australian Labor Party* (Canberra: Australian National University Press, 1973).

49. Ideally, preselection to 35 percent of winnable seats in Parliament by 2001. Practical efforts to move toward this goal have been unevenly impressive. One painful aspect of Labor's 1996 defeat was the unprecedentedly high number of women elected for conservative parties from marginal seats without resort to a quota system. My interest, however, is in the cultural shift entailed by the goal itself.

50. I argue elsewhere that corporatism as a political culture in Australia draws on Indonesian *exempla* and looks with ambivalent envy to Singapore's efficiency as a model; "'Non-Nationalism' and 'Post-Nationalism' in the Australian Republicanism Debate," *Trajectories II*, 1995 Proceedings, Institute of Literature, National Tsing-Hua University, Taiwan.

51. In response to those appalled by the idea of "managing" differences, this variety of neocorporatism is agnostic about difference philosophically construed. Setting aside incommensurables as exceeding negotiation, it points to the extreme violence of those nationalisms that treat differences as *un*manageable, challenges its critics to name alternatives available to government, and invites concrete proposals for improving the management process: that many a *différend* is activated at every moment of this process is not denied but frankly accepted as part of the way things work.

52. In this respect, Labor corporatism differs from the more intensively analyzed *fascist* variety of corporatism. On the latter, see Slavoj Žižek, *Tarrying with the Nega-*

tive: Kant, Hegel and the Critique of Ideology (Durham: Duke University Press, 1993), 200–37.

53. While there is little rigorous analysis of the feminist culture of "mateship," there is a large literature on Australian feminism's experience with "playing the state." Among the examples not so far cited, see: Ann Curthoys, "Australian Feminism and the State: Practice and Theory," *The State in Question: Transformations of the Australian State,* ed. Paul James (Sydney: Allen & Unwin, 1996), 138–60; Suzanne Franzway, Dianne Court, and R. W. Connell, *Staking a Claim: Feminism, Bureaucracy and the State* (Sydney and Boston: Allen & Unwin, 1989); Anna Yeatman, *Bureaucrats, Technocrats, Femocrats* (Sydney and Boston: Allen & Unwin, 1990).

54. See Masao Miyoshi, "A Borderless World? From Colonialism to Transnationalism and the Decline of the Nation-State," *Critical Inquiry* 19.4 (1993): 726–51.

55. Curthoys and Muecke, 190.

56. See Bain Attwood, ed., *In the Age of Mabo: History, Aborigines and Australia* (Sydney: Allen & Unwin, 1996); Murray Goot and Tim Rowse, *Make a Better Offer: The Politics of Mabo* (Sydney: Pluto, 1994); M. A. Stephenson and Suri Ratnapala, eds., *Mabo: A Judicial Revolution* (St. Lucia: University of Queensland Press, 1993).

57. In most cases at least two-thirds of all electors must vote "yes" to secure this result. Votes cast in the Northern Territory and the Australian Capital Territory count only in the poll of electors.

58. Forty-two proposals to amend the constitution were put to the electorate between Federation in 1901 and 1993. All but eight were rejected, as were two further proposals for military conscription in World War One. *Parliamentary Handbook of the Commonwealth of Australia* (1993), 26th ed., 689.

59. Marcia Langton, *"Well, I heard it on the radio and I saw it on the television . . . "* (North Sydney: Australian Film Commission, 1993), 84.

60. On the "specific" intellectual, see *Michel Foucault: Power/Knowledge,* ed. Colin Gordon (Brighton: Harvester, 1980), 126–33.

61. Langton, cited in David Leser's profile of Noel Pearson, "The Cape Crusader," *HQ* (March/April 1994): 80.

62. Langton, *"Well, I heard it on the radio and I saw it on the television . . . "*, 84 and 35 respectively.

63. See Catrina Felton and Liz Flanagan, "Institutionalised Feminism: A Tidda's Perspective," *Lilith* 8 (1993): 56; Langton, *"Well, I heard it on the radio and I saw it on the television . . . "*, 91–92; Stephen Muecke, *Textual Spaces: Aboriginality and Cultural Studies* (Kensington: New South Wales University Press, 1992).

64. Cited in "The Cape Crusader," 84; see also Sue Cant, "Aborigines Urged to Target Middle Class," *The Australian* 6 June 1994.

65. Cited in Keith Scott, "Last Chance to Translate Grievance into Change," *Canberra Times* 14 October 1993.

66. Tim Rowse, "Diversity in Indigenous Citizenship," *Communal/Plural* 2 (1993): 49.

67. In early 1996, conservative politicians ebulliently testing their strength in Aboriginal affairs were asked to stop interfering by the mining executives and graziers who are usually their allies. See Fiona Kennedy, "Aboriginal Consensus Reached on Cape York," *Australian* 6 February 1996; and Marcia Langton, "No Future in a Return to Racial Paternalism," *Australian* 18 April 1996.

68. Cited in Cameron Forbes, "How Green Can a Black Afford to Be?" *The Australian* 6 June 1994.

69. See Giorgio Agamben, *The Coming Community*, trans. Michael Hardt (Minneapolis: Minnesota University Press, 1993); Gilles Deleuze and Félix Guattari, *A Thousand Plateaus*, trans. Brian Massumi (Minneapolis: Minnesota University Press, 1987).

70. On the complicity between universalism and particularism that sustains the tenacity of this schema, see Naoki Sakai, *Translation and Subjectivity* (Minneapolis: University of Minnesota Press, 1997), ch. 5.

71. Hage, "Republicanism, Multiculturalism, Zoology," 132. Hage is glossing Susan Stewart, *On Longing: Narratives of the Miniature, the Gigantic, the Souvenir, the Collection* (Baltimore and London: Johns Hopkins University Press, 1984).

72. Bruce Robbins, *Secular Vocations: Intellectuals, Professionalism, Culture* (London and New York: Verso, 1993), 196.

73. These laws were repealed by the Tasmanian government in 1997 following a long campaign by gay and lesbian activists.

74. Kalantzis and Cope, "Republicanism and Cultural Diversity," *The Republicanism Debate*, ed. Hudson and Carter, 143.

75. On "the national interest" as sectarian abstraction, see Graeme Turner, *Making It National: Nationalism and Australian Popular Culture* (Sydney: Allen & Unwin, 1994). On the force of identity politics, see James Holston and Arjun Appadurai, "Cities and Citizenship," *Public Culture* 8.2 (1996): 195.

76. Rowse, "Diversity in Indigenous Citizenship," 52.

77. Beatrice Faust, "Cultural Clash of Women in Motion," *Weekend Australian* 15–16 Oct. 1994.

78. Helen Irving, "Swissterhood," *Arena Magazine* 11 (1994): 15.

79. On the media marketing of this "marketing image," see Martin Hirst, "The Coming Republic: Citizenship and the Public Sphere in Post-Colonial Australia," *Australian Journal of Communication* 22.3 (1995): 13–39.

80. See Terry Widders and Greg Noble, "On the Dreaming Track to the Republic: Indigenous People and the Ambivalence of Citizenship," *Communal/Plural* 2 (1993): 95–112.

81. Cited in Catherine Armitage, "Companies Urged to Halt Asian Exploitation," *The Australian* 11 October 1994.

82. Cited in Adele Horin, "Plea for Businesses to Combat Child Labour," *Sydney Morning Herald* 6 March 1996.

EPILOGUE

1. Friedrich Nietzsche, "On the Uses and Disadvantages of History for Life," *Untimely Meditations*, trans. R. J. Hollingdale (Cambridge and New York: Cambridge University Press, 1983), 72.

2. Cited in Frank Devine, "'Drab Mr Suburbia' Has the Last Laugh," *Australian* 27 February 1997.

3. Demographer Christobel Young, cited by Michael Stutchbury, "The Bizarre Anti-Migration Coalition," *Australian Financial Review* 14 November 1990.

4. See Gail Guthrie Valaskakis, "The Chippewa and the Other: Living the Heritage of Lac du Flambeau," *Cultural Studies* 2.3 (1988): 267–93.

5. Michael Gordon, "An Ordinary Success: Mainstream Man, One Year On," *The Australian Magazine*, 22–23 February 1997, 12–18. The article includes a photograph of Howard in a beach town wearing an open-necked shirt. See ch. 3 above.

6. On the tenacity of the belief that Anglo-Celtic citizens have more "right" than other citizens to define others' rights, see Ghassan Hage, "Anglo-Celtics Today: Cosmo-Multiculturalism and the Phase of the Fading Phallus," *Communal/Plural* 4 (1994): 41–77.

7. On the broad context shaping this perception, see Arif Dirlik, "The Postcolonial Aura: Third World Criticism in the Age of Global Capitalism," *Critical Inquiry* 20.2 (1994): 328–56, and Stuart Hall's response to Dirlik in "When Was 'the Post-Colonial'? Thinking at the Limit," *The Post-Colonial Question: Common Skies, Divided Horizons*, ed. Iain Chambers and Lidia Curti (London and New York: Routledge, 1996), 242–60.

8. I discuss the discourse of race apocalypse in "White Panic or, Mad Max and the Sublime," *Trajectories of Cultural Studies*, ed. Kuan-Hsing Chen (London: Routledge, forthcoming).

9. Donald Horne, *The Public Culture: An Argument with the Future* (London and Boulder: Pluto Press, 1994), vii.

10. Nietzsche, 72–73.

11. Cited in Devine. Again, I stress that "suburban" connotes modest material circumstances, and working- or lower-middle-class social struggles. See ch. 2, n. 3, and ch. 4, n. 28.

12. Les Murray, *Subhuman Redneck Poems* (Potts Point: Duffy & Snellgrove, 1996).

13. Margaret Harris and Ian Verrender, "How Sydney Became Asia's Middle-Class Sweatshop," *Sydney Morning Herald* 19 November 1995. The article discusses the move of Asian companies such as Cathay Pacific (one of the world's biggest airlines), and Asian-oriented American companies, to establish regional headquarters in Australia because of "our bargain-basement pay rates" ("cheap labour") relative to the salaries expected by executives in Hong Kong or Singapore.

14. These long-running serials, still popular during my adolescence in the 1960s, had titles such as "Blue Hills," "Portia Faces Life," and "When a Girl Marries." Clearly the forerunners of the popular TV series of the past twenty years (*A Country Practice*, *The Flying Doctors*, *Blue Heelers*) that focus, unlike U.S. soaps, on homely communities rather than rich and beautiful individualists, the radio serials in turn were rooted in a popular social realist literature: for example, Kylie Tennant's classic novel *The Battlers* (London and Sydney: Angus & Robertson, 1941).

15. Nietzsche, p. 73.

16. *Policies* for women, in contrast, began being discarded or neglected soon after the 1996 election.

17. On the "kynical," see ch. 5 above.

18. On the distinction between a poor true copy and a simulacrum, see ch. 4 above.

19. Walter Benjamin, "Theses on the Philosophy of History," *Illuminations*, ed. Hannah Arendt and trans. Harry Zohn (London: Jonathan Cape, 1970), 259–60.

20. Jane Goodall, "General Adaptation Syndrome: Hypochondrias of the *Fin de Siècle*," *Aesthesia and the Economy of the Senses*, ed. Helen Grace (UWS, Nepean: Faculty of Visual & Perfoming Arts, 1996), 80. Goodall is referring to, for example, the work of Paul Virilio. I should clarify that she writes this fine essay as a hypochondriac.

21. Goodall, "General Adaptation Syndrome," 79. Goodall focuses on images of invasive technological stress. Another model of immanent apocalypse is the "viral"

and, in an essay that remains one of the clearest expositions I know of what it means for activism to reclaim the temporality of experience and effort from an "end of" (gay sex) fantasy, Douglas Crimp points to the phobic function of the viral model in the work of Baudrillard, one of Goodall's "hypochondriacs": "Portraits of People with AIDS," *Cultural Studies*, ed. Lawrence Grossberg, Cary Nelson, and Paula Treichler (New York and London: Routledge, 1992), 130.

22. Dick Hebdige, "Training Some Thoughts on the Future," *Mapping the Futures: Local Cultures, Global Change*, ed. Jon Bird et al. (London and New York: Routledge, 1993), 275.

23. On the complex articulation of "climatology" in philosophy to racism, nationalism and, more specifically, hostility toward immigrants, see Naoki Sakai, *Translation and Subjectivity* (Minneapolis: University of Minnesota Press, 1997), chs. 3 and 4.

24. David Harvey, *The Condition of Postmodernity: An Enquiry into the Origins of Cultural Change* (Oxford: Blackwell, 1989).

25. On volatilized models of time, see ch. 1 above. On heterogeneous temporalities, see Homi K. Bhabha, *The Location of Culture* (London and New York: Routledge, 1994); Dipesh Chakrabarty, "Postcoloniality and the Artifice of History: Who Speaks for 'Indian' Pasts?" *Representations* 37 (1992): 1–26, and "Provincializing Europe: Postcoloniality and the Critique of History," *Cultural Studies* 6.3 (1992): 337–57; Luke Gibbons, *Transformations in Irish Culture* (Cork: Cork University Press, 1996).

26. Ruth Levitas, "The Future of Thinking about the Future," *Mapping the Futures*, ed. Jon Bird et al., 258.

27. Margaret Morse, "An Ontology of Everyday Distraction: The Freeway, the Mall and Television," *Logics of Television: Essays in Cultural Criticism*, ed. Patricia Mellencamp (London: BFI Publishing, 1990), 215.

28. Ian Hunter, *Culture and Government: The Emergence of Literary Education* (London: Macmillan, 1988). See ch. 3 above.

29. Michèle Le Doeuff, *The Philosophical Imaginary*, trans. Colin Gordon (Stanford: Stanford University Press, 1989), 45–56.

30. Ian Hunter, "Setting Limits to Culture," *New Formations* 4 (spring 1988): 103–25.

31. Tony Bennett, "Putting Policy into Cultural Studies," *Cultural Studies*, ed. Lawrence Grossberg, Cary Nelson, and Paula Treichler (New York and London: Routledge, 1992), 31–32. My emphasis. Further references in parentheses in the text. The definition of agency cited in the next sentence is from an unpublished paper by Barry Hindess.

32. Le Doeuff, *The Philosophical Imaginary*, and *Hipparchia's Choice: An Essay Concerning Women, Philosophy, Etc.*, trans. Trista Selous (Oxford, UK, and Cambridge, MA: Blackwell, 1991).

33. Most recently, *Outside in the Teaching Machine* (New York and London: Routledge, 1993). A critique of the role played in cultural theory by a phantom agent (the "self-knowing, politically canny subaltern") is explicitly the task of Spivak's most famous essay, "Can the Subaltern Speak?" *Marxism and the Interpretation of Culture*, ed. Cary Nelson and Lawrence Grossberg (Urbana: University of Illinois Press, 1988), 27–313.

34. Patricia J. Williams, *The Alchemy of Race and Rights: Diary of a Law Professor* (Cambridge, MA, and London: Harvard University Press, 1991).

35. Rey Chow, *Writing Diaspora: Tactics of Intervention in Contemporary Cultural Stud-*

ies (Bloomington and Indianapolis: Indiana University Press, 1993): "Strictly speaking, we are not only living in the age of 'traveling theories' and 'traveling theorists' ... but also of *portable oppressions* and *portable oppressed objects*" (146). Further references in parentheses in the text.

36. I refer to Ross Chambers's work on reading, desire, and change, *Room for Maneuver: Reading Oppositional Narrative* (Chicago and London: University of Chicago Press, 1991).

37. Chow herself picks up and carries further parts of Iain Chambers's essay, "A Miniature History of the Walkman," *New Formations* 11 (summer 1990): 1–4.

38. Deleuze and Guattari, *A Thousand Plateaus*, 6–7.

39. Hunter, *Culture and Government*, 288.

40. On genre understood as a rhetoric and thus as a practice rather than a rule, see Anne Freadman and Amanda Macdonald, *What Is This Thing Called "Genre"?* (Mount Nebo: Boombana Publications, 1992).

41. See Deborah McDowell's discussion of the charge of nativism in *"The Changing Same": Black Women's Literature, Criticism, and Theory* (Bloomington and Indianapolis: Indiana University Press, 1995), 113–17.

42. David Harvey, "From Space to Place and Back Again: Reflections on the Condition of Postmodernity," *Mapping the Futures*, ed. Bird et al. (London and New York: Routledge, 1993), 26. Harvey is citing H. Speier's work on *German White Collar Workers and the Rise of Hitler*.

43. Cynthia Enloe, *Bananas, Beaches and Bases: Making Feminist Sense of International Politics* (Berkeley and Los Angeles: University of California Press, 1989); Jamaica Kincaid, *A Small Place* (London: Virago, 1988); Eric Michaels, *For a Cultural Future: Francis Jupurrurla Makes TV at Yuendumu* (Sydney: Artspace, 1987), included in *Bad Aboriginal Art: Tradition, Media, and Technological Horizons* (Minneapolis: University of Minnesota Press, 1994), 99–125; Sally Morgan, *My Place* (Fremantle: Fremantle Arts Centre Press, 1987).

44. Laura Mulvey, *Visual and Other Pleasures* (Bloomington: Indiana University Press, 1989), 163.

45. This distinction is developed in detail by Doreen Massey in "Power-Geometry and a Progressive Sense of Place," *Mapping the Futures*, ed. Bird et al., 59–69.

46. Tucked away in small columns by most daily papers, the news was a big cover story for *Business Review Weekly*: "Keating Is Dead: Labor's New Guard Rejects His Faith in Free Markets," 3 March 1997.

47. Eric Michaels, *Unbecoming: An AIDS Diary* (Sydney: Empress Publishing, 1990), 192.

WORKS CITED

Abelson, Elaine S. *When Ladies Go A-Thieving: Middle-Class Shoplifters in the Victorian Department Store.* New York: Oxford UP, 1990.

Adorno, Theodor. "Letters to Walter Benjamin." *Aesthetics and Politics: Debates between Bloch, Lukacs, Brecht, Benjamin, Adorno.* Translation editor Ronald Taylor. London: Verso, 1977. 110–33.

———. "Progress." *The Philosophical Forum* XV.1–2 (1983–84): 5–70.

Agamben, Giorgio. *The Coming Community.* Trans. Michael Hardt. Minneapolis: U of Minnesota P, 1993.

Alexander, Jeffrey, and Piotr Sztompa, eds. *Rethinking Progress.* London: Unwin Hyman, 1990.

Alliez, Eric, and Michel Feher. "The Luster of Capital." *Zone* 1/2 (nd): 315–59.

———. "Notes on the Sophisticated City." *Zone* 1/2 (nd): 40–55.

"An Australian Non-Nationalism." *Sydney Morning Herald* 12 February 1994.

Anderson, Perry. "Modernity and Revolution." Nelson and Grossberg. 317–38.

Appleby, Joyce, Lynn Hunt, and Margaret Jacob. *Telling the Truth about History.* New York and London: Norton, 1994.

Armitage, Catherine. "Companies Urged to Halt Asian Exploitation." *Australian* 11 October 1994.

Artlink 10.1/2 (1990). "Contemporary Aboriginal Art."

Attali, Jacques. *Noise: The Political Economy of Music.* Minneapolis: U of Minnesota P, 1985.

Attwood, Bain, ed. *In the Age of Mabo: History, Aborigines and Australia.* Sydney: Allen & Unwin, 1996.

Augé, Marc. *Non-Places: Introduction to an Anthropology of Supermodernity.* Trans. John Howe. London: Verso, 1995.

Aurum Encyclopaedia of Science Fiction. Ed. Phil Hardy. London: Aurum Press, 1984.

"Aust. 'in Argentine Syndrome.'" *Australian Financial Review* 3 March 1992.

Australia Reconstructed: ACTU/TDC Mission to Western Europe. Canberra: Australian Government Publishing Service, 1987.

"Australia—Time to Get Serious." *Far Eastern Economic Review* 10 October 1991.

Australian Cultural History 10 (1991). "Travellers, Journeys, Tourists."

Australian House of Representatives, Daily Hansard 27 February 1992.

Badham, John. dir. *Dracula.* 1979.

Baker, G., and B. Funaro. *Shopping Centers, Design and Operation.* New York: Reinhold Publishing, 1951.

Bakhtin, M. M. *The Dialogic Imagination: Four Essays.* Ed. Michael Holquist. Trans. Caryl Emerson and Michael Holquist. Austin: U of Texas P, 1981.

"Bald Rock Highlight," *Tenterfield Star* 17 November 1986.

Ball, Desmond. *A Suitable Piece of Real Estate: American Installations in Australia.* Sydney: Hale & Iremonger, 1980.

Barry, Don, and Stephen Muecke, eds. *The Apprehension of Time.* Sydney: Local Consumption Publications, 1988.

Barthes, Roland. "Change the Object Itself." *Image-Music-Text.* Ed. and trans. Stephen Heath. Glasgow: Fontana, 1977. 165–69.

——. *The Eiffel Tower and Other Mythologies.* Trans. Richard Howard. New York: Hill & Wang, 1979.

——. *Mythologies.* Paris: Seuil, 1957.

——. *The Rustle of Language.* Trans. Richard Howard. Oxford: Blackwell, 1986.

Baudrillard, Jean. *America.* Trans. Chris Turner. London: Verso, 1988.

——. "The Ecstasy of Communication." *The Anti-Aesthetic.* Ed. Hal Foster. Washington: Bay Press, 1983. 126–34.

——. *L'effet beaubourg: implosion et dissuasion.* Paris, Editions Galilée, 1977.

——. *Fatal Strategies: Crystal Revenge.* Trans. Philip Beitchman and W. G. J. Niesluchowski. New York: Semiotext(e)/Pluto, 1990.

——. *Seduction.* Trans. Brian Singer. New York: St. Martin's Press, 1990.

——. *Simulations.* Trans. Paul Foss, Paul Patton, and Philip Beitchman. New York: Semiotext(e), 1983.

——. *La société de consommation.* Paris: Gallimard, 1970.

Beddington, Nadine. *Design for Shopping Centres.* London: Butterworth Scientific, 1982.

Beilharz, Peter. "Republicanism and Citizenship." Hudson and Carter. 109–17.

Bell, Diane. *Daughters of the Dreaming.* Melbourne and North Sydney: McPhee Gribble with Allen & Unwin, 1983.

Benjamin, Walter. "A Berlin Chronicle." *One-Way Street and Other Writings.* Trans. Edmund Jephcott and Kingsley Shorter. London: New Left Books, 1979. 293–346.

——. "Theses on the Philosophy of History." *Illuminations.* Ed. Hannah Arendt. Trans. Harry Zohn. London: Jonathan Cape, 1970. 255–66.

Bennett, Tony. "Coming out of English: A Policy Calculus for Cultural Studies." Ruthven. 33–44.

——. "Putting Policy into Cultural Studies." Grossberg, Nelson, and Treichler. 23–37.

——, Patrick Buckridge, David Carter, and Colin Mercer, eds. *Celebrating the Nation: A Critical Study of Australia's Bicentenary.* Sydney: Allen & Unwin, 1992.

Bensen, Susan Porter. *Counter Cultures: Saleswomen, Managers, and Customers in American Department Stores 1890–1940.* Urbana and Chicago: U of Illinois P, 1988.

Bensmaïa, Réda. "On the Concept of Minor Literature: From Kafka to Kateb Yacine." Boundas and Olkowski. 213–28.

Benveniste, Emile. *Problèmes de linguistique générale.* Paris: Gallimard, 1966.

Berlant, Lauren. "The Face of America and the State of Emergency." Nelson and Gaonkar. 397–439.

Berman, Marshall. *All That Is Solid Melts into Air: The Experience of Modernity.* New York: Simon and Schuster, 1982.

——. "The Signs in the Street: A Response to Perry Anderson." *New Left Review* 144 (1984): 114–23.

Bhabha, Homi K. *The Location of Culture.* London and New York: Routledge, 1994.

———, ed. *Nation and Narration*. London and New York: Routledge, 1990.

Bird, Jon, Barry Curtis, Tim Putnam, George Robertson, and Lisa Tickner, eds. *Mapping the Futures: Local Cultures, Global Change*. London and New York: Routledge, 1993.

Blainey, Geoffrey. *The Tyranny of Distance: How Distance Shaped Australia's History*. Melbourne: Sun Books, 1966.

Blanchot, Maurice. "Everyday Speech." *Yale French Studies* 73 (1987): 12–20.

Bogue, Ronald. *Deleuze and Guattari*. New York: Routledge, 1989.

Boorstin, Daniel. *The Image: A Guide to Pseudo-Events in America*. New York: Harper and Row, 1961.

Boundas, Constantin V., and Dorothea Olkowski, eds. *Gilles Deleuze and the Theater of Philosophy*. New York and London: Routledge, 1994.

Boyd, Robin. *The Australian Ugliness*. Ringwood and Harmondsworth: Penguin, 1963.

———. *Australia's Home*. Harmondsworth: Penguin, 1978.

Boyer, M. Christine. "The Return of Aesthetics to City Planning." *Philosophical Streets: New Approaches to Urbanism*. Ed. Dennis Crow. Washington, DC: Maisonneuve, 1990. 93–112.

Braidotti, Rosi. *Nomadic Subjects: Embodiment and Sexual Difference in Contemporary Feminist Theory*. New York: Columbia UP, 1994.

Brennan, Warwick. "ARM Hails Libs' win." *Sunday Telegraph* 10 March 1996.

Bringing Them Home. Report of the National Inquiry into the Separation of Aboriginal and Torres Strait Islander Children from Their Families. Commonwealth of Australia, 1997.

Bromfield, David. "Making the Modern in the Newest City in the World." *Aspects of Perth Modernism 1929–1942*. Ed. David Bromfield. Perth: Centre for Fine Arts UWA, 1988. 2–8.

Bruno, Guiliana. "Ramble City: Postmodernism and *Blade Runner*." *October* 41 (1987): 61–74.

———. *Streetwalking on a Ruined Map: Cultural Theory and the City Films of Elvira Notari*. Princeton: Princeton UP, 1993.

Bulbeck, Chilla. "Republicanism and Post-Nationalism." Hudson and Carter. 88–96.

Burchell, David. "The Virtuous Citizen and the Commercial Spirit: The Unhappy Prehistory of Citizenship and Modernity." *Communal/Plural* 2 (1993): 17–45.

———, and Race Matthews, eds. *Labor's Troubled Times*. Sydney: Pluto, 1991.

Burchill, Julie. *Ambition*. New York: Harper, 1989.

Burger, Peter. *Theory of the Avant-Garde*. Trans. Michael Shaw. Minneapolis: U of Minnesota P, 1984.

Burns, Wilfred. *British Shopping Centers*. London: Leonard Hill, 1959.

Bury, J. P. *The Idea of Progress: An Inquiry into Its Origin and Growth*. New York: Macmillan, 1932.

Camera Obscura 20–21 (1989). "The Spectatrix."

Cant, Sue. "Aborigines Urged to Target Middle Class." *Australian* 6 June 1994.

Carew, Edna. *Keating: A Biography*. Sydney: Allen & Unwin, 1988.

———. *Paul Keating: Prime Minister*. Sydney: Allen & Unwin, 1992.

"Carr Cuts Skyscraper Plans Down." *Sydney Morning Herald* 31 August 1987.

Carter, Erica, James Donald, and Judith Squires, eds. *Space and Place: Theories of Identity and Location*. London: Lawrence and Wishart, 1993.

Carter, Paul. *The Road to Botany Bay*. London & Boston: Faber and Faber, 1987.

"Cassandra." "Rationalists Winning Some, Losing Some." *Australian Financial Review* 19 November 1991.

Castle in the Clouds! 3 (1977), Marvel Comics.

Castles, Stephen, Mary Kalantzis, Bill Cope, and Michael Morrissey. *Mistaken Identity: Multiculturalism and the Demise of Nationalism in Australia*. Sydney: Pluto, 1988.

Chakrabarty, Dipesh. "Postcoloniality and the Artifice of History: Who Speaks for 'Indian' Pasts?" *Representations* 37 (1992): 1–26.

———. "Provincializing Europe: Postcoloniality and the Critique of History." *Cultural Studies* 6.3 (1992): 337–57.

———. "Trafficking in History and Theory: Subaltern Studies." Ruthven. 101–108.

Chambers, Iain. "Maps for the Metropolis: A Possible Guide to the Present." *Cultural Studies* 1.1 (1987): 1–21.

———. "A Miniature History of the Walkman." *New Formations* 11 (1990): 1–4.

———. *Popular Culture: The Metropolitan Experience*. London and New York: Methuen, 1986.

———, and Lidia Curti, eds. *The Post-Colonial Question: Common Skies, Divided Horizons*. London and New York: Routledge, 1996.

Chambers, Ross. *Room for Maneuver: Reading Oppositional Narrative*. Chicago and London: U of Chicago P, 1991.

———. "Strolling, Touring, Cruising: Counter-Disciplinary Narrative and the Loiterature of Travel." *Understanding Narrative*. Ed. James Phelan and Peter Rabinowitz. Columbus: Ohio State UP, 1994. 17–42.

Chang, Briankle. *Deconstructing Communication*. Minneapolis: U of Minnesota P, 1996.

Chen, Kuan-Hsing. "Voices from the Outside: Towards a New Internationalist Localism." *Cultural Studies* 6.3 (1992): 476–84.

Chow, Rey. *Woman and Chinese Modernity: The Politics of Reading between West and East*. Minneapolis: U of Minnesota P, 1991.

———. *Writing Diaspora: Tactics of Intervention in Contemporary Cultural Studies*. Bloomington and Indianapolis: Indiana UP, 1993.

Christensen, Jerome. "From Rhetoric to Corporate Populism: A Romantic Critique of the Academy in an Age of High Gossip." *Critical Inquiry* 16.2 (1990): 438–65.

Clark, C. M. H. *A History of Australia*, vol. V, *The People Make Laws 1888–1915*. Melbourne: Melbourne UP, 1981.

———. "The Ruins of the Ideologies." *The Australian Dream*. Ed. Ian Turner. Melbourne: Sun Books, 1968. 348–51.

Cleary, Paul. "Banana Republic Vision Comes True." *Sydney Morning Herald* 14 May 1996.

Clifford, James. *The Predicament of Culture*. Cambridge: Harvard UP, 1988.

Cockburn, Milton. "Voter Support Strong, but Only When They Decide Who Leads." *Sydney Morning Herald* 7 June 1995.

Coleman, Peter, ed. *Australian Civilization*. Melbourne and Sydney: Cheshire, 1962.

"Colquhoun." "How to Pick the Real Paul Keating." *Sydney Morning Herald* 4 November 1991.

———. "Once upon a Time . . . " *Sydney Morning Herald* 21 August 1989.

"Coming to Grips with the Debt Crisis." *Australian Financial Review* 20 November 1989.

Communal/Plural 2 (1993). "Republicanism/Citizenship/Community."

Connell, R. W. *Ruling Class Ruling Culture: Studies of Conflict, Power and Hegemony in Australian Life.* Cambridge: Cambridge UP, 1977.

Continuum 8.2 (1994). "Critical Multiculturalism."

Conway, Ronald. *The Great Australian Stupor: An Interpretation of the Australian Way of Life.* Melbourne: Sun Books, 1971.

———. *Land of the Long Weekend.* Melbourne: Sun Books, 1978.

Cot, Annie L. "Neoconservative Economics, Utopia and Crisis." *Zone* 1/2 (nd): 293–311.

Craik, Jennifer. *Resorting to Tourism: Cultural Policies for Tourist Development in Australia.* Sydney: Allen & Unwin, 1991.

Cramer, Sue, ed. *Postmodernism: A Consideration of the Appropriation of Aboriginal Imagery.* Brisbane: Institute of Modern Art, 1989.

Crawford, Norman. *Tenterfield.* Tenterfield District Historical Society, 1949.

Crimp, Douglas. "Portraits of People with AIDS." Grossberg, Nelson, and Treichler. 117–33.

Cronenberg, David, dir. *The Fly.* 1982.

Crozier, Michel J., Samuel P. Huntington, and Joli Watanuki, eds. *The Crisis of Democracy: Report to the Trilateral Commission on the Governability of Democracies.* New York: New York UP, 1975.

Cryle, Peter. *The Thematics of Commitment: The Tower & The Plain.* Princeton: Princeton UP, 1985.

Culler, Jonathan. "Semiotics of Tourism." *The American Journal of Semiotics* 1.1/2 (1981): 127–40.

Cultural Studies 6.3 (1992). "'Dismantling' Fremantle."

Cumming, Fia. *Mates: Five Champions of the Labor Right.* Sydney: Allen & Unwin, 1991.

Cunningham, Stuart. "The Cultural Policy Debate Revisited." *Meanjin* 51.3 (1992): 533–43.

———. "Cultural Studies from the Viewpoint of Cultural Policy." Turner. 126–39.

———. "Style, Form and History in Australian Mini-Series." *Southern Review* 22.3 (1989): 315–33.

———, and Elizabeth Jacka. "Cultural Studies in the Light of the Policy Process— A Curate's Egg?" *Australian Cultural Studies Conference: 1990 Proceedings.* U of Western Sydney, Nepean: Faculty of Humanities & Social Sciences, 1991. 26–56.

Curthoys, Ann. "Australian Feminism and the State: Practice and Theory." James. 138–60.

———. *For and against Feminism.* Sydney: Allen & Unwin, 1988.

———. "Single White Male." *Arena Magazine* 8 (1993–94): 28.

———. "What Is the Socialism in Socialist Feminism?" *Australian Feminist Studies* 6 (1988): 17–24.

———, and Stephen Muecke. "Australia, for Example." Hudson and Carter. 177–200.

Daly, M. T. *Sydney Boom, Sydney Bust.* Sydney: Allen & Unwin, 1982.

Dark, Eleanor. *The Timeless Land*. Sydney: Collins, 1941.

David, Abe, and Ted Wheelwright. *The Third Wave: Australia and Asian Capitalism*. Sydney: The Left Book Club, 1989.

Davila, Juan, and Paul Foss. *The Mutilated Pieta*. Sydney: Artspace, 1985.

Davis, Mike. "Urban Renaissance and the Spirit of Postmodernism." Kaplan. 79–87.

Dawson, John A. *Shopping Centre Development*. London and New York: Longman, 1983.

Dean, Kenneth, and Brian Massumi. *First and Last Emperors: The Absolute State and the Body of the Despot*. Brooklyn: Autonomedia, 1992.

De Certeau, Michel. *Heterologies*. Trans. Brian Massumi. Minneapolis: U of Minnesota P, 1986.

———. *The Practice of Everyday Life*. Trans. Steven F. Rendall. Berkeley and London: U of California P, 1984.

———. *The Writing of History*. Trans. Tom Conley. New York: Columbia UP, 1988.

De Lauretis, Teresa. *Alice Doesn't: Feminism, Semiotics, Cinema*. Bloomington: Indiana UP, 1984.

———, ed. *Feminist Studies/Critical Studies*. Bloomington: Indiana UP, 1986.

Deleuze, Gilles. "He Stuttered." Boundas and Olkowski. 23–29.

———. *The Logic of Sense*. Ed. Constantin V. Boundas. Trans. Mark Lester with Charles Stivale. New York: Columbia UP, 1990.

———. "Plato and the Simulacrum." Trans. Rosalind Krauss. *October* 27 (1983): 45–56.

———, and Félix Guattari. *A Thousand Plateaus: Capitalism and Schizophrenia*. Trans. Brian Massumi. Minneapolis: U of Minnesota P, 1987.

———. *Kafka: Toward a Minor Literature*. Trans. Dana Polan. Minneapolis: U of Minnesota P, 1986.

Denoon, Donald. *Settler Capitalism: The Dynamics of Dependent Development in the Southern Hemisphere*. Oxford and New York: Oxford UP, 1983.

Department of Environment, Housing and Community Development. *The Shopping Centre as a Community Leisure Resource*. Canberra: Australian Government Publishing Service, 1978.

Derrida, Jacques. *The Other Heading: Reflections on Today's Europe*. Trans. Pascale-Anne Brault and Michael B. Naas. Bloomington and Indianapolis: Indiana UP, 1992.

Deutsche, Rosalyn. "Architecture of the Evicted." *Strategies* 3 (1990): 159–83.

———. *Evictions: Art and Spatial Politics*. Cambridge, MA: The MIT Press, 1996.

Devine, Frank. "'Drab Mr Suburbia' Has the Last Laugh." *Australian* 27 February 1997.

De Weerdt, Jacques. "L'espace rural français: vocation touristique ou processus de touristification?" Paper to the 1990 World Congress of the International Sociological Association, Madrid.

Dictionary of Australian Quotations. Ed. Stephen Murray-Smith. Melbourne: Heinemann, 1984.

Diprose, Rosalyn, and Robyn Ferrell, eds. *Cartographies: Poststructuralism and the Mapping of Bodies and Spaces*. Sydney: Allen & Unwin, 1991.

Dirlik, Arif. "The Postcolonial Aura: Third World Criticism in the Age of Global Capitalism." *Critical Inquiry* 20.2 (1994): 328–56.

Docker, John. *The Nervous Nineties: Australian Cultural Life in the 1890s.* Melbourne and Oxford: Oxford UP, 1991.

———. *Postmodernism and Popular Culture: A Cultural History.* Cambridge: Cambridge UP, 1994.

Duncan, James, and David Ley, eds. *Place/Culture/Representation.* London and New York: Routledge, 1993.

Dutton, Geoffrey. *Sun, Sea, Surf and Sand—The Myth of The Beach.* Oxford and Melbourne: Oxford UP, 1985.

Dyster, Barrie, and David Meredith. *Australia in the International Economy in the Twentieth Century.* Cambridge: Cambridge UP, 1990.

Eagleton, Terry. *Walter Benjamin, or Towards a Revolutionary Criticism.* London: Verso and NLB, 1981.

"Eastville to Go West." *Maitland Mercury* 12 November 1969.

Edinburgh '76 Magazine 1 (1976). "Psycho-analysis/Cinema/Avant-Garde."

Edwards, Coral, and Peter Read. *The Lost Children.* Sydney and New York: Doubleday, 1992.

Edwards, John. "Paul Keating: A Lust for Power." *Sydney Morning Herald* 24 September 1988.

Eisenstein, Hester. *Inside Agitators: Australian Femocrats and the State.* Philadelphia: Temple UP, 1996.

Encyclopaedia of Aboriginal Australia. 2 vols. General editor David Horton. Canberra: Australian Institute of Aboriginal and Torres Strait Islander Studies, 1994.

Enloe, Cynthia. *Bananas, Beaches and Bases: Making Feminist Sense of International Politics.* Berkeley and Los Angeles: U of California P, 1989.

Ermath, Elizabeth Deeds. *Sequel to History: Postmodernism and the Crisis of Representational Time.* Princeton: Princeton UP, 1992.

Ewen, Stuart. *Captains of Consciousness: Advertising and the Social Roots of the Consumer Culture.* New York: McGraw-Hill, 1976.

"Exclusive: The Human Fly." *People* 23 March 1987.

Fabian, Johannes. *Time and the Other: How Anthropology Makes Its Object.* New York: Columbia University Press, 1983.

Farley, Rick. "The Political Imperatives of Native Title." *Australian* 15 May 1996.

Faust, Beatrice. "Cultural Clash of Women in Motion." *Weekend Australian* 15–16 October 1994.

Featherstone, Mike, ed. *Cultural Theory and Cultural Change.* London, Newbury Park, and New Delhi: Sage, 1992.

———. "The Heroic Life and Everyday Life." Featherstone. 159–82.

Felski, Rita. *The Gender of Modernity.* Cambridge, MA, and London: Harvard UP, 1995.

Felton, Catrina, and Liz Flanagan. "Institutionalised Feminism: A Tidda's Perspective." *Lilith* 8 (1993): 53–59.

Feminist Review 52 (1996). "The World Upside Down: Feminisms in the Antipodes."

Filmnews May 1988. "Remembering Claire Johnston."

Finch, Lynette. *The Classing Gaze: Sexuality, Class and Surveillance.* Allen & Unwin: Sydney, 1993.

Fiske, John. *Reading the Popular.* London and Boston: Unwin Hyman, 1989.

——, Bob Hodge, and Graeme Turner. *Myths of Oz: Reading Australian Popular Culture.* Sydney, London, Boston: Allen & Unwin, 1987.

Fletcher, Angus. *Allegory: The Theory of a Symbolic Mode.* Ithaca and London: Cornell UP, 1964.

Forbes, Cameron. "How Green Can a Black Afford to Be?" *Australian* 6 June 1994.

Forbes, John. *New and Selected Poems.* Sydney: Angus & Robertson, 1992.

Foss, Paul, ed. *Island in the Stream: Myths of Place in Australian Culture.* Sydney: Pluto, 1988.

——. "Landscape without Landscape." Foss. 1–3.

——, and Meaghan Morris, eds. *Language, Sexuality and Subversion.* Sydney: Feral Publications, 1978.

Fourmile, Henrietta. "Aboriginal Heritage Legislation and Self-Determination." *Australian-Canadian Studies* 7.1–2 (1989): 45–61.

Franzway, Suzanne, Dianne Court, and R. W. Connell. *Staking a Claim: Feminism, Bureaucracy and the State.* Sydney and Boston: Allen & Unwin, 1989.

Freadman, Anne. "Sandpaper." *Southern Review* 16.1 (1983): 161–73.

——, and Amanda Macdonald. *What Is This Thing Called "Genre"?* Mount Nebo: Boombana Publications, 1992.

Freeland, J. M. *Architecture in Australia: A History.* Ringwood and Harmondsworth: Penguin, 1972.

Freudenberg, Graham. *Cause for Power: The Official History of the New South Wales Branch of the Australian Labor Party.* Sydney: Pluto, 1991.

Friedburg, Anne. *Window Shopping: Cinema and the Postmodern.* Berkeley and Los Angeles: U of California P, 1993.

Frieden, Bernard J., and Lynne B. Sagalyn. *Downtown, Inc.: How America Rebuilds Cities.* Cambridge, MA: The MIT Press, 1989.

"From Dust to Shops." *Courier-Mail* 26 February 1969.

Frow, John. "Accounting for Tastes: Some Problems in Bourdieu's Sociology of Culture." *Cultural Studies* 1.1 (1987): 59–73.

——. *Cultural Studies and Cultural Value.* Oxford: Oxford UP, 1995.

——. "Michel de Certeau and the Practice of Representation." *Cultural Studies* 5.1 (1991): 52–60.

——. "Tourism and the Semiotics of Nostalgia." *October* 57 (1991): 123–51.

——, and Meaghan Morris, eds. *Australian Cultural Studies: A Reader.* Sydney and Urbana: Allen & Unwin and U of Illinois P, 1993.

Fussell, Paul. *Abroad: British Literary Traveling between the Wars.* New York and Oxford: Oxford UP, 1980.

Gallop, Jane. *Feminism and Psychoanalysis: The Daughter's Seduction.* London: Macmillan, 1982.

——. *Reading Lacan.* Ithaca and London: Cornell UP, 1985.

Garnaut, Ross. *Australia and the Northeast Asian Ascendancy: Report to the Prime Minister and the Minister for Foreign Affairs and Trade.* Canberra: Australian Government Publishing Service, 1989.

Garran, R. R. *Prosper the Commonwealth.* Sydney: Angus & Robertson, 1958.

Gatens, Moira. "Corporeal Representation in/and the Body Politic." Diprose and Ferrell. 79–87.

Gibbons, Luke. *Transformations in Irish Culture.* Cork: Cork UP, 1996.

Gibson, Ross. *The Diminishing Paradise: Changing Literary Perceptions of Australia.* Sydney and London: Angus & Robertson, 1984.

Gibson, William. *Idoru.* London: Viking, 1996.

Gibson-Graham, J. K. *The End of Capitalism (as We Knew It): A Feminist Critique of Political Economy.* Cambridge, MA, and Oxford: Blackwell, 1996.

Giddens, Anthony. *The Constitution of Society.* Cambridge and Oxford: Polity, 1984.

Gilroy, Paul. *The Black Atlantic: Modernity and Double Consciousness.* Cambridge, MA: Harvard UP, 1993.

Godzich, Wlad. *The Culture of Literacy.* Cambridge, MA, and London: Harvard UP, 1994.

Goodall, Jane. "General Adaptation Syndrome: Hypochondrias of the *Fin de Siècle.*" *Aesthesia and the Economy of the Senses.* Ed. Helen Grace. UWS, Nepean: Faculty of Visual & Perfoming Arts, 1996. 55–83.

Goot, Murray, and Tim Rowse. *Make a Better Offer: The Politics of Mabo.* Sydney: Pluto, 1994.

Gordon, Colin, ed. *Michel Foucault: Power/Knowledge.* Brighton: Harvester, 1980.

Gordon, Michael. "An Ordinary Success: Mainstream Man, One Year On." *The Australian Magazine,* 22–23 February 1997. 12–18.

——. *A Question of Leadership: Paul Keating, Political Fighter.* St. Lucia: U of Queensland P, 1993.

Goss, Jon. "The 'Magic of the Mall': An Analysis of Form, Function, and Meaning in the Contemporary Retail Built Environment." *Annals of the Association of American Geographers* 83.1 (1993): 18–47.

Grace, Helen, "Business, Pleasure, Narrative: The Folktale in Our Times." Diprose and Ferrell. 113–25.

——. "A House of Games: Serious Business and the Aesthetics of Logic." Frow and Morris. 69–85.

——, dir. *Serious Undertakings.* Ronin. 1983.

Grattan, Michelle. "Ideological Spectacles: Reporting the 'Rat Pack.'" *Media Information Australia* 60 (1991): 9.

Gratz, Roberta Brandes. *The Living City.* New York: Simon and Schuster, 1989.

"Great Moments in Philosophy." *Sydney Morning Herald* 30 June 1987.

Gregson, Nicky, and Louise Crewe. "The Bargain, the Knowledge, and the Spectacle: Making Sense of Consumption in the Space of the Car-Boot Sale." *Environment and Planning D: Society and Space* 15.1 (1997): 87–112.

Grewal, Inderpal, and Caren Kaplan, eds. *Scattered Hegemonies: Postmodernity and Transnational Feminist Practices.* Minneapolis: U of Minnesota P, 1994.

Grimshaw, Patricia, Marilyn Lake, Ann McGrath, and Marian Quartly. *Creating a Nation.* Ringwood: McPhee Gribble, 1994.

Grossberg, Lawrence. "Cultural Studies: What's In a Name?" B. Aubrey Fisher Memorial Lecture, October 1993. Department of Communication, U of Utah, Salt Lake City, Utah.

——. "The Formations of Cultural Studies: An American in Birmingham." *Strategies* 2 (1989): 114–49.

——. "The In-difference of Television." *Screen* 28.2 (1987): 28–45.

——. *It's a Sin: Postmodernism, Politics and Culture.* Sydney: Power Publications, 1988.

——. *We Gotta Get out of This Place: Popular Conservatism and Postmodern Culture.* New York and London: Routledge, 1992.

——, Cary Nelson, and Paula Treichler, eds. *Cultural Studies.* New York and London: Routledge, 1992.

Grosz, Elizabeth. *Jacques Lacan: A Feminist Introduction.* Boston: Unwin Hyman, 1990.

——. *Volatile Bodies: Toward a Corporeal Feminism.* Bloomington and Indianapolis: Indiana UP, 1994.

Gruen, Victor, and Larry Smith. *Shopping Towns U.S.A.* New York: Reinhold Publishing, 1960.

Guillermin, John. dir. *King Kong.* 1976.

Gunew, Sneja. "Home and Away: Nostalgia in Australian (Migrant) Writing." Foss. 35–46.

Gutman, G. O. "Rational View Needed on the Playing Field." *Australian Financial Review* 23 December 1991.

Habermas, Jürgen. *The New Conservatism.* Cambridge: MIT, 1989.

Haebich, Anna. *For Their Own Good: Aborigines and Government in the South West of Western Australia 1900–1940.* Nedlands: U of Western Australia P, 1992.

Hage, Ghassan. "Anglo-Celtics Today: Cosmo-Multiculturalism and the Phase of the Fading Phallus." *Communal/Plural* 4 (1994): 41–77.

——. "Racism, Multiculturalism and the Gulf War." *Arena* 96 (1991): 8–13.

——. "Republicanism, Multiculturalism, Zoology." *Communal/Plural* 2 (1993): 113–37.

Hale, David D. "Australia's Economy: Can It Survive Free Trade?" *Weekend Australian* 16–17 November 1991.

Hall, Catherine. "Histories, Empires and the Post-Colonial Moment." Chambers and Curti. 65–77.

Hall, Glen. *The Road to the River (1839–1939).* Lismore: Northern Rivers College of Advanced Education, 1975.

Hall, Stuart. "Cultural Studies and Its Theoretical Legacies." Grossberg, Nelson, and Treichler. 277–94.

——. "When Was 'the Post-Colonial'? Thinking at the Limit." Chambers and Curti. 242–60.

——, and Martin Jacques, eds. *New Times: The Changing Face of Politics in the 1990s.* London: Lawrence & Wishart in association with *Marxism Today,* 1989.

Halliday, Ken. *Call of the Highlands: The Tenterfield Story 1828–1988.* Tenterfield Shire Council and Australian Bicentenary Authority, 1988.

Haraway, Donna. *Primate Visions: Gender, Race, and Nature in the World of Modern Science.* New York and London: Routledge, 1989.

——. *Simians, Cyborgs and Women: The Reinvention of Nature.* New York: Routledge, 1991.

Harris, Margaret, and Ian Verrender. "How Sydney Became Asia's Middle-Class Sweatshop." *Sydney Morning Herald* 19 November 1995.

Hartcher, Peter. "Keating Becomes a Victim of the 'Intelligence Trap.'" *Sydney Morning Herald* 2 November 1991.

Hartley, John. "Suburbanality (in Cultural Studies)." *Meanjin* 51.3 (1992): 453–64.

Harvey, David. *The Condition of Postmodernity: An Enquiry into the Origins of Cultural Change.* Oxford: Blackwell, 1989.

———. "Flexible Accumulation through Urbanization: Reflections on 'Post-Modernism' in the American City." *Antipode* 19.3 (1987): 260–86.

———. "From Space to Place and Back Again: Reflections on the Condition of Postmodernity." Bird et al. 3–29.

———. *The Urbanization of Capital.* Oxford: Basil Blackwell, 1985.

Hawkins, Gay. *From Nimbin to Mardi Gras: Constructing Community Arts.* Sydney: Allen & Unwin, 1993.

Hayward, Phillip. "Culture, Logic and Criticism." *Media Information Australia* 61 (1991): 72–75.

Hebdige, Dick. *Hiding in the Light.* London and New York: Routledge, 1988.

———. "The Impossible Object: Towards a Sociology of the Sublime." *New Formations* 1 (1987): 47–76.

———. "Training Some Thoughts on the Future." Bird et al. 270–79.

Hillach, Ansgar. "The Aesthetics of Politics: Walter Benjamin's 'Theories of German Fascism.'" *New German Critique* 17 (1979): 99–119.

Himmelfarb, Gertrude. *On Looking into the Abyss: Untimely Thoughts on Culture and Society.* New York: Vintage Books, 1994.

Hindess, Barry. "The Very Idea of a Modern Republic." *Communal/Plural* 2 (1993): 1–15.

Hirst, Martin. "The Coming Republic: Citizenship and the Public Sphere in Post-Colonial Australia." *Australian Journal of Communication* 22.3 (1995): 13–39.

Holston, James, and Arjun Appadurai. "Cities and Citizenship." *Public Culture* 8.2 (1996): 187–204.

Honda, Inoshiro, dir. *King Kong No Gyakushu.* Toho. 1967.

hooks, bell. *Yearning: Race, Gender and Cultural Politics.* Boston: South End Press, 1990.

Hooks, Kevin, dir. *Irresistible Force.* 1993.

Horin, Adele. "Plea for Businesses to Combat Child Labour." *Sydney Morning Herald* 6 March 1996.

Hornbeck, James. *Stores and Shopping Centers.* New York: McGraw-Hill, 1962.

Horne, Donald. *The Great Museum: The Re-Presentation of History.* London and Sydney: Pluto, 1984.

———. *How to Be Australia.* Monash University: National Centre for Australian Studies, 1994.

———. *The Intelligent Tourist.* McMahon's Point: Margaret Gee Publishing, 1993.

———. *The Lucky Country.* Ringwood: Penguin, 1964.

———. *Money Made Us.* Ringwood and Harmondsworth: Penguin, 1976.

———. *The Public Culture: An Argument with the Future.* 2nd revised ed. London and Boulder: Pluto, 1994.

———, et al., eds. *The Coming Republic.* Sydney: Sun Australia, 1992.

Hudson, Wayne, and David Carter, eds. *The Republicanism Debate.* Kensington: New South Wales UP, 1993.

Huggins, Rita, and Jackie Huggins. *Auntie Rita.* Canberra: Aboriginal Studies Press, 1994.

Hughes, Robert. *The Fatal Shore.* London: Collins Harvill, 1987.

Hunter, Ian. *Culture and Government: The Emergence of Literary Education.* London: Macmillan, 1988.

——. *Rethinking the School: Subjectivity, Bureaucracy, Criticism.* Sydney and New York: Allen & Unwin and St. Martins Press, 1994.

——. "Setting Limits to Culture." *New Formations* 4 (1988): 103–24. Also in Turner. 140–63.

Huxley, Margo, and Kate Kerkin. "What Price the Bicentennial? A Political Economy of Darling Harbour." *Transition: Discourse on Architecture* 26 (1988): 57–64.

Huxtable, Ada Louise. *The Tall Building Artistically Reconsidered: The Search for a Skyscraper Style.* New York: Pantheon Books, 1984.

Huyssen, Andreas. *After the Great Divide: Modernism, Mass Culture, Postmodernism.* Bloomington: Indiana UP, 1986.

Hyams, Peter, dir. *Time Cop.* 1994.

"In the Know." *Weekend Australian* 24–25 June 1989.

Irving, Helen. "Feminists to Turn up Heat on the Republic." *Sydney Morning Herald* 20 August 2.

——. "Republicanism, Royalty and Tales of Australian Manhood." *Communal/Plural* 2 (1993): 139–51.

——. "Swissterhood." *Arena Magazine* 11 (1994): 15.

Jacobs, Jane. *The Death and Life of Great American Cities.* New York: Random House, 1961.

Jaensch, Dean. *The Hawke-Keating Hijack.* Sydney: Allen & Unwin, 1989.

James, Paul. "As Nation and State: A Postmodern Republic Takes Shape." James. 224–51.

——, ed. *The State in Question: Transformations of the Australian State.* Sydney: Allen & Unwin, 1996.

Jameson, Fredric. *Postmodernism, or, The Cultural Logic of Late Capitalism.* Durham: Duke UP, 1991.

Jardine, Alice. *Gynesis: Configurations of Woman and Modernity.* Ithaca and London: Cornell UP, 1985.

Jayamanne, Laleen, dir. *A Song of Ceylon.* Women Make Movies. 1985.

Jennett, Christine, and Randal G. Stewart. *Hawke and Australian Public Policy: Consensus and Restructuring.* South Melbourne: Macmillan, 1990.

Johnson, Colin. *Doctor Wooreddy's Prescription for Enduring the Ending of the World.* Melbourne: Hyland House, 1983.

Johnston, Claire, ed. *Dorothy Arzner—Towards a Feminist Cinema.* London: BFI, 1975.

——. "Femininity and the Masquerade: *Anne of the Indies.*" (1975) *Psychoanalysis & Cinema.* Ed. E. Ann Kaplan. New York: Routledge, 1990. 64–72.

——. "*Maeve.*" *Screen* 22.4 (1981): 55–63.

——, ed. *Notes on Women's Cinema.* London: SEFT, 1973.

——. "The Subject of Feminist Film Theory/Practice." *Screen* 21.2 (1980): 27–34.

——. "Women's Cinema as Counter-Cinema." Johnston. *Notes.* 24–31.

——, and Paul Willemen. "Brecht in Britain: On *The Nightcleaners.*" *Screen* 16.4 (1975/76): 101–13.

——, and Paul Willemen, eds. *Frank Tashlin.* Edinburgh: EIFF, 1973.

——, and Paul Willemen, eds. *Jacques Tourneur.* Edinburgh: EIFF, 1975.

Jones, Colin S. *Regional Shopping Centres.* London: Business Books, 1969.

Kalantzis, Mary, and Bill Cope. "Republicanism and Cultural Diversity." Hudson and Carter. 118–44.

Kaplan, E. Ann, ed. *Postmodernism and Its Discontents: Theories, Practices.* London: Verso, 1988.

Kaspar, Wolfgang. "The Revolution We Have to Have." *Weekend Australian* 12–13 October 1991.

Katz, Cindi. "Major/Minor: Theory, Nature, and Politics." *Annals of the Association of American Geographers* 85.1 (1995): 164–67.

"Keating Is Dead: Labor's New Guard Rejects His Faith in Free Markets," *Business Review Weekly* 3 March 1997.

"Keating? Welfare Boss Says: No Way." *Sydney Morning Herald* 24 October 1991.

Keating, Michael, and Geoff Dixon. *Making Economic Policy in Australia 1983–1988.* Melbourne: Longman Cheshire, 1989.

Keith, Michael, and Steve Pile, eds. *Place and the Politics of Identity.* London and New York: Routledge, 1993.

Kelly, Paul. *The Hawke Ascendancy: A Definitive Account of Its Origins and Climax 1975–1983.* Sydney: Angus & Robertson, 1984.

———. "Howard's Report Card: A year of governing cautiously." *Weekend Australian* 1–2 March 1997.

Keneally, Tom. *Our Republic.* Port Melbourne: Heinemann Australia, 1993.

Kennedy, Fiona. "Aboriginal Consensus Reached on Cape York." *Australian* 6 February 1996.

Kincaid, Jamaica. *A Small Place.* London: Virago, 1988.

"King Kong: The Moment of Final Decision." *Australian Financial Review* 15 June 1989. 47–49.

Kingston, Beverley. *Basket, Bag and Trolley: A History of Shopping in Australia.* Melbourne: Oxford UP, 1994.

Kirby, Michael. "Reflections on Constitutional Monarchy." Hudson and Carter. 61–76.

Kitney, Geoff. "Coarse Keating Put off Course." *Australian Financial Review* 31 December 1987.

Knevitt, Charles. "Towers of Power." *Weekend Australian* 2–3 November 1985.

Knight, Stephen. *The Selling of the Australian Mind: From First Fleet to Third Mercedes.* Port Melbourne: Heinemann Australia, 1990.

Knightley, Phillip. "The Real Keating Revealed." *Sunday Telegraph* 20 August 1989.

Kowinski, William Severini. *The Malling of America: An Inside Look at the Great Consumer Paradise.* New York: William Morrow, 1985.

Kroker, Arthur. *Technology and the Canadian Mind: Innis/McLuhan/Grant.* Montreal: New World Perspectives, 1984.

LaCapra, Dominick. *History and Criticism.* Ithaca: Cornell UP, 1985.

Lacoue-Labarthe, Philippe. *Heidegger, Art and Politics.* Oxford: Blackwell, 1990.

Lake, Marilyn. "Sexing the Republic: What Do Women Want?" *Age* 2 December 1993.

La Nauze, J. A. *The Making of the Australian Constitution.* Melbourne: Melbourne UP, 1972.

Lanfant, Marie-Françoise, John B. Allcock, and Edward M. Bruner, eds. *International Tourism: Identity and Change.* London, Thousand Oaks, and New Delhi: Sage, 1995.

Langton, Marcia. "No Future in a Return to Racial Paternalism." *Australian* 18 April 1996.

———. *"Well, I heard it on the radio and I saw it on the television . . . " An essay for the Australian Film Commission on the Politics and Aesthetics of Filmmaking by and about Aboriginal People and Things.* North Sydney: Australian Film Commission, 1993.

Laplanche, J., and J.-B. Pontalis. *The Language of Psycho-analysis.* Trans. Donald Nicholson-Smith. London: The Hogarth Press, 1980.

Lardeau, Yann. "Touche pas à la femme blanche." *Traverses* 8 (1977): 116–24.

Lash, Scott, and John Urry. *The End of Organized Capitalism.* Madison: U of Wisconsin P, 1987.

Laurence, Michael. "Now, the Billion-Dollar Game Comes to the Boil." *Sydney Morning Herald* 15 August 1987.

Lawrence, D. H. *Kangaroo.* Ringwood and Harmondsworth: Penguin, 1968.

Lawson, Sylvia. *The Archibald Paradox.* Ringwood and Harmondsworth: Penguin, 1983.

———. "Art in Bondage." *Australian Society* 8.8 (1989): 52–53.

Le Doeuff, Michèle. *Hipparchia's Choice: An Essay Concerning Women, Philosophy, etc.* Trans. Trista Selous. Oxford UK and Cambridge, MA: Blackwell, 1991.

———. *The Philosophical Imaginary.* Trans. Colin Gordon. Stanford: Stanford UP, 1989.

Lefebvre, Henri. *Critique de la vie quotidienne I: Introduction.* Paris: Grasset, 1947.

———. *Critique de la vie quotidienne II: Fondement d'une sociologie de la quotidienneté.* Paris: L'Arche, 1962.

———. *Everyday Life in the Modern World.* Trans. Sacha Rabinovitch. New Brunswick: Transaction Books, 1984.

Lentricchia, Frank. *Criticism and Social Change.* Chicago and London: U of Chicago P, 1983.

Leong, Wai-Teng. "Culture and the State: Manufacturing Traditions for Tourism." *Critical Studies in Mass Communication* 6 (1989): 355–75.

Leser, David. "The Cape Crusader." *HQ* (March/April 1994): 78–84.

Levitas, Ruth. "The Future of Thinking about the Future." Bird et al. 257–66.

Levy, James. "The Error in Argentina's Ways." *Sydney Morning Herald* 19 April 1995.

Lilith 8 (1993). "Dealing with Difference."

Lynch, Kevin. *What Time Is This Place?* Cambridge, MA: The MIT Press, 1972.

Lyons, John. "Our Prime Minister in Waiting." *Weekend Australian* 22–23 August 1987.

Lyotard, Jean-François. *The Postmodern Condition: A Report on Knowledge.* Trans. Geoff Bennington and Brian Massumi. Minneapolis: U of Minnesota P, 1984.

MacCannell, Dean. *Empty Meeting Grounds: The Tourist Papers.* London and New York: Routledge, 1992.

———. *The Tourist: A New Theory of the Leisure Class.* New York: Schocken, 1976.

McClelland, James. "A Moneybags Not a PM." *Sydney Morning Herald* 10 September 1987.

McClintock, Anne. *Imperial Leather: Race, Gender and Sexuality in the Colonial Context.* New York and London: Routledge, 1995. 9–15.

McCloskey, Donald N. *The Rhetoric of Economics.* Madison: U of Wisconsin P, 1985.

McDowell, Deborah E. *"The Changing Same": Black Women's Literature, Criticism, and Theory.* Bloomington and Indianapolis: Indiana UP, 1995.

McEachern, Doug. *Business Mates: The Power and Politics of the Hawke Era.* Sydney: Prentice-Hall, 1991.

McGrath, Ann. "Travels to a Distant Past: The Mythology of the Outback." *Australian Cultural History* 10 (1991): 113–24.

McGregor, Craig. *Headliners: Craig McGregor's Social Portraits.* St. Lucia: U of Queensland P, 1990.

Macintyre, Stuart. "Tall Poppies." *Australian Society* 8.9 (1989): 8–9.

McMullin, Ross. *The Light on the Hill: The Australian Labor Party 1891–1991.* Oxford: Oxford UP, 1991.

Macquarie Dictionary of Australian Quotations. General editor Stephen Torre. Sydney: The Macquarie Library, 1990.

McQueen, Humphrey. *A New Britannia.* Ringwood and Harmondsworth: Penguin, 1970.

——. "The Pineapple of Professional Correctness," *ABC Radio 24 Hours* Jun. 1996: 56–58.

McRobbie, Angela. "Settling Accounts with Subcultures." *Screen Education* 34 (1980): 37–49.

Maddox, Graham. *The Hawke Government and Labor Tradition.* Ringwood: Penguin Australia, 1989.

Manne, Robert. "The Future of Conservatism." *Quadrant* (January-February 1992): 49–55.

Marrie, Adrian. "Museums and Aborigines: A Case Study in Internal Colonialism." *Australian-Canadian Studies* 7.1–2 (1989): 63–80.

Martin, A. W. *Henry Parkes, a Biography.* Melbourne: Melbourne UP, 1980.

——, ed. *Letters from Menie: Sir Henry Parkes and His Daughter.* Melbourne: Melbourne UP, 1983.

Martin, Biddy, and Chandra Talpade Mohanty. "Feminist Politics: What's Home Got to Do with It?" De Lauretis. 191–212.

Masciarotte, Gloria-Jean. "C'mon Girl: Oprah Winfrey and the Discourse of Feminine Talk." *Genders* 11 (1991): 81–110.

Massey, Doreen. "Power-Geometry and a Progressive Sense of Place." Bird et al. 59–69.

——. *Space, Place and Gender.* Cambridge: Polity, 1994.

Massumi, Brian. "Realer than Real: The Simulacrum According to Deleuze and Guattari." *Copyright* 1 (1987): 90–97.

Mayne, Judith. "'King Kong' and the Ideology of Spectacle." *Quarterly Review of Film Studies* 1.4 (1976): 373–87.

Meanjin 51.3 (1992). "Culture, Policy and beyond."

Mellencamp, Patricia. *High Anxiety: Catastrophe, Scandal, Age, and Comedy.* Bloomington and Indianapolis: Indiana UP, 1992.

——. *Indiscretions: Avant-Garde Film, Video, and Feminism.* Bloomington and Indianapolis: Indiana UP, 1990.

——, ed. *Logics of Television.* Bloomington and Indianapolis: Indiana UP, 1990.

Mercer, Kobena. "'1968': Periodizing Politics and Identity." Grossberg, Nelson, and Treichler. 424–38.

Michaels, Eric. *The Aboriginal Invention of Television in Central Australia 1982–1986.* Canberra: Australian Institute of Aboriginal Studies, 1986.

——. *Bad Aboriginal Art: Tradition, Media, and Technological Horizons.* Minneapolis: U of Minnesota P, 1994.

——. *For a Cultural Future: Francis Jupurrurla Makes TV at Yuendumu.* Sydney: Artspace, 1987. Also in *Bad Aboriginal Art.* 99–125.

———. *Unbecoming: An AIDS Diary*. Sydney: EmPress Publishing, 1990.

Mikesch, Elfi, and Monika Treut, dir. *Seduction: The Cruel Woman*. 1985.

Millmow, Alex. "Profile: Paul Keating." *Australian Left Review* 130 (1991): 3.

"Mini-City to Open—July 8," *Courier-Mail* 7 April 1970.

Miyoshi, Masao. "A Borderless World? From Colonialism to Transnationalism and the Decline of the Nation-State." *Critical Inquiry* 19.4 (1993): 726–51.

Moffatt, Tracey, dir. *Nice Coloured Girls*. Women Make Movies. 1987.

———, dir. *Night Cries: A Rural Tragedy*. Women Make Movies. 1989.

Montag, Warren. "What Is at Stake in the Debate on Postmodernism?" Kaplan. 88–103.

Moore, Catriona, ed. *Dissonance: Feminism and the Arts 1970–90*. Sydney: Allen & Unwin, 1994.

Moorhouse, Frank. *Room Service: Comic Writings of Frank Moorhouse*. Ringwood and Harmondsworth: Penguin, 1985.

Morgan, Sally. *My Place*. Fremantle: Fremantle Arts Centre, 1987.

Morley, David, and Kuan-Hsing Chen, eds. *Stuart Hall: Critical Dialogues in Cultural Studies*. London and New York: Routledge, 1996.

Morris, Meaghan. "Afterthoughts on Australianism." *Cultural Studies* 6/3 (1992): 468–75.

———. "Banality in Cultural Studies." Mellencamp. 14–43.

———. "Crazy Talk Is Not Enough." *Environment and Planning D: Society and Space* 14.4 (1996): 384–93.

———. "Fear and the Family Sedan." *The Politics of Everyday Fear*. Ed. Brian Massumi. Minneapolis: U of Minnesota P, 1993. 285–305.

———. "A Gadfly Bites Back." *Meanjin* 51.3 (1992): 545–51.

———. "Life as a Tourist Object in Australia." Lanfant, Allcock, and Bruner. 177–191.

———. "The Man in the Mirror: David Harvey's 'Condition' of Postmodernity." Featherstone. 253–79.

———. "'Non-Nationalism' and 'Post-Nationalism' in the Australian Republicanism Debate." *Trajectories II*. Proceedings. Institute of Literature. National Tsing-Hua University. Taiwan.

———. "Panorama: The Live, the Dead and the Living." Foss. 160–87. Also in Turner. 19–58.

———. *The Pirate's Fiancée: Feminism, Reading, Postmodernism*. London: Verso, 1988.

———. "Sydney Tower." *Island Magazine* 9/10 (1982): 53–66.

———. "White Panic or, Mad Max and the Sublime." *Trajectories of Cultural Studies*. Ed. Kuan-Hsing Chen. London: Routledge, forthcoming.

———, and Paul Patton, eds. *Michel Foucault: Power, Truth, Strategy*. Sydney: Feral Publications, 1979.

Morse, Margaret. "An Ontology of Everyday Distraction: The Freeway, the Mall, and Television." Mellencamp. 193–221.

Mudrooroo Nyoongah. "Beached Party." *Sydney Morning Herald* 19 January 1991.

Muecke, Stephen. "Experimental History? The 'Space' of History in Recent Histories of Kimberley Colonialism." *The UTS Review* 2.1 (1996): 1–11.

———. *No Road (Bitumen All the Way)*. Fremantle: Fremantle Arts Centre Press, 1994.

———. *Textual Spaces: Aboriginality and Cultural Studies*. Kensington: New South Wales UP, 1992.

Mulvey, Laura. *Visual and Other Pleasures.* Bloomington: Indiana UP, 1989.

Murdolo, Adele. "Warmth and Unity with All Women? Historicizing Racism in the Australian Women's Movement." *Feminist Review* 52 (1996): 69–86.

Murray, Les. *Subhuman Redneck Poems.* Potts Point: Duffy & Snellgrove, 1996.

——. *The Vernacular Republic: Poems 1961–1983.* Sydney: Angus & Robertson, 1990.

Murray, Robert. *The Split: Australian Labor in the Fifties.* Melbourne: Cheshire, 1970.

Naas, Michael B. "Introduction: For Example." Derrida. vii–lix.

Nairn, Bede. *Civilising Capitalism: The Beginnings of the Australian Labor Party.* Canberra: Australian National UP, 1973.

"National Birthplace Goes off the Rails," *Sydney Morning Herald* 23 October 1989.

"National Independence a Far Cry from Virulent Nationalism." *Australian Financial Review* 14 June 1994.

Nava, Mica. "Consumerism Reconsidered: Buying and Power." *Cultural Studies* 5.2 (1991): 157–73.

Nelson, Cary, and Dilip Parameshwar Gaonkar, eds. *Disciplinarity and Dissent in Cultural Studies.* New York and London: Routledge, 1996.

——, and Lawrence Grossberg, eds., *Marxism and the Interpretation of Culture.* Urbana: U of Illinois P, 1988.

New Formations 17 (1992). "The Question of Home."

Newton, Judith. "History as Usual? Feminism and the 'New Historicism.'" *The New Historicism.* Ed. H. Aram Veeser. New York: Routledge, 1989. 152–67.

Niethammer, Lutz. *Posthistoire: Has History Come to an End?* Trans. Patrick Camiller. London: Verso, 1992.

Nietzsche, Friedrich. "On the Uses and Disadvantages of History for Life." *Untimely Meditations.* Trans. R. J. Hollingdale. Cambridge and New York: Cambridge UP, 1983. 57–123.

Nightingale, Virginia. "What's 'Ethnographic' about Ethnographic Audience Research?" Frow and Morris. 149–61. Also in Turner. 164–77.

Norris, Christopher. *Spinoza & the Origins of Modern Critical Theory.* Oxford: Blackwell, 1991.

Noyce, Phillip, dir. *Newsfront.* Roadshow. 1978.

O'Regan, Tom. *Australian Television Culture.* Sydney: Allen & Unwin, 1993.

——. "(Mis)taking Policy: Notes on the Cultural Policy Debate." Frow and Morris. 192–206.

Parker, Derek. *The Courtesans: The Press Gallery in the Hawke Era.* Sydney: Allen & Unwin, 1990.

Parkes, Henry. *Studies in Rhyme.* Sydney: J. Ferguson, 1870.

Parkes, Menie. *Poems, Printed for Private Circulation.* Sydney: F. Cunninghame, 1867.

Parliamentary Handbook of the Commonwealth of Australia. 26th ed. (1993).

Pateman, Carole. *The Sexual Contract.* Cambridge: Polity, 1988.

Pearson, Noel. "Mabo and the Humanities: Shifting Frontiers." *The Humanities and a Creative Nation: Jubilee Essays.* Ed. Deryck M. Schreuder. Canberra: Australian Academy of the Humanities, 1995. 43–62.

Perkin, Corrie. "Store Wars." *Good Weekend* 7 June 1986: 16–23.

Petro, Patrice. "Feminism and Film History." *Camera Obscura* 22 (1990): 9–26.

——. *Joyless Streets: Women and Melodramatic Representation in Weimar Germany.* Princeton: Princeton UP, 1989.

Phillips, A. A. *The Australian Tradition: Studies in a Colonial Culture.* Reissue with an introduction by H. P. Heseltine. St. Kilda: Longman Cheshire, 1980.

Phillips, Anne. *Democracy and Difference.* Cambridge: Polity, 1993.

Picard, Michel. "Cultural Heritage and Tourist Capital: Cultural Tourism in Bali." Lanfant, Allcock, and Bruner, 44–66.

Pollock, Griselda. *Vision and Difference: Femininity, Feminism and the Histories of Art.* London and New York: Routledge, 1988.

"Poor Performance 'Shooting Aust [sic] in the Head.'" *Australian Financial Review* 26 October 1989.

Prato, Paulo, and Gianluca Trivero. "The Spectacle of Travel." *The Australian Journal of Cultural Studies* 3.2 (1985): 25–43.

Pringle, Rosemary. "Octavius Beale and the Ideology of the Birthrate: The Royal Commissions of 1904 and 1905." *Refractory Girl* 3 (1973): 19–27.

Pusey, Michael. *Economic Rationalism in Canberra: A Nation-Building State Changes Its Mind.* Cambridge and Melbourne: Cambridge UP, 1991.

Quarry, Neville. "Knox City Shopping Centre: A Review." *Architecture Australia* 67.5 (1978): 68.

———. "A Shopping Guide." Unpublished paper.

Rainer, Yvonne, dir. *The Man Who Envied Women.* 1985.

Ramsey, Alan. "Black, Blue and Deep in the Red." *Sydney Morning Herald* 1 December 1990.

Rapoport, Amos. *The Meaning of the Built Environment: A Nonverbal Communication Approach.* Beverly Hills: Sage Publications, 1982.

Redstone, Louis G. *New Dimensions in Shopping Centers and Stores.* New York: McGraw-Hill, 1973.

Reekie, Gail. *Temptations: Sex, Selling and the Department Store.* Sydney: Allen & Unwin, 1993.

Reiger, Kerreen M. *The Disenchantment of the Home: Modernizing the Australian Family 1880–1940.* Melbourne: Oxford UP, 1985.

Reynolds, Henry. *The Law of the Land.* Ringwood and Harmondsworth: Penguin, 1987.

———. *The Other Side of the Frontier: Aboriginal Resistance to the European Invasion of Australia.* Ringwood and Harmondsworth: Penguin, 1982.

———. *With the White People.* Ringwood and Harmondsworth: Penguin, 1990.

Robbins, Bruce. *Secular Vocations: Intellectuals, Professionalism, Culture.* London and New York: Verso, 1993.

Robert, Marthe. *Roman des origines et origines du roman.* Paris: Gallimard, 1972.

Roberts, Peter. "Rich to Get Richer at the Expense of the Poor." *Australian Financial Review* 22 November 1991.

Robinson, Peter. "Fair Go, We're All Bludgers." *Sun-Herald* 18 June 1989.

———. "In Search of Elusive Economic Panacea." *Australian Financial Review* 11 December 1991.

———. "Take a Good Look at Keating and Co." *Sun-Herald* 30 August 1987.

———. "Time to Rotate the Top Job." *Sun-Herald* 10 November 1991.

Rodriguez, Ileana. *House/Garden/Nation: Space, Gender and Ethnicity in Postcolonial Latin American Literatures by Women.* Durham and London: Duke UP, 1994.

Rolls, Eric. *Sojourners: Flowers and the Wide Sea.* St. Lucia: U of Queensland P, 1992.

Romero, George, dir. *Dawn of the Dead.* 1979.

Rosaldo, Michelle Z. "Toward an Anthropology of Self and Feeling." *Culture Theory: Essays on Mind, Self and Emotion.* Ed. Richard A. Shweder and Robert A. LeVine. Cambridge: Cambridge UP, 1984. 137–57.

Rose, Gillian. *Feminism and Geography: The Limits of Geographical Knowledge.* Cambridge: Polity, 1993.

Rose, Jacqueline. *Sexuality in the Field of Vision.* London: Verso, 1986.

Ross, Andrew. *The Chicago Gangster Theory of Life: Nature's Debt to Society.* London and New York: Verso, 1994.

———. *No Respect: Intellectuals and Popular Culture.* New York and London: Routledge, 1989.

Rowley, Sue. "The Journey's End: Women's Mobility and Confinement." *Australian Cultural History* 10 (1991): 69–83.

Rowse, Tim. "Diversity in Indigenous Citizenship." *Communal/Plural* 2 (1993): 47–63.

Ruddick, Susan. "Heterotopias of the Homeless: Strategies and Tactics of Placemaking in Los Angeles." *Strategies* 3 (1990): 184–201.

Ruthven, K. K., ed. *Beyond the Disciplines: The New Humanities.* Canberra: Australian Academy of the Humanities, 1993.

Sakai, Naoki. *Translation and Subjectivity.* Minneapolis: U of Minnesota P, 1997.

Sandercock, Leonie. *Cities for Sale: Property, Politics and Urban Planning in Australia.* Melbourne: Melbourne UP, 1977.

Sanders, Noel. "Azaria Chamberlain and Popular Culture." Frow and Morris. 86–101.

Schaffer, Kay. *Women and the Bush: Forces of Desire in the Australian Cultural Tradition.* Cambridge: Cambridge UP, 1988.

Schepisi, Fred, dir. *Evil Angels* a.k.a. *A Cry in the Dark.* 1988.

Schirato, Tony. "My Space or Yours? De Certeau, Frow and the Meaning of Popular Culture." *Cultural Studies* 7.2 (1993): 282–91.

Schlesinger, John, dir. *The Falcon and the Snowman.* 1984.

Schoedsack, Ernest B., and Merian C. Cooper, dirs. *King Kong.* 1933.

Schulte-Sasse, Jochen. "Electronic Media and Cultural Politics in the Reagan Era: The Attack on Libya and *Hands Across America* as Post-modern Events." *Cultural Critique* 8 (1987–88): 123–52.

Scott, Andrew. *Fading Loyalties: The Australian Labor Party and the Working Class.* Sydney: Pluto, 1991.

Scott, Bonnie Kime. *The Gender of Modernism: A Critical Anthology.* Bloomington and Indianapolis: Indiana UP, 1990.

Scott, Joan W. "'Experience.'" *Feminists Theorize the Political.* Ed. Judith Butler and Joan W. Scott. New York and London: Routledge, 1992. 22–40.

Scott, Keith. "Last Chance to Translate Grievance into Change." *Canberra Times* 14 October 1993.

Scott, Ridley, dir. *Blade Runner.* 1982.

Seccombe, Mike. "From Paul to John, Special Delivery." *Sydney Morning Herald* 25 October 1989.

Sedgwick, Eve Kosofsky. *Between Men: English Literature and Male Homosocial Desire.* New York: Columbia, 1985.

———. *Epistemology of the Closet.* Berkeley and Los Angeles: U of California P, 1990.

Sennett, Richard. *The Fall of Public Man.* New York and London: Norton, 1974.

Shapiro, Gary. "From the Sublime to the Political: Some Historical Notes." *New Literary History* 16.2 (1985): 213–35.

Shepard, Sam. *Motel Chronicles.* San Francisco: City Lights Books, 1982.

Sharp, Rhonda, and Ray Broomhill. *Short Changed: Women and Economic Policies.* Sydney: Allen & Unwin, 1988.

Shopping Center Development Handbook. Washington, DC: Urban Land Institute, 1977.

Shopping for a Retail Policy. A.I.U.S. Publication 99. Canberra: Australian Institute of Urban Studies, 1982.

Sieburth, Richard. "Sentimental Travelling: On the Road (and off the Wall) with Laurence Sterne." *Scripsi* 4.3: 197–211.

Singleman, Glenn, and Chris Hilton, dirs. *A Spire.* A Spire Productions/ABC-TV, 1988.

Sloterdijk, Peter. *Critique of Cynical Reason.* Minneapolis: U of Minnesota P, 1987.

Slutzkin, Linda. "Spartans in Speedos." *Creating Australia: 200 Years of Art 1788–1988.* Ed. Daniel Thomas. Adelaide: International Cultural Corporation of Australia Ltd. and Art Gallery Board of South Australia, 1988. 176–77.

Smith, Bernard. *European Vision and The South Pacific 1768–1850.* Oxford: Oxford UP, 1960.

Smith, Kevin, dir. *Mallrats.* 1995.

Social Text 31/32 (1992). "Third World and Post-Colonial Issues."

Soja, Edward W. *Postmodern Geographies: The Reassertion of Space in Critical Social Theory.* London and New York: Verso, 1989.

Sommerlad, E. Lloyd. *The Migrant Shepherd: Ober-Rosbach to Tenterfield,* 1986.

Somol, R. E. "' . . . You Put Me in a Happy State': The Singularity of Power in Chicago's Loop." *Copyright* 1 (1987): 98–118.

Spillers, Hortense J., ed. *Comparative American Identities: Race, Sex, and Nationality in the Modern Text.* New York: Routledge, 1991.

Spivak, Gayatri Chakravorty. "Can the Subaltern Speak?" Nelson and Grossberg. 271–313.

——. *Outside in the Teaching Machine.* New York and London: Routledge, 1993.

Steedman, Carolyn. "Culture, Cultural Studies, and the Historians." Grossberg, Nelson, and Treichler. 613–22.

Steinberg, Michael P. "Cultural History and Cultural Studies." Nelson and Gaonkar. 103–29.

Stephenson, M. A., and Suri Ratnapala, eds. *Mabo: A Judicial Revolution.* St. Lucia: U of Queensland P, 1993.

Stern, Lesley, Laleen Jayamanne, and Helen Grace, "Remembering Claire Johnston." *Framework* 35 (1988): 114–29.

Sternlieb, George, and James W. Hughes, eds. *Shopping Centers, U.S.A.* Rutgers, NJ: Center for Urban Policy Research, 1981.

Stewart, Susan. *On Longing: Narratives of the Miniature, the Gigantic, the Souvenir, the Collection.* Baltimore and London: Johns Hopkins UP, 1984.

Stone, Oliver, dir. *Wall Street.* 1987.

Stratton, Jon. "Deconstructing the Territory." *Cultural Studies* 3.1 (1989): 38–57.

——, and Ien Ang. "Multicultural Imagined Communities: Cultural Difference and National Identity in Australia and the USA." *Continuum* 8.2. (1994): 124–58.

Straub, Jean-Marie, and Danielle Huillet, dirs. *Too Soon Too Late*. 1980.

Stutchbury, Michael. "The Bizarre Anti-Migration Coalition." *Australian Financial Review* 14 November 1990.

Summers, Anne. *Damned Whores and God's Police: The Colonization of Women in Australia*. Ringwood and Harmondsworth: Penguin, 1975.

Swain, Tony. *A Place for Strangers: Towards a History of Australian Aboriginal Being*. Cambridge, New York, and Melbourne: Cambridge UP, 1993.

"Swan Steels ARC for Competition." *Sunday Telegraph* 26 November 1989.

"Sydney's Human Fly." *Daily Mirror* 2 February 1987.

Sykes, Roberta. *Black Majority*. Hawthorn: Hudson, 1989.

Tanaka, Yuki. "The Japanese Political-Construction Complex." *Technocratic Dreaming: Of Very Fast Trains and Japanese Designer Cities*. Ed. Paul James. Melbourne: Left Book Club, 1990. 71–77.

Tanner, Lindsay. "Labourism in Retreat." Burchell and Matthews. 71–79.

Taylor, Paul, ed. *Juan Davila: Hysterical Tears*. Melbourne: Greenhouse, 1985.

Tennant, Kylie. *Australia: Her Story*. London: Pan Books, 1964.

——. *The Battlers*. London and Sydney: Angus & Robertson, 1941.

Thomas, Julian. "Heroic and Democratic Histories: Pioneering as a Historical Concept." *The UTS Review* 2.1 (1996): 58–71.

Thompson, Elaine. "Giving Ourselves Better Government." Horne et al. 148–60.

Thompson, Ronald, Andrew Joshua, Kevin Rogers, Raymond Geoffrey, and Brian Burkett, dirs. *Ngukurr: Weya Wi Na*. Ngukurr School Council, Ngukurr Adult Education Committee, and Yugul Manggi Media. 1988.

Trollope, Anthony. *Travelling Sketches*. London: Chapman and Hall, 1866. Reprint ed. 1981.

Tuan, Yi-Fu. *Morality and Imagination: Paradoxes of Progress*. Madison: U of Wisconsin P, 1989.

Turner, Graeme. "Dilemmas of a Cultural Critic: Australian Cultural Studies Today." *Australian Journal of Communication* 16 (1989): 1–12.

——. *Making It National: Nationalism and Australian Popular Culture*. Sydney: Allen & Unwin, 1994.

——, ed. *Nation, Culture, Text: Australian Cultural and Media Studies*. London and New York: Routledge, 1993.

——. "Of Rocks and Hard Places: The Colonized, the National and Australian Cultural Studies." *Cultural Studies* 6.3 (1992): 424–32.

——. "Return to Oz: Populism, the Academy, and the Future of Australian Studies." *Meanjin* 50.1 (1991): 19–31.

——. "Two Faces of Australian Nationalism." *Sydney Morning Herald* 25 January 1997.

Urry, John. *The Tourist Gaze: Leisure and Travel in Contemporary Societies*. London, Newbury Park, and New Delhi: Sage, 1990.

Valaskakis, Gail Guthrie. "The Chippewa and the Other: Living the Heritage of Lac du Flambeau." *Cultural Studies* 2.3 (1988): 267–93.

van den Abbeele, Georges. "Sightseers: The Tourist as Theorist." *Diacritics* 10 (1980): 2–14.

van Rossum-Guyon, Françoise. "Questions à Julia Kristeva—A partir de Polylogue." *Revue des sciences humaines* 168 (1977): 495–501.

Venturi, Robert, Denise Scott Brown, and Steven Izenour. *Learning from Las Vegas:*

The Forgotten Symbolism of Architectural Form. Cambridge, MA: The MIT Press, 1977.

Virilio, Paul. *Esthétique de la disparition.* Paris: Balland, 1980.

———. "The Overexposed City." *Zone* 1/2 (nd): 14–31.

———. *Speed and Politics.* Trans. Mark Polizzotti. New York: Semiotext(e), 1986.

———. "Véhiculaire." Jacques Berque, et al. *Cause commune: Nomades et vagabonds.* Paris: UGE, 1975. 41–68.

———. *The Vision Machine.* Trans. Julie Rose. London and Bloomington: BFI and Indiana UP, 1994.

———. *War and Cinema: The Logistics of Perception.* Trans. Patrick Camiller. London: Verso, 1989.

———, with Sylvere Lotringer. *Pure War.* Trans. Mark Polizzotti. New York: Semiotext(e), 1983.

Wallace, Michele. *Invisibility Blues: From Pop to Theory.* London: Verso, 1990.

Walsh, Max. "Menzies Was Right, After All." *Sydney Morning Herald* 21 December 1995.

———. "Now, It's a Question of Pride for Paul." *Sydney Morning Herald* 11 October 1990.

———. *Poor Little Rich Country: The Path to the Eighties.* Harmondsworth and Ringwood: Penguin, 1979.

Walsh, Peter. See "Cassandra."

Ward, Russel. *The Australian Legend.* Melbourne: Oxford UP, 1958.

Waring, Marilyn. *Counting for Nothing: What Men Value & What Women Are Worth.* Sydney: Allen & Unwin, 1988.

Watson, Don. "Birth of a Post-Modern Nation." *Weekend Australian* 24–25 July 1993.

Watson, Sophie, ed. *Playing the State: Australian Feminist Interventions.* Sydney: Allen & Unwin, 1990.

———, and Katherine Gibson, eds. *Postmodern Cities and Spaces.* Oxford and Cambridge, MA: Blackwell, 1995.

Wenders, Wim, dir. *Paris, Texas.* 1991.

Werckmeister, O. K. *Citadel Culture.* Chicago: U of Chicago P, 1991.

Wernick, Andrew. "Sign and Commodity: Aspects of the Cultural Dynamic of Advanced Capitalism." *Canadian Journal of Political and Social Theory* 8.1–2 (1984): 17–34.

Widders, Terry, and Greg Noble. "On the Dreaming Track to the Republic: Indigenous People and the Ambivalence of Citizenship." *Communal/Plural* 2 (1993): 95–112.

"Will Maitland Retain Its Entity or Become a Newcastle Suburb?" *Newcastle Morning Herald* 24 January 1969.

Willemen, Paul. *Looks and Frictions: Essays in Cultural Studies and Film Theory.* London and Bloomington: BFI and Indiana UP, 1994.

———. "Response to Donzelot." *The Apprehension of Time.* Barry and Muecke. 28–32.

———. "Rotterdam." *Framework* 20 (1983): 41–44.

Williams, Patricia J. *The Alchemy of Race and Rights: Diary of a Law Professor.* Cambridge, MA, and London: Harvard UP, 1991.

Willmot, Eric. *Australia: The Last Experiment.* Sydney: ABC Enterprises, 1987.

———. *Pemelwuy: The Rainbow Warrior.* Sydney: Weldons, 1987.

Wilson, Elizabeth. *Adorned in Dreams: Fashion and Modernity.* London: Virago, 1985.

Wilson, Robert Anton. "Project Parameters in Cherry Valley by the Testicles." *Semiotext(e)* 14 (1989): 337–43.

Wilson, Tikka Jan. "Feminism and Institutionalized Racism: Inclusion and Exclusion at an Australian Feminist Refuge." *Feminist Review* 52 (1996): 1–26.

Wiltshire, Kenneth. *Tenterfield Revisited: Reforming Australia's System of Government for 2001.* St. Lucia: U of Queensland P, 1991.

Windschuttle, Keith. *The Killing of History: How a Discipline Is Being Murdered by Literary Critics and Social Theorists.* Sydney: Macleay Press, 1994.

Wolff, Janet. "The Invisible Flâneuse: Women and the Literature of Modernity." *Theory Culture & Society* 2.3 (1985): 37–46.

Yeatman, Anna. *Bureaucrats, Technocrats, Femocrats.* Sydney and Boston: Allen & Unwin, 1990.

Yiftachel, Oren. "The Dark Side of Modernism: Planning as Control of an Ethnic Minority." Watson and Gibson. 216–42.

Young, Robert. *White Mythologies: Writing, History and the West.* London: Routledge, 1990.

Zahalka, Anne. "The Tourist as Theorist 1: (Theory Takes a Holiday)." Photo-essay. *Cultural Studies* 2.1 (January 1987): 17–28.

Žižek, Slavoj. *For They Know Not What They Do: Enjoyment as a Political Factor.* London: Verso, 1991.

——. "The King Is a Thing." *New Formations* 13 (1991): 19–37.

——. *The Sublime Object of Ideology.* London: Verso, 1989.

——. *Tarrying with the Negative: Kant, Hegel and the Critique of Ideology.* Durham: Duke UP, 1993.

Zukin, Sharon. *Loft Living: Culture and Capital in Urban Change.* Baltimore: Johns Hopkins University Press, 1982.

INDEX

MEAGHAN MORRIS is the author of several works of feminist cultural theory, including *The Pirate's Fiancée: Feminism, Reading, Postmodernism*, and co-editor (with John Frow) of *Australian Cultural Studies: A Reader*. Formerly a film critic, she is now an Australian Research Council Senior Fellow at the University of Technology, Sydney.

Lightning Source UK Ltd.
Milton Keynes UK
UKHW021920140221
378607UK00018B/813